HOW TO BE A
SMART
INVESTOR

$\$\$\$\$\$\$\$\$\$\$\$\$\$\$\$\$\$\$$

**LEARN HOW
TO TURN A
SMALL STAKE
INTO A
BIG
PAYOFF**

By RON DAVIS

and The Hume Group, Inc. Editors

The Hume Group, Inc.
2839 Paces Ferry Road, NW, Suite 1170
Atlanta, GA 30339-5770

ISBN 0-9660073-0-1 hardcover

59100

Table of Contents

Chapter 1: What Is Wealth? A 21st Century Perspective

Chapter 2: A Financial Test to Help You Get Ready

Chapter 3: Stocks + Compounding = Wealth

Chapter 4: How to Acquire Additional Investment Funds

Chapter 5: The Risk Factor: Be Careful Out There

Chapter 6: How the Experts Do It

Chapter 7: Asset Allocation—Finding the Right Combination

Chapter 8: Action Plans for the Small Investor

Chapter 9: Dividend Growth: A Consistent Winner

Chapter 10: Matching the Market

Chapter 11: Real-Estate Investing for the Small Investor

Chapter 12: How to Know When You've Hit Pay Dirt

Chapter 13: The Quest for Winners

Chapter 14: Profiting from Turnarounds

Chapter 15: How to Tax Shelter Your Money

Chapter 16: Protecting Your Assets

Chapter 17: Some Guidelines to Get You Where You're Going

Chapter 18: Launching into Investor Cyberspace

Chapter 19: How to Recession-Proof Your Investments

Chapter 20: The Amazing Power of Compounding

Foreword

A lot of folks write books, but unless they bring something of value to the table, something truly insightful and practically beneficial for the reader, they are not worth our reading time. My experience in the financial-services industry goes back 35 years, and during that time, I have read volumes on the subject of investing, personal finance, and financial planning. Unfortunately, too many of them appeared to be self-serving and offered little in the way of immediate benefit to their readers.

I have written three books on personal finance and the financial-services industry, and I look back on these experiences with gratitude. The extensive feedback I have received is appreciated because it has affirmed my conviction that the measure of a book is the degree to which it contributes to the knowledge and progress of humanity.

That was the feeling I had as I read the manuscript of *How to Be a Smart Investor*—a sense that it had the great potential to improve the lives of its readers. It provided a clear and practical road map for reaching the goals of the reader more than that of the author. Too few personal-finance books accomplish that task with a minimum amount of clutter. This book provides answers readers seek, not questions they don't.

But back to the future and the book *How to Be a Smart Investor*. Whether you are novice or sophisticate, wealthy or of modest means, young or old, male or female, every page of this book will make you more financially and, therefore, personally more successful. Written in easy-to-understand language, readers can immediately apply the ideas and advice to their own unique situation—and with a high probability of outstanding results.

I take personal pride in recommending this book to just about everyone. My hat is off to Ron Davis and The Hume Group for their writing and publishing such a practical, user-friendly work. When all is read and said, you too will have found it more than worth your reading time. It may even change your life!

> Harold W. Gourgues, Jr.
> Publisher
> *The Gourgues Report*

Introduction

Almost all of us regret the portion of our lives we've squandered. Instead of years of focused, dedicated production, we allowed ourselves to be caught up in uncharted, haphazard, and indiscriminate actions that ultimately resulted in little, if any, success or gains.

And so it was with me and wealth production. For most of my life, I had no financial plan, no goals. As expected, I accumulated little more than debt and worry.

That changed in 1978 when I joined the company that was to become The Hume Group, Inc. As an editor, I was actively involved in research and inquiry into financial matters. I worked closely with some of the top investors and personal-finance experts in the nation. It didn't take long for me to realize that I had to use my newly acquired knowledge—or risk a lifetime of paycheck-to-paycheck existence.

Fortunately, I didn't start too late. I found the key to financial success. But I know now that had I found that key, say, 10 years—or even five years—sooner, I would be in substantially better shape today. As it is, I've had only about 15 years to become financially independent and free of debt.

The key I found, incidentally, is that the technique for accumulating wealth is pretty simple. So simple, in fact, that it can be reduced to a single concept. As I learned, wealth relies on nothing more than the acquisition of equity-type investments. That's it. Once you concentrate on acquiring such holdings, you will be doing what more than 99 percent of the millionaires in the world have done to become rich.

Obviously, there's more to it than just that. You have to know *which* equity investments to own. And that's what this book is all about. In the next 20 chapters, I have taken the ideas and information that I and a lot of financial and investment authorities and professionals have used to attain monetary success. And those ideas and information are not all that complicated. You don't even need a high-school education to put them to work for you.

I hope you will learn from this book and apply its formulas and advice as soon as possible. I guarantee you will be glad you did. I only wish I had had instruction in a book like this 30 years ago.

Ron Davis

Chapter 1: What Is Wealth? A 21st Century Perspective

"Wealth may be an excellent thing, for it means power, it means leisure, it means liberty."

— James Russell Lowell

Why You Need to Be Smart

When you think of making money, compare it to a touchdown in a football game. You can score a touchdown—maybe a lot of touchdowns—but you still may not win the game. Money is the same way. You can acquire a lot of money in your lifetime, yet you may not achieve your goals of security, independence, and lifetime income. Like touchdowns in football, money is a means to an end, but not the end itself. You have to have a game plan, a defensive strategy, and some coaching skills.

In other words, you have to be *smart*. Let's consider for a moment why smarts are so important.

At any point in your life, you may want material possessions that could enrich your life as well as the lives of the people you love. Maybe you're fed up with renting a cramped, noisy apartment and would give anything for a peaceful, spacious house of your own. Maybe your precocious 10-year-old daughter already reads better than many older kids, and you're concerned about how you'll pay the astounding tab for a four-year college education. The possibilities are many.

What you need is a smart way to reach those goals. In short, what you need is a "personal financial plan that works" — a plan that can help you turn a small stake into a big payoff.

Those "wants" you have are very important. They are the starting point. The Chinese philosopher Lao-tsu, in the *Tao De Ching* wrote that a journey of a thousand miles begins with the first step. Think of a financial plan in terms of a road map that you've just spread across your kitchen table. Before you pick a route that will get you to your destination, you must have an idea of where you want to go.

How This Book Will Help

The contents of this book can make you a lot smarter. It can give you direction. If you were going big-game hunting for the first time in the African wilds, you would want the help of an experienced tracker. Well, consider this as a journey into the unexplored territory of investing and wealth building. You want to be escorted on that journey, but you also want to be smart enough to bag the game yourself when the opportunity arises.

Here, for example, is what you will find in the following chapters to teach you those smarts:

Chapter 2: A Financial Test to Help You Get Ready

This chapter offers some fun tests (and, no, you won't be graded) to provide you with a self-evaluation—a point of embarkation. You may find out things about yourself that you weren't aware of.

You'll discover :

➤ How to prioritize your needs and aspirations.

➤ Six simple techniques for setting up a workable budget.

➤ Three budgeting myths that you probably believe.

➤ Nine sure-fire strategies for handling a cash crunch.

➤ How much money you'll need to reach certain long-range goals in life.

➤ The key to success in staying on a budget.

This is what is meant by being a smart investor.

Chapter 3: Stocks + Compounding = Wealth

Want to know how to pick the right stocks at the right time?

Well, so would every other investor. After all, that is a big key to investment success. Obviously, stock selection is not simple, but if you use the ideas and principles contained in this chapter, you will improve your investment performance.

You'll learn 14 tell-tale signs of a growth company. The 10 growth-stock super stars of 1996. Two factors that determine what a company's shares are worth and will be worth over time. The three major advantages of common stock. A simple way to measure a stock's "I.Q." And see how the amazing power of one investing tool contributes to your wealth-building efforts.

Chapter 4: How to Acquire Additional Investment Funds

It takes money to make money. And if you are starting an investment program with limited funds, you must know how to get the money you'll need. Do you know the secret? And this is not about simply becoming a better food or clothes shopper. Instead, this chapter gives you ideas for reducing your expenses for such things as insurance, a home mortgage, banking, and credit cards.

You'll learn how banks trick you into paying higher interest rates than you have to. A sneaky way credit-card companies use snob appeal to rip you off. Fifteen ways to get a discount on your auto and homeowners policy. How to cash out your whole-life policy and earn a higher return.

You'll also discover how to earn interest on money you've already spent...reduce your credit-card interest charges with a simple phone call...and eliminate the costs of buying stocks.

Chapter 5: The Risk Factor: Be Careful Out There

In this chapter, you'll find that there's no such thing as a riskless investment. Even investing your cash by stashing it under your mattress involves risk of fire or theft, plus the erosion of your money's value through inflation. But even though risk is always present, this chapter shows how to reduce it, yet realize a high return.

You'll discover an often-overlooked way to investigate a company's risk potential. What to watch out for when reading a prospectus for a stock-index fund. How to protect your money so that only a part of it has short-term risk. A secret way that diversification can work against you. How inflation can actually work to your advantage. And the one financial risk you can *never* afford to take.

It's tempting to panic when your investments suddenly turn sour. But you'll learn here how to become what some investment experts call a "self-less" investor.

Chapter 6: How the Experts Do It

Maybe the name Benjamin Graham doesn't mean much to you. What about the name John Templeton? Or John Neff? Or Warren Buffett? But in professional investment-advisory circles in this country, all four are legends.

Despite their prominence, however, you may not know that each of the four accumulated great wealth solely through investing. And their impact on American investment analysis and selection has been truly monumental.

In this chapter, you'll discover 10 secrets of investment success from the now-famous Beardstown Ladies Investment Club. Meet an eccentric recluse who turned $5,000 into several million dollars—by simply following a few basic investment rules. And learn about ordinary people who were able to take a modest amount of money and turn it into millions—even billions. Using the proven techniques in this chapter, almost anyone can turn a small stake into a sizable payoff.

Chapter 7: Asset Allocation—Finding the Right Combination

In this chapter, you'll discover a valuable way to spread your money among different types of investments while also spreading the risk.

Inside tips and secrets show you the one sure way to make money—even in a bear market. The "5-percent allocation system" followed by two of the world's wealthiest men. How to tell if the market is headed for a dive by following the all-important "Rule of 35." Where most big money in a diversified portfolio comes from. Four recommendations for investors new to asset allocation. Plus eye-opening ways the experts allocate investments.

If stocks start doing well, do you simply put a larger portion of your funds into the stock market? If real estate seems headed for better times, do you shift your money around so you can put more into real-estate investments? You'll also learn when and why investments should be exchanged to enhance the chances of making you more money.

Chapter 8: Action Plans For the Small Investor

How can you use short selling effectively—during a bull market or even when you spot a stock headed for a fall? In this chapter, you'll learn the pros and cons of selling short. How to increase your holdings and cut your risk. A trick for buying shares for less than the average market price. And a small-investment and lower-risk alternative to selling short.

You'll find out how to sell something you don't own. Discover a powerful technique that lets you combine your money with borrowed funds to create a profitable situation for both you and the lender. And learn why value investors are so successful.

In this chapter, you'll also learn other valuable investing tactics, all designed to help you improve your investment performance.

Chapter 9: Dividend Growth: A Consistent Winner

Dividends are an important means of increasing your wealth through stock-market investing. But how do you pick those companies that will pay you high dividends—and offer a promise of capital gains (that is, stock-price increase) as well? That's an easier question to answer than you think. When a company pays a high dividend, for example, do you know what that means? Is the company in distress? Or is it one you should invest in? And what about a company that is expecting slower growth and is paying out dividends rather than retaining them to finance future expansion or product research? Is that a good sign or a bad sign? This chapter shows you how steady increases in a company's dividend can be a plus rather than a minus—if you know what to look for.

You'll also learn about a cost-saving plan to increase the size and the value of your stock portfolio—even in down markets. Many companies—especially the blue-chip firms—will allow stockholders access to these plans. By taking advantage of them, you can pyramid your holdings in a company over the years, even earning extra dividends. You'll learn specifically which companies these are.

You'll also learn about another investment strategy that produces above-average results. It's the Dow Dividend Plan, sometimes also called "The Dogs of the Dow." Learn why this plan has outperformed the market in many of the past 20 years—and how you can take advantage of it.

Chapter 10: Matching the Market

Here you'll learn about stock-index funds. What is a stock-index fund? In fact, what is a stock index? Ever hear of the Dow Jones Industrial Average? Of course you have. That's a stock index. The Dow follows the fortunes of 30 blue-chip stocks. But there are other indexes that over time have performed better for investors.

discover the surprising tax benefits of index funds.
atch out for when reading a prospectus for a stock-
How index funds signal a bull market flattening
arn the secrets of using indexes to improve your

overall investment performance.

Chapter 11: Real-Estate Investing for the Small Investor

Maybe you've ruled out real estate as part of your investment portfolio. That's probably not a good idea. Did you know that real-estate investing doesn't always take big bucks? In this chapter you'll learn that you don't have to come up with at least $50,000 to get into real estate.

What if you could buy shares in a real-estate project—or several real-estate projects—just like you'd invest in shares of corporate stock? Safe havens when the general stock market falls, REITs let you invest in apartment buildings, shopping centers, and other rental properties without the hassle of being a landlord. In the past 10 years, REITs have paid an average annual yield of 7.8 percent—comparing favorably with the Dow Jones Utility Average.

You'll discover three keys to choosing a winning REIT. The secret of buying real estate with no money down. The best way to buy shares in a real-estate project. The top 20 cities in which to buy residential property. Plus other real-estate-related investments aimed at the smaller investor.

Chapter 12: How to Know When You've Hit Pay Dirt

Do you have what it takes to spot a stock that will make you wealthy? Without such knowledge, you will never be able to distinguish between a winner and a loser.

In the past, you may have been intimidated by the columns of facts, figures, and notes in published financial statements. But with just a few pointers that you'll learn in this chapter, you can evaluate a company quickly and easily—just by the information contained in its annual report.

You'll discover the components of a good balance sheet. Get a fix on assets. Understand the important relationship between current assets and current liabilities. And learn to recognize companies headed for trouble.

With the valuable lessons you'll learn in this chapter, you'll make more reasoned—and more profitable—investment decisions.

Chapter 13: The Quest for Winners

Here you're going to explore certain companies that can make you money. Their stocks can help you accumulate wealth in a way that could be the surest and the quickest—and perhaps even the safest. The best part is that such stocks are commonplace in investing. That's right. Commonplace. In this chapter, you'll discover how to find them.

You'll learn the four characteristics of a "best-bargain" stock. How to track down undervalued "gems" before they take off in the stock market. The opportune time to find a stock with high earnings and low share prices. *Forbes* list of the top 20 small companies in America. And a secret way to spot hot stocks that may be hiding right under your nose.

Find out about an out-of-favor fund that offers cash-dividend yields of 7 percent and up. The pros and cons of initial public offerings. Nine technologies that will revolutionize our lives. Where to spot under-researched or undiscovered stocks on the financial pages of your newspaper.

Chapter 14: Profiting from Turnarounds

Under some circumstances, the failure or near-failure of a company can be transformed into opportunity—for you. Here you'll see how the hope and the ability of managers and workers to regain control of their shattered companies can multiply the holdings of savvy investors. And you'll learn the important signals that mean the difference between a company's success and failure.

Investors like you can often see trouble coming—if they know what to look for. In this chapter, you'll discover 10 proven principles for detecting a turnaround in the making. A good place to start if you're unsure whether the company you're interested in needs a turnaround effort. Why spinoffs are worth a closer look. The easiest—and perhaps most deadly—quick fix that failing companies try to use. Five reasons why a company can find itself in deep trouble. And nine warning signs that a company may not be able to pull off a turnaround.

You'll also focus on one of the nation's premier companies

to see how it floundered, then, in remarkable fashion, not only revived, but also prospered. You'll learn how many investors foresaw the turnaround and took advantage of it. By knowing how to spot those turning signs, you too can enjoy the outstanding profits.

Chapter 15: How to Tax Shelter Your Money

Every adult person in the United States, almost without exception, can reduce his or her tax burden. That is a bold statement. But it's true. Whether you're a 17-year-old part-time worker at a fast-food restaurant, a 75-year-old retiree living on Social Security and a pension, or someone in between, there's always something you can do to cut taxes.

In this chapter, you'll pick up dozens of winning ways to outwit the tax man, including: How to get "free money" from the IRS...reap big benefits from a Keogh...earn interest income that's free of both state and federal taxes...and, thanks to the 1997 tax-law changes, eliminate tax obligations on retirement savings.

You'll discover how to make an early withdrawal on your IRA—and still come out ahead. Eight smart questions to ask when calling a fund's investor-service department. And how your 401(k) contribution may entitle you to an IRA tax deduction you couldn't otherwise take.

Chapter 16: Protecting Your Assets

Nobody has to sell you on insurance. But do you know its value in the overall scheme of things? Do you know the best way to protect yourself and others you choose from the daily hazards of life? How to prevent the loss of your savings, your investments, your possessions—everything you own?

If you don't, and before you can begin accumulating sizable wealth, make sure you learn from this chapter how to have adequate insurance coverage. Note the word "adequate." It means that you have enough, but not too much. You want to avoid spending money for protection you don't need almost as much as you want to assure that you don't underinsure.

Here, you'll learn an easy way to calculate your life-insurance needs. Five tips to cut your property-insurance costs. What to buy if you can only afford one insurance. Four easy steps to follow when comparison shopping for insurance. Why you shouldn't use the market value of your home to calculate your insurance needs. Two big drawbacks to whole-life insurance. The insurance most people overlook but most people need.

You'll find the right insurance that not only protects you and your family financially in case of sickness, injury, or death, but keeps you from having to overpay for the coverage you need.

Chapter 17: Some Guidelines to Get You Where You're Going

What's your investment personality? How does your financial situation size up against others who are also trying to accumulate wealth? Here, you'll take a look at three typical investors, ages 25, 40, and 55. Even if you fall in between those ages, you may still identify and learn from their examples.

The three situations represent critical "ages" of Americans:

At 25, do you chose conservative investments? And can you benefit from the amazing power of compounding? Should your investments emphasize top-quality bonds, bank certificates of deposit, high-quality preferred shares, and Treasury and government-agency securities? Can you also afford to be aggressive, with a large portion of your portfolio consisting of growth stocks and mutual funds.

At 40, should investments be in blue-chip stocks, quality bonds, real estate? Should you consider including growth stocks or growth mutual funds?

At 55, should you now look for higher returns by adding a few more growth-oriented investments? As you near retirement, do you really need to protect your investment nest egg by cutting back on your riskier investments in favor of those that will protect your capital and provide good income?

This chapter provides the answers to all those questions.

Chapter 18: Launching into Investor Cyberspace

Crucial to your making rewarding investment decisions is information. But where can you get that information?

You could use a home computer for facts and figures about investing and money management. But do you need to be "online"? Can you find what you are looking for with an online service? Can you sift through all these data and determine exactly which investments and financial plan are right for you?

You start with the assumption that you have never used your home computer with an investing objective in mind. If that is the case, will you have much trouble using your computer for investing purposes? Do you have enough computer "savvy" to go the next step upward.

You'll explore in detail how to find information and track your investments online. For example: Which full-service brokerage firms don't want you to know about online stock trading. Eight discount brokers that can save you up to 80 percent on trading costs. The Internet's "Big Four"—where really active traders get their investment information. The very best sites for business lists. And a free service that gives you all the information you need to keep up with the stock market.

Chapter 19: How to Recession-Proof Your Investments

Do you know how to successfully deal with a recession? First, you have to have a starting point, but where's the best place to start? After all, you don't want to try to contend with a recession until you find out what it does and how it affects you personally.

And are recessions really a certainty? Do they result from our excesses? Are they part of some immutable universal law that we must endure? And how can you survive—and prosper?

In this chapter, you'll find out what goes on during those critical weeks before a recession begins. Ten warning signals that a recession-induced bear market is ready to roar our way. Three tools the Fed uses to control the money supply. And what happens to your money when the Fed drops the discount rate.

Even if a recession is predestined, we still need to be able to cope with it. And successful confrontation is indeed possible—if we know how to react and do the right things.

Chapter 20: The Amazing Power of Compounding

Compounding puts at your command one of the most potent wealth-accumulating weapons. Compounding heightens the act of investing from something commonplace into something extraordinary. It can singly transform a modest return on investment into millions of dollars.

But do you know how to calculate simple interest and compound interest? You learn in this chapter how to make these calculations—simply and quickly.

Two Big Questions

At any point in life, you must be able to answer two questions:

1. What do I want?

2. When do I want it?

Those are simple questions that are at the heart of any personal financial-planning program. They also reflect an important concept about financial planning: It's a very personal procedure. Also always remember that it is your financial plan. It's not your friend Bill's or your aunt Mary's or your Dad's or your son's or daughter's. While you may have others help you with its creation and implementation, and parts of it may affect someone else (such as paying for a child's college tuition), its focus is on you and on what you want. Feel good about that. It means having a clear idea of what you want, taking inventory of what you have now, and mapping a way to get the things you seek. It means taking control of your finances and acknowledging that you have choices.

'Will I Have Enough?'

Unless you're filthy rich, you may have asked yourself—maybe quite often—if you are putting aside enough money. In other words, you wonder, will I ever be wealthy? For most people, the answer is no, simply because they don't know, and may never know, how to accumulate wealth.

WHAT YOU'LL NEED TO ACHIEVE MINIMUM WEALTH

Married Couple*

Annual Income	— At this age you should have this amount —			
	35	45	55	65
$ 30,000	$ 1,010	$ 14,920	$ 50,254	$ 81,330
$ 50,000	3,790	33,620	114,690	180,760
$ 75,000	8,290	64,580	208,500	325,240
$100,000	30,530	102,050	259,840	469,040
$150,000	61,830	198,810	463,150	769,910

Single Man**

Annual Income	—At this age you should have this amount—			
	35	45	55	65
$ 30,000	$ 3,130	$ 25,050	$ 60,200	$ 88,310
$ 50,000	2,990	37,130	122,210	175,150
$ 75,000	14,850	69,060	174,440	304,340
$100,000	27,480	115,940	270,810	455,360
$150,000	64,730	222,170	432,950	671,820

Single Woman***

Annual Income	—At this age you should have this amount—			
	35	45	55	65
$ 30,000	$ 18,770	$ 41,320	$ 70,130	$ 96,842
$ 50,000	34,620	66,570	116,100	173,040
$ 75,000	59,700	123,690	219,030	323,810
$100,000	89,720	192,390	338,980	499,290
$150,000	159,750	334,800	523,300	728,840

*Spousal benefits from Social Security mean that a married couple needs a lesser amount per individual than does a single person.

**Men usually experience more wage growth later in life, allowing for greater contributions at that time to retirement.

***Women normally live longer than men, resulting in greater amounts needed at all stages of life, but especially when they are younger and earn less.

Source: *Chicago Tribune*, Merrill Lynch & Co.

Obviously, for some, wealth may have an entirely different meaning than the definition others give it. A lot depends on your needs and your aspirations. But generally, no matter how old you are, your wealth requirements are about the same as those of your peers. The previous page shows what the experts say the minimum level of savings/investments (excluding home equity) you should have at each stage of your life.

So raise your hand if you've reached or surpassed the money goals exemplified.

That's okay if your hand isn't up. That's why you bought this book, isn't it? You're concerned that you haven't kept pace with your friends and neighbors, so now you want to know how to catch up with them.

Well, catch up you can. You can in fact accumulate wealth—no matter what age you start trying to do so. All you really need is an innovative strategy (which I'll explain to you), then the determination to implement that strategy and the sheer will power to stick with it through good times and bad.

And don't get the idea that you're going to have to start a life of self-denial and sacrifice to achieve your wealth objective. That's not what wealth accumulation is about—not at all. You can still enjoy life to the utmost, yet realize the financial targets you set. Here's how one person did just that:

Jerry Bradshaw is not typical of most Americans who reach the Big Five-Oh. He has accumulated a small fortune and looks forward to early retirement and, after that, travel and golf in the North Carolina mountains where he is currently building a home in a swank resort area. But 12 years ago, Bradshaw (and he prefers that I not use his real name) had less than $1,000 in savings and no investments. But he went to work for a then-small home-supply company, mixing paint for do-it-yourself customers of the store at which he was employed.

The company he worked for has almost from the start of operations offered its employees a stock-purchase plan, and Bradshaw took advantage of it to the fullest. He saw his investment quickly multiply, so he wisely started buying the company's stock on his own and outside the confines of the stock-purchase plan. Soon, he had accumulated equity in the

company to the tune of $750,000. Not bad for a paint sales-
man.

Bradshaw was fortunate, of course. He got in on the
ground floor of an operation that would soon become one of the
corporate giants of the nation. And that company just happened to offer its employees a piece of the growth it enjoyed.
Today, many of the company's employees—perhaps some who
wait on you when you visit your local store—are millionaires.

This is an example of what can result from an investment
in an emerging company. Bradshaw was and is an employee of
one such company. But many employees of similar companies
have also become wealthy by investing with their employer,
and they accomplished that trick not through merely being in
the right place at the right time, but through careful analysis
and dogged resolve.

You too can spot a company when it's in the embryonic
stage of growth. And once you have made a shrewd choice,
know that you can eventually reap the fortune that you right-
ly deserve.

Devising Your Game Plan

You can work toward accomplishing several goals through
financial planning. Planning not only helps you bring your
goals into crisp, clear focus, but also helps you prepare for economic downturns or the loss of a job. If you are part of a couple, planning can vastly diminish money battles with your
partner. For example, you'll be able to pinpoint your respective
strengths and weaknesses—and to reinforce each other's good
habits while mitigating the bad ones.

You'll also be better prepared should one partner take time
off from work to care for young children or an aging relative.
And if you're single, you'll have a much better handle on your
own money style and thus be able to spot weaknesses you had-
n't noticed or admitted to before.

Whatever your marital status, you'll be able to take your
financial future into your own hands. Imagine how you'll feel
when you get your bank and brokerage statements showing
your ever-increasing account balances. Now contrast that sen-
sation with the inevitable stomach-churning you experience

every time those abrupt letters on pink paper—signifying yet another overdue bill—arrive. It is really any contest as to which you'd rather have?

Another important point to consider: Financial planning does not have to be complex, difficult, a drag, a chore, or any other negative image you might conjure up. Financial planning can be as simple as thinking about what you'll do tomorrow. It's a process that lets you take control.

One way to think of it is to imagine you're going to build a house. You'll need an idea of what you want that house to contain. (Two bedrooms? Three bedrooms? A formal dining room? A fireplace?) What style will you want? (Colonial? Ranch? Contemporary?) How big? What color? Then you'll need to decide if you want to help build it, and, if so, how much you'll do. Then when it's done, you'll need furnishings. Finally, you'll need to consider taxes, maintenance, and insurance on the house.

Maybe you think you don't need goals. If you're a diehard hedonist, you'll sacrifice your future willingly in order to enjoy that compact-disc player, that new luxury car, that Caribbean cruise, that frequent dining out at expensive restaurants. But if your mindset leans toward deferral, you feel far more comfortable putting off your rewards until you're certain you've earned them—perhaps many times over.

Presumably, you'll be working toward both current and future goals: having enough money to keep up the lifestyle you want while saving enough for your children's education and your and your partner's comfortable retirement. The objective is to cover your monthly bills while still setting aside a sufficient amount for future expenses. It's this ability to invest that will allow you to get ahead at last.

In fact, setting aside a percentage of your monthly income—no matter what percentage rate you choose—should be just as important as paying your bills. For example, if you feel you can set aside only 1 percent of your monthly income, that's okay. But be sure you get in the habit of paying yourself that 1 percent no matter what. After all, isn't your future at least as important as that big night out on the town?

Immediate Goals Versus Future Goals

In most cases, saving a percentage of each month's income may not be a sufficient goal. As mentioned, having a goal of being rich isn't as realistic as focusing on a new Porsche in your favorite color. The solution: Sort your goals into short-term and long-term. Long-term goals are those that take considerable money and/or time: buying a car or a house, or building up a fund for education, a wedding, or vacations, for example. Short-term goals are those you'd like to accomplish this month or this year, like lowering the balance on your credit card by a few hundred dollars or buying that new set of towels to replace the threadbare ones your mother gave you a decade ago.

Your short-term and long-term goals will vary depending on your priorities and the stage of your life cycle. If you're just out of school, work on paying off college loans quickly and on starting a savings fund. If you're considering getting married and you're in your thirties, consider growth investments like stocks and real estate.

Once you've started your family, you'll need to think about beginning college-savings accounts and buying life insurance. In your forties, you'll probably be ready to trade up for a bigger house, fill in any shortfall in your college fund, and begin seriously planning your retirement. You'll probably want to spend more on luxuries like vacations and cruises once the children have moved out. And during your retirement years, you'll be more oriented toward preserving your hard-earned capital than increasing it further.

Throughout these stages, your short-term goals will be easier to identify than will your long-term ones, largely because short-term goals are more pressing: It's easier to conceptualize paying the rent without a scramble every month than to think about having a spacious home years from now.

Writing down your goals is a time-proven way to bring them into a clearer picture. Making a list of what you want (some of those things you jotted down earlier) is a good place to start. But once you've done that, you'll need to start prioritizing them. And here's where you begin setting realistic goals. Which ones do you want to accomplish first? In Chapter 2, you'll see how to determine what you really want in this regard.

Just a Matter of Organizing Yourself

Let's pause here to consider a very important subject: record keeping. The benefits to you of keeping good records are numerous. Record keeping actually begins at...well, the beginning. That means with your check register, because that's where you start your financial journey: through knowing your expenses (by writing checks) and your income (by making deposits). It's a good idea to pay everything you can by check and hold onto your canceled checks and old check registers. Note your checks and automatic-teller-machine withdrawals and deposits immediately; many would-be financial plans are sabotaged by forgetting to record that $40 or $60 withdrawal you make. If your spouse or partner also writes checks on the same account, create a system for recording who's written checks for what amount.

Be honest with this question: What do you do when your bank statement arrives? If you're like most people, you toss it in a drawer or on top of a dresser, then balance it in a month or two, if at all. Don't wait. The sooner you reconcile your statement, the better your cash records will be. If you belong to a credit union that issues "share drafts" rather than returning your canceled checks, make certain to save the carbon copies and file them in order, just as you would canceled checks. The best canceled-check file: still the proverbial shoe box.

It's also a good idea to designate a specific day for paying bills, either once or twice a month. Record the due dates of your major bills—credit cards, local and long-distance phone companies, insurance, utilities—on a single sheet. Post the sheet above your desk at home, on the refrigerator, or someplace else where you're not likely to miss it. If for some reason you can't pay bills on your designated days, you'll know which are due imminently and be able to avoid late fees and interest charges as a result.

Also, be certain to keep a running log of tax-deductible

expenditures. You can do this by listing potentially deductible items (if you itemize them) in a notebook. For easier access later, separate them into charitable contributions, medical expenses, business expenses, home improvements, etc. If you own rental housing, records of painting and repairs, contractors you've hired, and late-night phone calls from tenants could be valuable if you later have to prove to the IRS that you're an active investor—and thus entitled to significantly larger tax breaks than a so-called "passive" investor.

If you can't bring yourself to keep a log, at least write deductible expenses in your check register in a particular color ink when you make each entry or mark them in that color when you pay bills. Assuming that you have a running list, you may want to do this anyway just to make sure you don't forget anything.

If you don't keep a datebook already, start one. Loose-leaf datebooks, highly fashionable these days, actually can be quite useful. If yours accepts loose-leaf pages, look for inserts relating to financial matters: expense logs, travel-recorder forms, etc. Use them and periodically add the pages to your other financial records. Some datebooks also come with self-sealing or zippered plastic pockets to hold receipts.

In any case, devise a simple, clear system for filing your financial records. There are only two keys to good organization: (1) Your system should make sense to you and (2) it should be as organized as you need it to be. If you have relatively few assets, filing bank statements, credit-card statements, and insurance data together may be perfectly reasonable.

If your assets are more substantial, however, you'll probably want to file each of those items in separate categories—and even may want to separate information within a single category, such as among different bank accounts or insurance policies. The objective is not to create a burdensome system for yourself if you don't need one—but not to wind up with a slew of messy documents if you do.

Select a single place to keep bills, and file them by due date. Or you could try keeping an accordion file with at least 12 pockets—one marked for each month. Note due dates on your calendar as bills arrive, then file them in the appropriate pocket. Move receipts to a different pocket once you pay bills. But if filing your bills in such a way provokes an "out-of-sight-out-of-mind" reaction, neatly stash them in a tabletop container instead. However, bills should still sit vertically, so that you can slip newly arrived ones into appropriate order. Vertical file folders—whether in an accordion file, suspended in a file cabinet or resting in a drawer or on a desktop—will make access to the contents easy.

If categories correspond with those you'll need for taxes, your receipt-filing system will be most useful to you. Check your last tax return for broad categories and create subcategories for areas in which you have a lot of activity. Your filing system also can include folders for items that don't involve your finances directly but will benefit from better organization. For instance, a basic filing system could have variations on the following categories:

- ➤ Auto.
- ➤ Banking records/correspondence.
- ➤ Bonds.
- ➤ Credit cards.
- ➤ Household bills.
- ➤ Insurance.
- ➤ Medical receipts (assorted).
- ➤ Mutual funds.
- ➤ Real-estate holdings.
- ➤ Reference (owners' manuals, personal-finance data, frequent-flier statements, etc.).
- ➤ Stocks.

Such a simple system gives you the basic information you need to prepare your tax returns—or if yours are prepared by an accountant, saves you paying for his or her time to wade through a disorganized jungle of papers every year. You'll be able to find records easily should you need them during the year: say, a receipt and warranty entitling you to free repairs should that new, high-tech telephone you bought suddenly go dead.

A good record-keeping system also helps you cultivate the discipline you need to save money en route to financial independence. And just by knowing where your records are, you'll feel far more in control of your financial condition. In fact, the more organized you become, the easier your financial odyssey will be. In addition to your filing system, you also might take these steps:

➤ Rent a safe-deposit box. In it put your stock and bond certificates, insurance policies, titles to cars, property deeds, mortgages, and other property records. Your safe-deposit box should also contain such documents as birth certificates, marriage licenses, divorce decrees, and passports. It can also house expensive jewelry, collector coins, and other small items of high value.

➤ Buy a fireproof strongbox for the important records you'll keep at home, but can't afford to have destroyed in a fire.

➤ Denote a single place to keep records of stock, bond, mutual-fund, and real-estate transactions. On such records, include information on purchase dates and prices, number of shares or properties held, current market values, etc.

➤ Keep a list handy of the contents of your safe-deposit box.

➤ Keep a list handy of the contents of your wallet. If it should be lost or stolen, you'll be able to produce your driver's license numbers, the numbers of your credit cards, and the numbers of your long-distance phone company.

➤ Keep a list of the serial numbers of your electronic equipment, to include dates of purchase and model numbers. It's a good idea to videotape or make regular camera shots of all the rooms in your home, then store the tape or prints in your safe-deposit box.

Now you're ready to go. With your goals set and your records organized, you can take on the challenge of making and saving money. The remainder of this book contains action plans that show you how through steady investing—even with small amounts—you can accumulate real and lasting wealth.

Chapter 2: A Financial Test to Help You Get Ready

"A man is least known to himself."

– Cicero

An Introduction—To Yourself

The next few pages will "introduce" you to yourself. That seems like a silly statement, but for many people, they often know spouses, relatives, and friends better than they know themselves. And until you know yourself, you can never get a handle on what you really want in life.

That's what this chapter is designed to do: tell you some things you may not know about your real wants, needs, and objectives.

The following chart, for example, will help you pattern a worksheet so you can define—and set—your short-term and long-term goals. And in the process you'll gain a lot of self-knowledge. You'll find 10 goals and one left blank for you to fill in.

Call this worksheet "mental pump priming" if you like. All you have to do is circle the number corresponding to this list of priorities:

(0) Don't want or need.

(1) Already have; don't want a better one.

(2) Have, but want to replace or improve.

CHART 1

A GOAL-SETTING MODEL

1. House or Condo: (0)(1)(2)(3)
   Time period: ( ) years
   Cost now: $
   Estimated cost at time of purchase: $
   Down payment required: $

2. Education: (0)(1)(2)(3)
   Time period: ( ) years
   Cost now: $
   Estimated cost: $
   Cost per year: $

3. Car: (0)(1)(2)(3)
   Time period: ( ) years
   Cost now: $
   Estimated cost at time of purchase: $
   Down payment, if you plan to finance: $

4. Furniture: (0)(1)(2)(3)
   Time period: ( ) years
   Cost now: $
   Estimated cost at time of purchase: $

5. Home computer: (0)(1)(2)(3)
   Time period: ( )
   Cost now: $
   Estimated cost at time of purchase: $

6. Home renovations (name type): (0)(1)(2)(3)
   Time period: ( )
   Cost now: $
   Estimated cost at time of repairs: $

7. Boat, plane, RV, etc. (name type): (0)(1)(2)(3)
   Time period: ( )
   Cost now: $
   Estimated cost at time of purchase: $

8. Collections (art, stamps, etc.): (0)(1)(2)(3)
   Time period: ( )
   Cost now: $
   Estimated cost at time of purchase: $

9. Wedding (for yourself or children): (0)(1)(2)(3)
   Time period: ( )
   Cost now: $
   Estimated cost at time of purchase: $

10. Vacations: (0)(1)(2)(3)
    Time period before departure: ( )
    Cost now: $
    Estimated cost at time of vacation: $

11. Other (specify): (0)(1)(2)(3)
    Time period: ( )
    Cost now: $
    Estimated cost at time of purchase $

(3) Don't have, but do want one.

If you answer (2) or (3), specify the time period as—

(0)	Now
(1-5)	One to five years.
(5-10)	Five to 10 years.
(10-20)	10 to 20 years.
(20+)	More than 20 years.

Naturally, the longer term your goals are, the less exact your financial estimates of their costs will likely be. Try to predict what something will cost when you're ready to buy it by factoring in a reasonable sum for inflation—say, 4 percent to 6 percent annually. If inflation calculations make you dizzy, just estimate in today's dollars. But do bear in mind that costs are bound to escalate over time. Now try filling out the following worksheet to get you on your way. Keep in mind that you'll need a retirement reserve in addition to these long-range plans.

CHART 2

EXPECTED FUTURE OUTLAYS

Year	Item(s)	Anticipated Expenditure
1997		$
1998		$
1999		$
2000		$
2001		$
2002		$
2003		$
2004		$
2005		$
2006		$

Now add up your totals for all the categories. For expenses that have down payments, such as buying a house or car, add in just the down payment—but obviously you'll have to allow for monthly payments somewhere (and you'll learn how to make such an allowance later). This enables you to determine how much you'll need every year to meet your long-range goals. Based on the year you'd like to meet each goal, fill in Chart 2.

This is your ongoing challenge. You'll usually want to redo this worksheet every year or two because goals change over time and you'll accomplish some and reject others. But that's what planning is all about. It grants you more control over your financial future, but, at the same time, it gives you enough flexibility to change when conditions warrant.

The Ball's in Your Court

You probably have a lot of ideas about the things you want out of life. But if you're like most people, your vision remains hazy. And when you can't or won't focus on those ideas, they remain unaccomplished.

The first step to creating your personal financial plan is to begin writing down on paper the objectives you want to reach. Don't worry that what you write down may seem totally unrealistic. Write them down anyway. The important thing is to put your wants and desires in writing. As you move through this financial-planning assignment, you'll begin to sift until you find the goals you really want to achieve. To get things started, use the worksheet that follows in Chart 3.

Obviously, your objectives will change as you progress through life. For example, there are some typical objectives for each age group (excluding, of course, some of the pipe dreams you may have).

Now here's a key point to make this exercise meaningful: You must be able to tune out other distractions—that is, other expenses and nonessentials—that prevent the achievement of your goals, especially those of high priority. Think of the sheer determination and singleness of purpose that a sprinter affixes to the finish line or a mountain climber attaches to the summit of a vertical ascent. In much the same way, the more

CHART 3

OBJECTIVES I WANT TO REACH

	Goal	Priority*	Date Hope to Reach
Age 20-30			
	Buy a home	1	Within two years
	Purchase more life insurance	2	Within five years
	Invest in mutual fund	3	Within one year
	Put aside maximum in IRA	2	Next tax year
	Buy a boat	2	Within two years
	Have a baby	4	Within four years
Age 31-40			
	Buy larger home	2	Within three years
	Take vacation to Europe	2	Within three years
	Set up college fund for children	1	Within one year
	Start a business	4	Within 10 years
	Add to disability-insurance coverage	2	Within two years
	Build a second home	4	Within 10 years
Age 41-50			
	Start a business	1	Within one year
	Take vacation to Hawaii	2	Within two years
	Buy retirement home	3	Within five years
	Devise plan for early retirement	2	Within two years
	Change careers	4	Within seven years
	Buy classic MG	5	Within seven years
	Reduce investment-asset risk	3	Within five years
Age 51-60			
	Relocate to Santa Fe, NM for retirement	2	Within five years
	Expand business nationwide	3	Within five years
	Make specific plans for retirement	1	Within two years
	Create estate plan	2	Within two years
	Take cruise around world	5	Within five years
	Reduce investment-asset risk further	3	Within four years
Age 61-70			
	Retire	1	Within three years
	Take on son as business partner	2	Within two years
	Take cruise around world	2	Within two years
	Begin gift-giving program for children and grandchildren	2	Within next year

*1, 2, 3, 4, or 5, with 1 the most desired.

you're able to concentrate on what you want, the more likely you are to achieve your financial and life goals.

So the key to knowing *what* you want is knowing *when* you want it. If you have a 10-year-old daughter, for example, she's just eight years away from college, and that's not a very long time when you consider how much you'll need to put away in the interim. Having a definite time constraint allows you to work backward. You can figure out what you'll need to do now to meet your goals later. Otherwise, you'll only have too vague a sense that you'll get what you want some time in the distant future—a frustrating scenario at best. At worst, it's practically tantamount to admitting you're not likely to achieve those goals at all.

Which leads to another goal-setting maxim: The more specific you can be about your financial aims, the better. Very few people are capable of saying, "I want to be rich," and actually becoming so. That's not because the goal is unrealistic, but because it's too unfocused. On the other hand, wanting to own a spacious suburban home and a Jaguar, to vacation in Europe, and to be able to send your children to Yale certainly equates with a privileged lifestyle.

But such goals are much more attainable precisely because they're distinct and well-defined. To use the football analogy again, you can't simply say your goal is to win a particular game; you must design specific plays that will overcome certain defenses and others that will stop certain offenses. You must, in fact, have a *total game plan*.

A Word You Don't Want to Hear

Now get ready for a bit of embarrassment. You're going to see the dreaded "B" word. You know this word well, even if you don't like to use it in mixed company. The "B" word is of course "budget." And perhaps the reason it embarrasses you to say it even to yourself is because you've always known you should have a budget, but you probably have never really bothered to create a detailed one. Or if you have had a budget, maybe you used it for a while, then discarded it once you found yourself unable to stick to it. So now the word represents failure to you.

But you can stop feeling that way and start thinking of a budget differently. A budget is really nothing more than a type of map. If you were going on a trip by car to someplace you've never been, you wouldn't walk out the door without a map. Sure, you could stop for directions occasionally, but then you're trusting the judgment of others. With a map, however, you can go where you want, and even if you make a wrong turn a couple of times, you should be able to reach your destination eventually. Obviously, the better you plot your course, the fewer wrong turns you'll make and the greater the likelihood that you'll arrive when you predicted.

Maybe by looking at some misconceptions about budgeting, you'll get a better understanding of the true value of that process to you.

Some Budgeting Fallacies

The first fallacy about budgeting is that it makes life deadly boring. That it restricts you to a spartan lifestyle. That gone are the things that make life pleasurable.

Second, there's the one that budgets are only for people in truly desperate straits. Someone deep in debt, having their car repossessed, or defaulting on a mortgage loan.

Third is the misconception that since you're doing okay—paying your bills each month and occasionally setting aside a little for savings—you don't need a budget.

If you believe such fallacies, then you'll probably never reach your goals. Yes, you'll spend a little time on creating a budget, and the hour of so that you're involved won't be as much fun as, say, going to a World Series game. But you can make it interesting if you work at it.

Moreover, you may find that your budget won't allow some purchases that you occasionally make. But all you really need to do is make some substitutions. If, for example, you have to forgo an evening of entertainment once a month, on the night you would normally go, don't just stay at home. Instead, plan a walk in your local park or a drive to a section of your city or town that you've always wanted to explore.

And consider this: The $250 bread maker, the $100 spent on cosmetics you rarely use, or the $4,000 vacation you took at a time when you couldn't afford it are indulgences that don't really enrich your life. They only hamper your efforts to meet your real goals.

Sticking to a budget is much the same. You don't have to stop buying good wines, the designer clothes that make you look and feel terrific, the expensive skateboard that your son wants more than anything. Budgeting simply means recognizing that many things in life are tradeoffs. Being aware of that fact empowers you to choose the things you want over those you don't. It also means recognizing that you will have a way of paying for those things, or to substitute less costly purchases for expensive ones that really don't matter much to you in the long run.

Budgeting is a process that allows you to control your money, not the other way around. It may not sound as dreamy or romantic as simply spending money when the urge seizes you. But remember that for every person who achieves his or her goals by sheer determination, hundreds more spend their time wondering where they went wrong—and without really ever knowing why they failed to succeed.

Key to Budgeting: The Cash-Flow Statement

Now that you know that a budget is not some formidable obstacle that you can't hurdle, your next step will be simple. That step is a personal cash-flow statement.

Such a statement merely records where your cash comes from and goes each month. It helps you become aware of income you may not realize you have. For instance, you may be earning interest and dividend income in addition to your monthly paycheck. More often, a cash-flow statement helps you track the expenses that, when added together, can break the best-intentioned budget.

Chart 4 is an actual cash-flow form so you can get a better idea of what is meant.

As you can see, a cash-flow statement shows all your sources of cash: salary, wages, business income, investment dividends and interest, for example, plus the amount you receive from each category every month.

Next, you record all your monthly expenses, from necessities, such as shelter and food, to telephone bills, car insurance, taxes, credit-card payments, tuition, restaurant tabs, alimony, and anything else that separates you from your money.

And don't brush aside those "little items," such as the 50 cents you pay each day for the newspaper at the news stand. Consider that in a year, that 50 cents each workday adds up to about $125 a year. And if you could reduce the price of a daily lunch from $6 to $4, you would save $500 a year—a savings that would, for most people, equate to income totaling nearly $700.

So you don't want to overlook such "petty" expenditures. Otherwise, your snapshot of your cash position at that moment in time will be slightly out of focus. A cash-flow statement must give you an accurate accounting of your financial condition.

This immediate summary can save you from being deceived into thinking you have more or less cash on hand than you really do. You'll be able to see your biggest sources and uses of cash, a boon for making and evaluating financial decisions. And you'll clearly see the distinction between cash and profits. For example, let's say the value of your house is rising in a spiraling real-estate market, but unless you have cash to spend on your day-to-day needs, the growing equity in your house won't relieve the misery that you are suffering in your life.

You will find it tough to know whether you're winning the game unless somebody's keeping score. In the financial-planning arena, you're both player and scorekeeper. But that's not such a bad thing. Good records are your progress report for achieving your financial goals—the way you tell precisely how close you are and how far you've come. They give you a sense of control, and in the often-intimidating realm of money, that's no small psychological edge. What's more, good records are immensely useful for monitoring business expenses reimbursable by your employer and for preparing your tax returns. By extension, keeping records can save you money. Sometimes lots of it. More on this important subject later.

CHART 4

STATEMENT OF CASH FLOW
Period: From _____ To _____

	MONTH	1	2	3	4	5	6	7	8	9	10	11	12	TOTAL
	OPENING CASH BALANCE cash on hand and in checking account from box 7 of last month 1													
SOURCES OF CASH	salary, wages, income from business													
	dividends from investments													
	interest from investments													
	rents													
	loans													
	bonuses, gifts, prizes													
	government allowances													
	other sources													
	total sources 2													
	TOTAL CASH AVAILABLE (1+2) 3													
USES OF CASH	**NECESSITIES**													
	food													
	clothing													
	HOUSING													
	rent or mortgage for house													
	utilities													
	PROTECTION													
	life insurance													
	medical insurance & expense													
	dental insurance & expense													
	auto insurance													
	other													
	TAXES													
	income													
	property													
	other													
	LOANS													
	repayment													
	installment debts													
	EDUCATION													
	for children													
	EMERGENCY SAVINGS													
	special savings account													
	LIVING EXPENSES													
	transportation													
	recreation & development													
	home furnishings													
	spending money													
	MISCELLANEOUS													
	gifts, etc.													
	TOTAL USES 4													
	EXCESS CASH AVAILABLE (3-4) 5													
	Less normal planned savings 6													
	NET EXCESS CASH 7 (on hand and in checking account)													

A Moment in Time

You're not quite through with the tools you'll need to begin your wealth accumulation. At this point, you need to know about another valuable exercise in this learning process. This exercise involves creating a balance sheet.

A balance sheet shows you your total financial picture at a given moment in time. That makes it fundamentally different from a cash-flow statement, which, as you recall, shows only your sources and uses of cash. A balance sheet, however, clearly portrays the value of all your assets, such as your house, car, jewelry, fine art, stock and bond investments, and even that collection of rare, vintage jazz records. The total of these items—along with the cash in hand—is known as your total assets. Adding up all your debts—the sum of your current bills for medical care, credit cards, car loans, taxes, and the like—gives you your total liabilities. Your assets minus your liabilities equal your net worth—what you'd be worth if you had to settle up with all your creditors right this moment.

What can you use a balance sheet for? If you've ever applied for a loan, you know how useful it can be to have such information already compiled when you fill out loan-application forms. A balance sheet also helps you manage your cash by showing where you may have funds idling—like a low-interest savings account—while you're simultaneously paying high interest on credit-card debt.

Just as important, a balance sheet also helps drive home the reality that all your assets are investments. That's obvious with assets traditionally considered investments, like securities and real estate. But the cash in your wallet also qualifies. Other assets are difficult to quantify in dollars and cents: the college education that boosts your earning power, for instance. Or they may be quantifiable, but not tangible: the shares of stock you buy but never actually see or the $100 owed to you by a friend.

So now take a look at the personal balance-sheet form shown in Chart 5.

As you see, the balance sheet has two columns: assets on the left, liabilities on the right. This is standard balance-sheet procedure. You'll find the same thing when you look at the balance sheet of General Motors. The reason: The total in the assets column always equals the total in the liabilities-plus-net-worth column. That's because net worth equals assets minus liabilities; thus, net worth and liabilities must equal assets.

Here's an example to explain. Suppose you borrow $100. When you do, your assets increase by that amount. But so do your liabilities. After all, you owe the money to someone. Likewise, if you lend $100 to a friend, your cash on hand decreases by that amount—but because the debt is still an asset, the sum in your asset column remains unchanged. Hence, the name "balance sheet."

Also standard is the grouping of assets and liabilities by maturity, as shown on Chart 5. Anything due in one year or less is considered "short term," while anything due in more than one year is "long term"—for instance, cash, bank accounts, and shares of a money-market fund. A mortgage is long term—and in fact probably the most long-term liability you'll ever have.

Credit-card debt is deceptive. Even if you stretch your payments over a period of months or years, this is still a short-term liability. That's because the balance theoretically is due in full each time a bill arrives.

This distinction between short-term and long-term liabilities can be a real boon for managing debt. Once you know when all your loans are due, you can tackle your higher-interest, short-term debts before those with less punishing terms. You can earmark funds for specific purposes, like paying off a three-year car loan or five-year student loan. And you'll know whether you can benefit by restructuring your debt with, say, a consolidating low-interest home-equity loan.

Keep in mind that you won't need to create a balance sheet very often. Once a year is usually adequate for most people, although you may want to redo your balance sheet if your financial status changes considerably in the interim—like when you buy a house or pay off a substantial loan.

CHART 5

PERSONAL BALANCE SHEET

ASSETS	LIABILITIES AND NET WORTH
Short-term:	**Short-term:**
Cash:	Total Current Bills:
Cash on hand	Medical
Checking account	Dental
Savings account	Utility
Money-market account	Credit cards
Investments:	Miscellaneous
Brokerage account	Total Installment Debt:
Bonds	Charge accounts
Stocks	Personal loans
Mutual funds	Car loans
Pension or Retirement Plans:	Furniture loans
Life insurance (cash value)	Other
Receivables	Taxes owing:
Amounts owing to you	Income tax
Property tax	Other
Long term:	**Long term:**
Personal Property (Resale Values):	Other Loans:
House/vacation home	Loans against stocks, bonds
Auto	Loans against insurance policies
Jewelry	Other loans
Art collections	Mortgage debt:
Furniture	Home −1st
Other	−2nd
Investments:	Other (boat, etc.)
Real estate (other than above)	Total Liabilities $
Other	
Pension or Retirement Plans:	Net Worth $
Company pension plan	
Other	(Assets − Liabilities)
	Total Liabilities
Total Assets	**and Net Worth $**

Handling a Cash Crunch

All your planning efforts still may not prevent you from experiencing an occasional cash crunch. (Businesses call this "negative cash flow.") The cause could be a favorable one: Maybe you and your spouse learn that you're expecting a baby, or maybe your daughter is accepted at one of the Ivy League universities. Or you could be moving to another city to take a better job and you must sell your house at a loss.

More likely, however, the cash crunch results from a less welcome situation. You or your partner might lose a job, be disabled, decide on a divorce, or suffer any number of other problems. In such cases, you'll need a quick financial fix by securing additional funds or sharply reducing your living expenses. And the amount of money you need or the scaling back you endure will depend on your circumstances. Scrounging around for $100 when your son accidentally socks a baseball through a neighbor's window is far different from covering several thousand dollars in unexpected medical bills.

Under such crises, you'll find it difficult to stay level-headed. But as with every other aspect of planning, you must be realistic—and determined—to find a way to meet the challenge. These strategies can help:

> **Review your financial statements.** When planning your future, you must have useful financial information. This means a cash-flow statement and income statement, prepared within the last three months. Pay special attention to your variable and fixed expenses.

> **Determine your "crunch" line.** Add up your fixed expenses to see what you can't possibly live without, then create a budget to ferret out everything you don't absolutely need. Shoot for the most gain with the least pain. Refer to Chapter 4 for tips on ways to cut expenses.

> **Change your spending habits.** It doesn't make sense to buy that expensive suit when you're not sure you'll be able to pay the mortgage. Make an effort not to buy anything you could live without. Before making any purchase, ask this

question of yourself: Do I need this item, or do I merely want it?

➤ **Keep critical bills current.** These are payments for housing, utilities, car, and insurance. You can't function without them, so make sure you have enough in reserve to pay them at least three months in advance.

➤ **Control the use of credit cards.** You simply have to reach the point where you can pay off all credit-card outstanding balances each month as they come due. You'll pay dearly if you don't. More on this later.

➤ **If you run into problems paying your bills, call your creditors.** If you believe your creditors won't notice you're in arrears, think again. They will, and they will notify the credit bureaus. Call or write to explain your situation and, if possible, arrange to make partial payments. Also, if you need to have your bills spread out over the month instead of receiving them all on, say, the first, let your creditors know; most will be accommodating.

➤ **Determine what you can liquidate.** Take a close look at your possessions. What about that ruby brooch you inherited from your aunt? Or the baby grand piano you own and never play? By selling them, you could free up some money for investing.

➤ **Involve your family.** Get everyone in on the act. Make them all—even the children—active participants in the planning process. This is especially true if you undergo a crisis. By doing so, you'll make it both a learning experience and a way to provide some reassurance.

➤ **Consider a career change.** If you are in a dead-end job or career, weigh the options of making a change. The objective is to increase your income while gaining employment fulfillment.

Do You Need a Financial Planner?

The task of accumulating wealth is daunting. So daunting, in fact, that you may think you need professional help. You've heard that financial planners will take on the job of designing you a tailor-made strategy, including helping you select the proper investments, if need be.

Well, that's true—to a certain extent. But keep in mind that financial planners come in an assortment of types and styles. There are those who will charge you thousands of dollars to handle financial planning for you. And there are those who will design you a plan for as little as $50. What you'll receive in return varies as much as the price.

Your brokerage firm, for example, may assign a financial planner from its staff to handle your account, especially if you have a substantial amount of assets. But obviously such a person will recommend those investments offered by his or her firm. Objectivity often is questionable: Brokerage firms that offer financial planning tend to push their own managed underwritings.

Much the same is true of insurance-company-related financial planners, who generally will push their firm's insurance and annuity products. And financial planners associated with commercial banks will likely favor money-market accounts and certificates of deposit.

So you might think that an independent financial planner might be your best bet. But most of them are subject to blatant conflicts of interest because they rely partially or totally on financial-product commissions for their income.

Worse, anyone who wants to call himself or herself a financial planner can do so. Planners aren't required to be licensed or pass qualifying examinations, nor are they governed by any regulatory agencies. The result sometimes has been wholesale fraud in the name of financial planning.

If you are considering using the services of a financial planner, then, just be wary. A "fee-only" planner is usually your best choice. In most cases he or she doesn't rely on commissions for compensation. You can find fee-only planners by contacting their association and asking for a listing of those in your area. Here are the address and telephone number:

National Association of Personal Financial Advisors
355 W. Dundee Road, Suite 200
Buffalo Grove, IL 60089
800/366-2732

The following checklist can help you make a choice:

☐ 1. Ask about the planner's educational background. Determine if he or she holds any degrees in finance from recognized institutions.

☐ 2. Check on the planner's professional credentials. The Denver-based College for Financial Planning offers a curriculum leading to a "Certified Financial Planner" designation; some major colleges and universities have equivalent programs. Membership in the Atlanta-based International Association for Financial Planning isn't meaningful in itself, since the trade association has minimal criteria. But its Registry program is more analogous to the CFP designation.

☐ 3. Ask about the number of years of experience the planner has in this field.

☐ 4. Ask how much he or she initially charges and if there are annual fees.

☐ 5. Ask about the planner's other clients, what his or her track record is with them, and if you can talk with any of them.

☐ 6. Ask questions about the planner's experience with your particular situation. If, for example, your goal is to provide for your children's college education, does the planner ask the right questions as to when they'll be attending and where?

☐ 7. Make sure the planner attempts to pinpoint the level of risk you're comfortable with.

☐ 8. Make sure he or she knows your goals, thinks they are realistic, and is determined to help you reach them.

☐ 9. Check the planner's written communications and reports to make sure they are neat, well-organized, and comprehensive.

☐ 10. Make sure you fully understand the planner's recommendations. They should make sense to you and your family.

In this chapter, you have perhaps learned some things about yourself, your goals, and your ambitions. This is essential information if you are to succeed as an investor. You have also seen how to use this information to establish a budget and set up your cash flow. And you have filled in a personal balance sheet—a document you will find yourself referring to many times. Finally, you have resolved whether or not you need the help of a professional financial planner and how much you can expect to pay if you retain one.

Chapter 3:
Stocks + Compounding = Wealth

"Don't gamble! Take all of your savings and buy some good stocks. Hold onto them until they go up. Then sell them. If they don't go up, then don't buy them!"

— Will Rogers

"'Buy low, then sell when stocks go up.'
You'll prosper if you try it.
What if a stock refuses to rise?
The answer's simple: don't buy it."

—Paul Richards

Tomorrow's Winners – Today

The problem with the above advice, of course, is that no investor can tell in advance which stocks are going to go up. Such fortune-telling capabilities simply don't exist or we'd all be fabulously rich.

So this chapter is not the proverbial one about how to make a million or how to get rich quick. The only sure way of doing that is to win a lottery or receive a large inheritance. And although fortunes have been made in the stock market by those who got in on a stock early and stuck with it through numerous declines and bear markets, such instances are not all that common.

You can of course become rich by investing in baby IBMs or Xeroxes, but most of these infant companies fail. The majority are high-risk speculations to which few national investors would commit huge proportions of their savings.

In fact, the only sure way to improve your results is to adopt sound investment principles that have withstood the test of time.

In all probability, the principles that have made investors successful in the past will continue to do so.

This chapter will explain those principles and guide you toward your ultimate goal: picking the right stocks and significantly increasing the value of your portfolio. Successful implementation of the approach outlined requires neither exceptional intelligence nor access to inside tips. Any moderately enterprising investor can employ these guidelines successfully, at least on a limited scale. In any case, they'll help you avoid the costly stock-market pitfalls that snare so many unwary investors.

Why Common Stock

Common stock is an exceptional investment because it offers you three major advantages. First, because of its variable-income nature, you can participate in the economic progress of the company. Should the company experience extraordinary expansion, the shareholder will often participate in it through an increase in the value of his or her shares. Secondly, common stock offers you the best possibility of capital growth when the nation's economy is healthy.

Finally, common stock is considered by many experts as a good long-term hedge against inflation. As the general price level rises, so, theoretically, do stock prices. An investment of 100 shares of Sears, Roebuck, bought in 1906 at $5,700, would now be worth more than $2.5 million. The value of the dollar worth 100 cents in 1939 is worth 15 cents today, but the Dow Jones Industrial Average climbed above 8200 recently from about 160 in 1939.

The reason for this remarkable increase in value lies in the process of compounding. In almost magic-like manner, an

investment that seems meager can, with time, become boun-
teous. Let's digress for a moment to explain.

The Wonder of Compounding

When you add compounding to your arsenal for accumulating wealth, you have at your command one of the most potent
weapons that exist. Compounding heightens the act of investing from something commonplace into something extraordinary. It can singly transform a modest return on investment
into millions of dollars.

Let's look at some examples of compounding as it applies
to common stocks:

Suppose you are 25 years old and have invested a thousand dollars in the stock market. Let's also assume you can
save $50 a month and can obtain a 15-percent total return on
your common-stock investments. Here's what you can accomplish with this amount and enough time:

Age	$1,000 + $50 a Month
25	$ 1,000
30	8,663
35	18,054
40	40,967
45	87,054
50	179,745
55	466,185
60	741,183
65	1,495,435

Of course, income taxes would normally take a huge portion of your accumulation if you haven't invested in something
that is tax-free. But we're assuming that you have invested
through an individual retirement account, which does provide
you with tax protection.

Now assume that you're 30 years old. You'll need a slightly
larger stake to begin with: $10,000. But this time, you're just
going to let the initial amount earn its own way (at 15 percent) without adding anything more. As you can see, the

results you'll get from compounding are just about as good.

Age	$10,000 + Nothing a Month
30	$ 10,000
35	20,113
40	40,456
45	81,371
50	163,670
55	329,190
60	662,120
65	1,331,800

Next, suppose you open an IRA. In it, you invest $145 a month for 20 years in common stock. That's a total of $34,800. The contributions to common stock in the IRA do well, yielding 10 percent compounded annually. How much do you think you will have accumulated over the 20 years?

☐ $50,000   ☐ $75,000   ☐ $104,000

The answer is $104,000, give or take a few dollars. If you keep this up for another five years, incidentally, the total will increase to $178,967.

Finally, if you had an opportunity to invest $5,000 per year in common stock for 10 years, how much do you think you would accumulate at the end of that time if your stock earned 12 percent compounded annually? (Leave taxes out of your calculation.)

☐ $51,200   ☐ $76,512   ☐ $87,744

The correct answer is $87,744. And if you continued the same process for another 10 years, you'd have $360,262!

Little wonder that the compounding effect has always been one of the major concerns of investors. And as you have seen in the previous examples, rates of return are the pulse of investing. Mastering the concept in its various calculations is consequently fundamental to understanding much of what goes on in money and portfolio management. In Chapter 20 of this book, you can spend more time to fully understand what compounding is all about. For now, just remember what Benjamin Franklin had to say about compounding: "Money is of a prolific, generating nature. Money can beget money, and its offspring can beget more." Franklin was probably merely agreeing with one of his contemporaries, Baron Rothschild, who called compound interest the "eighth wonder of the world."

Going with Growth

Good growth potential is always a plus. This is not to say that all common stocks are growth stocks. Rather, on average, common stock offers you better growth than other types of securities. With regard to income, common stocks vary. Dividends are not guaranteed. And investment in common stock is riskier than investment in preferred stocks or bonds.

To invest in common stocks for growth, and to attain superior results, you need to understand and appreciate these key points:

➤ Selectivity is the key to consistent profits.

➤ The right information is essential.

➤ There is no substitute for quality.

➤ Finding good value provides your margin of safety.

➤ Excellent companies improve your odds.

➤ Investing in "super" stocks can build wealth.

You'll be looking at each one in some detail in a moment, but first, expand on the definition of common stocks to include growth stocks.

The Concept of a Growth Stock

The term "growth stock" is applied to the stock of a company that has increased its earnings per share for a period of years at a rate much higher than most companies generally— and is expected to continue to do so in the future. It is assumed that the earnings growth of the company will have a steady and predictable effect on the company's share price over time.

THE GROWTH-STOCK DREAM TEAM

Many growth stocks enjoyed unparalleled success in 1996. Here, for example, are the best performers during that boom year:

Company	12/31/96 Closing Price	Change from 1995
TSR	$28.00	966.7%
VIASOFT	47.25	695.7
Zitel	44.38	639.6
ISG Int'l Software Group	27.75	516.7
Federal Agricultural Mortgage	30.75	515.0
Finish Line	21.13	463.3
PMR	26.13	435.9
Williams Energy	17.38	434.6
Maxwell Technologies	22.00	433.3
Medicis Pharmaceutical	44.00	375.7

But earnings-per-share growth rates vary widely from one sector to another. So what constitutes an above-average return? There is no single answer, but in your search for growth stocks you're looking for earnings growth that is superior to the aggregate rates of return of the companies listed in such broad market averages as the Standard & Poor's 500 and the Dow Jones Industrial Average. Generally speaking, a stock is not a growth stock unless earnings per share have been growing at a rate of at least 15 percent a year, on average, for the previous five years.

Another hallmark of a growth stock is a high return on shareholders' equity. A return of more than 15 percent is necessary for a stock to be considered a growth stock.

For growth stocks, these two variables—earnings per share and return on shareholders' equity—are the major factors in determining what the company's shares are worth and will be worth over time. Companies with above-average growth in earnings and a high return on shareholders' equity will tend to show above-average share-price performance in the market. As mentioned, most growth stocks must maintain at least a

15-percent return on equity and an annual 15-percent EPS growth rate to remain growth stocks.

A great many investors buy groceries more carefully than they buy stocks. Frequently they will buy a stock because it's been recommended by somebody, and hence is expected to go up. Beyond that, they acquire little knowledge of the company involved, its financial characteristics, or its operating record.

In your search for bargain-priced super stocks, though, you'll have to know how to "read the label" to get exceptional value for your money. Now take a look at how to do just that.

Be Selective

Stocks can be divided into two vastly different categories. The first contains a large number of bad or mediocre stocks that are not worth buying and that should be scrupulously avoided. They may be of insufficient quality, carry excessive risk, or have limited growth potential. The second category contains a tiny number of superior issues that are well worth buying boldly.

The task of the selective investor is to identify the stocks in the latter group, invest in them, and wait patiently. Painstaking selectivity is one of the keys to consistent profits.

The problem is that there are thousands of publicly traded companies in America, and each one is a potential investment for your portfolio. How does an investor select the good stocks—the potential super stocks—from among the thousands of candidates in the marketplace?

Many investors, especially beginners, are looking for a magic formula or strategy that will enable them to "beat the market" and make a lot of money fast. They have a strong tendency to get caught up in stories about how someone supposedly made a lot of gains by following brokers' tips, a guru, or the latest stock-market fad.

But experienced investors know that there are no sure and easy paths to riches in the stock market. Making the really large gains in growth stocks demands a high degree of staying power in the right stocks.

Every successful investment practitioner has a philosophy and a method, along with a battle plan to make it all work.

There are dozens of investment styles and strategies. And there are numerous quantitative and qualitative approaches to the stock market. But generally there are three types of strategists:

1. **Value investors:** They select companies that are selling in the marketplace for considerably less than their true worth or intrinsic value. This value is determined primarily by balance-sheet analysis. Consideration is given to the value of future dividends and earnings, but more attention is paid to the realizable value of the company's assets.

2. **Growth investors:** They select companies that are expected to experience continued increases in sales revenue, earnings, profitability, or market share. They anticipate that the continued growth in earnings, assets, and profitability of such companies will produce a corresponding growth in share prices over time.

3. **Market timers:** They select stocks that will change favorably in price. Attention is paid to charts or other largely mechanical means of determining the right moments to buy and sell. The objective is to make a profit buying and selling in advance of stock-price swings on the basis of "technical" factors, such as volume and price, chart patterns, and cycle analysis.

Which method is best? Historically, the value approach to stock selection has proven *most* successful and the market-timing approach the *least* successful. The strategy outlined in this book is a value-oriented approach to growth investing—in other words, a combination of the two methods. Your objective is twofold: to identify growing companies and to invest in them as cheaply as possible.

The Search for Facts

Accurate, reliable information is essential to the stock-selection process. Basing investment decisions on bad information can be a disaster. These are the key data you'll need, including:

➤ Current annual sales.

➤ Current assets.

➤ Current liabilities.

➤ Current book value.

➤ Current earnings per share.

➤ Earnings per share for the past 10 years.

➤ Preferred and common dividends for the past 10 years.

➤ Annual growth rate in earnings for the past 10 years.

➤ Compounded annual earnings growth rate for the past five or 10 years.

➤ Yearly high and low market prices for the past three years.

From your public library, you should be able to obtain most, if not all, of these figures, especially if you are investigating a major company. There, you can obtain a variety of sources, too, such as Standard & Poor's, Moody's, and Value Line. If you have access to an online computer service, such as America Online or CompuServe, you can also readily get this information.

Testing for Quality

Quality-conscious investing depends on selecting companies with good operating and financial track records, manageable debt, and sound management. You can avoid a large percentage of potentially serious investment mistakes by buying only high-quality blue-chip or investment-grade stocks.

Start by examining and comparing companies within a specific industry. The leaders will be financially strong, visibly profitable, and have demonstrated long-term growth in earnings and assets. Such companies frequently are large and have a high profile in the marketplace. Holding their shares gives you a margin of safety.

Here are the key areas to investigate when testing for quality:

➤ **Size.** Consider only medium to large corporations with

annual sales of at least $100 million. This rules out small, speculative companies.

> **Financial condition.** Current assets should be at least twice current liabilities. Long-term debt should not exceed the net current assets or working capital.

> **Earnings stability.** The company must have had earnings for the common stock in each of the past 10 years.

> **Dividends.** The company must have paid dividends for the common or preferred shares in each of the past 10 years.

> **Earnings growth.** A minimum increase of at least 30 percent in earnings per share in the past 10 years.

Testing for Value

As you've already learned, value investors (and you'll learn more about this type of investor later in this book) concentrate on identifying companies that are selling in the marketplace for considerably less than their true worth or intrinsic value. A value-oriented investor looks for companies that are undervalued. In such cases, the stock price has been driven low enough for the value investor to consider the shares a true bargain. Usually the cause of this condition is disappointing earnings, protracted neglect, or unpopularity. Value investors buy a bargain stock believing that conditions will improve and they will be able to sell the shares at a much higher price.

At least a dozen different quantitative approaches measure value. Most of these are of interest only to the security or business analyst. Each measure attempts to relate the current share price of the company to some other financial characteristic, such as earnings, cash flow, dividends, book value, or sales revenue.

Depending on the company or the industry in which it operates, some ratios or "multiples" are more important than others. And a multiple that is high for one type of company might be considered low for another.

A complete and detailed discussion of all the tools of a value investor will be presented later. But suffice to say that no investor (whether of the value school or the growth school) can reasonably expect to make lasting gains by overpaying for stocks.

How do you avoid buying a stock priced too high? Simple: Don't pay more than it's worth. Here are three tests of value that will help you determine just how much is too much:

➤ **The price/earnings multiple.** This number is obtained by dividing the market price of the stock by the company's latest 12-month earnings per share. The p/e multiple, or ratio, indicates how much investors are willing to pay for a company's earnings. In general, it is not advisable to pay more than 15 times current earnings or 12 times future earnings. The lower the multiple, the better the value.

➤ **The price/book-value multiple**. This number is obtained by dividing the market price of the stock by the company's net worth, or total assets minus total liabilities. It indicates how much investors are willing to pay for a company's shares in relation to its theoretical liquidation value. In general, it is not advisable to pay more than 1.5 times book value for a stock, unless the price/earnings multiple is less than 15.

➤ **The price/sales ratio.** To obtain this number, first multiply the stock price by the total number of shares. Then compare that figure with the company's revenues in the most recent 12-month period. In general, pay no more than 75 percent of sales unless the price/earnings multiple is less than 15 or the price/book-value ratio is much less than 1.5.

A word of caution goes with these screening techniques, however: They are all sound and useful, but beware of relying on just one, by itself—it may lead you astray:

➤ A low price/earnings multiple might simply mean the company's earnings have temporarily bulged.

➤ A low price/book-value ratio might camouflage an overinflated book value, owing to needed but untaken asset write-downs.

➤ A low price/sales ratio might signal tough times for the next few years, or very low profitability.

It's a good idea to use two of these tests—ideally all three. By using them all, you assure that you're not paying high prices in relation to earnings, to book value, or to the company's sales size.

This is really the sum and substance of value investing. Study after study proves that above-average returns are often traced to a rigorous use of value criteria in stock selection.

Value investors search for discrepancies between the value of a business and the price of small pieces of that business in the market. Then they exploit the difference between the market price of the business and its intrinsic value. Like all attempts to beat the market, value investing is a search for pockets of inefficiency.

While looking for value is important, never rely solely on value criteria for selecting a stock. Such an approach is an invitation to disaster: A very cheap stock may look like a good investment, even though it is on the edge of bankruptcy. No investment tactic should be used in isolation.

Testing for Excellence

A great deal of sound investment advice has the clear ring of common sense. It has long been the prevalent view that the art of successful investing lies first in the choice of those industries that are most likely to grow in the future and then in identifying the most promising companies in those industries.

But don't follow this strategy blindly and slavishly. Obvious prospects for growth in a business do not always translate into obvious profits for investors. And even the experts don't have infallible ways of selecting the most promising companies in the most promising industries.

How do you reconcile the importance of investing in excellent companies with the importance of buying value? Simply put, make outstanding quality one of your stock-selection criteria.

The key idea here is that you can make a lot of money by investing in an outstanding enterprise and holding it for years and years as it becomes bigger and better. The market price of your shares almost certainly will rise over time to reflect their higher intrinsic value.

As a growth investor, you must be willing to "pay up" for first-class companies that have the best research, forward-looking competent management of high integrity, effective cost-cutting programs, and the other hallmarks of a superior enterprise. (Just remember to apply your value-investing criteria to ensure you don't pay too much.) It's primarily these excellent companies that are able to maintain long-term superior earnings growth, the key to consistent long-term share-price appreciation, which is the touchstone of a superior stock.

There are three key indicators of excellence:

➤ **Growth orientation**, because senior management has an overriding desire to maximize growth in the business.

➤ **Marketing excellence.** A broad understanding of the company's market along with an organization capable of generating customer satisfaction.

➤ **Competitive superiority over current or potential competitors:** for example, in being the lowest-cost producer or the company with the largest market share.

The shares of excellent companies have the potential to be growth stocks or even superior stocks. More important, they can keep you out of serious trouble.

The logic of investing in excellent companies with excellent management cannot be overestimated in today's extremely competitive, changeable economy. Savvy investors always take a hard look at management before risking their money. Stocks will fluctuate, but managerial excellence is a commodity that endures. Over the long run, it will offer outstanding rewards to those investors who recognize it.

Measuring a Stock's 'I.Q.'

To aid you in your search for bargain-priced super stocks,

you need a method of measuring a stock's investment merits. One such method is to determine the stock's "investment quotient," or I.Q.

Stated simply, the I.Q. relates the price of a stock to either the company's growth rate or to its profitability. Its purpose is to identify pockets of inefficiency in which the price may be too low compared with other financial characteristics that are important in predicting superior share-price performance.

Just as an individual's intelligence quotient may be used to predict someone's success in performing certain tasks, a stock's investment quotient may be used to predict its tendency to perform well in the stock market.

There are two ways to determine a stock's investment quotient. In the first method, a company's growth in earnings is compared with the price the market is willing to pay for those earnings. In the second method, a company's profitability or return on equity is compared with the price the market is willing to pay for the profits the company generates.

The growth I.Q. is determined by dividing a company's latest 12-month gain in earnings by its price/earnings ratio:

$$\frac{\text{Earnings gain over previous year (EG)}}{\text{Price/earnings multiple (PE)}}$$

The "profitability I.Q." is determined by dividing a company's latest 12-month return on equity by its price/earnings ratio:

$$\frac{\text{Return on equity for current year (ROE)}}{\text{Price/earnings multiple (PE)}}$$

In both cases, a ratio greater than 2 indicates superior value. For example, if a company experienced a 20-percent gain in earnings in the previous year and its price/earnings ratio was 9.5, then its growth I.Q. would be 20÷9.5, or 2.1.

Or, if a company had a 25-percent return on equity in the previous year and its price/earnings ratio was 12, then its profitability I.Q. would be 25÷12, or 2.08.

Obviously, a high investment quotient may be a result of either very high growth/profitability, or a very low price/earnings multiple.

It can be very useful to compare the average five-year or 10-year earnings-growth rate or return on equity with the current price/earnings multiple. Using the I.Q. in this manner is a superb way to determine which stocks are undervalued.

Of course, all this talk about past performance is, unfortunately, mostly academic. Very little can be reliably determined by looking just at last year's results. It is the trend of growth and profitability that is the key to a stock's future.

For this reason, the best use of the I.Q. is to plot a trend over time, going back as far as possible. The latest five-year to 10-year period, however, will be of the greatest significance. For example, a positive sign for a company, and a signal that something good is happening for the stock, is an earnings growth rate or return on equity that is rising while the price/earnings multiple is steady or rising at a slower rate. A negative sign for a company, and a signal that something bad is happening for the stock, is an earnings growth rate or return on equity that is slowing down and a price/earnings multiple that has taken a sudden drop.

If the I.Q. is not quite 2 but is trending toward it, the stock is becoming an excellent value. If the I.Q. is near 2 but declining, the stock is becoming a poorer value. But in either case, the I.Q. by itself isn't foolproof. One needs to determine the cause of the change in I.Q. This can usually be determined by studying the earnings growth over time and the return on equity from year to year.

Your Super-Stock Selection Summary

As a value-oriented growth investor, you're looking for companies that have been experiencing favorable trends in earnings growth and profitability and that will, you hope, continue to experience such trends in the future. You're interested in buying superior growth stocks, but only when the price is right.

In your search for a super stock, bear in mind that one of the tell-tale signs of a growth company is the ownership of the stock. It's a good sign when officers and directors, who are, of course, the most "in the know" about the company, own shares. If a large proportion of the shares of a company is held by the insiders, it indicates that the smart money is confident about the company's business prospects.

You want management that thinks the way an owner would. After all, as a shareholder, you are an owner and you want people running your company whose interests are the same as yours.

Use this checklist to help you find those bargain-priced super stocks:

- ❏ Rising unit sales volume.

- ❏ Rising pre-tax profit margins.

- ❏ Above-average return on shareholders' equity.

- ❏ Strong earnings-per-share growth.

- ❏ Rising dividends, but a low payout ratio. (Don't be wooed by mediocre companies offering high dividends. As a shareholder, you're better off if dividends are retained within the company and reinvested intelligently.)

- ❏ Low debt.

- ❏ Low institutional holdings.

- ❏ Increasing price/earnings multiple.

- ❏ High share ownership by strong, owner-oriented insiders.

- ❏ A leading position in an attractive industry; a strong business franchise.

- ❏ Better products or services than the competition.

- ❏ An understandable business that sees its profits in cash.

- ❏ Predictable earnings.

- ❏ Low inventories and high asset turnover.

This chapter details the principles of sound investment strategies using common stocks. You learned ways to pick the right stocks to increase the value of your portfolio. You also saw that a successful investor requires neither exceptional intelligence nor access to insider tips. You should now be able to implement a strategy of stock selection that will produce meaningful and lasting results.

Chapter 4:
How to Acquire Additional Investment Funds

"A penny saved is a penny got"—
Firm to this scoundrel maxim keepeth he.

– James Thomson

Finding Buried Treasure

After you start concentrating on ways to accumulate money, you'll soon recognize the many advantages of controlling your spending habits and taking other actions to make extra money. In effect, you will "uncover" money that you can use to benefit from the investment opportunities explored in this book. This is not about supermarket-shopping tips or ways to save money buying a car. Consumer-type information abounds from other sources. (In fact, The Hume Group Inc. offers some of the best advice in that regard through its MoneyFiles series.) Instead, in this chapter—and in the entire book—you deal strictly with financial- and investor-related information. So with that in mind here are just a few potential methods for finding buried treasure:

Capitalize on Your Insurance:

If you have a whole-life policy, or any other type that has built up a sizable cash-surrender value, you can put that money to more-productive use. The insurance company will "lend" (and keep in mind that the money is technically yours) most of the cash value to you at an attractive interest rate. You can then invest that money, earning a much higher return than any interest the insurance lender charges. (Under current tax law, the interest expense on a loan from your life-insurance policy may be considered consumer-loan interest, which is not deductible.)

If you can't borrow the cash value on your life-insurance policy (or you have no cash value), still take a closer look at the policy. Eliminate unneeded coverage to reduce your premiums, and use the savings for investment. But it's the same story as with bankers: Few insurance agents will be inclined to tell you that you need less coverage. The initiative must be yours.

Here are three ways to save money on other insurance premiums:

1. Increase deductible limits for auto and home losses, perhaps from $250 to $1,000. Often, the higher premium you pay year after year to have a low deductible is not worth the few extra hundred dollars you'd get with your claim in the unlikely event of damage or loss of your property. (Many people don't even make a claim for less than a large damage loss because they fear their premiums will rise.)

    You can make an even larger savings by raising the deductible on your health-insurance plan (unless your employer pays for your coverage). So-called "first-dollar coverage" is the most expensive health insurance you can buy, and the price tag for having the insurer pay for routine doctor visits and occasional prescriptions may be greater than it is worth. A policy with a $250 or $1,000 deductible generally will cost hundreds of dollars a year less.

2. If your car is more than five years old, take the maximum deductibles on comprehensive and collision coverages. Or

you may want to eliminate these coverages altogether if the repair/replacement reimbursement will be relatively low due to the vehicle's age. (Some insurance companies allow you to insure against damage to your vehicle with a few-dollars premium that applies only if you don't carry regular collision coverage and the damage is proven to be the fault of the driver of another vehicle.)

3. Discuss your policies with your insurance agent to be sure you are receiving all discounts to which you are entitled. Make sure any changes in status since you acquired your coverage are reflected in your policies.

Some of the things for which auto owners can get premium discounts include:

➤ Being over age 55.

➤ Being retired.

➤ Driving less than 8,000 miles per year.

➤ Being married.

➤ Having two or more cars on the same policy.

➤ Having student drivers in the family take a driver's education course.

➤ Installing a security system.

➤ Having a driving record free of accidents and traffic violations.

➤ Living in a low-risk (for accidents) area.

Homeowners can benefit on their insurance from—

➤ Being nonsmokers.

➤ Having smoke detectors.

➤ Living near a fire station.

➤ Having a home-security system.

➤ Living above the ground floor.

➤ Using the same company to insure both their residence and motor vehicles.

Depending on the insurance company or companies you use, these factors can make you eligible for premiums lower than those with which you started. And if they don't, then consider changing companies. By comparison shopping among reputable companies, you may save hundreds of dollars each year on auto, life, and homeowner policies. You're entitled to full value for what you pay.

Now let's turn to insurance expenses and consider them in a slightly different light, using the example of Jack Oliver.

We all probably have a bit of Jack Oliver's mode of behavior in us, at least when it comes to insurance. Jack is 43, is married, and he and his wife have three children, two of them teenagers. He has worked for the same company since he graduated from high school. When he was 25, he bought a $10,000 whole-life insurance policy and has been paying premiums on it ever since. He also has some term insurance through a plan at work.

Jack would be hard-pressed to tell you exactly how much term insurance coverage he has. It's something multiplied by his salary, he thinks. As for his whole-life policy, he isn't even sure where it is. He does know that it would pay a lump sum of $50,000 at death. But ask Jack about its cash value, and he'd be out in left field. Ask him if he's getting nonsmoker's rates (Jack doesn't smoke) and he's be as curious as you are. Then to really embarrass him, ask him if he's ever really looked at his insurance as both protection and an investment.

As stated, there's probably a little bit of Jack Oliver in all of us. Most of us know distressingly little about our own personal-insurance situation. Yet, like everything else in our financial portfolio, choosing insurance and managing it is a key to personal success.

Try this brief self-analysis quiz to see how much you know about your current insurance policies:

➤ Have you reviewed your life-insurance situation carefully in the past year? Past two years?

➤ Do you have term insurance? Do you know how much?

➤ Do you have a whole-life policy? Do you know what its face value is? Does it have a cash value? If so, do you know how much?

➤ Do you know whether nonsmoker's rates are available from your current insurer?

➤ Are you confident that your current policies are good investments as well as good forms of protection for your family?

How many of these questions did you answer with a "yes"? Consider coverage for nonsmokers. The savings can be considerable. There are plenty of nonsmokers who, having bought insurance some time ago when they smoked, now may be paying a higher premium than they should be.

YOUR GUIDE TO LOWER PREMIUMS

The following states offer shopping guides with auto-insurance rate comparisons:

State	Telephone #	State	Telephone #
Alabama	334-269-3550	Nebraska	402-471-2201
Alaska	907-269-7900	Nevada	800-992-0900
Arizona	602-912-8444	New Jersey	800-446-7467
California	800-927-4357	New York	800-342-3736
Colorado	303-894-7499	North Dakota	800-247-0560
Connecticut	203-297-3867	Ohio	800-686-1526
Delaware	800-282-8611	Oregon	503-378-4484
Florida	904-922-3132	Pennsylvania	717-787-2317
Hawaii	808-587-1234	Rhode Island	401-277-2223
Kentucky	502-564-3630	South Carolina	800-768-3467
Louisiana	800-259-5300	Texas	800-252-3439
Maine	207-624-8475	Utah	800-439-3805
Maryland	800-492-6116	Vermont	802-828-3301
Massachusetts	617-521-7777	Virginia	800-552-7945
Michigan	517-373-9273	Washington	800-562-6900
Minnesota	800-657-3602	West Virginia	800-642-9004
Missouri	800-726-7390	Wisconsin	800-236-8517
Montana	800-332-6148	Wyoming	800-438-5768

Let's say you're a 40-year-old male smoker who wants a $250,000 yearly renewable-term life-insurance policy. Such a policy, paid monthly, could run to something like $930 a year. If you were a 40-year-old nonsmoker, you might pay about $510 for the same coverage. So if you're a nonsmoker and you have some insurance coverage that you haven't looked at in some time, dig it out and review what you're paying. Even if the difference to you is only $100, that's money you could be putting to use in your investment program.

That's only one example of potential savings. What about the bigger picture? Do you have the right type of life insurance? Does the insurance you have contain an investment feature? Could you do better? You need to deal with all these questions and learn how to provide the best coverage for your situation.

For now, here are three additional ways to save money on insurance:

1. You have some excellent insurance bargains available to you if you're a nondrinker. If you aren't getting special rates by being in that group, talk to your insurance agent. Incidentally, the bargains aren't confined to life insurance. Some firms offer special rates for auto and property insurance as well.

2. The difference in insurance premiums among companies can be astounding. A recent survey of guaranteed whole-life policies for a 35-year-old male seeking $100,000 in coverage showed a broad range in costs, from around $500 annually to about $1,600 annually. With that kind of spread, you can't afford not to shop the market for the best rate.

3. Life insurance isn't for everyone. If you're single and have no dependents, you may not need life insurance at all. Examine your situation closely.

CUTTING LIFE INSURANCE COSTS

Keep in mind that life-insurance-agent commissions can run anywhere from 70 percent to more than 100 percent of the initial premium you pay, plus another 5 percent on renewals. But now available are so-called "low-load" policies. They eliminate big sales commissions.

Two companies that offer such policies are USAA in San Antonio (800-531-8000) and Ameritas Life Insurance in Lincoln, Neb. (800- 255-9678). Or you can call Ameritas' largest distributor, Veritas in Houston (800-552-3553).

USAA sells its own policies through a staff of salaried personnel. Ameritas sells through agents whose modest 10-percent fee (plus 2 percent on renewals) is not deducted from your premium; it's simply built into the policy price. Fee-based financial planners also sell Ameritas policies.

Control Impulse Buying:

Regular buying on impulse will torpedo any type of money-management program. Are you one of those shoppers who finds, too often, that items you don't need have just "followed you home from the store"?

From surveys by the Point of Purchase Advertising Institute, we learn that more than 40 percent of all in-store purchases are unplanned. So if you spend $100 a week in the grocery store, there's a good chance that at least $40 of that will go for impulse items. That's $2,080 a year!

Certain products are sold largely on their impulse, and retail-merchandising techniques encourage such impulse buying. It's no accident that such items as candy, gum, tabloid newspapers, and magazines are displayed at the checkout counter.

If you plan your shopping in advance (make a list and stick to it), you're much less likely to react on impulse. Another proven way to combat impulse spending is simply to pace yourself when shopping. Put the brakes on before a shopping frenzy builds.

Know your limits, and when you feel yourself pushing them, play a little mind game. Tell yourself, "I'll buy this, but first I'll have a cup of coffee," or, "I'll get it tomorrow." Chances

are you'll forget about the purchase or, with time to reflect, it
will not seem such a "necessity."

Before making a purchase, ask—

➤ Do I really need this item?

➤ Can I really afford it?

➤ Have I comparison shopped?

➤ Is now the best time to make this purchase?

➤ Should I pay cash or go into debt on the installment plan?

➤ Should I use a credit card?

➤ Is there a less expensive way to "borrow" the money?

A prime time to shop for many expensive consumer goods
is just after Christmas. Big postseason sales start in January,
but February can be even better for shopping. In February
consumers begin to receive their deferred-payment bills for
goods they charged at Christmas. They make a point not to go
shopping. Retailers anticipate the corresponding drop in sales
and mark inventory down to keep it moving. This is the time
to make your move.

Structure Your Spending:

Before making a major purchase, research the product and
have an idea of what the item should cost, setting a fixed
amount aside (mentally or actually) for that purpose. Paying a
few extra cents or even dollars now and then shouldn't do
much damage; sometimes convenience or some other benefit of
making the purchase then and there warrants paying a little
more. But on major purchases, overpaying can mean a significant loss of future purchasing power—and funds with which to
invest.

You get nothing extra for the additional money you spend.
That money becomes a higher gross profit to some retailer,
extra cash in his pocket, and less for you to invest or to spend
on yourself or your family and friends. Put yourself in control
of your purchases rather than letting merchants, other people,
powerful advertising, or random impulses dictate how much

you should spend or on what.

As mentioned, this is not the place to get consumer-type information. But you are aware of the advantages of seasonal fluctuations in retail sales. Buying a new car when dealers advertise rebates or low-interest financing or when you can get attractive loan terms from your bank or credit union also makes sense. As well, it's wise to buy cars in the late fall, when dealers offer major discounts on existing inventory to make room for next year's models.

Moreover, most shoppers know it pays to buy your wardrobe out of season. You can predict shifts in demand for many goods and services and structure your spending accordingly. Electronics, furniture, heating/cooling systems—sales of these and most other items move in seasonal cycles.

Stretch Your Banking Dollars:

It's an unfortunate fact that it's not enough that you work hard. To grow wealthy, you have to make your money work hard, too. You can start this process by making better use of your bank. Here's how:

1. Eliminate unnecessary service charges. Service fees vary widely from bank to bank. Study your bank statement. See how much you are being charged for specific services. Then call around to your bank's competitors to see what they charge for the same services. Or the same bank may be able to offer you a better deal. For example, you may have opened your checking account with $500. At that time the only checking plan available to you carried a flat-fee service charge of $5 a month. Six years later your balance may have risen so that you now qualify for free checking. The bank won't automatically alter your plan so long as it can keep collecting its (your) five dollars. One fast call, in this case, could save you $60 a year.

2. Never let funds accumulate in a noninterest-bearing account, such as most checking accounts. Instead, ask your bank for a checking account that pays interest so long as you maintain a minimum balance.

3. Set up a money-market checking account in addition to, or instead of, a regular savings account. Money-market accounts usually pay you a return greater than regular savings accounts, with an interest rate tied to movement in the prime rate. You can then write a monthly check (out of the handful of checks you're allowed to write each month with a money-market account) to your regular checking account to pay your bills.

4. Once you've chosen a high-interest account, make regular deposits into it. Your paycheck and any other receipts should go to this account. Transfer to the lower-paying checking account only the amount needed to cover regular expenses. A realistic goal for most people is to hold on, for savings, to at least 10 percent of all the money deposited to a money-market account.

5. Consistency is important. It's easier (and better) to set aside $85 each month for one year in a high-interest account than to try to come up with a $1,000 deposit once a year. The pattern (and the financial judgment it implies), rather than the amount of the deposits, will better serve your financial growth.

6. Look for investment alternatives to "accounts." Checking accounts are fully liquid (that is, you can withdraw money any time you want without penalty), but they're designed to hold small sums of money. If you have the minimum required (usually more than $1,000) and you can get along with less liquidity, put a block of money into a six-month or one-year certificate of deposit, short-term government securities, or money-market mutual fund. These vehicles pay rates substantially higher than regular savings or checking accounts and offer almost immediate liquidity.

SOME TYPICAL BANK ATM SURCHARGES

Here are 10 of the nation's largest banks and the surcharges that customers pay to access their automatic teller machines:

Bank	Surcharge Amount	Fee for Using Another Bank's ATM
Bank of America	$1	$2
Wells Fargo	$1 to $1.50	$.50 to $2
NationsBank	$1 to $1.25	$1
Banc One	$1.50	$.50
First Union	$1	$1.25 to $2
First Bank	N/A	$2
Norwest	$.75 to $1.50	$1.50
PNC Bank	$.50 to $2	$.50 to $2
Fleet	$1 to $2	$1.50
Citibank	N/A	$1 to $1.75

Establish a Routine:

Let's say it's January 1. You've made up your mind to start investing next year at this time, and you decide to save $1,000 (plus interest) especially for that purpose. If you're not used to parting with $1,000 in cash all at once, you may have trouble meeting your regular expenses. You can reach your goal by December if you put $85 per month ($85 x 12 = $1,020) into, say, a 5.5-percent money-market account, compounded monthly.

But then you start thinking about giving up that $85 each month. So you don't deposit the $85 for the entire 12 months. In December, you take a deep breath and plunk down $1,000 into the money-market account. Great. You've got the investment money you promised yourself, and you haven't lost a penny. Or have you? December is the twelfth month of your savings year. Because of the way interest is computed, your $1,000 will earn one month's worth of 5.5 percent, or $4.58 (1/12 x .055 x $1,000).

Compare this with 12 regular $85 deposits, January through December, earning 5.5 percent in that same money-market account. If you deposit $85 per month, you get a total of about $26 in interest. This may not seem like a lot of money. But look at what that $26 really is: almost a third of one month's $85 deposit. Money that you don't have to earn for your money-market account.

That's what consistent deposits can do for you.

Earn Extra Interest:

Suppose you end up with $100 each year in extra interest by finding the highest-paying interest account available and holding the most you can in that account. If you transfer the $100 into a 6-percent investment vehicle each year and reinvest it for 25 years, that original $2,500 will grow to $5,486, almost $3,000 of it interest!

If you shop around for a better-paying investment vehicle and increase your interest rate from 6 percent to 8 percent, the two extra percentage points initially will earn you an extra $20 per $1,000 per year. You might think that's not much at all, right?

It may hardly seem worth taking time to shop for the higher rate, but the extra return compounded at 8 percent for 25 years will grow to $7,311. That is almost $2,000 more than would be earned at the lower rate. Not bad for a bit of extra work. And this is only an 8-percent rate of return. Percentages and gains can be even higher as you move into other types of investments.

Consolidate Debts:

You may have debts with many creditors and at varying interest rates. Debt consolidation may save you a great deal of money. Check the debts you owe: auto loans, credit cards, finance companies, remembering that loan charges may vary from year to year and among financial institutions.

Interest on auto loans has been known to vary as much as 10 percent. Finance companies often charge much higher rates than banks and credit unions. Credit cards and department-store accounts can be insidious ways of incurring additional debt—unless you use them properly.

Also, it is a fact of the modern financial system that small loans generally incur higher interest rates. When General Electric and Ford Motor Co. go to their bank, they pays interest at the prime rate (the rate banks charge their favorite customers). You probably are paying several points over the prime, even if you bank where GE and Ford do. You may not be able to change the fact that the bank gives GE and Ford a better interest rate than it gives you. But you can control, to some degree, the interest rate you pay based on the amount of money you borrow. Look at the interest-rate schedules on your credit-card bills. You'll see information that tells you something like this: On the balance up to $2,000, the finance charge is 16 percent annually, while on the balance over $2,000, you pay 12 percent. (These numbers are generalized.)

You may owe $2,000 or more in credit-card bills, but if it's spread over several cards with low but lingering balances, you're paying the 16 percent on every penny. And if you pay the minimum amount due to each creditor every month, you will carry 16 percent until all balances go to zero.

Here's how to shop for a consolidation loan:

1. Call the loan department at three different financial institutions in your area. Find out whether they make consolidation loans. (Some institutions call such loans a "personal line of credit.") Not all financial institutions charge the same rates. Credit unions frequently offer lower rates than banks or thrift institutions. If you have savings at a credit union (usually called a "share account"), you may be able to borrow as much as you have deposited at a rate below prime.

2. Ask whether the institution charges any difference in interest, based on the amount of the balance. If so, then compare the interest that would be charged on the total of what you owe with the interest you're currently paying on each of your credit cards. The interest on a consolidated loan will probably be less than the cumulative interest on a series of credit cards.

3. If you are an established customer with a good credit rat-

ing, apply for a lower-interest consolidation loan or a line of credit for the total of the individual credit-card balances due. Use that new line of credit to pay off the individual balances this month—and you will reduce the interest you pay on the gross amount of your credit-card debt. It is best not to use the credit cards again until the loan is paid off.

Refinance Loans:

You can renegotiate and refinance smaller loans as well as larger ones. But be careful. Make sure you can benefit from the refinancing before you renegotiate.

Suppose you have an auto loan at 10 percent, and your bank is willing to lend you the money to pay it off at 7 percent. Good deal, right? Maybe.

If a big part of the loan has been paid off, refinancing may not be worthwhile, because the new debt is usually paid off over a longer period of time and will ultimately cost more.

Quick rule of thumb: The more recently the loan was made, the better chance refinancing has to work for you. Get out the papers, look into your loans today. Look to see if you can make some changes that will get your money in motion, working for you.

Control Credit Cards:

Credit cards come in three basic types:

Department-store cards: Most major retailers have their own credit cards. Typically, they do not charge an annual fee, but often charge interest rates higher than do bank cards: up to 20 percent (if state usury laws allow).

Travel and entertainment cards, like American Express, Carte Blanche, and Diners Club. They charge annual fees ranging to $300. Generally, you pay off what you owe each month, and there is no finance charge.

Bank cards, like Visa and MasterCard. They charge a yearly fee of perhaps as much as $35 (or as much as they can get away with), with the average around $20. Interest rates vary from state to state, from about 10 to about 18, with the average around 16 percent.

Credit cards are pure money makers for the institutions issuing them. Besides the 8- to 18-percent interest they charge the consumer, they receive another 1 to 6 percent in account-service fees from merchants who buy a credit-card "franchise." It should be no surprise when you become "preapproved" for a new credit card. The financial institution stands to make as much as a whopping 24-percent return on the credit it hopes to extend to you.

For too many consumers, a wallet full of credit cards is a status symbol. They have Visa and MasterCard, American Express and Diners Club or Carte Blanche. That is pointless. Visa won't do anything MasterCard won't do. American Express is taken almost anywhere Carte Blanche and Diners Club are taken.

Credit-card issuers also make it easy for you to pyramid your debt by offering to let you pay off only a small portion of the outstanding balance each month. While these smaller payments seem to allow you to hold onto more cash each month, they really add up to a major expense.

Suppose you have a balance of $500 at the beginning of the month and the credit-card company allows you to make a minimum payment of $35. During the month, you charge another $100. The interest on this account is, say, 18 percent, which is computed as 1.5 percent of the unpaid balance. (For simplicity's sake, assume that the interest charges are added after you make your payment. In practice, however, many credit-card companies compute interest on the average daily balance, which results in even higher charges.)

Your minimum payment reduces the balance to $465. Adding the interest raises it to $471.98, and your new purchases take it to $571.98. If you make another $35 payment, the next month's interest charge will be based on $536.98. For the second month, your interest will be $8.05—nearly one-fourth of your minimum payment—part of which will be interest on interest! If you continue to charge more than you pay off, you will continue to accumulate interest on interest, as well as on your charges, and you will have virtually no chance of paying off the debt.

So long as you are making the minimum payment regularly, the lender will encourage you to borrow more—even offering to raise the maximum line of credit if you get too close.

To reduce your credit costs and accumulate more money for investment purposes, try not to charge more than you can pay in a month. If you have to charge a larger amount, don't just make the minimum payment; pay off at least 40 percent or 50 percent of the outstanding balance. And if you have to make a larger purchase, look for a cheaper loan from a bank or credit union.

One way to beat credit-card psychology is to think of plastic as a source of instant cash that you have already put away somewhere. Use the instant money only for a limited, premeditated set of purchases (for example, dining-out funds or auto repairs). Or consider a credit card as a lender (for that's what it is) of last resort. The key is to limit the categories of spending you do with the card.

You can control your plastic starting today if you take a hard look at what it's costing you. Take a moment to fill in Chart 6. Enter the user fee (if there is one) in the first column for the credit cards you carry.

WHEN YOU NEED HELP WITH DEBT

The following are excellent sources of assistance if you are in debt and can't seem to find your way out:

➤ Consumer Credit Counseling Service (800-388-2227). Their offices, located in major cities, offer help in setting a budget and negotiating with creditors. The cost is about $9 a month.

➤ Debtors Anonymous (P.O. Box 400, Grand Central Station, New York, NY 10163). These support groups conduct regular meetings in most major cities.

➤ Bank Rate Monitor's Website (http://www.bankrate.com). This service helps you find low-rate, low-fee credit cards.

➤ How to Get Out of Debt, Stay Out of Debt and Live Prosperously (Bantam, $5.99). This easy-to-follow guide helps you find answers to debt problems.

➤ Rebuild Your Credit; Solve Your Debt Problems (Nolo Press, $14.95). This kit includes worksheets and sample letters to creditors and tells you how to deal with debts and reestablish your credit.

THE BEST CREDIT-CARD DEALS

Issuer	Annual Rate	Annual Fee
For Cardholders Who Carry Balances...		
Arkansas Federal	7.75%	$35
Federal Savings Bank (Ark.)	7.92	33
Central Carolina Bank of Ga.	8.50	29
AFBA Industrial Bank (Colo.)	8.50	35
Oak Brook Bank (Ill.)	8.90	50
For Cardholders Who Pay in Full...		
Oak Brook Bank (Ill.)	11.90	0
Amalgamated Bank (Ill.)	12.00	0
USAA Federal Savings Bank (Texas)	12.50	0
AFBA Industrial Bank (Colo.)	12.50	0
Transflorida Bank	12.90	0

In the second column, enter your interest charges for the past 12 months. Most credit-card companies make this figure easy to obtain for tax-reporting purposes. They put on your December or January statement how much interest they charged you during the previous year. If you can't find your last 12 statements easily, take the interest charge on your most recent statement, multiply it by 12, and enter the result.

You may want to adjust it a bit up or down for accuracy. But be honest with yourself. In the third column, enter your annual cost for carrying the card—the number you get by adding columns one and two. Then total all your credit-card costs at the bottom. If the number at the bottom is a shock to you (and it is to many people), then take the advice in the "Credit-Card Action Checklist"—pronto.

Here's the Credit-Card Action Checklist:

1. Keep one bank card, one travel-and-entertainment card, and just the most useful department-store cards. Then cut up the others. That's right. Cut them up. Multiple cards only encourage unnecessary spending.

2. Avoid "upscale" cards: gold, silver, platinum, etc. An American Express green card costs $55 a year, the gold

card $75, and the platinum $300. Their value begins and ends with snob appeal. A higher line of credit for a higher fee at credit-card interest rates is no bargain.

3. Shop for bank cards. As mentioned, all MasterCards and Visa cards are the same. What you pay for them is not. The highest annual percentage rate (APR) is often charged by major bank-card advertisers; you bear the cost of those ads in user fees.

4. If you belong to a credit union, apply for a member's credit card. Terms are usually more favorable than a bank's.

5. Charge only what you can afford to repay in full every month. This way you avoid finance charges altogether.

6. Avoid using department-store cards for purchases like television sets or furniture. You can often borrow the money for these purchases from your bank or credit union at lower rates. Better still, save in advance and pay cash. You may even get a lower price that way.

7. Compare monthly finance charges on cards you choose to keep. For example, J.C. Penney and Macy's both have their own credit cards, but also accept Visa and MasterCard. You may be paying a lower interest rate on your bank card than on the store card.

Float Your Credit:

While on the subject of credit cards, consider a way most persons can use them to the greatest advantage. One of the toughest tricks in financial life is to earn interest on money you've already spent, but a peculiarity of credit-card business practices allows you to do just that.

When you buy an item with your credit card, there usually is a gap between the time you make the purchase and the time the charge appears on your credit-card bill. For example, if your credit-card bill closes on the 15th of the month and you buy something on the 16th, that charge won't appear on your bill until the following month.

CHART 6

YOUR PERSONAL-CREDIT PROFILE			
CREDIT CARD	USER FEE	INTEREST CHARGE	ANNUAL COST
		TOTAL	

Once the bill is prepared, there is another gap between the date you receive it and the date on which the credit grantor starts charging you interest. This may range from 10 to 25 days. Your credit contract states, however, that if you pay the balance in full before the end of that period, you won't be charged interest. Suppose you have 25 days from the billing date to make your payment. A charge on the 16th of July would be carried on the books interest-free until September 10. During that period, you have free use of the credit-card company's money.

You could even make a profit on the difference. Suppose you charged $1,000 worth of goods on your credit card the day after the closing date for the bill. With a 25-day grace period after you receive the bill with that charge on it, you'll have use of the money for about 45 days. That's known as a "float." If you pay the bill in full when it is due, you'll avoid interest charges and make some money on your own. If you pay only the minimum amount on the bill, you'll be charged interest on interest by the next month.

The interest of $1,000 in a money-market account paying 5 percent is about 14 cents a day. Not very much? After 45 days, that adds up to about $5.85, which while not a great profit is not bad for the privilege of using someone else's money for a month and a half.

Remember, too, that checks don't clear the day they are written, or even the day they are deposited in the recipient's bank account. The check for $1,000 you write to pay the credit-card issuer may take several days to be deducted from your account. If you have a checking account that pays interest, you'll earn a few cents extra while the check is being processed. Admittedly, none of this amount to much by itself, but over a year's period and 20 or 30 transactions, it can mean serious money.

Keep an 'Interest' in Your Checking Account:

Are you paying someone for the privilege of using your own money? You are if—

➤ You are paying a service charge for your checking account.

➤ You have money in a checking account that doesn't pay interest.

The first case is fairly obvious. If you have to pay a bank a monthly fee or a per-check charge for using your own funds, you're losing money. Ordinary service charges for a bank checking account can run $5 to $10 a month—or more. That's at least $60 you're spending every year for the use of your own money.

But even if your bank doesn't charge you, if it is not paying interest on your checking account, you are losing money. The $500 you keep in your checking account to handle monthly bills, small purchases, and emergencies could be earning you $25 a year or more. If your balance is higher, of course, your return will be, too.

Interest-bearing checking accounts have been around since the late 1970s. First came the Negotiated Order of Withdrawal

(NOW) accounts, which were really savings accounts with check-writing privileges. Then came the Insured Money-Market Deposit Account (MMDA), which pays interest rates tied to current yields of money-market instruments, but offer only limited check writing. Super NOW accounts made their debut in 1983; they require a higher minimum balance than MMDAs, but allow unlimited check writing.

Most banks and credit unions offer some form of all three kinds of accounts. In many cases, your average daily balance during the month determines whether or not you qualify for the highest rate of interest—or any interest at all. Some require minimum deposits and minimum balances, but the checking-account balance may be combined with your savings balance to calculate the minimum. With MMDAs and Super NOWs, interest rates fluctuate with the market. When interest rates rise, so will your funds.

As a rule, you don't want to keep a large balance in your checking account, even if you are earning money-market rates on the funds. But there's no reason you can't make every dollar work for you. Earning interest on your checking account is one step toward maximizing your return on all your capital. Just be sure to shop around before you open an account. Don't simply depend on a colorful advertising campaign to lure you through the doors.

Save on Credit:

Getting the best credit terms means more than shopping for the best annual percentage rate (APR). It also can mean designing a loan that will put money back in your pocket. Changing the down payment, the length of the loan, or the interest rate will save you money. By negotiating with the lender, you'll be dollars ahead.

Suppose you want to buy a $20,000 car. If you put 10 percent down and finance the $18,000 balance, your payments (over 48 months) will be $474, and you'll pay $4,752 interest over four years (assuming a 12-percent APR). However, if you can afford to put 25 percent down, your monthly payments on the $15,000 balance will be $395. Over four years, you'll pay $3,960 in interest, and your out-of-pocket monthly costs will be $79 less.

You may feel you'll be better off putting the $3,000 in a savings account instead. In four years, at a 5-percent passbook rate, $3,000 will grow to $3,663. But if you put the $79 a month you'd save by making the larger down payment in a passbook account, it would grow to $4,188—$525 more than the $3,000 would grow to. In addition, you would have saved another $792 in interest payments on the original loan. Added to the savings growth, a higher down payment would result in a total savings of $1,317 over the life of the loan.

Perhaps you can't afford to make a larger down payment, but you can swing larger monthly payments. If you finance that same $18,000 over 36 months instead of 48, your payments would be $598 a month. The interest cost during that period would be $3,522—a savings of $438.

Unless you are a major depositor or a long-time customer at your bank, you probably won't be able to influence interest rates as easily as you can change the loan terms. But you can shop around for the best available rate, and it will save you money. Cutting the interest rate on your $18,000 loan by 1 percent will save you $422 over the life of the loan. If you can shave the rate to 10 percent instead of 12, you'll save yourself $839 in four years.

Credit unions generally offer lower rates than banks. The highest rates are often charged by finance companies—including those your dealer may use when you buy your car.

Use Leverage When You Borrow:

Leverage is frequently discussed in this book. In an investment sense, leverage simply means buying with borrowed money: using what you have to get more, then using both to earn higher investment income and generate larger capital growth. Not only is that technique both shrewd and effective, but also it's even reinforced by government tax policy.

Consider this comparison of two investors. One used leverage; the other did not. The difference in their results, even though they operated from much the same base, is quite profound.

Our subjects—let's call them Phil Reese and Ramona Brownlee—decided a few years ago that they would each formally begin their investment programs when they had accumulated $5,000. Phil changed his spending patterns so he could save money each month without radically changing his lifestyle. It took him awhile, but after getting a bonus from his employer, he finally had $5,000.

Meanwhile, Ramona, whose income and tastes were pretty much the same as Phil's, was also successful in amassing the $5,000, but she went at it a little more intensely. She quit smoking, "brown-bagged" her lunch a couple of days a week, and joined a car pool. The result was that she not only had the $5,000, but she also found that without smoking and without the extra expenses of lunches and commuting, she could turn up $600 extra every year.

At that point, Phil and Ramona went different financial routes. Both used their $5,000 to set up investments, but Ramona levered her program into a much bigger venture. Here's what happened:

Both bought units of a stock mutual fund with a good history of annual return: 17 percent.

But Ramona did not stop there. With the $600 a year, she knew she would be able to service a loan for investment purposes. At a credit union, her solid credit record got her an unsecured loan of $5,000 at 12 percent, and she put that money to work along with the $5,000 in the same investment, so that she had $10,000 working for her.

Here's how things worked out for Phil and Ramona in our example:

Year 1 Transaction	Phil	Ramona
Cash investment	$5,000	$ 5,000
Loan	—	5,000
Total invested	$5,000	$10,000
Gain 17% yearly growth	$ 850	$ 1,700

After one year they did reasonably well. The mutual-fund return matched its past performance of 17 percent. But look at the table to see the difference in the gains.

Of course, Ramona spent an extra $600 to finance the loan, but because she had cut back on expenses by that amount, she had the funds to apply to loan repayment and didn't have to disturb her investment assets.

Leverage allows an investor to pay for a portion of an investment—often the lion's share—with borrowed money. It allows for the purchase of more of an investment, or a bigger investment (like property), than you could buy with your personal funds. In the same way that a person can use a steel rod to pry up a rock many times his or her own weight, that same person can use borrowed money to generate a lot more profit.

Naturally, the investor counts on the investment's growth in value to cover the leverage costs and provide gain. But with intelligent investing in partnership with intelligent borrowing, a minimal cash outlay can buy a sizable investment.

Here's what leverage can do:

1. Leverage can dramatically increase the size of an investment with a minimum outlay of cash.

2. Leverage helps an investor make a larger investment earlier than might otherwise be possible or at a time that might otherwise be *impossible*. Leverage gives flexibility.

3. Leverage can help reduce the time it takes to realize a significant profit.

4. A successfully levered investment instrument can boost investment potential by providing opportunity for yet further leverage.

Yet another exciting element of leverage is the way it can accelerate your wealth-building power. Back up a moment and review the gains achieved by Phil ($850) and Ramona ($1,700). Remember that if both now choose to leave their money in the mutual fund, they still have their original $5,000 each, to be added to their totals. But look what would happen if Ramona maintained her loan for two more years—all things being equal—under exactly the same conditions as last time:

Year 2

Transaction		Phil	Ramona
Gain after 1 year	$	850	$ 1,700
Cash investment		5,000	5,000
Loan		–	$ 5,000
Total invested		5,850	$ 11,700
Gross profit @ 17%			
average yearly growth	$	994.50	$ 1,989

Year 3

Transaction		Phil	Ramona
Gain after 1 year	$	850	$ 1,700
Gain after 2 years		994.50	1,989
Cash investment		5,000	5,000
Loan		–	$ 5,000
Total invested	$	6,844.50	$ 13,689
Gross profit @ 17%			
average yearly growth	$	1,163.57	$ 2,327.13

Notice how Ramona's total is not only much greater than Phil's, but, compared with the first time they invested, Ramona's total is made up of much more of her own money. The first time, only $5,000 of Ramona's $10,000 was her own (50 percent). The second time, about 57 percent ($6,700 ÷ $11,700) of the total was her own, and by the end of the third year, 63 percent ($8,689 ÷ $13,689) was her own money.

What does that mean? Basically, flexibility and choice. Ramona could opt for lower risk and stay with the total she has now. Or she could use some of her net worth to make an even larger loan and lever her total to a greater amount. The question is this: Which is the better strategy? The answer will lie in some of the cautions one must consider when using leverage.

Basically, there are only two good reasons to borrow money: One, as you've seen with this "what-if" situation, is to invest to earn taxable income. This is strategic borrowing—using other people's money as part of your wealth-building program. If an investment seems to have good potential returns, after taking interest payments and taxes into account, and you can afford to carry the loan, then borrowing to invest is a reasonable risk.

The other reason to borrow is need. You may experience times when money is required to meet unexpected expenses. But be sure you have no alternative before you proceed. And if you apply for a consumer loan, make repayment a priority; the interest isn't tax-deductible.

A school of thought also suggests that you should borrow even if you don't need the money. A good record of repayment establishes a credit rating. Better yet, repay the loan promptly. The argument is that this will validate you even more as a good credit risk and will enable you to borrow more easily in the future if you need money for an emergency.

That's an interesting idea—but an unnecessary expense in most cases. If you pay your utility bills on time or have a credit card that you pay promptly, you already have a good credit rating established. If your credit rating isn't so good, then a cheaper and easier route is to apply for a Visa or MasterCard and acquire a solid credit rating by paying your bills by the due date each month. In fact, one of the first things any bank will look at when you apply for a loan is your credit-card payment record.

But are you in a position to borrow money? If so, how much? The analysis below will give you some idea:

1. Enter your monthly gross pay:_____

2. Enter your spouse's monthly gross pay: _____

3. If anyone else contributes to your family income, enter his or her monthly gross pay:_____

4. Enter your monthly investment income:_____

5. Add lines 1 through 4 and enter the total:_____

6. Multiply the figure on line 5 by 35% and enter the result:_____

7. Enter the net monthly cost of any current debt-repayment program, including a mortgage: _____

8. Subtract line 7 from line 6 and enter the result:_____

The figure on line 8 is the amount of additional debt repayment that experts say you could afford each month. It's based on the commonly used criterion that no more than 35 percent of household gross pay should be earmarked for debt repayment.

Remember that this is the absolute maximum you should commit to debt repayment. If you want to be more conservative, repeat the exercise using a 25-percent or 30-percent maximum. The final figure should be one that you and your family feel comfortable with, not one that will leave you strapped or compromise your lifestyle.

Make Payments to Yourself:

This brings us to one of the most effective and painless ways of finding money to invest, without altering your standard of living. It's called "earmarking." Earmarking money can add thousands of extra dollars that give an unusually strong boost to an investment plan. When you get down to the last coupon or two in your payment book, don't just think of the extra cash you're going to have. Think instead of a specific investment vehicle into which you can divert it, or of a high-interest account where you can hold it while you analyze your investment prospects. Keep writing a check for the amount you've been making in payments, but write it to yourself and deposit it or invest it where it will do you some good. You won't miss the money, since it has been going out anyway, and you'll be surprised at how fast you accumulate extra funds.

Now take a look at all the sources of investment capital you have available to you. The earmarked money that will come when the intermittent obligations are gone; the account interest and fees earned (or saved) by shopping for the best deal at your bank—and among the financial institutions and credit-card companies available to you; the savings from refinanced loans or consolidated debts; the newly discovered discounts on your insurance premiums; the money you might save by buying big-ticket items when the demand is low and by taking steps to eliminate impulse shopping.

Get the Best Deal on Mortgages:

Owning a home is one of life's traditional goals. That's natural, since most of us would rather see those monthly payments go toward buying our own property than helping someone else buys theirs. Homeownership is a good financial goal, it's a good investment, and it can help you from a tax standpoint. But if you are a homeowner, or aspire to be one, you've got to know how to handle your mortgage loan. You can save large sums of money by getting the right type of loan and paying it off fast. Remember, the more money you save in one sector of your personal financial portfolio, the more money you can make in another.

To help you understand this important subject, put yourself in the following situation:

Let's say you're out shopping for a mortgage loan. The manager at your bank wants your business and offers you a 25-year loan at 8 percent. He's been helpful to you in the past, and you'd like to deal with him. But on the way to your car, you pass a savings-and-loan association that has a big sign in the window promoting 25-year mortgage loans at $7^1/_2$ percent.

Do you—

❑ Forget about the savings-and-loan and stay with the bank?

❑ Walk in and sign a deal with the savings-and-loan?

❑ Look for other alternatives?

Answering "yes" to any of those questions would not be wrong. But let's say you decide that because of your past relationship with your bank, you'd rather place your mortgage there. That may be the right course, but before you make up your mind, take time to calculate what that loyalty is going to cost.

Suppose you want to borrow $70,000. At 8 percent, amortized over 25 years, your monthly payment would be $540.27; at $7^1/_2$ percent, you'd pay $517.29. That a difference of only $22.98. But the argument for switching becomes a bit more compelling when you multiply the monthly difference by 12 and realize you've given your 8-percent mortgage lender an unnecessary $275.76 over a year. While that's not a vast sum, it's a credit that would look better on *your* personal balance sheet than it would in the *bank's* annual report.

But wait, let's take a look at just how astonishing those numbers really get. You're looking at a 25-year term for your mortgage. So over that time, you'll have to pay $6,894 more by taking the bank mortgage loan. If you signed with the savings-and-loan, you could put that money aside.

Now that you've seen the difference just half a percentage point can make, let's look at some even more amazing numbers.

Mortgages are set up in such a way that for the first several years, most of the money you're paying is interest. Very little goes toward reducing your principal. What does that mean to you? Simply that any additional payments you can make in the early stages of a mortgage will have an almost unbelievable impact on the total interest you'll have to pay to make your house your own.

But there's another factor that enters into the picture. Current federal income-tax laws allow you to deduct mortgage interest you pay. So you will have to take that into consideration when you determine the net savings after you find a cheaper rate of interest. You'll see elsewhere in this book how to make after-tax calculations.

Cut (or Eliminate) Your Commission Costs:

When you think of your stockbroker, you probably picture someone who executes your buy and sell orders and who occasionally gives you investment advice. But there's more to the brokerage business than is readily apparent. And one of the most important elements is the way brokers charge for their services.

A SAMPLING OF DISCOUNT BROKERS

The following are some of the major discount brokers with phone numbers and a sampling of the typical fees charged:

Company	200 Shares @ $50	500 Shares @ $25	1000 Shares @ $30
Fidelity (800-544-7558)	$109	$118	$166
Olde (800-956-1100)	60	100	125
Quick & Reilly (800-837-2497)	84	90	128
Schwab (800-435-4000)	110	118	166
Scottsdale (800-619-7283)	40	55	80
Waterhouse (800-288-9097)	53	70	138

Years ago, brokerage commissions were set by regulation. But today brokers can charge whatever they feel they can get by with. Thank goodness for competition. Discount brokers and the growing trend toward direct purchase of stocks have kept the big brokerage houses from raising rates excessively. Deep-discount brokerages have in fact created quite a stir in the business; their commissions may be less than a third of that of the full-service companies. On a 100-share order, you may be able to save as much as $60 on commissions; on a 500-share order, the savings could be $300 or more.

However, when you use a discount broker, you may get considerably less attention than you would from a traditional full-service broker. The way discounters keep their prices low is by eliminating "frills," such as research departments. Your full-service broker could call on the reports of his firm's analysts in deciding whether to recommend a stock. The discount broker is primarily in business to execute trades and normally has no research support to give.

This is fine if you are accustomed to picking your own stocks anyway. You may spend enough time following market trends, reading earnings reports, and digesting investment news to make intelligent choices. If that is true, you don't need the advice of your broker. Instead you simply need someone who can buy and sell for you. Discount brokers offer that. In general, their ability to execute orders is as good as a full-service broker's. There is no sacrifice there. Most discounters have their own floor traders and direct lines to the trading floor. In recent years, discounters have become more aggressive in their marketing, and several of them are available by computer through online database systems.

Charles Schwab, a leading discount brokerage, has, for example, combined online information access and trading with a proprietary software package called "Streetsmart." You buy the software and get free access to Schwab's portfolio-management and trading services and discounted access to Dow Jones News/Retrieval and Standard & Poor's MarketScope, which provides news and commentary on stocks and bonds, updated periodically through the trading day. Trading and portfolio-management services are free, though you do pay a commission for your buy and sell orders. But for most people, this service is a bargain.

Direct purchase of stocks is for those who really want to buy and sell as cheaply as possible. In fact, you can avoid commissions altogether with "no-load" stocks, as this method of acquiring stocks is called.

With no-load stocks, you buy directly from the issuing company without using a broker at all. At last count, more than 100 companies were offering no-load stocks, and the number was rapidly increasing. The procedure works like this: You buy your first shares from the company, with the initial minimum typically set somewhere between $50 and $1,000. The shares you purchase are then put into a dividend-reinvestment plan (more on this in a moment), so that your dividends automatically buy additional shares. If you want to buy additional shares, however, you can, simply by sending in optional cash payments.

Page 88 displays 75 companies (plus telephone numbers) that currently offer their stocks on a no-load basis.

COMPANY	TEL. #	COMPANY	TEL. #
ABT Building Products	800-774-4117	Imperial Chemical Industries	800-711-6475
AFLAC	800-774-4117	Integon	910-770-2000
AirTouch Communications	800-233-5601	Johnson Controls	414-228-2363
American Recreation Centers	916-852-8005	Kellwood	314-576-3100
Ameritech	888-752-6248	Kerr-McGee	405-270-1313
Amoco	800-774-4117	Madison Gas & Electric	800-356-6423
Arrow Financial	518-745-1000	McDonald's	800-774-4117
Atlantic Energy	609-645-4506	MidAmerican Energy	800-247-5211
Atmos Energy	800-774-4117	Mobil	800-648-9291
Bard, C.R.	800-828-1639	Morton International	800-774-4117
Barnett Banks	800-328-5822	National Westminster Bank	800-711-6475
Bob Evans Farms	800-774-4117	NorAmEnergy	800-843-3445
British Airways	800-711-6475	Norsk Hydro	800-711-6475
British Telecommunications	800-711-6475	Oklahoma Gas & Electric	800-395-2662
Cadbury Schweppes	800-711-6475	Pacific Dunlop	800-711-6475
Capstead Mortgage	214-874-2323	Pharmacia & Upjohn	800-774-4117
Carpenter Technology	800-822-9828	Philadelphia Suburban	800-774-4117
Central & South West	800-774-4117	Piedmont Natural Gas	800-774-4117
Comsat	310-214-3200	Pinnacle West	800-774-4117
Conrail	800-243-7812	Portland General	503-464-8599
Crown American Realty	800-278-4353	Proctor & Gamble	800-742-6253
DeBartolo Realty	800-850-2880	Rank Organisation	800-711-6475
Dial	800-453-2235	Reader's Digest	800-242-4653
DTE Energy	800-774-4117	Regions Financial	800-446-2617
Eastern Co.	800-774-4117	Reuters Holdings	800-711-6475
Energen	800-774-4117	Scana	800-774-4117
Enron	800-662-7662	Telefonos de Mexico	800-711-6475
Exxon	800-252-1800	Tenneco	800-446-2617
Fiat	800-711-6475	Texaco	800-283-9785
First Commercial	501-371-6716	Tyson Foods	800-822-7096
First USA	800-524-4458	Urban Shopping Centers	800-774-4117
General Growth Properties	800-774-4117	U. S. West Communications	800-537-0222
Grand Metropolitan	800-711-6475	U.S. West Media Group	800-537-0222
Home Depot	800-774-4117	Wal-Mart Stores	800-438-6278
Home Properties	716-546-4900	Western Resources	800-774-4117
Houston Industries	800-774-4117	Wisconsin Energy	800-558-9663
Illinova	800-750-7011	WPS Resources	800-236-1551
		York International	800-774-4117

Beware of the Rule of 78s:

Paying off a big debt early seems like a good idea. You'll reduce your monthly outlay and be able to set aside more for savings or investments. But don't count on getting a big break on your interest payments. You may find out you owe more than you expect.

Let's look at a one-year loan for $1,000 at a simple 10-percent interest rate. Your finance charge will be $100, and your monthly payments will be $91.67. Now let's suppose you decide after six months to pay off the outstanding balance. You've paid $550 so far. You assume each monthly payment included 1/12 of your finance charge, or $8.33. Multiplying that by six = $50. You subtract $50 from what you've paid and wind up with a figure of $500, leaving a balance owing of $500. But the lender says you owe more than that. Why?

Interest charges are not spread equally over the life of a loan because as you make payments you actually have less of the principal available. Lenders use a formula called "the Rule of 78s" to determine how much of each payment is credited to interest and principal. You pay more interest at the beginning of the loan, which means your principal is paid off more slowly than you anticipated.

If you add up the numbers one through 12, the result is 78, which gives the rule its name. That total then becomes the denominator, or bottom number, in your interest fraction. The numerator, or top number, is the number of payments remaining. For a one-year loan, it starts at 12 and goes down as you make each payment.

In the first month, 12/78 of your payment is credited to interest, so you multiply $100 x 12/78. That equals $15.38. In the second month, multiply $100 x 11/78. That equals $14.10. In two months, you've paid $29.48 in interest, or nearly 30 percent of your total finance charge. You've reduced your principal by only $153.84.

At the end of six months, you've paid $73 in interest and only $477 toward the principal. Your unpaid principal is $523. If you paid the lender $500, you still owe $23. By paying off the loan after six months, you save only $24 of your finance charge.

At the end of six months, you've paid $73 in interest and only $477 toward the principal. Your unpaid principal is $523. If you paid the lender $500, you still owe $23. By paying off the loan after six months, you save only $24 of your finance charge.

The same formula works for any loan period. If you have two years to pay off your debt, the sum of the months is 300. Your first month's payment would include 24/300 of your total finance charge.

Incidentally, the Rule of 78s is not a prepayment penalty. The rule is simply a fee the lender tacks on to discourage early payoffs.

❅❅❅❅

You've now been exposed to the ideas and techniques that top professional investors and counselors advise using to find additional investment funds. As you've seen, you can save big bucks without sacrificing the quality of life you're used to. And remember that money saved is like tax-free income. It's all yours to keep, to spend (wisely, of course) or to invest. Don't waste time putting the things you've learned to work.

Chapter 5: The Risk Factor: Be Careful Out There

"Chance governs all."

– John Milton

Why Risk Is Good for You

As we age, the investment opportunities for wealth accumulation decrease. And in this lesson, you'll learn how to compensate for the fact that time is the enemy.

You'll see, for example, how a person who begins his investment program by putting $1,000 a month into municipal bonds yielding 8 percent cannot hope to attain great wealth by the time he or she is 70. But a 25-year-old person, having invested $1,000 a month consistently in 8-percent munibonds, accumulates more than $5 million by age 70.

Moreover, you'll see how age plays a part in the options that are available to us. At age 25, a person can choose from practically the entire spectrum of investments and expect to achieve wealth by age 70. But at 60, only a few ways remain for achieving wealth—and those ways, as the following chart shows, are fraught with risk:

CHART 7

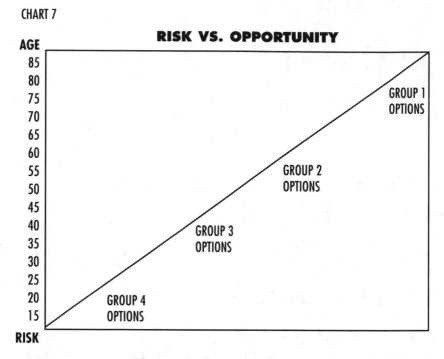

RISK VS. OPPORTUNITY

AGE: 85, 80, 75, 70, 65, 60, 55, 50, 45, 40, 35, 30, 25, 20, 15

GROUP 1 OPTIONS

GROUP 2 OPTIONS

GROUP 3 OPTIONS

GROUP 4 OPTIONS

RISK

Group 4 options: Group 3 options plus Treasury securities, bank certificates of deposit, U.S. Savings Bonds, high-grade municipal bonds.

Group 3 options: Group 2 options plus corporate bonds, blue-chip common stocks, preferred stocks, mutual funds.

Group 2 options: Group 1 options plus high-growth stocks, stock options, junk bonds, commercial real estate, precious metals, rights and warrants.

Group 1 options: Ownership of a business, commodities, currency speculation, undeveloped real estate.

However, no one should let risk be an obstacle. Almost every day, one or more Americans pass the magic barometer of wealth: Their net worth exceeds $1,000,000, allowing them to call themselves "millionaires." And many started their investment programs either late in life or attained that status within less than 10 years. Obviously, risk was involved.

So your return on investment depends in large part on the risk you take. In a nutshell, if the company you invest in fails, you lose your money. As the chances of loss lessen, your likelihood of getting a better return becomes greater. So if there's no chance of losing your money, you probably won't get a very high return, if any at all.

There is no such thing, however, as an investment that does not entail some degree of risk, no matter how remote. Even investing your cash by stashing it away under your mattress involves risk of loss through fire or theft, plus the almost-certain erosion of your money's value through inflation. Risk then is always present. And before we start accumulating money, we simply need to learn that risk takes many forms that can be described, foreseen, evaluated, and minimized—if not avoided altogether.

If you follow the suggestions in this book, you will of course be exposed to some risk. You can't avoid it. But by no means will that risk be so great that you chance losing your entire holdings. In harm's way will be only a portion of your investment—and then only for the short term. Over the long term—and that's what you should think in terms of—you should be able to accumulate the funds necessary to attain the wealth you seek. Keep in mind that the greatest risk lies in not being able to control your emotions. It's tempting to panic when your investments suddenly turn sour. As you've heard probably many times before: The only thing you have to fear is fear itself (and maybe that your new next-door neighbor might be a drummer in a rock band).

Now let's look at risk in more detail. Here are the primary types of risk:

➤ Purchasing-power risk.

➤ Financial risk.

➤ Interest-rate risk.

➤ Market risk.

Plus, there are a few lesser types that we need to know about: political, social, monetary, and one called "brokerage risk." Before discovering ways to deal with risk problems, let's look at how they pose a dilemma for an investor.

WHAT FEAR AND EMOTION CAN DO

Using the current bull market as a point of comparison, here's how such emotions as fear and panic can play havoc with investment returns:

Stock investors are obviously enjoying the market to the utmost. They are actually neglecting other investments so they can put as much money as possible into common shares. But if you had your money in the stock market a decade ago, you would have experienced quite a different scenario—one that could certainly repeat in the future.

Let's return to 1987 and visualize what could have happened to you at that time. Like millions of other people, you would have been sitting back and watching your riches grow. And as the spring of 1987 turned to summer, your excitement would have turned to elation. When the Dow Jones Industrial Average broke through the 2700 market, most experts were predicting it would hit 3000 by the end of the year.

In early October, however, the market began a steep slide, which could have been accounted for by sellers taking profits. Just a minor correction, most people said. But when the Dow plunged 508 points on Monday, October 19, wiping out billions of dollars of wealth, panic would have probably gripped you, as it actually did in the case of most other investors.

In reality, most small investors on that frightening day futilely attempted to sell or switch their stock holdings over to money-market funds. But you most likely wouldn't have been successful in your attempt. The telephone lines to brokers and mutual-fund companies stayed tied up all day. During the greatest avalanche of stock values in history, you would have been powerless to get out of the way.

As it turned out, however, you would have been fortunate you didn't get through to sell your stocks or switch your mutual-fund shares. The next day, the market underwent a strong rebound in prices. The market did not recoup all its losses that day, but over the next several weeks it did recover from its crash low. By the end of 1987, stock prices were higher than they had been at the beginning of the year.

Moral: Over the long run, stock investments will suffer from minor corrections—and maybe even a crash or two—but in the end, investors like you will contain risk and enjoy profits that will consistently outpace those of almost every other type of investment.

It's an Unpredictable World We Live In

When you think about risk, you really are considering the fact that this world is unpredictable. If you knew what was going to occur tomorrow, or next week, or next year, you could avoid the problems and take advantage of the solutions. In other words, you could live in—and prosper from—a risk-free environment.

But that's not going to happen. The best you can do is assemble all the facts and figures, then try to make a reasonable choice. Obviously, the more information you have, the better your chances of making the right decision.

When you are evaluating the risks inherent in a given investment, your first questions should be:

➤ "What kind of risk is involved?"

➤ "What is the extent of this risk?"

➤ "Is the potential return worth this risk?

The answers you arrive at will be highly personal, especially in regard to the return. A risk that seems worthwhile to one person may seem far too great to another. No one else can tell you what your response should be in any given situation. For each person, the return offered by an investment must be carefully weighed against the risk he or she is prepared to take.

On the surface, the relationship between risk and return seems straightforward. In general, you will find that risk and return move in the same direction. Chart 8 shows that if you are prepared to accept greater risk, you stand to receive greater returns. But keep in mind that this is talking generalities here. You will not necessarily be in a position to acquire great wealth by taking extraordinary risks. If that were so, you could assure yourself of millionaire status simply by showing up at the race track every day and betting all your money on the long shots.

The relationship between risk and return perhaps can be expressed more realistically by turning the statements around to read this way: If there is a high degree of risk, you should expect a potentially high return. And, indeed, you will find that high-risk investments almost invariably offer a high return. And from this it follows, of course, that investments entailing little risk generally pay the lowest returns. Whether you perform as a high roller or a conservative investor will depend on many factors, not the least of these will be the makeup of your own personality.

Now let's look in detail at the various types of risk and see if we can find some ways you can deal with them.

CHART 8

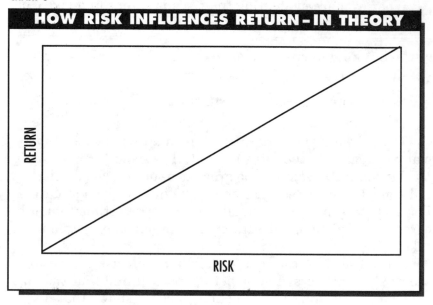

Purchasing-Power Risk

Two hundred years ago you could walk into a good restaurant and order a full-course meal—soup, beefsteak, potatoes, bread, tea or coffee—and receive a bill for 11 cents. If you felt like splurging, you could order veal cutlets or lamb chops instead of beefsteak, and your bill would total a penny more. But the purchasing power of those pennies would be commensurate, more or less, with your earning power in those days. Chances are that your wages or salary would have been about $6 a week.

What has happened in the two centuries since, of course, is that inflation has devalued U.S. currency. As a consumer, you can do nothing to prevent inflation from eroding the purchasing power of the dollar. But as an investor, your control of the situation lies largely in your hands. That means that when you are considering an investment, you must be careful to calculate its return not merely in terms of dollars, but in terms of purchasing power. And the longer the term of the investment, the more important this calculation becomes.

The old cash-under-the-mattress concept is an ideal example of how not to cope with inflation. The $1,000 you stash there today may have spending power of only $500 when you recover those greenbacks a few years later. Changes in the cost of living are usually measured by the government's Consumer Price Index, which has been rising, almost without interruption, for decades.

Most people these days recognize that principle quite readily when it is expressed in such stark terms. The principle is less obvious, however, when an investment appears to offer an attractive return. You may be inclined to invest in a certain issue of bonds that pays 9 percent per year. After all, if you invest $1,000 in them, you will have $1,090 just a year later. But if inflation is running at 10 percent during that year, your investment, expressed in actual purchasing power, will be worth less than it was the day you bought the bond. That 9-percent interest will be more than canceled by the 10-percent inflation. Of course, that bond purchase was nevertheless a better investment than, say, leaving the $1,000 in the bank, where it might have yielded only 5 or 6 percent.

Since most of us are consumers first and investors second, we are inclined to think of inflation more in terms of rising prices than in terms of shrinking dollars. You can begin right now to sharpen your perception as an investor if you remind yourself from time to time of this bit of wisdom: "It isn't the price of goods and services that has gone up; it's the value of the dollar that has gone down."

Even moderate inflation, if it persists year after year, can cause considerable erosion of the value of the dollar. For example, inflation of only 4 percent a year means that the cost of living will double in 18 years. In some years, of course, inflation has been much more severe than that. So when you plan for the long term, you must give full consideration to the purchasing-power risk. Always ask yourself what the dollars you own will be worth when the term of the investment is up.

Investments with fixed values and fixed returns are more

vulnerable to inflation than investments whose value and returns may fluctuate. Bonds, long-term mortgages, and annuity contracts, along with nonconvertible preferred stocks, are poor hedges against inflation because they offer stated returns and fixed principals over their life.

For example, suppose you acquired a single-premium annuity contract in 1997 that guarantees to pay you $1,000 a month beginning in 2017, when you plan to retire. But if inflation averages just 5 percent over the course of that 20 years, the payment you receive each month ($1,000) will be worth only about $377 when you go to buy goods and services in 2017. Worse, as inflation persists, the value of the annuity payments will continue to decline.

Investments that offer variable returns are better hedges against inflation. Common stock, mutual-fund shares, and real estate fall into that classification. Over the longer term, the indexes of stock prices normally rise faster than consumer prices. In addition to capital appreciation, common stock offers you the opportunity to share in the earnings of the company. During many years over the past three decades, the dividend returns of the average company have outstripped the increase in the cost of living. Keep in mind, however, that such trends may not continue. And while it is true that prices of variable-return investments have risen, bull markets don't last forever. The future may present us with a totally different phenomenon than we now experience.

Something else to keep in mind: Inflation can work to your advantage when you become a long-term borrower instead of a long-term investor. On a fixed-yield contract, as the dollars shrink in value, they become increasingly easy to repay. Suppose you secured a $100,000 mortgage loan, amortized over 30 years at 7 percent. You would make payments of $665.30 a month. Ten years later, if the rate of inflation averages 5 percent a year, you would need to earn today's equivalent of $408.44 to make your monthly mortgage payments. And even though the mortgage is amortized so that you repay a portion of the principal each year, you still benefit from the effect of the dollar's shrinking value.

Financial Risk

A second type of risk—and perhaps the most important one—is financial risk, which is also known as "credit risk," "business risk," or "operating risk." By whatever name, this is a risk that focuses on the simple uncertainty: "If I put my money into this investment, will I get it back, along with whatever returns I expect?" It's like being approached by an acquaintance who wants to borrow $500. Unless you are in the habit of throwing your money away on risky ventures and lost causes, you are likely to ponder such questions as: "Will he repay me on time?" "Is he earning enough to do so?" "Is he secure in his job?" "Is he a reckless spender?" "What if he becomes ill or even dies?" And so on.

Comparable questions need to be asked about the financial risk involved in any investment you may be considering: How stable is the company? How competent is the management? And what is the company's financial capacity—its income-generating power? If you have put your money into a corporation that becomes insolvent and can't pay its debts when they come due, then you know—too late–that the company's financial capacity is virtually zero. At the other end of the scale, a company may be earning so much that it could pay its fixed charges several times over, in which case its financial capacity is obviously very good.

To decide whether a given investment is likely to have low or high financial capacity, you must study its current and past condition. Even a good past performance doesn't guarantee a sound future. But it's important to take such an indicator into account.

Some investments, by their very nature, carry a higher degree of financial risk than others. Preferred stocks, for instance, are riskier than bonds, simply because corporations are not required to declare and pay dividends, whereas they are pledged to pay bond interest and failure to do so is a serious matter of default.

Commons stocks carry an even higher degree of financial risk. If you own common shares and something happens to the company's fortunes, you are last in line among the creditors and investors entitled to recoup their money.

With real estate, financial risk is also there, but in different form. Your tenants may fall behind in their rent. They may damage your property. Or they may simply disappear in the dead of the night.

The degree of financial risk inherent in various types of investments are illustrated in Chart 9. If you consider some of the examples, you will realize that the investments with relatively low financial risk are the very ones that have a high purchasing-power risk—and vice versa. Government bonds, for instance, are shown in the chart to have low financial risk. Yet, as we have seen, they carry a high purchasing-power risk because their fixed value is almost certain to be eroded by inflation.

At the other end of the spectrum, an investment like commodities futures entails a relatively high financial risk but offers a relatively low (and thus counterbalancing) degree of purchasing-power risk. That's because commodities futures tend to ride with inflation, increasing in value as prices rise. So they can offer substantial protection against purchasing-power risk.

These illustrations emphasize the advantages and disadvantages that every investor must either accept or avoid, depending upon individual needs and objectives.

CHART 9

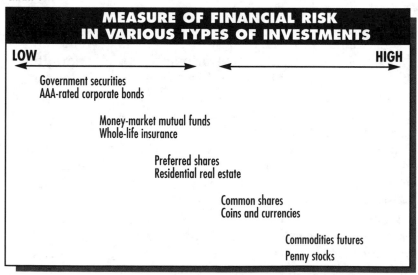

MEASURE OF FINANCIAL RISK
IN VARIOUS TYPES OF INVESTMENTS

LOW   HIGH

Government securities
AAA-rated corporate bonds

Money-market mutual funds
Whole-life insurance

Preferred shares
Residential real estate

Common shares
Coins and currencies

Commodities futures
Penny stocks

Interest-Rate Risk

This form of risk is defined roughly as "the uncertainty of future returns due to changes in the market rates of interest" and is associated with fixed-return investments. In 1995, Duke Power (now Duke Energy) Co., a regional utility firm based in Charlotte, N.C., sold $1,000 bonds offering a yield of $6^{3}/_{4}$ percent and maturing in 2025. By the next summer, you could buy one of those bonds for $875. Duke Power was and is financially sound. What forced the price of those bonds down by $12^{1}/_{2}$ percent? The answer has to do with interest-rate risk. Here's what happened:

When the company issued its bonds in 1995, $6^{3}/_{4}$ percent was about the current market rate of interest for such securities. And while the rate of interest on such bonds is fixed, the market rate of interest generally varies over time. Only at the time of issue can you be sure that the coupon rate will equal the market rate of interest. A year or so after the Duke Power bonds were issued, market rates for interest were far higher (at just over 8 percent) than they had been only a few months earlier. Duke Power had issued bonds earlier in the 1990s at coupon rates of $7^{3}/_{8}$ percent and $8^{3}/_{8}$ percent. No one in his or her right mind would pay $1,000 for a bond paying only $67.50 in annual interest when he or she could buy equally secure bonds earning $73.75 or $83.75. Yet the rate of interest, as shown on the bond coupon, remained fixed, and the company was not obliged to pay a penny more than that.

Therefore, if you owned one of those 1995-issued bonds, the only way you could attract a buyer would be to reduce the price from the face value of $1,000 to an amount that would produce a return equal to current market rates in mid-1996. In other words, you would have to offer your bond at a discount—which in this case works out to a price of $875 when two factors are taken into account. One factor is the interest of $67.50 the bond holder would collect each year; the other factor is the extra $125 he would recover in 2025, when he is able to cash in the $1,000 bond at full face value. Those two factors together are worth the equivalent of the yields being offered currently.

As you can see from this example, interest-rate risk is the

chance you take that, if market interest rates rise, they will drive down the price of your security. Conversely, if interest rates fall, the price of your security will rise.

Since World War II, interest rates have been unstable. From 1945 until 1959, long-term rates increased. From 1960 to 1964, they declined slightly, only to rise again from 1965 to 1970. They leveled off in 1971, then underwent several years of increase. Toward the end of the decade and into the 1980s, they underwent a series of rapid dips and rises, creating a confusing pattern, especially for people committing themselves to large, long-term personal expenditures, such as the purchasing and mortgaging of a home. By 1990, rates were heading downward and into a period of relatively stability, where they stayed until they began rising again slightly in the mid-1990s. Generally, however, the longer the maturity period of a debt security, the greater the fluctuation in price due to changes in interest rates, as Chart 10 shows.

CHART 10

TABLE OF VALUES*

Current Market Yield	Years to Maturity						
	1	2	3	4	6	8	10
7%	101.90	103.67	105.33	106.87	109.66	112.09	114.21
8%	100.94	101.81	102.62	103.37	104.69	105.83	106.80
9%	100.00	100.00	100.00	100.00	100.00	100.00	100.00
10%	99.07	98.23	97.46	96.77	95.57	94.58	93.77
11%	98.15	96.49	95.00	93.67	91.38	89.54	88.05
12%	97.25	94.80	92.62	90.69	87.42	84.84	82.80
13%	96.36	93.15	90.32	87.82	83.68	80.46	77.96
14%	95.48	91.53	88.08	85.07	80.14	76.38	73.51
15%	94.61	89.95	85.92	82.43	76.79	72.58	69.42

* Figures are as quoted, which is on the basis of a bond selling for $100; add a zero to the price to reflect the fact that they are actually $1,000 bonds. For example, a bond quoted at $109.66 is actuallly valued at $1,096.60

The analysis above applies as well to income stocks and mortgages. Any shares that offer little growth potential but steady dividend income are similar to bonds. Typical of this category are utilities. Let's say AT&T offers a steady 7.5-percent dividend rate on its common stock. If the market rate of interest rises above 7.5 percent and should there be no change in dividends, you will find your stock price declining slightly to equate a new dividend rate with the new market rate.

For example, suppose the stock sells for $50 a share, and you receive $3.75 a share in dividends. This is a 7.5-percent dividend rate. The market rate then rises to 9 percent. If you still receive $3.75 a share, your stock price should, in theory, decline to $41.67. In this way, the ratio of income to share price equals the new interest rate of 9 percent.

As you might suppose, changes in interest rates can create risks for the borrower as well as for the investor. Consider a long-term mortgage at 10 percent. Let's say interest rates fall to 9 percent. Unless you can renegotiate the mortgage, you are forced to pay interest greater than the going market rate. And if you sell the property, an astute buyer who assumes your mortgage might expect you to reduce your selling price to compensate him for the interest he will have to pay in excess of the going market rate. On the other hand, if you acquire a mortgage on a property and interest rates later rise, you enjoy the benefit of the "cheaper" money.

If you find yourself paying too high a rate of interest on a mortgage, you may want to refinance by taking out a new mortgage and paying off the old one. Such refinancing, however, costs money and may include payment of a penalty for retiring the old mortgage.

Market Risk

A fourth important type of risk is market risk, which is simply the uncertainty of future prices due to changing investor attitudes or other unknown factors. The waves of optimism and pessimism that sweep the markets are typical of this form of risk. Obviously, you can do little to protect yourself in such an instance. You cannot anticipate investor attitudes. "Market psychology" plays an important role in determining security prices. Traditionally, the Dow Jones Industrial Average of stock prices has fluctuated over time, reflecting in part varying market attitudes.

What can you do to guard against market risk? You can

select those investments that might be the least susceptible to investor whims. On the whole, government and corporate bonds are less affected by market risk that are real estate and common shares. The higher the grade of the security (that is, the lower its financial risk), the better it will be in fending against market risk.

Political, Social, and Monetary Risk

Other, less common risks may also have to be taken into account, depending on the nature of the investment. These fall into the following categories:

➤ *Political risk* becomes a concern when you are investing in politically unstable nations. The potential return may be higher than that of similar investments in more tractable nations, but the risk is high because of possible explosive internal conditions in the less stable situation. A mining venture in a Latin American nation, for example, may seem attractive in other respects, but that country's government may be ripe for a political coup followed by a seizure of all foreign investments—yours included.

➤ *Social risk* involves such concerns as pollution-control, overpopulation, the energy crisis, and the threat of civil disorder—any of which can cause a shift in consumption and production patterns that affect potential investments adversely.

➤ *Monetary risk* can also influence your global investments. If the exchange rate of a currency you have invested in changes sharply and unfavorably, you stand to lose two ways—in loss of capital and loss of the income from your investments.

Brokerage Risk

Investors who use brokerage firms to handle transactions are at risk that orders won't get filled when made, that they won't get the "tips" and other current information necessary to make a astute decision, and that they will be ignored when a hot investment prospect becomes available. You can do something about such service transgressions, however.

Here are some suggestions on what to seek from a brokerage firm to reduce brokerage-service risk:

> *Responsiveness.* Will a "personal representative" or account manager oversee your account and act quickly as an advocate for your interests? Does the designated employee offer solutions for helping you with your concerns rather than simply attending to the mechanics of trading? How easy is it to see or talk to the officers of the brokerage firm when necessary?

> *Organization.* Will someone be available at all times to handle the account regardless of vacation or other unavailability of the designated person? How is the brokerage firm organized to support your contact?

> *Market orientation.* Does the firm have a strong, well-defined orientation toward investors of your size? How much experience does it have in your particular interests?

> *Foreign trading.* Does the firm have the capability of handling foreign-stock needs? Will it be able to help you develop and increase foreign holdings, either through an affiliated foreign office or a similar arrangement?

> *Special services.* Does the firm offer cash-management services, consulting, and seminars of interest to small investors? Sometimes the little things count: Does the firm give immediate credit to sales, or are they put on "hold" for a few days? And to complement stock-trading accounts, which personal services does it offer?

> *Charges.* What are the costs involved? Obtain a copy of the firm's fee schedule, which should be readily available, and compare it to other firms you are considering.

If your risk evaluation narrows to several too-close-to-call brokerage firms, there's nothing wrong with establishing more than one relationship.

Matching Risks With Needs

Once you have surveyed all investment risks, you need to determine which risks you can afford to accept. Then you need to decide how you can keep the acceptable risks to a minimum. Both assessments will depend on your individual goals and circumstances. For example, if you are interested in growth and are not dependent for your livelihood on the safety of your capital, you will not want to spend a lot of time and energy minimizing your financial risk. Instead, you will be attracted to growth stocks or other growth investments that are likely to protect you against purchasing-power risk.

On the other hand, if you are about to retire and are relying on your life savings to produce the income you will need, you will be greatly concerned about keeping financial risk to a minimum. With that aim in mind, you would probably be willing to tolerate the interest-rate risk in return for a guaranteed, steady income.

Young persons and middle-aged heads of families may need investments that are easily liquidated so that they are well-prepared to pay for the purchase of a house or for tuition at an expensive university. Such people want investments where the market risk is minimal. Generally, purchasing-power risk should concern every investor. As for other risks, your ability to accept them changes as your situation and needs change.

Every investment has some element of risk—some uncertainty of future returns. The trick of course is to minimize those risks to whatever extent you can. To reduce your vulnerability to the risks that cannot be eliminated, you can try various combinations of investments. By so doing, you will lessen your overall risk and broaden the objectives you can expect to achieve through your investment program. This is known as "diversification."

Dealing with Risk Through Diversification

You touch on this important subject elsewhere in this book.

But let's consider it in light of its importance in reducing exposure to various risks. After all, the most common and most consequential reason for diversification is to spread risk. When you consider the advantages of diversification, you can easily see how foolish it would be for you to take the opposite position by consolidating all your capital into one investment. One reason is that the investment that seems best for you at a given moment may not be best next month or next year. As a logical investor, you should purchase several investments that will together meet your needs and outperform the average. This way, you spread your risk.

Suppose, for example, that a few years ago you invested in one or more of five promising selections: Swiss francs, gold bullion, art, bank shares, and rental property. And let's also suppose that each of these selections underwent certain specific changes in value:

➤ For reasons of international trade and certain political happenings, Swiss francs went up by 55 percent in relation to the U.S. dollar.

➤ Gold bullion, reflecting lack of investor confidence in certain currencies and commodities, jumped by 68 percent.

➤ The works of art you chose—three paintings by the eccentric and controversial Andy Warbucks—dropped in value by 20 percent when rumors began circulating that Warbucks was farming out some of his assignments to second-year students at a certain Manhattan art college and that some works in circulation were in fact counterfeit.

➤ In the same period, the bank shares you had in mind made a modest gain of 3 percent.

➤ The rental property you considered suffered from unforeseen vacancies and tenant problems, consequently dropping in value by 40 percent.

If you had picked the right investment from among those five, you could have made a capital gain of $6,800. Or if you had picked the one that proved to be the worst of the lot, you would have lost $4,000. By investing $2,000 in each of those five selections, however, you would have spread the risk and emerged with a profit of $1,320, or 13.2 percent.

Of course, there's always the chance that all five investments could drop in value. But it is considerably less likely, especially when you have made your choice from among many promising possibilities—and especially when your choices are as dissimilar as these are.

Different Kinds of Diversification

The practice of spreading dollars among different types of investments is a common and effective way of diversifying, but by no means is it the only way. You can diversify entirely within the realm of business and industry: manufacturing, real estate, utilities, mines, oil, and so forth. Or you can diversify on a geographical basis to spread your risk over several areas or throughout several countries. You can even diversify in terms of time by arranging to have portions of your investment capital committed for various periods, either by initiating buying and selling according to a predetermined schedule or by placing your money in bonds or similar securities that mature at various prearranged dates.

In some cases, it's possible to combine two or more forms of diversification. It's up to you to make the choices that best suit your personal needs. Once you have diversified, however, review your investments often. Certain investments may suit your needs for a given period, but are then made unsuitable by changing conditions. If you let that happen without reviewing and modifying your investment position, you will have diversification working against you instead of on your side.

Diversifying with Foreign Investments

Some Americans think of foreign investments as too remote, too complex, too risky, or even too un-American. They are none of those things. They are as accessible, easy to understand, and safe as U.S. investments. As for being un-American, if you are comfortable buying a Swiss watch, a Japanese car, or a pair of Italian shoes, then what's wrong with buying the shares of a foreign company? After all, many of our strongest and most important industries depend on both the export and import of raw materials and finished products. Without international trade, most countries around the world, including the United States, would be deprived of essential goods and income vital to their economic health and prosperity. Investment involving both the inflow and outflow of capital is simply an extension of this same trading relationship. In other words, foreign investments undertaken in peacetime are no reflection on the investor's patriotism.

You can use foreign opportunities, as mentioned, to broaden your diversification. Certain foreign companies present investment opportunities that are not available in this country (coffee, tin, and rubber production, for example). Through foreign investment, diversification can be carried out in a richer market and a larger, more extensive area. You will also find that in the broader world market, comparable investments will often sell for less than they do at home. This makes it not only easier for you to buy, but also easier for you to sell.

You may wonder whether it's practical to try keeping track of an investment in some other country. In fact, figures are available through the news media. So are reports of the companies and industries you invest in. And your investment broker should have access to information from abroad, including perhaps, overseas affiliations through which he can obtain accurate, up-to-date information.

In short, don't make any unwarranted assumptions about foreign investments. Being foreign doesn't automatically make an investment either better or worse than a comparable investment at home. Like any other, it should be subject to your careful scrutiny and evaluated by the criteria that are important to you.

DON'T BE A FOREIGNER TO FOREIGN COMPANIES

Many investors have shied away from foreign stocks because of recent downtrends overseas. If you are one, take a look at these European regional and Latin American funds:

Fund	1-Year Yield Through 4/1/97
Fidelity Nordic	37.05%
INVESCO Int'l-European	28.50
Fidelity Europe Cap. Appre.	26.64
Scudder Greater Europe	26.49
Vista: European, A	25.70
Pioneer Europe, A	25.17
DFA Group: UK Small Company	24.49
Fidelity United Kindgom	24.42
Merrill Eurofund, B	24.06
Wright Equi: Nordic	24.03

Fund	1-Year Yield Through 4/1/97
Morgan Stanley Int'l: Latin Amer.	48.69
Morgan Stanley Funds: Latin, A	47.32
Federated Latin Amer. Growth, A	35.79
Fidelity Latin America	32.83
BT Inv.: Latin American	32.35
TCW/DW Latin Amer Growth	32.35
Merrill Latin America, B	29.96
INVESCO Spec. Latin Amer. Growth	29.81
Scudder Latin America	29.30
Excelsior: Emerging America	29.09

Here are listings of the top-rated international funds based on performance during a recent 12-month period:

Fund	1-Year Yield Through 4/1/97
Oppenheimer Int'l Growth, A	31.23%
Artisan: International	29.73
Janus Overseas	27.81
Waddell & Reed: Int'l Growth, B	24.85
Massmutual Inst: Int'l, 4	23.41
Oakmark International	23.16
Aetna: Int'l Growth, Sel	22.75
N&B International	22.07
Brandes Inv: Int'l, A	21.88
Harbor: International	21.78

Source: Lipper Analytical Services

Leverage and Risk

No discussion of risk would be complete without some reference to the effect known as leverage, which you briefly learned about earlier. As mentioned, under the right circumstances, this technique can multiply the profits that accrue from a given investment. Leverage can work either for you or against you, however. It can magnify a return or magnify a loss, and it can also increase or decrease an investment risk.

Let's look at the impact of leverage on profit. The most pointed example involves the use of borrowed funds. Consider a company that has the following profit:

Sales	$1,000
Operating cost	800
Profit	$ 200

If the company has share capital of $1,000, the return to the shareholder is 200÷1000, or 20 percent. On the other hand, if the company had borrowed $500 at 5 percent and had share capital of $500, the leverage effect would come into play, with the following result:

Sales		$1,000
Operating costs	$ 800	
Bond interest	25	825
Profit		$ 175

In this case, the return to the shareholder is 175÷500, or 35 percent. See how leverage has substantially increased the return on investment?

Of course, leverage can work the other way. Suppose the company has a profit of only $40. If the company has share capital of $1,000 and no debt, the return is 40÷1000, or 4 percent. But if the company has a $500 debt at 5 percent, as in the previous case, and only $500 in share capital, the interest on the debt will eat up most of the meager profits. From the $40 return, the company has to pay $25 in interest. So the net profit is $40 - $25 = $15. Now the return to the shareholder is

15÷500, or 3 percent.

Certain other investments, because of the cyclical nature of the businesses concerned, have an added risk due to the leverage effect. Consider how leverage affects the company in the next example, as operating conditions vary over a five-year period. (For purposes of simplicity, ignore the income-tax effects here.)

	YEARS				
	1	2	3	4	5
Profit before interest	$100	$200	$ 30	$100	$ 50
Interest at 5%	25	25	25	25	25
Net profit	$ 75	$175	$ 5	$ 75	$ 25
Shareholder's return					
(equity: $1,000)	7.5%	17.5%	.5%	7.5%	2.5%
(equity: $500)	15 %	35 %	1 %	15 %	5 %
Percentage change in profits before interest from prior year	–	100%	–85%	233%	–50%
Percentage change in net profit from prior year	–	133%	–97%	1,400%	–67%

The impact of leverage is clear. It amplifies the cyclical changes in profits. For example, from Year 3 to Year 4, profits before interest rose by 233 percent, while profits after interest rose 1,400 percent. It is like the tail end of skaters in the game of "crack the whip." The end skater will slow down much more abruptly than the inside skater when the chain slows down. When the chain speeds up, the end skater will attain a much higher speed. Consider this volatility when you invest in a leveraged venture. It is certainly reflected in the value of your investment.

Leverage is not something you should gloss over. It can be just as dangerous as it is rewarding. As a wise investor, you should be fully aware of the impact of this strategy. Carefully investigate leveraged investments, then choose them only if prospects are good.

Small sums of money are more difficult to raise. A loan for less than $100,000 is usually more difficult to raise than amounts of $1 million or more. Among the main reasons:

➤ Investing in a small company requires the same time as a large one, and often longer, because records are less detailed. And a large company, if publicly held, has its audited annual report readily available.

➤ If things go wrong in a small company, it's often the end of the road. There are fewer assets to fall back on and less momentum in the marketplace. Murphy's Law tells us that "anything that can go wrong will go wrong—and at the worst possible time." If it's true of any situation, it's true of the owner-managed business.

➤ Although larger loans are more profitable, a small loan costs the lender more in paperwork and administrative time.

Lenders and investors need time to investigate a new client. If you leave it to the last moment, you probably won't get the money unless it is a very short-term and self-liquidating inventory loan, an overdraft from your existing bank, or the short-term deferral of an interest or repayment sum to an existing lender.

Not only will lenders not have the time to carry out an investigation, but they will be suspicious of your management ability if you wait until the last minute or do not have the necessary information to enable you to anticipate your cash needs. The only good way to foresee future cash needs is through the preparation of a financial plan and cash-flow projection.

Judging Risk and Reward

You seek a return on your investment in relation to the risk you take. Basically, risk in a financial sense can be divided

CHART 11

AN INVESTMENT-RISK CHECKLIST

Always determine the downside risks and potential problem areas of an investment. There are risks in any situation; identify them and understand them. Find out if the company or investment subject is prepared to deal with them. Ensure that negatives are completely dealt with in a positive manner. Too negative a projection should make you think twice. A lot of information is available from most companies to help in your quest. Here, for example, are some of the data available to investors:

➤ Description of the business (outline on one page).
➤ History of the company or investment.
➤ Management biographies and responsibilities.
➤ The product or service
  ➤ description;
  ➤ patents, licenses, etc.;
  ➤ trademarks and copyrights;
  ➤ applications and uses;
  ➤ the market;
  ➤ competition;
  ➤ historical development and growth; market and position in that market;
  ➤ your investment's market share (if applicable);
  ➤ distribution channels;
  ➤ pricing;
  ➤ customers.
➤ Production or product sourcing
  ➤ facilities;
  ➤ costing and control;
  ➤ employees (numbers, union);
  ➤ plant overhead and how allocated;
  ➤ gross margins;
  ➤ sources of supply;
  ➤ purchasing;
  ➤ shipping restrictions, tariffs.
➤ Finance and control
  ➤ under whose control?;
  ➤ financial structure;
  ➤ balance sheet: present and over past five years.
➤ Projections
  ➤ sales, cost of sales, gross profit, G&A, and net profit before taxes: for five

(continued)

into liquidity, the ease with which the money can be collected and is or could be available in cash; and security, the protection that is required by the investor (you) to ensure that the money will, in fact, be returned. If you were lending the money to a company, your security could be in the form of a specific lien against a building or piece of equipment; it may be a debenture (like a bond), placed against all assets and ranking after specific charges, to a finance or leasing or mortgage company; or it could be a simple "promise to pay" with some collateral unsecured. When you buy a stock, however, you in fact own a piece of the company, so there's no real assurance you'll ever recoup your investment.

So the factors that will interest you as an investor are the ability of the company to sell its product or service and pay its bills on time without straining cash flow and basic stability (measured in availability of working capital and retained earnings). In other words, you want to know what resources the company has to fall back on when business is slow.

Chart 11 can help you judge the ability of a company to handle its affairs—and ensure that you, as an investor, will not be assuming too much risk

CHART 11, CONTINUED

> years, preferably with high, low, and medium projections;
>> ➤ cash flow by month for one year and by quarters for at least three years;
>> ➤ give full explanation of major assumptions;
>> ➤ low net-profit projection should not fall below the total projected for taxes, principal and interest payment, plus reasonable profit.
> ➤ Basic data
>> ➤ bank, with name of manager;
>> ➤ line of credit;
>> ➤ legal advisers;
>> ➤ accountants;
>> ➤ incorporation, authorized and issued stock;
>> ➤ directors of company;
>> ➤ shareholders' list;
>> ➤ detailed descriptions of services offered and promotional literature;
>> ➤ detailed product literature;
>> ➤ detailed description of buildings and other assets owned;
>> ➤ projections (assuming summary only in report), including projected balance sheets, based on profit-and-loss statements and cash-flow projections.

Guidelines for Your Approach To Risk Appraisal

Before you start looking at specific investments and how to approach them, consider the following general guidelines:

1. Go to appropriate sources. A public library or a computer-linked information service can help, but don't be shy about seeking information from the company itself.

2. Go to those who know the industry. Sometimes investors are reluctant to approach industry sources. This is faulty reasoning. You will usually get better information, a quicker answer, and more professional treatment from those who are familiar with the risks and conditions in the industry.

3. Risk assessment involves an understanding of not only the industry, but also the individual running the company. Approach the most appropriate sources before you go to total strangers. If they cannot help you, get them to introduce and refer you to others.

4. Do not be too precise in your demands. For the type of investment you think you should make, be flexible—at least at the beginning of the process. Investment sources and government officials are as human as you; it is better to work with them and through them, asking them to help you find the answer, than it is to present them with a detailed proposition, saying (or implying), "Give it to me." The better attitude is: "Here's the information I need. Can you help me get it?" Along with credit checks and analyzing the business's ability to operate profitably, sources are more likely to provide information when they are certain that an investor has legitimate needs and goals.

5. Prepare a one-page summary. In the written presentation of your investment selection, define your objectives in keeping with the risks you can tolerate.

6. An investment is favorable only when mutually beneficial. By the time negotiations are completed, the investor should understand the risks thoroughly—there must be no surprises left at the end.

7. Always check on the people of the investment you are about to acquire. A good way, if you have time, is not just to check the references from the company (these will always be good), but also, if possible, those from competitors. Then talk, at random, to other investors, especially those who have experienced difficulties.

Measuring Risk

How can you gauge the amount of risk in a given investment? Since this is a fundamental question that you will probably ask yourself each time you consider an investment decision, let's examine it in some detail.

The risk-quantifying methods are all based on the following assumption: Once you thoroughly research an investment, you will possess far more information than you realize. This information sometimes shows itself in "gut feelings," which are difficult to accept as a basis for rational decision making. Yet this information is valuable. Therefore, let's look at several ways that can help you to extract such information from your own "memory banks." The methods are all based on the research conducted at Stanford Research Institute (SRI) in California, and they are widely used in industry.

Assume that you have done some diligent research on a company we'll call International Ventures, Inc., now trading at $20 a share. You have read the financial statements of the company, the press releases, the newspaper clippings, and all the material you could find on its product line. You are now a reasonably informed investor and have an intuitive "feel" for the company's prospects. How do you now translate that feel into hard data?

First, pose a series of questions, then try to answer them to the best of your subjective knowledge. The answers may not be precise, but if your research has been good, chances are your answers will be close to the real prospects of the company. These prospects will be reflected in the "risk-profile" table for the stock. Second, ask about the chances that the stock (now at $20) will rise within a year to more than $22? Assume you have answered (after some soul searching) that the chances are about 50 percent. Now, what are the chances that the stock will rise above $24 within a year? Twenty percent? And above $25? Ten percent? And $28? Zero percent?

Next, do the same for the downside risk. What are the odds that the stock will remain above $20? You decide it is about 60 percent. And above $18? You estimate 80 percent. And above $16? Perhaps 100 percent.

The results are summarized in the following table:

Your estimate of the lowest price of the stock after one year of holding it	Percent chance for an occurrence
$16	100
$18	80
$20 (current price)	60
$22	50
$24	20
$26	10
$28	0

Some of the elementary meanings of the list: Your chances of gaining are 60 percent; or, to express that differently, you have three chances out of five of selling the stock for more than you bought it. Also, you estimate that there is no chance that the stock will trade above $28, or below $16. Note that the figure of, say, 80 percent in the $18 row means two related things: (1) either the chances of the stock trading above $18 are 80 percent or (2) the chances of the stock trading below $18 are 20 percent.

You can devise some uses for this "information" about the stock, dealing in absolute dollars. Suppose you intend to invest $1,000 in the stock. You subsequently choose an arbitrary point of 20-percent failure (you may choose another at your convenience) and see that with the chance of gain being four out of five, you may turn an investment of $20 per share into either $24 or $18. This is based on your innate feeling, clothed with numbers.

Assuming you purchase 100 shares with your $1,000 (at a

margin of 50 percent), you could either gain $400 or lose $200. Would you enter into such a game? Would you risk $200 to gain $400? Only you can decide if this degree of risk is acceptable to you personally, but at least you have a concrete question on which to base your decision.

Another way of using the information in the table is to decide in advance on a required rate of return. If you are greedy and want a return of 40 percent on your investment, you would require a gain of $400 on your $1,000. You would look at a similar table you've created to see that you have a four-out-of-five chance on making this profit. Assume that you decide that this chance is acceptable. But what about the risk? From the table, you can see that you would risk losing up to $200. (Basically, this is the same example as the one used above, except you start by considering the potential or desired gain rather than the potential or acceptable loss.) Again, only you can decide if the potential gains outweigh the potential losses.

You can see, then, that the table you've constructed will not provide you with the "final" answer to the investment question. But it will help you put your own research to use. In other words, forcing yourself to quantify your gut feeling for the stock's prospects will not guarantee you a surefire method of correctly guessing whether the stock will go up. However, if you have researched the stock properly, you will be able to use more of your knowledge than you would otherwise have done.

This decision making in risky circumstances is widely used by several large corporations. It does not ensure that any particular project will be successful, but rather that in the long run the total portfolio of investments will be successful. In the same way, you could not say with certainty that any particular acquisition of stock will be successful. But in the long run, over several purchases of stock, your ability to make money will improve, since you will be basing your investment decisions on more information.

Refining Your Risk Measurement

Another way of using the table you have constructed is a refinement called "a convergence toward a fixed value" (if you want to get technical). The concept is simple. You determine at which point you stop studying the facts you have gathered about a company and start looking for new information. That usually occurs when you have extracted the full value of the information you have on hand. Throughout the research of the stock, you query yourself and modify your estimates for that stock.

For example, you discover that the prospects of a new product are rosier than you had previously imagined. Therefore, you upgrade your prospects for the company's stock. The moment your refinement (still based on nothing more than your gut feeling) does not lead to appreciable change in the table of probabilities, you have probably reached the point where the information on hand is fully digested. If you still feel you need to study the company a bit more, by all means do so, but look for new information to supplement the information you already have.

Suppose you have thoroughly studied the company and constructed your "final" risk table. The decision is easy if your table shows that the risk is worthwhile. You invest. But suppose it shows that the risk involved in investing in that company is greater than you would like to accept. What should you do? Most likely you would return to your final risk table to have one more look at it—to see if you could upgrade your estimates to make the risk more acceptable. If you can do this—legitimately and with a clear conscience—then you may invest.

If you cannot bring yourself to change your opinion of the stock's prospects, and you still feel like investing in the stock, then you may have to admit that you are going to accept a risk not commensurate with the reward. You can then invest—so long as you know what you are doing and understand that you are taking more risk than you would normally like. If you decide that the potential reward does not justify the risk and choose not to invest, then you may later find you have avoided a costly error.

A Risk-Reduction Epilogue

In this chapter, you've seen how risk can be a friend as well as a foe. Keep in mind that unless you are buying 100 shares of a stock trading at less than $5 each, you will be spending hundreds, or even thousands, of dollars on stock purchases. So review carefully the basic research steps take before buying a security. For purposes of clarity, consider common stocks and the research needed for their selection.

Before you buy a stock, picture yourself as intending to buy the whole company, not just a piece of it. This will force you to assess it properly. Remember that you are depositing your money in the hands of strangers. Wouldn't you like to know first what they are up to? As mentioned, learn as much as you can about the company, its affairs, its management, and its finances.

Also learn about the areas of business that the company is in. This might mean a trip to your local business library to find as much background material as you can. It would certainly involve a call to your broker, a lengthy conversation with an analyst who follows the company's fortunes on a regular basis, and an examination of the company's most recent financial statements. All this is standard practice, and a routine outlined in greater detail elsewhere in this book.

But there is something else you should do that most investors overlook. If possible, make an effort to have physical contact with the company—with some of the employees, an officer, the CEO (why not?). If guided tours are offered, go on one; usually you can ask questions of key personnel at that time.

Finally, use the products or services of the company and compare them with those of competitors. Talk to friends and neighbors about how they like and use the products and services. Find a consensus, then go with it.

Chapter 6: How the Experts Do It

"Nothing succeeds like success."

– Alexandre Dumas

Measures of Success

Investment success comes in many forms to many people. As the following vignettes in this chapter show, however, such success is best achieved through hard work and dedication. Luck plays a part, of course, but only a very small part. In fact, the most outstanding accomplishments in the investment world have little to do with good fortune, but derive mostly from knowledge and perspiration.

The 'Father' of Investors

Maybe the name Benjamin Graham doesn't mean much to you. But in professional investment-advisory circles in this country, he's a true legend.

Despite his current prominence, however, Graham was actually a product of the early part of this century. Moreover, he wasn't even born in the United States. He was a native of England, though his family did move here when he was very young.

But the impact he made on American investment evaluation and selection during his lifetime (he died in 1976) was so monumental, that he is known today as the "Father of Fundamental Analysis." And that designation is well-deserved. His book, *Security Analysis: Principles and Techniques,* which he coauthored with David L. Dodd, is still considered the classic authority—some call it "The Bible"—for serious investors. Multibillionaire Warren Buffett, quite an astute investor himself, chose Graham as his mentor and was one of his most ardent disciples.

Graham's position of high esteem results from the principles that he espoused and that were so original. In *Security Analysis*, he outlined a way to determine the true value of a stock, and if that stock met his criteria, he advised buying it. Moreover, he was not just a theorist; he proved that his principles work in practice. His investment performance was an amazing 17.4 percent during a period when the market as a whole went through a series of major bearish as well as minor bullish sequences.

Since his methodology was based on determining the value of a stock, his approach became known as "value investing." Surprisingly, that often meant avoiding growth-type stocks. That's because growth stocks usually have high price/earnings ratios, and high price/book-value ratios, meaning that they tend to be overpriced in good markets and underperform in bad ones.

Graham also differed with conventional wisdom that contended that investors must take on greater risk to get a better return. He believed that by seeking out the best values—the bargains—investors would keep risk at a minimum.

So what exactly did Graham look for when analyzing stocks? First, he advised finding stocks selling for substantially less than their current assets per share (after subtracting all liabilities). Such stocks, he said, are the same as purchasing a dollar's worth of assets at discounts of 30-40 percent.

He also advised investors to buy a stock as if they were buying the entire company and look for those so good that buyers would be willing to own their shares forever. That means, generally, blue-chip stocks with long records of steadily rising earnings. It also means investing in the "best" industry, then investing in the "best" company in that industry (and with little concern for the stock's price).

To help value-governed investors, Graham, assisted by James B. Rea, developed 10 basic guidelines for finding bargain stocks. A bargain stock, he said, has the following attributes:

1. The price is less than two-thirds of net quick assets (current assets less total debt).

2. The price is less than two-thirds of tangible book value.

3. Earnings per share are greater than 20 percent of price—a p/e ratio of 5 or less.

4. The p/e ratio is no higher than 40 percent of its five-year high.

5. The dividend yield is greater than two-thirds of the prevailing AAA bond yield.

6. The earnings yield (that is, the rate of return from earnings alone) is greater than double the current AAA bond yield.

7. The compound 10-year earnings growth exceeds 7 percent—with two or fewer earnings declines under 5 percent in the period.

8. The current ratio (current assets divided by current liabilities) is 2 or more.

9. The total debt is less than tangible book value—a debt-equity ratio below 1.

10. Total debt is less than twice net liquidation value—net quick assets.

Graham recognized, of course, that very few stocks satisfy every one of these criteria. So he suggested that four (numbers 1, 3, 5, and 9) were predominant (and he later reduced those four to just two: 1 and 3). At that point, he raised his p/e ratio standard (number 3) to 7.5.

Currently, most value investors aim for a p/e of 10 or less. But the real point of Graham's criteria is that they provide specifics on what makes a bargain: low price relative to earnings, dividends, and book value, and low debt in relation to book value.

Okay, all this explains when to buy a stock, but what did Graham have to say about selling? First, he chose to ignore temporary price drops of a stock, especially if the company continues to satisfy the expectations that signaled the purchase. But time hasn't been kind to some of his selling rules based on fundamentals (sell if the price is up 50 percent, if you've hung on for two years or if the dividend is omitted). Nevertheless, value investors who have done their buying can begin thinking about selling when:

➤ A company ceases to qualify as a value-investing opportunity.

➤ Earnings drop enough to make the stock overpriced by 50 percent or more relative to buying criterion number 3 above.

➤ Return on investment displays a declining trend.

➤ The stock has moved up and is no longer a bargain, and a better value-investment buy comes along.

Graham was also in favor of diversification among types of securities. For example, he suggested dividing an investment portfolio so that at least a fourth of it is in bonds and at least a fourth of it is in stocks. Graham felt that when the stock market is precipitously high, bonds are a better value than stocks, but that never should either type of security fall below the 25-percent level.

But don't get the impression that Graham was simply a cold and calculating investment scientist, devoid of feelings or emotion. In fact, he was a charismatic and caring person, given to bursts of elation (especially when his stock holdings were faring well) and merriment.

He was also illustrative when attempting to explain his theories. In his book *The Craft of Investing*, John Train tells of a parable about market cycles that Graham was fond of telling. In Train's words, the parable went like this:

"Think of yourself as owning your stocks in a joint venture with a virtual lunatic—the tens of millions of market participants transformed into a single eccentric. Every day your manic-depressive partner gets out of bed, and depending on how he feels, he offers either to buy out your share of the venture or sell you his. The offers are emotional and ill considered. For instance, one day he'll say, 'Oh, God, what a mess!

Look, take the whole thing at half price.' And if he feels optimistic he'll say, 'I feel great! How about letting me buy you out at twice market?' You need never accept any of his propositions. And except for his offers, your interest in the joint venture—the stream of profits you receive—is completely unaffected by these fits of enthusiasm or gloom. But if you want to take advantage of them, you always have that possibility. So he's a very convenient partner to have around."

The Contrarian's Contrarian

John Neff makes money by bucking the trend. He's called a "contrarian," and that means he might sell when everyone else is buying or buy when everyone else is selling. Like most contrarians, he believes that an investor should look to value—that is, determine whether a stock is overvalued, in which case, don't buy, or undervalued, in which case a closer scrutiny is deserved.

Neff is a very wealthy man. And he's made a lot of other people wealthy, too. As manager of Vanguard's Windsor Fund, he earned a name for himself in a field that is dominated by investment advisers with a decided herd mentality. His record shows, however, that in the sea of run-with-the-wind mutual-fund managers, a policy of investment "tacking" can do wonders.

So how does Neff do it?

There's no real secret. He simply looks for turnaround stocks, the stocks that most investment advisers would shun. Neff calls them "uncomfortable stocks...that make you twitch a bit." In other words, he looks for hidden value where others have found little or nothing worthwhile at the moment.

In a recent interview with *Kiplinger's Personal Finance Magazine*, Neff explained that when assessing a stock, he looks at the rate of earnings growth plus the dividend yield to determine total return. He compares that to the stock's price/earnings ratio. If, for example, a stock shows a growth in earnings this year compared to last year of 10 percent and a dividend yield of 4 percent, that would add up to 14 percent. Then he would attach a p/e ratio of seven, or half the rate of total return, a year from now. If the p/e ratio drops to seven, he would be ready to buy.

Neff treats cyclical stocks a bit differently. Recall that cyclical stocks are those of companies whose earnings move in tandem with the economy or business cycles and which thus have lower earnings when the nation is in an economic slide and higher earnings when the economy is recovering. Metals, automobiles, home building, heavy machinery, airlines, travel, and leisure are examples of cyclical industries.

For such stocks, someone following the Neff system would try to determine what a company is capable of earning near the peak of a cycle. With auto-company stocks, for example, he calculates their "normalized earnings": what they would earn under normal conditions. Let's say the economy is in a slump and General Motors stock reflects that slump with lower sales and lower earnings. An investor would take that situation into account and base his decision to buy on a calculation of what earnings per share would be during normal conditions. And if normal conditions seem imminent, he would buy General Motors stock at the current "depressed" price with the expectation that it soon would rise.

So when does Neff sell?

Apparently, he's not married to any stock. As mentioned, he's a contrarian, and that means when the market embraces a stock and its price starts rising, Neff will usually start selling. The higher the price goes, the more he will sell.

But his system is not infallible. In 1989 and 1990, for example, Windsor fund failed to keep pace with the market as a whole. In fact, 1990 was a losing year for him—his only one, though. He explains that in that year and the preceding one, he had overloaded with 30 percent of Windsor's assets devoted to financial stocks. Plus, he missed out on the stocks of some industries—tobaccos, drugs, foods, and communications—that did quite well. They simply did not comply with standard contrarian theory and practice.

He's a patient man, however, and he doesn't panic easily. Even when he got angry letters from Windsor investors critical of his tactics, he listened, but stayed the course he had plotted. He knows that such criticism is based on conventional wisdom, which flies in the face of contrarianism, and which in the long run is almost always wrong.

The Worldly Wise Investor

How do you describe an investor who searches for global-type stocks that most other investors dismiss as too risky or lacking in potential? Well, you might call him a "worldly skeptic."

For John Templeton, however, such a description would probably please him. Call him skeptic, pessimist, contrarian. He shows the symptoms of all those traits. And by taking advantage of them, he has become about as successful financially as a person can become. How successful? From humble beginnings in Winchester, Tenn., he recently yielded his position as head of the Templeton funds to retire in the Bahamas as one of the world's wealthiest men.

So we obviously can learn a lot from Templeton, a fascinating personality who borrows from principles he gleaned from such diverse teachers as Ben Franklin, Ralph Waldo Emerson, John D. Rockefeller and *The Bible*. From them, he has shaped an investment philosophy that works—and works well. He explained it this way in an interview in *Forbes* magazine a couple of years ago:

"In almost every activity of normal life, people try to go where the outlook is best. You look for a job in an industry with a good future, or build a factory where the prospects are best. But my contention is if you're selecting publicly traded investments, you have to do the opposite. You're trying to buy a share at the lowest possible price in relation to what that corporation is worth. And there's only one reason a share goes to a bargain price: because other people are selling. There is no other reason.

"To get a bargain price, you've got to look for where the public is most frightened and pessimistic."

So that's why Templeton doesn't object when someone calls his philosophy "maximum pessimism," even though it bears all the earmarks of contrarianism. But Templeton carries his brand of the philosophy to worldwide dimensions, so much so that if we could invest in companies located on Mars, he would likely have already taken a close look at some Martian prospectuses. He has, for example, invested in stocks of Peru when that country was undergoing political upheaval during the mid-1980s. Soon after that, Peru achieved stability, and the Peruvian stock-market index realized a twentyfold increase. Templeton's personal investment of $2 million grew to well over $20 million by the time he finally took his profits from the Peruvian stocks he had selected.

Templeton's feelings toward the markets of other countries result from his early years, when as a student on a Rhodes scholarship studying law at Oxford, he journeyed through 27 nations. He explains that even though America dominated the world at that time, American investors were generally uninformed about markets elsewhere. To Templeton, such a constricted view of the world doesn't make sense. He feels that in searching on other continents, you are likely to find more bargains, better bargains, and less risk.

Nevertheless, Templeton picks stocks, not countries. He recently told *Changing Times* magazine that his analysts, based in six cities around the globe, keep close tabs on 20 percent of stocks worldwide—without regard to country—that have the lowest price/earnings ratios. If selections come from one country, it only indicates that conditions there are favorable for employment of Templeton's "buy-cheap-and-wait-for-a-comeback" theory. He added, however, that the catch is picking stocks that will come back. "You only get a bargain when people are selling, and it has to be for a temporary reason," he told *Changing Times*.

But Templeton's feelings toward stocks are not the same as they are toward bonds. He believes that inflation will not always stay at the low level of the last few years. As a result, inflation, combined with high taxes, will ultimately produce a negative yield for bonds, even long-term types. Consequently, he would buy them for trading rather than holding them for the income.

So that pretty much sums up the logic behind Templeton's buy strategy. But what about his decisions on selling? When does he suggest that you take profits on a stock? On that subject, he recently explained his doctrine in a *Forbes* magazine article. He said he has worked hard to overcome the tendency to either sell too soon or too late. And several years ago he came up with what he believes is the right answer to when to sell. "The solution," he said, "is never to ask when to sell a stock. Instead, you should sell only when you have found a

new stock that is a 50-percent better bargain than the one
that you hold." Many people call that "comparison shopping"—
a search for *relative* bargains as much as a search for *absolute*
bargains. In that sense, selling and buying are almost one and
the same.

Also ingrained into Templeton's investment philosophy is
his deep-rooted religious convictions. His mother believed, for
instance, that spiritualism and positive thought are a foundation of prosperity. And putting such training into practice, he
has established the Templeton Foundation Prize for Progress
in Religion, which each year awards $1 million to someone
selected as a deserving world spiritual leader.

J. Michael McGowan, a Los Angeles attorney, Certified
Financial Planner, and obvious protégé of Templeton, recognizes
the role religion plays in his mentor's investment philosophy.
Recently writing for *ABA Journal*, he pointed to 10 basic guidelines that Templeton uses when making investment decisions:

1. **Bargain hunting.** To find a good investment, first find a
   good bargain. To Templeton, a bargain means high value
   combined with low price.

2. **Diversification.** As explained previously, Templeton looks
   for buys almost anywhere in the world.

3. **Economic/political awareness.** Templeton avoids investments in nations where the political or social environment
   is so unstable that successful investing is unlikely.

4. **Flexibility.** Templeton believes in staying open-minded
   and tolerant, while standing ready to change strategies
   when such change is called for.

5. **Patience.** Templeton probably is more patient with an
   investment than most fund managers. Believing that a
   bargain "remains a bargain for a long time," he reports
   that the average holding period for a stock in his portfolio
   is nearly six years.

6. **Analytical research**. The phrase "due diligence" takes on
   new meaning with Templeton. He advocates quantitative
   analysis to evaluate a company's performance. His chief

tools: Value Line, *The Wall Street Journal*, and SEC 10K reports.

7. **Extensive networking.** Templeton has built a structure of contacts, or "friends," as he calls them. Such individuals are located in every country he has visited and in every industry he has studied. As a result, he has always been able to get on the phone to ask questions about an investment of interest to him.

8. **Positive thinking.** Despite his philosophy of maximum pessimism, Templeton is a decided optimist about the future. For instance, he considers all bear markets to be temporary, and when he suffers a setback, he doesn't really worry but simply takes his lumps and presses forward.

9. **Simplicity.** As noted, his investment philosophy is neither complex nor contrived from complicated formulas. To him, the best ideas are very plain and unpretentious.

10. **Prayer.** Also as noted, Templeton's strong religious beliefs influence both his life and his investment philosophy. In fact, his view on the subject, as passed along to us by J. Michael McGowan is, "If you begin with prayer, you can think more clearly and will make fewer mistakes."

The World's Most Successful Investor. Period.

Warren Buffett is a billionaire. A *self-made* billionaire, by the way. And along the way to achieving that honored position, he has made a lot of other people rich, too. In fact, Buffett frequently receives thank-you notes and gifts from followers who made millions of dollars because of his investment savvy.

Buffett didn't become the world's most successful investor (a term *Forbes* magazine gave him in 1994) by good fortune, however. He worked at it throughout his life, beginning in early childhood, when, at about age four, his favorite "toy" was a money changer someone had given him. Later, he bought Coca-Colas (the soft drink, not the stock; that would come later) at wholesale, then sold them at a substantial markup to thirsty patrons at a local lake.

But resourceful, materialistic children of all backgrounds have done similar things. After all, this is a capitalistic society, and we teach our children early in life through example. Most eventually see money as a means to an end, not the end itself, so they become teachers, carpenters, and technicians (thank goodness!). In Buffett's case, however, he obviously always had every intention of becoming very rich. His mentor, for example, was Benjamin Graham, whose techniques he carefully studied at Graham's Manhattan investment firm.

Soon, Buffett had perfected a style of investing based on finding and buying undervalued securities. At 25, with $100,000, he started an investment partnership, which, some 15 years later, listed assets at $3 million. It was during the life of that partnership (which was dissolved in 1969) that Buffett acquired controlling interest in a textile firm named Berkshire Hathaway. He soon used that company as a holding company for buying stocks that met his simple, but stiff investing criteria.

His selections, for instance, were based merely on finding companies whose intrinsic value is greater than the market value of the stock. That's it. That's why he selected Coca-Cola (the stock, not the drink), Gillette, Capital Cities/ABC, and the Washington Post Co., among others.

Of course, such finds are not all that common. To locate them, you must do your homework. (Buffett is a math whiz, which has helped him.) But it also calls for someone who is not afraid to defy conventional wisdom. Buffett, like most other successful investors, is a contrarian. He buys the stocks of companies that other investors ignore or shy away from.

Oh, yes, and he believes in holding onto a stock till he has totally exhausted its potential. And he believes in owning the stocks of only a few companies. Eighty percent of the gains in Berkshire Hathaway have come from just six issues, for example. In fact, the last time he disposed of a major position was 1986, when he abandoned Handy & Harman, a precious-metals firm, and Lear Siegler, an auto-parts manufacturer. (In 1993, he sold a third of his position in Capital Cities/ABC, though he later admitted to a mistake in doing so.)

So you would think he has a record of detecting, then buying, the fledgling Intels, Microsofts, and Wal-Marts. But that's not the case. A study by *Time* magazine recently found that none of Buffett's holdings made the list of the top 50 performers over the past 20 years.

(As an adjunct to that study, research disclosed that investment portfolios with the fewest stocks and the lowest amount of trading outperform portfolios with more stocks and a higher turnover. And even more startling was the finding that randomly selected portfolios of 10 stocks each do just as well as the average mutual fund. Buffett apparently perceived such revelations many years ago.)

So you might say that Buffett avoids risk like other people avoid exposure to ebola. True, he probably wouldn't be a prime candidate for speculating in the penny-stock market, but at the same time he won't run from danger. Consider, for instance, that he doesn't diversify to a great extent, and most investment experts advise diversifying broadly as a way to reduce risk. In fact, Buffett at any given time will own the stocks of only nine or 10 companies.

Buffett seems to believe that most people—himself included—are capable of making only a very few smart decisions in their lifetime. So once those few decisions are made, he would suggest sticking with them and trying with all your might to resist making wrong ones.

On that subject, here, in a letter to shareholders of Berkshire Hathaway, is a brief expression of his investment philosophy on risk and diversification:

"The strategy we've adopted precludes our following standard diversification dogma. Many pundits would therefore say the strategy must be riskier than that employed by more conventional investors. We disagree. We believe that a policy of portfolio concentration may well *decrease* risk if it raises, as it should, both the intensity with which an investor thinks about a business and the comfort level he must feel with its economic characteristics before buying into it. In stating this opinion, we define risk, using dictionary terms, as 'the possibility of loss or injury.'

"Academics, however, like to define investment 'risk' differently, averring that it is the relative volatility as compared to that of a large universe of stocks. Employing databases and statistical skills, these academics compute with precision the 'beta' of a stock—its relative volatility in the past—and then build arcane investment and capital allocation theories around this calculation. In their hunger for a single statistic to measure risk, however, they forget a fundamental principle: It is better to be approximately right than precisely wrong.

"For owners of a business—and that's the way we think of shareholders—the academic's definition of risk is far off the mark, so much so that it produces absurdities. For example, under beta-based theory, a stock that has dropped very sharply compared to the market—as had Washington Post when we bought it in 1973— becomes 'riskier' at the lower price than it was at the higher price. Would that description have then made any sense to someone who was offered the entire company at a vastly reduced price?

"In fact, the true investor *welcomes* volatility...because a wildly fluctuating market means that irrationally low prices will periodically be attached to solid businesses. It is impossible to see how the availability of such prices can be thought of as increasing the hazards for an investor who is totally free to either ignore the market or exploit its folly."

No doubt, Buffett had little argument from those receiving his letter. After all, many of them probably remember when the stock of Berkshire Hathaway sold for $38 a share. Recently, the stock was selling for *$47,000* a share.

The Eccentric Investor

If anyone ever creates an Investors' Hall of Fame, Anne Scheiber is almost assured of charter membership. And why not? When she died recently, she was a multimillionaire, and she supposedly started her investment pursuits with only $5,000.

Yet, while we might admire her investment acumen, most of us would shudder when we consider the self-sacrifice and denial that helped Scheiber attain her investment fortune. She was in life a recluse, an eccentric, a spinster who lived in such a Spartan manner that she gives new meaning to the word "frugal." She always dressed in the same bargain-basement coat and hat, for instance. She allegedly spent less than $2 a day on food. She probably never bought a single piece of furniture for the Manhattan studio apartment where she resided for most of her life. And refusing to spend her money on such "frivolous" purchases as newspapers and magazines, she depended on the public library for the news and investment information she received.

Ironically, she probably could have lived a near-normal life and still achieved great wealth. But she was greatly influenced by the Depression—and perhaps from working in a low-paying job for the Internal Revenue Service most of her professional life. So she seemed driven to live as economically as possible. And after she retired in 1944 (with only a meager pension from the IRS) she continued her tightfisted life of self-imposed penury.

Gifted with great intelligence, however, she had learned to invest through reading and observation. *Time* magazine points out that during her IRS career, while auditing the returns of affluent taxpayers, she had noticed that most who had left large estates had accumulated their assets through common-stock investments. As a result of that finding, she began an intense study of the stock market, its movements and its cycles.

With $5,000 she had put into a savings account, she systematically invested in blue-chip stocks in the industries and businesses with which she was most familiar and comfortable: entertainment, beverages, and pharmaceuticals. For example, a lover of movies, she invested in such Hollywood studios as Universal and Paramount, and her background with figures helped her keep tabs on their productions and performances. And one "luxury" in life she enjoyed was an occasional soft drink, so she invested in Coca-Cola and PepsiCo. As for pharmaceuticals, she chose such familiar names as Bristol-Myers Squibb and Shering-Plough. (Incidentally, her 1950 Shering-Plough purchase of 1,000 shares eventually multiplied her $10,000 investment in that stock to 60,000 shares worth $4 million.)

How good was she compared to other investing gurus? Well, less than 30 years after she invested that first $5,000, Scheiber reportedly was worth several million dollars, and her annual return was alleged to be 22.1 percent. If so (and some dispute that figure), that compares to John Neff's 13.9 percent, Benjamin Graham's 17.4 percent, and Warren Buffett's

22.7 percent. She is definitely in the investors' big leagues. Moreover, she accomplished that track record by simply following a few basic investment rules. *Money* magazine summed up those rules as lessons we can learn from. They are:

1. "Invest in leading brands." Scheiber, for example, owned, in addition to Coca-Cola, Bristol-Myers, and PepsiCo, stocks of Exxon, Rockwell, and Apple (though she reportedly disliked the latter because it is a technology stock, and she just wasn't comfortable with technology).

2. "Favor firms with growing earnings." Rather than a stock's price/earnings ratio, Scheiber concentrated on a company's ability to increase profits. She apparently felt that despite normal stock-price fluctuations, a company should be able to grow profits. If not, she would avoid it.

3. "Capitalize on your interests." As mentioned, she felt most comfortable with companies that offered her a product or service she was familiar with and could identify with.

4. "Invest in small bites." She rarely bought more than 100 shares at a time, her broker disclosed after her death, and only once bought more than 200 (the previously mentioned Shering-Plough purchase of 1,000 shares). Such a rule not only allowed her to add diversity to her portfolio, but also prevented her from buying too many shares when they were overvalued.

5. "Reinvest your dividends." Such a rule permits the "compounding" effect with stock purchases. Or as one financial publication explains, "It [dividend reinvestment] is the same principle as playing with the house's money in gambling, with this advantage—it's a sure moneymaker in long-term investing."

6. "Never sell." Scheiber experienced periods when some of her stocks—especially the pharmaceuticals in the 1970s—suffered through agonizing bear markets. But she never panicked, believing that such stocks were basically sound and would come back. They almost always did.

7. "Keep informed." Both before and after a purchase, Scheiber was relentless in her pursuit of knowledge, She read voraciously and attended shareholder meetings, where she grilled executives of companies in which she had invested.

8. "Save with tax-exempt bonds." Dismayed by the big cut that Uncle Sam took each year from her investment return, she developed a system of shifting the dividends she collected each month into tax-protected securities. At one time, she was earning as much as $750,000 a year, tax free, in that way.

9. "Give something back." Before she died at age 101, she made provisions to donate her millions to a worthy cause. An orthodox Jew, she chose Yeshiva University in New York City because she felt that it would assist young Jewish women in their struggles against ethnic and gender discrimination—both of which she had endured during her lifetime.

10. "And finally, enjoy your money." This lesson, which Scheiber obviously failed to learn, would have put into her life some meaning that was less materialistic. As it was, we can only think that all she had in the end were a box of stock certificates and perhaps a few regrets.

The Groupie Investors

This is about a group of ordinary people who achieved extraordinary investments results. The group is the Beardstown (as in Beardstown, Ill.) Ladies, 16 women who a decade or so ago started an investment club that has been so successful that Wall Street's top experts marvel at its exploits. And well they should. The annual average return of the Beardstown Ladies' investment club is 23.4 percent, an accomplishment that places them among the ranks of the Buffetts, the Templetons, and the Grahams. They became so famous, in fact, that, by demand, they coauthored a book, *The Beardstown Ladies' Common-Sense Investment Guide*, that was on the best-seller list for three months.

These women say that their investment feats were byproducts of nothing more than common sense and that anyone can do what they did. Don't you believe that for a second. The Beardstown Ladies are a bunch of shrewd investors. They work—and work long and hard—at buying and selling stocks. But they are correct that a methodical and prudent approach to investing can work wonders. As groupies to that idol of conservatism, they exude patience and perseverance, two qualities that have allowed them to master the complexities of investing.

The stock market is of course the key to their success. Their rationale: "two centuries of growth." In fact, the market has been insulated for the most part from worldwide panics, wars, depressions, and dozens of lesser disasters, not to mention some very antibusiness American Presidents. At least, that seems to be the thinking of the Beardstown Ladies. So that's where they put their money: in the stock market.

First, the Beardstown Ladies advise getting your financial affairs in order. That means assessing your current situation, then setting goals for yourself and your investments. After that's done, only then can you make worthwhile investment choices.

Next, they recommend that you "pay yourself first"—that is, put aside money for investment purposes *while* you are paying your bills. Then with that money you've put aside, even if it's only $5 or $10, tuck it into a bank account for temporary safekeeping. By trying to save money the other way—waiting to set aside money until *after* you pay your bills—you almost guarantee that you won't have anything left over for yourself. Moreover, make sure the savings amount goes in on a regular basis.

If you have a decent income and still can't do anything but pay your bills, the Ladies recommend that it's then time for some serious budgeting, which may mean cutting back on eating out or giving up some other nonessential purchases.

Eventually you'll be ready to pick and buy stocks. The Beardstown Ladies call themselves "fundamentalists," which, in contrast to "technicians," depends on looking for value inherent in a company, then holding on while that value grows. Traders the Ladies aren't. They buy for the long term, ignore the daily fluctuations, and sell only when absolutely necessary.

The Ladies note the performance of the market over the past few years, then try to better that performance. For example, if the market as a whole has grown an average of 11 percent each year, they strive to earn higher. Their goal: an annual return of at least 14.7 percent, which means they double their money every five years.

Through trial and error, the Ladies perfected a system for choosing potentially profitable stocks. When considering an investment, they advise, test it using the following 10 screens:

1. **Industry ranking:** First, investigate a company's ranking within its industry by consulting Value Line's Investment Survey. Don't invest if the company is not in the top third or preferably in the top 25 in its industry.

2. **Timeliness:** Using Value Line, which ranks stocks for timeliness (a measure of "relative price performance for the next 12 months"), make sure your company has a rating of 1 (highest) or 2 (above average) on the timeliness scale of 1 to 5.

SHOULD YOU JOIN AN INVESTMENT CLUB?

The United States has more than 18,000 investment clubs that are essentially like that formed by the Beardstown Ladies. And like the Beardstown Ladies, many of them consistently have better return records than the average stock mutual fund.

Moreover, investment clubs are excellent ways to initially get involved in investing. In fact, none other than investment savant Peter Lynch is a great supporter of investment clubs and encourages individuals to join one. In fact, he maintains that members of investment clubs have an advantage over Wall Street experts when it comes to picking stocks. He explains, "Any normal person using the customary 3 percent of the brain can pick winning stocks....If you stay half alert, you can pick the spectacular performers right from your place of business or out of the neighborhood shopping mall, and long before Wall Street discovers them."

To form an investment club or find out about those in your locale, write to the National Association of Investors Corp., 711 W. Thirteen Mile Road, Madison Heights, MI 48071, or call 810-583-6242.

---

3. **Safety:** Again using Value Line, check the safety rating, which indicates the volatility of a stock's recent price compared to its long-term trend. A stock should have a rating of 1 (highest) or 2 (above average).

4. **Debt:** Determine whether the company has total debt that is equal to no more than a third of total assets. The Ladies believe that the lower the debt, the better the investment. Standard & Poor's Stock Reports, as well as Value Line, can furnish this information.

5. **Beta:** Don't consider a stock a prime candidate for investment unless its beta, as specified by Value Line, is between .90 and 1.10. (The beta of a stock indicates its price volatility, so that a stock whose beta is 1 will move up and down in price at the same rate as the Standard & Poor's 500 stock index, but a stock with a beta of 2 will move up and down twice as much as the S&P index.)

6. **Sales and earnings:** Make sure the companies you're considering have at least five years of solid growth in sales and earnings. They should also show that they grow by double digits in the next few years. ("A small company should be projected [by Value Line] to grow 12 percent to 15 percent or even higher; a medium-sized company should grow 10 percent to 12 percent; for a large established company, 7 percent to 10 percent growth is a good rate." Then evaluate the company's prospects for future growth by determining whether its industry is growing.

7. **Stock price:** Try to buy 100 shares of the stock—even if you must limit your purchases to low-priced selections. If you buy in "odd lots" of less than 100 shares (100 shares and multiples of 100 are called "round lots"), you'll pay more in broker's fees.

8. **Price/earnings ratio:** Track the price/earnings ratio of the company for the past five years. Make sure the ratio is at or below the average for that period. (The p/e ratio is the price of a security divided by earnings per share and indicates the cost of a stock relative to its projected earnings.) Value Line lists average annual p/e ratios for the previous 15 years.

9. **"Upside-down" ratio:** This indicator tells you the relative
   odds of potential gain as compared to the risk of loss for a
   given price per share. You want your company to have a
   three-to-one potential upside in projected growth. Value
   Line lists projected highs and lows. The Ladies give this
   example: "Determine the projected high price (say, $40).
   Subtract the present cost (say, $15). This leaves you with
   $25. Take the present cost ($15) and subtract the projected
   low ($10). This leaves you with $5. Divide the $25 (upside
   potential) by $5 (downside risk). This gives you a ratio of
   5:1, a good buy."

10. **Management:** The company should be run by people with
    solid track records. Review business publications for arti-
    cles about the management's performance. Other good
    sources for this information are Value Line, analysts'
    reports, and materials and presentations prepared by the
    company officials themselves. Top management should be
    in control of any problems and have well-devised plans for
    the next few years.

And that's all there is to buying—at least in principle. But
what about selling? When do the Ladies unload when a stock
isn't performing? Or do they simply hang in there through
thick and thin?

As mentioned, they prefer to invest for the long term, and
that means ignoring market and single-stock daily fluctuations. But they do occasionally sell when they think a stock
has no further potential for growth. Keep in mind that they
purchase a stock only because they expect it to appreciate 100
percent in the next three to five years.

But they've had some duds. One was Fur Vault, a fur-stor-
age company that suffered from the reaction to animal-rights
supporters. They eventually took a loss of $853.66 on 100
shares less than two-and-a-half years after buying them.
That's a 29-percent loss on an annual basis.

But such disasters as Fur Vault have been few and fur between.
(Please excuse the pun.) Selections such as A. G. Edwards,
Glaxo Holdings, McDonald's, Rollins, RPM, and Wolverine
Worldwide have more than made up for the Fur Vault debacle.

But selling is important, and the Ladies closely follow the guidelines provided by the National Association of Investors Corp. Those guidelines are as follows:

1. Don't sell just because the price hasn't moved. As long as the fundamentals are strong, have patience.

2. Don't sell because of a "paper loss." (A paper loss or paper profit is a loss or profit that you would make if you sold your stock at a particular price. These gains or losses are nothing more than calculations made on a piece of paper; they do not become "real" until your stock is actually sold.)

3. Don't sell because of a paper profit. If you sell automatically when a stock hits a predetermined price, you risk missing out on even more profit. If the fundamentals and growth prospects remain strong, don't part with that stock!

4. Don't sell on temporary bad news. If the long-term view looks bright, hold on for the ride.

5. Don't sell just to take action. Holding is as meaningful an action as buying or selling.

6. Don't sell a stock that has fallen so far that your remaining downside risk is small compared to the upside potential. You might have nowhere to go but up.

Before we leave these awe-inspiring Ladies, remember two other important components of their success. First, by necessity they invested using the dollar-cost-averaging method. In other words, they made regular purchases simply because they contributed money for investing on a regular basis. That has meant buying regardless of the market's level. If stock prices are low, they receive more shares for their money, and when stock prices are high, they receive fewer shares. But over an extended time during which stocks have moved both up and down, they have noticed that the average price per share has been lower than the average price for that period. That's because, as any mathematician can tell you, they bought more shares when prices were low and fewer shares when prices were high.

Second, the Ladies *reinvested their dividends*. As they so

well explain, "Automatically reinvesting your dividends is an excellent method of ensuring continued, steady investment growth over time. Using these funds to add to your investment naturally is one of the best and easiest ways to build up your portfolio. And you will be compounding your income because you will garner income from your initial investment and from the income itself."

But Can You Do It?

In this chapter, you've seen how some of the nation's top investment minds buy and sell stocks. And you've also seen how ordinary people of ordinary means can match the performance of the experts. The process isn't that complicated, probably no more so than the job you have. There are no gimmicks, no special tools used. The key is diligence, expertise (yours or someone else's), and persistence.

Chapter 7: Asset Allocation—Finding the Right Combination

"To be prepared is half the victory."

– Miguel de Cervantes Saadvedra

Bad Name, Good Idea

Perhaps you've read or heard someone mention the term "asset allocation." No one seems sure about the derivation of that phrase, but the words spoken either separately or together don't exactly excite. Perhaps some diabolical financial planner first used them to make his service to a client seem erudite and sophisticated, thus allowing him to charge a higher professional fee. In any case, we are apparently now at the mercy of the asset allocators.

But the idea behind asset allocation isn't all that bad. So in this chapter let's grudgingly use the term.

As you'll see, asset allocation is really nothing more than properly mixing your investments. You simply emphasize those that stand the best chance at any one time of making you the most money. If stocks start doing well, put a larger portion of your funds into the stock market. If real estate seems headed for better times, shift your money around so you can put more into real-estate investments.

Okay, you see how it works. You've probably already been doing that all along, even if you haven't known what asset allocation is about. It seems easy enough. But it isn't. In fact, effective asset allocation can mean the difference between successful investing and unsuccessful investing. If you invest most of your funds in stocks when the market is in a bear phase, you can lose your shirt—or worse. And if you've invested mostly in bonds when the real-estate market is going ballistic, you've missed the ride, even if bonds are doing okay.

So how do you know the right proportions? Well, a lot depends on you. Not so much on how much you know or how good you are at reading a crystal ball. Rather on your investment philosophy. But we're getting ahead of ourselves. Let's start with some basics of asset allocation.

First, draw a large circle, then run a line the length of the circle's equator. Next, draw a line from top to bottom. Now you've got a pie-shaped object divided into four equal parts, something like this (and don't worry if yours is a little lopsided; we strive to be Warren Buffett, not Michelangelo):

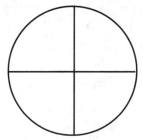

Now let's say you want to put 25 percent of your funds into stocks, 25 percent into bonds, 25 percent into real estate, and 25 percent into cotton-futures contracts. Simply label each quarter of the pie with the name of each of those four investments. Now your circle should look like this:

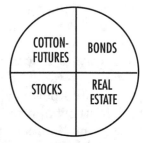

Rarely, however, would you commit your funds equally to

four investments. Sometimes you're going to sense that the bond market is the place to be. At other times, you're going to want more of your money to go into stocks. And so forth. So let's say the cotton-growing season looks like a bad one, and cotton futures don't look promising at the moment. So you want to reduce your holdings in those and put more into bonds, which are currently offering a high yield. And now you draw your pie so that you have only 10 percent in cotton futures, but 40 percent in bonds. You continue to hold 25 percent in the other investments. So at this point your circle should look like this:

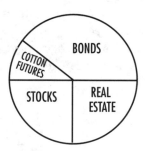

You probably didn't think asset allocation was so easy. Well it's not. Still, it's easier than driving a car in heavy traffic. And you have probably mastered that. In fact, think of asset allocation as driving an automobile. Most of the time, you drive along without really worrying about changing lanes or needing to speed up or slow down. You know where you're going, and you know what time you have to arrive. But suddenly traffic starts backing up, then stops. Now you have to make a decision. Do you take a chance that the traffic tie-up is only temporary and that you'll start moving again in a moment? Or do you hang a right and go a different but longer route to your destination?

Two vital factors are involved in such a decision. And they are the same decisions you have to make when considering asset allocation. (1) You have to know the *location* of your destination and (2) you have to know approximately when you must *arrive* at that destination. So if you take a detour, you must make sure you don't get lost and therefore never find your way. And if you pretty much know your way around, you still have to make sure your new route will get you where you're going *on time*.

With asset allocation, you must have a goal. It may be to build a nest egg of $500,000, or protect your funds against loss of capital, or double your worth in 10 years. Whatever, the goal must be realistic (not, "I want to accumulate a billion dollars"), and it must not expose you to excess risk (not, "Is this the line to buy lottery tickets?")

Back to our auto-driving analogy. If you don't have a destination in mind, you could aimlessly wander forever. Or if you know your destination but you drive like a maniac, you also may never get there—or at least not get there safe and sound. So now you know you have to have a goal and a reasonable amount of time to reach that goal.

But we aren't through with our auto analogy yet. This time, let's say you have at your disposal a fleet of cars, each with a driver, and you can, if you like, direct them all to a certain destination. This destination is important because you're sending money there and every dollar you send returns you two dollars—but only if the money gets there by 5 p.m. that day.

You could send all your money in one car, of course. But you see the fallacy of that strategy. A wreck, a car-jacking, or your driver deciding to take off to South America with your money means you've lost everything. So you wisely divide your money among your cars and tell each driver to take a different route to the destination. That way, if one or two run into a heavy traffic, you won't have everything tied up. Most of the cars will make it on time, and you'll at least double the money they are carrying.

But if you're really smart, you will evaluate the different cars in your fleet. You know that some of them are more dependable vehicles. Their drivers are sharper, more reliable, and know their way around. Other vehicles in the fleet have seen their better day, their drivers aren't familiar with the route, and they may decide to take their sweet time getting to their destination.

So naturally you put most of your money into the vehicles that stand the best chance to getting to the destination on time. You may put some into the other vehicles, but you're going to follow them, and if they don't perform as you like, you'll stop them, take some money or all of their money, then summon one of the better vehicles to transport it to the destination.

Enough with the analogy. By now, you surely understand what asset allocation is all about. And you also now understand the value of diversification. If you've learned anything to this point, it's this: Don't put all your eggs in one basket because if you do, you're making it easy for some crook with a serious craving for an omelette.

FOR THE ASSET-ALLOCATION NEWCOMER

If you're new to asset allocation, you may like the recommendations outlined by Ellsworth Davis when he was a vice president with a former capital-management subsidiary of American Express. His suggestions involve self-appraisal of personal holdings and assume that the investor is a stranger to asset allocation:

➤ First, compile a list of current assets. Break down assets into two categories: (1) corporate-related assets, such as pensions, salary-reduction/savings plans, and stock options, and (2) personal assets, such as stocks, bonds, CDs, and real estate. (A home may be included if you anticipate selling it or converting its equity into cash.)

➤ Second, determine short-term financial needs. Estimate how much money you will need for such purposes as your children's education or the support of an aging parent. Put assets for those needs in safe investments, such as bank CDs or short-term Treasuries.

➤ Third, set long-range financial goals. Calculate how much retirement income you will need and how much your survivors will need. If retirement is many years away, you might put at least a portion of your assets into riskier investments, such as growth stocks or low-grade bonds.

➤ Finally, determine the rate of return you will need so that you meet your requirements. If the rate seems unrealistically high, you may have to downgrade your goals—or find a way to increase your asset base. The higher the return needed, the greater the degree of risk you might have to accept.

A Widespread Following

But don't take just our word for it. Here's what Frank Cappiello, author of *New Guide to Finding the Next Superstock* says about diversification:

"Diversification remains the single most important step you can take to insulate yourself from market ups and downs."

Cappiello advocates dividing investments among various asset types: bonds, real estate, and perhaps some gold in addition to stocks. He feels that because each of those assets has a different investment cycle, some will do well when others don't.

He concludes, "Asset diversification assures you that in any investment climate you will make money—even in a bear market. That very fact allows you peace of mind and contributes to your sense of objectivity so that you can pursue a long-term strategy."

George Sterne, author of *The Dynamics of Personal Financial Planning*, says it this way: "If you buy a group of fundamentally sound stocks with good earnings, the chances are that in a good market you will catch at least some of the big winners. Most big money in a diversified portfolio comes from one or two big winners. Don't be deceived into thinking that 10 oil stocks is diversification; it is not. You should have a portfolio covering a wider range of industries. For example, you may have some stocks in the soft-drink industry, the retail area, drugs, home furnishings, electrical equipment, brewing, agricultural machinery, gold mining, and others."

But Sterne has also found that *over*diversification is not wise. He explains that the best strategy is to limit investments in stocks, for example, to 10 regardless of the amount of money available to invest. That would mean that rather than own 100 shares in 100 stocks, he adds, you would own 1,000 shares in 10 stocks.

Charles L. Fahy, author of *The Streetwise Investor*, also believes that diversification is absolutely necessary. He explains, "You can create a large degree of tolerance in your portfolio when you diversify. For example, if you have one stock that goes down, obviously your entire system performs poorly."

Fahy points to the "5-percent allocation system" followed by John Templeton and Warren Buffett—that is, don't put more than 5 percent of your investment capital into any one stock investment. By using this formula, you reduce risk to a minimum and take advantage of the one stock issue that might go tenfold.

Fahy suggests combining diversification with self-discipline, which, he says, is derived from a technique of identifying individual investments in a diversified portfolio and refraining from trying to predict the course of the market. "Remember," he concludes, "instead of forecasting or predicting, simply diversify,"

Benjamin Graham, coauthor of the previously mentioned *Security Analysis: Principles and Technique,* also recommended diversifying with both stocks and bonds by keeping at least 25 percent of holdings in bonds and cash reserves and a minimum of 25 percent in stocks. He based that advice on his belief that most investors really don't have the skills to determine whether stocks or bonds are the better bet at any one time, so both types should always be in an investment portfolio.

Equities or Debt—Which is Best for You?

Graham obviously didn't have much faith in the average investor's intelligence. But he did have a good point: Establish a mix of investment types based on market conditions, but never totally neglect any one type. He would probably also warn that there is no mix that is perfect for everyone.

In that regard, *Money Advisory*, a publication of the Research Institute of America (RIA), explained a few years ago that all too often financial planners and other experts give the impression that, depending on market conditions, there is an ideal combination of assets—say, 10 percent in cash, 20 percent in bonds, 30 percent in stocks, 40 percent in real estate—that is best for all investors. But, RIA notes, people vary widely in their objectives, circumstances, and tolerance for risk. In other words, RIA was saying that the effective deployment of capital depends on market conditions, but personal considerations are the controlling factor.

Still, asset-allocation guidelines are important. For some

people, in fact, they are essential. Without some direction, the average investor wouldn't even know how to *start* selecting investments. She might buy a stock on the advice of a brother-in-law when that stock has nothing to do with the goals she has in mind. Or during a period of disinflation she might have 80 percent of her holdings in gold, a strategy that would be financial suicide.

Many financial planners themselves depend on asset-allocation specialists for assistance. And one of the very best is Harold W. Gourgues, Jr., who publishes the influential *The Gourgues Report*, a newsletter whose subscribers for the most part are financial planners. Gourgues is generally regarded as one of the top asset-allocation strategists in America, and his advice carries a lot of weight in cities and towns throughout the nation.

Gourgues explains that any investment will fit into one of two categories: (1) direct and (2) indirect. Indirect investments are securities, such as stocks and bonds, and are generally quite liquid and offer "psychological" leverage, usually by way of the corporate ownership structure. Their value in the marketplace reflects both the underlying asset values and the temperament or mood of buyers and sellers. Direct investments, on the other hand, attach assets, or what Gourgues describes as "cash-flow streams"—or both—to the investor more directly. Real estate and precious metals are examples.

Gourgues then assigns each investment a percentage, but by no means does he suggest that all investors should blindly follow his model to the letter. Instead, he merely wants his percentages used as guidelines. Moreover, the Gourgues asset-allocation model is designed to change according to anticipated conditions. He is a contrarian and thus often buys when most others are selling and sells when most others are buying. Recently, Gourgues, based on expectations of a bear stock market and a bull real-estate market, told his readers to lighten up on stock holdings to 10 percent, while increasing their holdings in real estate and other direct investments to 75 percent. But at other times (like in the mid-'80s), the technical signals he uses may tell him to put as much as 40 percent into bonds, 25 percent into stocks, and a mere 5 percent into real estate.

Gourgues has an amazing record of forecasting the peaks

and valleys associated with investing. He knows that all investments follow certain cycles (which he likens to the pendulum of a clock), and that it's therefore just a matter of time before the cycle reaches its apex and starts its reversal. He cautions against trying to capture the last bit of profit from each cycle and prefers selling off before the peak occurs.

Explains Gourgues, "The avoidance of a major investment setback is in the long run far more important to asset accumulation and preservation than any attempt to squeeze out the last one-third to one-fourth of every investment bull market."

The system of asset allocation he espouses signaled the beginnings of the current long-term bull market in stocks in August 1982, when the Dow bottomed at about 769. That was when Gourgues' all-important "Rule of 35" was triggered. That Rule—a stock-market signal that has not erred since 1860—warns of a stock-market bottom when short-term interest rates decline by 35 percent from a previous high.

Incidentally, Gourgues' technical signals have recently warned that the bull market was peaking, so he has taken a lot of heat from those who followed his instructions to get out of stocks while the market was still a raging bull. But for a lot of investors his advice will probably yet prevent the loss of significant portions of their capital. Plus, his advice to get into real estate during the early stages of a seemingly inevitable bull market will certainly make many of his readers firm believers again.

In any case, you see the value of diversification. It pays to diversify among types of investments—that is, under the Gourgues system you would have cash equivalents, such as money-market funds, savings accounts, or short-term CDs, stocks (or funds), bonds (or funds), real estate, etc. Such diversification gives you some hedge against movements in interest rates, inflation, or the investment markets.

Next, diversify within each of your types of investments. For example, two stocks are better than one. Two bonds are better than one. Finally, diversify based on your risk tolerance, temperament, and personal philosophy. You don't want to lose sleep at night because you've speculated in pork-belly

HOW THE EXPERTS ALLOCATE INVESTMENTS

Almost all brokerage firms recommend diversifying investments. Here are some typical asset-allocation blends on March 31, 1997:

Broker	Recommended Mix (%)			
	Stocks	Bonds	Cash	Other
Goldman Sachs	60	25	10	5
Dean Witter	65	20	15	–
Prudential	70	0	30	–
PaineWebber	50	40	10	–
Lehman Brothers	65	35	0	–
Smith Barney	45	40	15	–
Merrill Lynch	40	55	5	–
Bear Stearns	55	35	10	–
First Boston	60	30	10	–
A.G. Edwards	55	30	15	–

futures. Nor do you want to invest in a furrier if you believe in animal rights. Just make sure you can handle an investment emotionally as well as financially.

Doing Something About Risk

But here's a strange fact about asset allocation and diversification: Recently, investors have found that by adding more volatile, higher-yielding foreign stocks to a portfolio of U.S. stocks, risk actually decreases (to a point) while return increases. Statistics show that while the U.S. stock market is going down, foreign stock markets (other than those of Canada) often go up. So if you have both types of holdings, the swings tend to moderate each other, but because both types of assets increase in value over time, your portfolio continues to increase in value—only without as much volatility.

You can, however, overdo this foreign-stock-holdings thing. If, for example (and we're talking averages here), your portfolio during the period January 1985-June 1994 comprised all stocks and 90 percent of them were foreign types, your average return was 17 percent, but your risk factor was 16 percent. But by lightening your load to a 50-50 ratio, foreign to domestic stocks, your annualized return during that period dropped slightly to 15.7 percent, but your percent risk declined to a much more tolerable 14.1 percent.

By the same token, by owning a bond portfolio with no stocks, you'll increase your return while reducing your risk if you add stocks. This was proved by Anthony Gallea, who is in charge of Smith Barney's Gallea Team in Pittsford, N.Y., and who wrote a book entitled *The Lump Sum Handbook: Investment and Tax Strategies for a Secure Retirement*. Gallea found that from 1976 through 1991, the Standard & Poor's 500 stock index had an average total return (appreciation plus dividend income) of 14.5 percent a year, and a bond portfolio produced a return of slightly more than 10 percent. However, a portfolio that contained 30-percent S&P stocks and 70-percent bonds returned about 1.5 percentage points more than a portfolio composed of bonds alone—and with less risk.

Asset allocation has even more meaning for investors who stubbornly avoid stocks and stay with bonds exclusively. One study discovered that overseas bonds yield an average of 2 percentage points more than domestic bonds. So such investors can still practice asset allocation by simply keeping about 20 percent of their bond investments overseas.

Some Words About Timing

Stock traders constantly attempt to buy and sell when the market or an individual issue is at a peak or valley, depending on the situation. To a degree, that makes sense. During the course of a single year, the price of a typical stock can vary by 10 percent or more. So you wouldn't want to buy Home Depot at $80 a share, only to see it drop to $75 a few weeks later. Nor would you want to sell Compaq at $55 a share, then watch as it jumps to $60 a share the next month. Few things in life are more irritating than that.

As the successes of prominent investors show, however, timing isn't all that important. It is a part of active trading, and active traders usually don't fare all that well in the long run. For many, their gains are eaten up in broker commissions they pay. Moreover, major turns in stock prices are usually triggered by unpredictable events. Most important, many investors are guided by their emotions: They refuse to ease up on buying stocks when the market is seemingly headed upward—and vice versa when the market is headed south. In other words, they want to swim with the tide, not against it. And that would make sense except for the fact that going with the flow means you'll eventually go crashing onto the shore.

So what's the answer? Should you try to time investment purchases and sales or not? Well, of course you should—but only within reason. Let's face facts. Every stock share is bought to be sold. Warren Buffett buys at what he thinks is the best time to buy, then sells when he figures that a particular holding is no longer pulling its weight. Much the same is true of Peter Lynch, Benjamin Graham, and John Templeton. They all have been able to pick a thoroughbred from the herd—much the same as they also could recognize an old nag that's ready for the glue factory.

How to Stay Current on Asset Allocation

We live in a fast-changing world. That means an asset-allocation formula that's good for today may not be appropriate in a few months. So how can you stay up-to-date? Try these publications:

➤ **Morningstar Inc.** publishes numerous guides to mutual funds, but it also advises as to the type of funds that are best at any particular time. Morningstar publications are available at public libraries or from Morningstar at 1-800-876-5005.

➤ *Forbes* magazine keeps you current on asset allocation, with columnists that rank investments (plus contrarian recommendations) and select investment types. Your public library probably subscribes to *Forbes* or you can subscribe yourself by calling 1-800-888-9896.

Asset Allocation: A Summary

As you've seen, asset allocation is a practical means of investing that you can put into practice. By doing so, you diversify your holdings and reduce your risk. The top money managers and brokers recommend such a system. And also as you've seen, timing plays a key role in enjoying the fruits of its success.

Chapter 8: Action Plans For the Small Investor

"He who sells what isn't his'n must buy it back or go to prison."

–Daniel Drew

Some Go-Go Strategies

The following action plans will show you the way to take advantage of some of the market strategies used by top investors. As you will see, none are very difficult to implement. Once you get the hang of them, you will be selling short, using leverage, trading options, dollar-cost averaging, and employing the techniques of value investors. First, selling short:

Selling Short

Investors use short selling when they think the price of an investment will drop. So during a bear market—or even when you spot a single stock during a bull market headed for a fall—you can use this strategy very effectively.

Selling short is simply selling something you don't own. But don't worry that, as the above quotation suggests, you may go to prison for this. When you sell stocks short, you pay your broker to borrow shares from someone else. Then you sell the borrowed shares, and later you go into the open market and buy (you hope at a lower price) the same number of shares and return them to the person you borrowed them from—thus avoiding any problems with the law.

Here's an example: You learn that the stock of a telecom-munications company named Realcom has enjoyed a fantastic increase in price after introducing a product known as the Realcom 1000 and is now selling at a price/earnings ratio of 28. But you know that Realcom is basically a one-product com-pany and that one of its market rivals is ready to bring to market a revolutionary product that will directly compete with the Realcom 1000.

Based on that information, you arrange with your broker to borrow 500 shares and sell them at $20. Within a couple of months, Realcom, suffering from plummeting sales as a result of its rival's new product, announces lower profits and the stock falls to $10 a share. You then buy 500 shares and walk away with a $5,000 profit (less commissions, of course).

That's how short selling works in principle. And on paper it sounds great. But the technique has its detractors. Plus, dangers lurk (though never a prison sentence).

Obviously, investors usually "go long," hoping stocks will rise after buying them. And most people never sell short. The reason is probably psychological. Perhaps they think it unethi-cal to wish that a company will fall on hard times. Also, the short seller has unlimited risk, because the stock's price could soar indefinitely. People who go long, however, risk losing only their investment.

Another disadvantage of selling short is that the seller cannot receive dividends. Any that are paid must go to the stock's owner.

One approach to allow you to profit from a short position is to sell a trend and hope for its extension. And don't count on contrarian theory in every case. A company that is badly man-aged or has a lackluster record will sometimes be acquired by a stronger company. Even the rumor of such an acquisition can run up the price of the stock you have shorted.

Success in taking a short position in the market means capitalizing on a negative. Most stock-market speculators seem to do much better taking a positive position. Time and just sitting on the shares of an established company can often pull an investor out of an initial mistake. He or she may even collect some dividends while waiting. But sitting on short sales can be expensive. The short seller receives no dividends, and there are other possible costs and difficulties. Emotionally, it is disconcerting to most people if the market starts going against them.

The availability of options (puts and calls) has greatly reduced the need to use short selling as a hedging device. With options, the risk can be limited only to the cost of the option. In other words, to limit a potential loss, you purchase a call option as a hedge against your short position. (More on options later.)

Or you can simply use a stop order. For example, with Realcom, when you sell short at $20 a share, you enter an order to buy 500 shares at $22 stop. If the stock price advances to $22, you'll limit your loss to $1,000.

If you think you want to use short selling, here's some advice: Don't sell short the stocks that have advanced the most; they frequently advance still further. Most short sellers tend to sell too soon and have to take losses later at higher prices.

Also, find out about insider trades. These are trades made by officers and directors of the company. (You can get this information from financial publications.) When the number of insiders selling exceeds the number buying, that's a good sign that the stock is priced too high and those in the know expect a decline in the near future.

Some investors also go by the volatility of a stock based on the stock's beta. In other words, when the historical relationship between the price movement of the stock and the overall market is awry, you may have a candidate for short selling. You are looking for volatility: more is better when you are considering a short position.

Selling short isn't for everyone. As you have seen, risk is involved. So if you are retired or if you are conservative in your investment viewpoint, you may want to use this strategy sparingly, if at all. Otherwise, it can add to your investment weaponry.

Using Leverage

Leverage, as stated earlier in this book, lets you combine your investment funds with borrowed funds to create a potentially profitable situation for both you and the lender. Let's say you buy a house with $10,000 down and a $90,000 mortgage, then sell the $100,000 house for $120,000. Your $20,000 profit is not 20 percent ($20,000 divided by $100,000), but 200 percent ($20,000 divided by $10,000). The profit percentage is calculated on the amount you put up, and this is leveraged with the borrowed money.

Leverage therefore is the technique of increasing your potential return (or loss) on an investment by providing less than the full purchase price for a financial asset from your own resources. Hence, leverage is sometimes called "trading on your equity."

Leverage can take a number of forms: borrowing from brokerage firms (called investing on "margin") or financial institutions; using paper profits to buy more securities (pyramiding); or trading in items that require only a small cash deposit or performance bond (commodity or currency margin). You use leverage to increase your possible returns—but of course with the understanding that you also increase your possible losses.

Margin investing is highly popular nowadays. If you intend to use this technique, however, you must open a margin account at a brokerage firm. Then when you buy on margin, an order is placed with a broker to purchase a number of shares of the stock in the usual way. However, you do not pay the full amount for the shares. Instead, you pay the broker some fraction of the amount due—and the broker lends you the remainder.

The shares you buy are then left in the broker's name. In actuality, the broker is simply acting as a financial intermediary, providing you with a secured loan. As security, you are leaving your shares.

WHEN NOT TO SELL SHORT

Professional investors sometimes sell short, and when they do they observe several rules:

➤ They avoid selling short the stock of a company that has a favorable outlook for earnings or sales. That's a buy signal, not a sell signal.

➤ They don't sell short the stock of any company that is too "thin"—that is, has only a few hundred thousand outstanding shares. A small amount of buying can push the stock price upward and put a squeeze on a short seller.

➤ They avoid selling short the stock of a company that has already suffered a price drop of 60 percent or more. Much of the profit from the transaction is gone.

➤ They don't sell short more than three or four stocks at a time. More than that means spending too much time keeping up with them.

➤ They don't sell short the stock of any company that is a candidate for a merger. Even rumors of a merger could mean a price rise.

➤ They don't buck the trend. If the overall market is headed up, chances are that even the market dogs will experience a uptrend.

Here is a typical margin trade:

Melvin Adams, an investor, buys 200 shares of General Widgets at $25 a share. The total cost of this investment would be $5,000. Then add, say, $150 for commission, and the total cost is $5,150. Now suppose Melvin has a margin account at the brokerage house. He could take a margin loan of 50 percent of the $5,000, which would be $2,500. He would then be putting up $2,650 from his cash resources, for a total of $5,150.

Now assume Melvin holds the shares for only one year and pays interest at a rate of 10 percent on the $2,500 loan, for a cost of $250. The anticipated dividend he'll receive on the stock is $250. Thus, in order for Frank to break even in that one-year period, the price of General Widgets must rise to at least $25.75 from its $25 level to cover the cost of commission and interest, less dividends.

The trade looks like this:

You buy 200 shares of General Widgets at $25 a share on margin. Assume that you hold the shares for one year and pay interest (at 10 percent a year) on the $2,500 loan.

Cost of 200 shares at $25	$ 5,000
Commission — to buy	150
Interest on $2,500 margin loan	250
Cost	$ 5,400
Less anticipated dividend	250
Net cost	$ 5,150
Net cost per share	$ 25.75

The price of General Widgets stock must rise to at least $25.75 per share from $25 in order to put you at a breakeven point. Keep in mind, however, that interest costs are tax deductible and would have a bearing on the net result.

As you can see, margin lending is the broker's version of revolving credit. Buying stocks on margin lets you put up part of the price, while the broker lends the rest at rates generally 2 percent more than the prime rate. (Actually, the rate is scaled up from the "broker call loan rate," but this rate is usually close to the prime rate.)

Buying stock on margin produces huge leverage and potential profits, but like credit, it can also encourage you to buy more than you can afford. But don't worry. Brokers won't let you get in too far over your head. Each broker has a "maintenance-margin level" for margin accounts. When the cash and stock value in a margin account drops below a certain percentage of the current market value, a margin call occurs. You'll need to put up more security (cash, etc.), otherwise the broker can liquidate part of your holdings.

So who is a candidate for using leverage? Again, this technique involves more risk than you may want to assume. So limit your leverage exposure to only a small portion of your portfolio, especially if you are at or nearing retirement.

Options Trading: High-Leveraged Action

You previously contemplated the use of options to prevent excessive losses when you sell short. But options trading is a world in itself. Instead of buying a portion of a company's assets and earnings potential, as when you buy stock, you buy only the right to buy the company's stock. Are you getting dizzy?

In fact, an option is merely a choice that may or may not happen. When investors buy options, they are really looking at the choices available to them.

Let's digress for a moment to consider another type of option. Suppose you want to buy a new home and you've narrowed your choices to just two houses. The thing is, you're not sure which way housing prices are headed. If you wait six months, prices might go down. Or they might go up. Builder A is offering you an attractive colonial for $100,000. You decide to go to the bank, take out a mortgage, and buy the house. If you do, that's just like buying stock. You get ownership for your money.

Before you hand over the cash for the colonial, however, Builder B makes you a different sort of offer on an equally valuable, stylish contemporary. Here's the deal. If you pay Builder B $500 now, he'll guarantee that you can buy his house for $100,000 six months from now. For a $500 fee you get the right to pay $100,000 for the contemporary no matter what happens to housing prices. And that right (or option) will last for six months.

But before you buy that option, notice two things. First, paying for the option does not convey ownership. You're only buying the right to buy something, nothing more than that. Second, note that buying the option doesn't obligate you to purchase the contemporary house. You've paid for a right that's yours to exercise—only if you choose to do so.

Let's see what happens if you go with Builder B. (1) If housing prices are higher in six months, you can exercise your purchase option and buy the contemporary house for $100,000. By purchasing the option, you've locked in the cost of the house. (2) If prices go down, you don't have to exercise your option. You can make a deal with Builder B to pay $95,000 for his house, or you can go to Builder A, who's now willing to take less for his colonial. Or you can try to find a better bargain. (3) If housing prices stay the same, you're out $500, but that's the cost of six more months of shopping time, which could have saved you several thousand dollars. (4) You

– 163 –

can sell the option if you suddenly have to move to another area.

And that's generally the way options on stocks work. Instead of a builder, however, you get them from a broker. They actually trade on the Chicago Board Options Exchange (CBOE), along with the New York Stock Exchange, and a couple of other exchanges.

The price specified in an options contract is known as the "strike" price. The option you bought from Builder B had a strike of $100,000. That is the price at which the option writer (seller) must do what's called for in the options contract. The strike price is not the cost of the option to its buyer. The price a buyer pays for an option is its premium. The premium you paid for Builder B's option was $500. You might pay a $2 premium for an option with a strike price of 90, which obligates the writer to perform at a stock price of $90 per share.

The strikes of standardized options are set at $5 intervals (though low-price stocks and stocks that have split may have strikes set at intervals of $2.50. The time component of an options contract is determined by the date of expiration. Standardized options contracts expire monthly, but the options traded on a single exchange don't all expire in the same month. Expirations come in cycles, so you may find that an option you're tracking expires in January, while a different option trading on the same exchange expires in February.

Recall that Builder B sold you an option on a specific house, with a $100,000 strike and a June expiration, for a premium of $500. From a writer you've never met, who has offered his option for sale through his broker, let's say you're considering the purchase of a company's February 90 option. That's a contract on the stock, with a 90 strike, that expires on the third Saturday in February—one month from now. The premium on this option is $2, which means the contract that covers 100 shares will cost you $200. But there's one thing missing from the contract you're considering. It doesn't specify what action the writer is bound to perform at the strike of 90 anytime in the next month. Builder B's promise was to sell you his house for the specified strike within the specified expiration. But with stock options you can require two kinds of behavior.

Depending on the option, the buyer obligates the writer either to buy or to sell. This is where puts and call come into the picture. A put is a contract that forces the writer to *buy* stock at the specified strike price. A call is a contract that binds the writer to *sell* at the specified strike.

If you buy a February 90 call, you're buying a contract that binds its writer to sell you 100 shares of the company's stock for $90 a share anytime before the third Saturday in February. In this example, we'll say that you want this option because you expect the stock to go higher than 90. Once you buy it, the writer is obligated to sell at $90 a share, 100 shares per contract, anytime prior to expiration.

It the stock rises to $100 a share, you can use the option to buy it for only $90 a share. Then you can turn around and sell the 100 shares you bought for $9,000 at their current market value of $10,000, and you'll make a profit of $1,000, less brokerage fees and the $2-a-share option premium.

You buy calls when you're hoping that a particular stock will climb past the strike price. You want to "call away" stock from the writer at a price that's less than the current market share price and sell it at the higher current market share price.

A put, on the other hand, obligates the writer to buy stock from you at the contract strike price. You want a put because you expect a drop in a stock's market price. Let's say you buy a February 90 put. That means you're buying a contract that binds its writer to purchase 100 shares of stock from you at $90 a share anytime prior to expiration. If the stock's market price falls to $80 a share, you would buy 100 shares through your broker for $8,000, then sell them to the writer for $9,000, and you'll again be ahead $1,000, less brokerage costs and the option premium you paid the writer.

The leverage is high because an option can often be bought for under a dollar per share (in 100-share units). The broker's commission, in percentage terms of the total dollar amount of your option, is extremely high. And brokers charge both when you buy the option and when you sell, or exercise it. Nevertheless this type of investment can bring excellent rewards.

Most people who buy options buy a call. Perhaps the unpopularity of puts is due to a desire to root for higher prices on the investments we own. In that way, puts are reminiscent of short selling. But puts enable you to make money, too, and that is important to the investor.

Puts or calls usually cost under 10 percent of the stock price. And the price of the option, plus the broker's commission, is the most you can lose when trading. With an option to buy (a call), you make money if the price of the underlying stock rises. Puts can be used as an alternative to selling short, and puts cost less in brokerage commissions than short selling. But for you to make a profit, the put stock must fall lower in price than the shorted stock.

The advantages of buying puts over short selling are:

➤ **Lower risk.** A put owner risks only the cost of the option, while the short seller has unlimited risk if the stock keeps rising in price.

➤ **Smaller capital investment.** The short seller must place up to 50 percent of the stock price as margin. The price of a put is far lower than that, usually less than 10 percent of the stock's price.

You can use puts not only to speculate in stock you believe will fall in price, but also as a sort of insurance on stock you have bought. Buying 100 shares of stock while at the same time buying a put on 100 shares of the same stock will ensure you against losing more money than the cost of the put, plus broker's fees. If the price goes down, the gain on the put offsets the loss on the stock. All you lose is the cost of the put plus broker's fees.

So why not use a stop-loss order with your stock instead of getting a put? Because though the stop-loss order on the stock you own is free, the stock will be sold if it drops to that designated stop-loss price. With a put, you can sit back for the term of the put and wait for the stock to rebound upward without taking a loss.

A "straddle" combines a put and a call and allows you to make money regardless of the direction of the stock's price, so long as it goes high or low enough to offset the costs of both the options and the brokerage commission. A straddle costs more than a put or call because it is two options rather than one.

If you think a stock is more likely to rise, you may want to buy two calls and one put as insurance. If you think a stock is more likely to fall, you may want to buy two puts and one call as insurance. Of course, with both strategies, you don't recoup your investment and start making profits until your stock swings high (or low) enough to recover the cost of all three options plus brokerage fees.

Keep in mind that for every person buying a put or call, someone must sell it. A put seller (writer), for example, must come up with at least 50 percent of the price of the stock, minus the price of the put, minus the difference between the stock's price of the put. If the price falls below the strike price, the put seller loses money and the put buyer gains. The opposite is true if the price rises above the strike price. With a spread, a speculator can sell one put and buy another on the same stock in different option months.

Options trading has some inherent risk, of course, and many investors, especially those with modest portfolios, may use this strategy only occasionally—and as merely a way to protect their assets.

Watch for Lots of Odd Lots

Experienced stock traders have a theory that the small investor constantly does the wrong thing at important turning points in the stock market. In fact, some traders believe so strongly in that theory that they use the "odd-lot trading index" (that is, the rate of purchases to sales made in less than "round," or 100-share, lots—presumably by small investors unable to afford round lots) as a guide to their trading strategies.

These traders therefore sell when the odd-lotter is buying, and they buy when the odd-lotter is selling. The underlying assumption to odd-lot trading is that the average small investor is emotional, frightened, and, most importantly, uninformed. They believe that small investors don't sell short because they do not grasp the concept, or they misinterpret inherent signals in news about companies and the markets.

But, most of all, the small investor is reputed to misunder-
stand the basic concepts of market trading.

Whatever the reason, the odd-lot theory generally works.
And when combined with the technique of selling short, a
savvy investor can make some money.

You can set up an odd-lot selling indicator on your own. You
simply divide the total odd-lot sales into the odd-lot short sales,
then chart a 10-day moving average. When the indicator drops
below 1.0 and stays there for several months, get ready to sell
short. But wait until it reaches 0.5 to actually start selling.

So what if the indicator rises above 1.0? Stop selling short
and start covering your positions. In fact, make sure you cover
all shorts when you calculate a one-day reading above 3.0.

A Primer for Value Investors

Some of the most successful investors and portfolio managers are faithful to a strategy you've learned a bit about earlier in this book: "value investing." When an investor invests
in value, he or she aims to profit from each stage of a company's earnings life cycle. They buy stocks *out* of favor and sell
them when they come back *into* favor. In that way, they earn
generous profits, but a safety net is built in.

Here are some of the typical value-investing criteria, as
formulated by William Nasgovitz, portfolio manager of the
Heartland Funds, and excerpted from a recent interview published in *Bloomberg Personal* magazine:

1. **A low price/earnings ratio.** "A stock's p/e ratio should be
   less than the market's multiple, if the stock is then 'discovered' by Wall Street, the low p/e provides opportunity for a
   sharp price increase. Also, if the market drops, low p/e
   stocks have less downside risk."

2. **Plenty of cash on hand.** "Cash flow should be substantially higher than the earnings per share. A strong cash
   flow permits expansion to be financed internally, shares to
   be repurchased, or the dividend to be increased."

3. **Earnings that are increasing.** "A sure sign of growth."

4. **A discount to book value.** "A company's book value—its assets minus liabilities—is what it would be worth if liquidated."

5. **A sound financial position.** "How much debt does a company have relative to its equity? Heartland likes low-debt balance sheets, with no more than 25 percent debt to total capital."

6. **Significant internal ownership.** "Executives who invest in their own stock have more incentive to work for the company's success."

7. **Competent management.** "Do the top decision makers have a realistic vision for the company, as well as a history of success and the drive to accomplish their goals?"

8. **"Hidden" assets.** "Does the company have undervalued assets? These can include understated natural resources, overfunded pension plans, or fixed assets that are worth substantially more than their stated book value."

9. **Positive technical analysis.** "How has the stock's price moved over time? Heartland looks for stocks that have built long-term bases."

10. **An impending major development.** "Is there a factor—a new product, for instance—that could potentially ignite interest in the stock and close the gap between the stock's price and what Heartland's managers believe is its intrinsic value?"

Value investing has merits for just about anyone. Many investors make all buy decisions based on its criteria. And it can be a useful strategy whether you are a conservative or aggressive type.

Dollar-Cost Averaging: A Trusty Companion

Like most investors, you probably worry when the market makes a move that seems contrary to a trend. Almost always in such a case, the movement is down when the overall trend is up. Suddenly, you wonder if the stock market will continue to be the inviting and dependable friend it has been of late. And then there's that nagging fear that it might end up becoming your worst enemy.

That's all right. Concern—even fear—is not all that bad. You will stay more alert to what's happening around you. Nevertheless, life could be a bit easier if you have some technique or strategy that will let you sleep a little better at night and prevent your making any big mistakes.

After all, hindsight has shown you that when the price of stocks seems headed down, that's the time to not only hold on to those you own, but also buy more. But if you're like most investors, you find that hard to do. In that case, a dollar-cost-averaging strategy is probably wise.

Under an investment system using dollar-cost averaging, an investor commits a fixed dollar amount at prescribed intervals during a long period of time. The investor makes purchases as frequently as possible to avoid seasonal or other variations. A suitable plan would call for, say, purchases four times a year for 10 years. The dollar amount is fixed—when prices are high, the investor buys fewer shares and when prices are low, he or she buys more shares. Hence, the weighted-average cost of the shares should be lower than the average price prevailing in the market at any time, unless prices plummet.

Let's say, for example, that you commit yourself to purchasing $4,000 worth of a stock on a periodic basis. Let's assume that you make four purchases over a period of time. The first time you buy, the price per share is $20, so you buy 200 shares. The next time you buy, the price has risen to $25, so you get 160 shares for your money. The third time, the price has risen to $40, and you buy 100 shares. Finally, the price falls to $32, so you buy 125 shares. Your total investment is $16,000. You will have purchased 585 shares at an average price of $27.35. With a market price of $32, you have "dollar-cost averaged"—your average price per share is lower than the market price.

That's great, you say. But now let's look at an even more favorable pattern of prices. Again, we'll assume a $4,000 periodic purchase plan. The first time, the price is $20 and you buy 200 shares. For the second purchase, the price has risen to $40, and you buy 100 shares. The price then rises to $50, and you buy 80 shares. Finally, the price rises to $80, and you buy 50 shares. Obviously, dollar-cost averaging yields spectacular results when the price rises steadily, since the process is identical to pyramiding. The total investment in this case is $16,000. You would have purchased 430 shares at an average price of $37.21, compared with the current market price of $80.

Prices don't always rise, of course, and if they continually fall, the strategy will not work in your favor. Let's again follow the example of a $4,000 plan. You buy 200 shares at $20 a share for the first purchase. Then the price falls to $16, and you buy 250 shares. Later the price falls to $10, and you buy 400 shares. Finally, the price falls to $8 and you buy 500 shares. Your total investment is $16,000, or 1,350 shares bought at an average price of $11.85, compared with the market price of $8. However, if the stock price were to recover to, say, $20, the results would be spectacular. On the other hand, should the price continue to fall, say, to $5, you would suffer a severe loss.

Let's look at another example: You commit yourself to a 10-year plan at $4,000 per period. No discernible pattern develops. The stock starts at $20, falls to $10, rises to $20, rises to $32, falls to $25, to $20, to $16, back to $20, up to $32, down to $20. The share price ends up exactly where it started. You would have made a total investment of $40,000 and purchased 2,060 shares at an average price of $19.42, and now the market price is $20.

The results aren't spectacular, but now take a close look at the share prices over the period. In five of the periods, the price was at $20, exactly where it started. In two of the periods, the price was below $20, and in three of the periods, the price was above $20. In the periods in which the price was below $20, the price had fallen to $10 and $16, for a total $14 below the $20 price. The periods in which the price was above $20 was when the purchase price was $25 and $32, for a total of $17 above the $20 price. In spite of the unfavorable rating in this dollar-cost plan, you still received a modest profit, as shown below:

CHART 12

DOLLAR-COST AVERAGING IN A VACILLATING MARKET				
Period	Price Per Share	No. Shares Purchased	Total Cost	Average Cost Per Share
1	$20	200	$4,000	$20.00
2	10	400	4,000	13.33
3	20	200	4,000	15.00
4	32	125	4,000	17.30
5	25	160	4,000	18.43
6	20	200	4,000	18.67
7	16	250	4,000	18.24
8	20	200	4,000	18.44
9	32	125	4,000	19.35
10	20	200	4,000	19.42

The advantages of dollar-cost averaging are quite clear: You wind up with a relatively low average price for securities in the long run. Plus, the plan is easy to implement. And you have a timing strategy that is quite mechanical, preventing you from getting emotionally involved. Over time, dollar-cost averaging should produce a lower price for shares you buy than the average market price—and a lower price than the final price unless the stock has been in a horrid bear trend.

As you can imagine, the more volatile the stock, the better the results of dollar-cost averaging. Constant or rising stock prices produce only a constant average price or a rising average price with each additional purchase. Conversely, a constantly declining price produces a lower average price with no profit opportunity. Therefore, the more volatile the share price, the more shares you'll pick up when the price is high. A volatile stock also gives you more opportunity to pick up shares cheaply, yielding even better results.

DOLLAR-COST AVERAGING WITH LIMITED FUNDS

If the dollar amounts you invest are relatively low, such as $1,000 a year or less, purchases made once a year will be best. Otherwise, you will be purchasing in small lots, of, say, $500 each, and you will be subject to minimum commissions from the brokerage firm.

If the dollar amount you invest is between $2,000 and $3,000 a year, you could make two purchases, one every six months. If the dollar amount you invest is $3,000 to $4,000, consider three purchases. And if the amount is between $4,000 and $5,000.... Well, you get the picture.

The point is that you wish to avoid making purchases of less than about $1,000 to minimize the possibility of being stuck with large percentage brokerage commission or odd lots. At the same time, you want to increase the number of purchases made per year to avoid the chance of a aberration. (For example, a day of the year when prices are invariably and inexplicably high.) By spreading your purchases over the year, you reduce the probability of this type of occurrence.

Keep in mind, however, you'll pay high transaction costs when you make frequent, possibly small purchases. Similarly, small purchases usually mean odd-lot trades, particularly when you fix a periodic purchase amount. But you can use dollar-cost averaging for the direct purchases of stocks, especially if you are in a dividend-reinvestment plan.

Before leaving the subject of averaging, consider some variations on the theme.

FREQUENT CONTRIBUTIONS ARE BEST

If you decide that dollar-cost averaging works for you, keep in mind that when investing, say, semiannually, or even quarterly, you may forego some of the advantages of this technique. The time span, especially for semiannually investing, is simply too great. You will likely, for example, miss out on the volatility that makes dollar-cost averaging such an excellent investment tactic.

Monthly contributions are probably best for most people.

The Constant-Dollar Plan

Some investors may want to make use of, at least to some extent, a conservative trading strategy known as constant-dollar investing. However, this mechanical-type plan works only if you can start with a fixed amount of money to invest in selected stocks, bonds, or a combination of the two. Then, if the value of the securities rises, you sell a sufficient dollar amount to return the total value of the portfolio to the original dollar amount.

Let's say you start with a $20,000 portfolio of stocks and bonds and its market value rises to $30,000. You would sell $10,000 worth of selected securities (investing the proceeds in riskless assets) to reduce the portfolio back to $20,000. If the market value were to fall to (heaven forbid) $12,000, you would buy $8,000 worth of additional securities to bring the portfolio back up to $20,000.

You constantly shift between risky assets (your portfolio) and riskless assets. You select the dollar amount that you want to have committed to a portfolio of risky assets of stocks and bonds and maintain the remainder in riskless assets, such as U.S. Treasury securities. With this plan, the major feature is that it provides an automatic process that forces you to shift from stocks and bonds to less risky assets in a rising market. Of course, it also means that you shift from riskless assets into stocks and bonds during a declining market. Since bull markets (and bear markets as well) do not last forever, you have a buffering process to let you liquidate stocks during a bull market by taking profits and adding to stock positions during a declining market.

This is not a perfect world, however, and this strategy has a couple of major flaws:

(1) Since the amount invested is maintained at this constant level, profits are severely constrained during a long-term bull market.

(2) You are also constantly adding to your portfolio during a long-term bear market, following a principle that is curiously similar to averaging down.

CHART 13

THE CONSTANT-DOLLAR PLAN IN ACTION

Portfolio of stocks and bonds	$20,000
Portfolio value rises to	30,000
Sell	10,000
OR	
Portfolio of stocks and bonds	$20,000
Portfolio value falls to	12,000
Buy	8,000

The shift is constantly between risky assets and riskless assets; the strategy thus yields automatic countercyclical buy and sell signals.

The Constant-Ratio Plan

If you want to maintain a specific ratio of stocks, bonds, or cash in a portfolio as prices change, then a constant-ratio plan is for you. As an example, suppose you choose to hold 40-percent stocks, 50-percent bonds, and 10-percent cash as a long-term portfolio target. If the value of the stocks rises so that they exceed 40 percent of the portfolio's total value, you would sell sufficient stocks to reduce the proportion back to 40 percent again. If the value of your bonds rises to, say, 60 percent, you'd sell sufficient bonds to reduce the proportion back to 50 percent.

Obviously, you shouldn't go overboard with this strategy. If you're buying and selling stocks and bonds on every quarter-point shift in your portfolio's value, your transaction costs will soon get way out of hand in relation to the small dollar amounts involved. But as you probably have figured by now, the major attraction of this plan is that it provides an automatic mechanism that forces you to adjust to changes in your portfolio balance. The method is particularly useful if stocks and bonds are moving in opposite directions for reasonably long periods of time. As a result, you get a countercyclical approach to investment. You are constantly shifting from rising stocks to lower-priced bonds, and vice versa.

Constant-ratio investing does not work well, however, if both stocks and bonds are moving in the same direction. During a high-interest-rate period, both will tend to move in the same direction, probably downward, and there is virtually no advantage to shifting from stocks to bonds if, during a downturn, the prices of both securities decline.

If you're structuring a portfolio of conventional and nonconventional investments, the constant-ratio method is particularly useful. Consider a constant-ratio plan that strikes a balance between gold, common stocks, real-estate investment trusts (more on these later), and Treasury bonds. Since those assets do not move in perfect lockstep (that is, they are not perfectly correlated), the automatic mechanism of constant-ratio investing is particularly useful.

The Variable-Ratio Plan

The variable-ratio plan is similar to the constant-ratio plan except that at varying levels in the market price, you change the proportion of the ratio. When the price of stocks in the portfolio increases, you simply adopt a new ratio, decreasing the amount of stocks in the portfolio and increasing the amount of fixed-income or other securities. This type of program is quite complex and requires that you often resort to estimates; however, it is a sophisticated and useful mechanical strategy.

First, you must determine a norm, or average, for equities. This norm can be a long-term expected trend of stock-market prices or it could be the long-term or expected level of price/earnings multiples. Many investors use the former, but it can be unreliable because it hinges on an accurate forecast of long-term stock prices. It's better to use the price/earnings ratio method instead. You do that by estimating price/earnings- multiples over the next time period. Current interest rates are the best indicator of which way interest rates are predicted to go. If you think interest rates will fall, expect the average price/earnings ratio of stocks to increase. Let's assume that you estimate an average price/earning ratio of 10. Based on that figure, you develop your trading strategy.

Chart 14 shows a typical strategy for a variable-ratio plan:

CHART 14

THE MECHANICS OF A VARIABLE-RATIO PLAN		
	RATIO	
Deviation from norm	Equities	Fixed-income securities
+100%	0%	100%
+ 80%	5%	95%
+ 60%	10%	90%
+ 50%	15%	85%
+ 40%	20%	80%
+ 30%	25%	75%
+ 20%	30%	70%
+ 10%	40%	60%
0%	50%	50%
- 10%	60%	40%
- 20%	70%	30%
- 30%	80%	20%
- 40%	90%	10%
- 50%	100%	0%

If the level of average price/earnings ratios deviates from the norm by 100-percent or more, you simply shift out of equities entirely and hold 100-percent fixed-income or other defensive-type securities. If the deviation from the norm is 80-percent or more, you would hold 5-percent equities and 95-percent fixed-income securities. At a 60-percent deviation from the norm, you would hold 10-percent equities and 90-percent fixed-income securities, and so on. If there is no deviation from the norm, you keep 50-percent equities and 50-percent fixed-income securities. This is your assumed starting point: a 50/50 balance under normal conditions. Of course, you can use any starting point that suits your needs.

Next, you have to determine the deviation from the norm associated with the expected trend of the average price/earnings multiple. For instance, a 100-percent deviation in the norm would be associated with a price/earnings ratio of 20. If the price/earnings ratio actually rises to 20, you would sell all your equities and hold only fixed-income securities. If the price/earnings ratio rises to 18, you would hold only 5-percent equities. If it rises to 16, which would represent 60-percent deviation from the norm, you would hold 10-percent equities, and so on.

If, however, the price-earnings ratio goes down, say, to 8, the deviation from the norm is -20 percent. You would hold 70-percent equities and 30-percent fixed-income securities. If the price/earnings ratio drops all the way down to 5—a -50 percent deviation from the norm—you'd hold only equities and no fixed-income securities at all. Chart 15 illustrates this example.

Obviously, the norm can change. That means that the deviations and associated price/earnings level will change as well. If you change the "norm" to a p/e of 12, for example, the price/earnings average would have to rise to 24 before you would switch entirely into fixed-income securities. By the same token, a drop in the average p/e to 6 would mean you hold only equities. Chart 16 gives the particulars for a "normal" p/e ratio of 12.

The major advantage of this plan is its automatic nature. It forces you to shift debt and equity securities when necessary and in a countercyclical manner. Keep in mind that you don't have to adhere precisely to the strategy. You might use a wider range of zones to cut down on the number of trades that take place. It's an unemotional strategy; you make your decisions by simply following the mechanistic process of the strategy. This is quite a sophisticated plan and can be a valuable device for portfolio-revision tactics.

CHART 15

DESIGNING A VARIABLE-RATIO PLAN WHEN THE AVERAGE P/E RATIO IS 10			
Deviation from norm	**Average P/e level**	**Equities**	**Fixed-income securities**
+100%	20	0%	100%
+ 80%	18	5%	95%
+ 60%	16	10%	90%
+ 50%	15	15%	85%
+ 40%	14	20%	80%
+ 30%	13	25%	75%
+ 20%	12	30%	70%
+ 10%	11	40%	50%
0%	10	50%	50%
- 10%	9	60%	40%
- 20%	8	70%	30%
- 30%	7	80%	20%
- 40%	6	90%	10%
- 50%	5	100%	0%

CHART 16

DESIGNING A VARIABLE-RATIO PLAN WHEN THE AVERAGE P/E RATIO CHANGES TO 12			
Deviation from norm	**Average P/e level**	**Equities**	**Fixed-income securities**
+100%	24.0	0%	100%
+ 80%	21.6	5%	95%
+ 60%	19.2	10%	90%
+ 50%	18.0	15%	85%
+ 40%	16.8	20%	80%
+ 30%	15.6	25%	75%
+ 20%	14.4	30%	70%
+ 10%	13.2	40%	60%
0%	12.0	50%	50%
- 10%	10.8	60%	40%
- 20%	9.6	70%	30%
- 30%	8.4	80%	20%
- 40%	7.2	90%	10%
- 50%	6.0	100%	0%

A Technique for the Aggressive

You will sometimes find a need to switch the asset mix of your investments. An aggressive method used by Richard Croft, a highly successful investor who specializes in portfolio management and asset allocation, goes by the irresistible title of "The Buy-Low, Sell-High Approach."

Croft's technique can be used any time you feel that the price of one asset has drifted too far astray relative to the other asset classes in the portfolio. Moreover, it does not require the investor to forecast changes in the economy or business cycle. It is activated only when the asset weightings within the portfolio begin to shift.

Following the contrarian philosophy of using an asset-allocation model to govern investment decisions (see chapter 7), you would buy assets that have performed poorly while selling those assets that have moved significantly higher. And over the long term, buying quality assets at bargain-basement prices should yield some fairly consistent risk-adjusted returns. The key, of course, is deciding when an asset has moved "significantly" higher or lower. You want to sell the better-performing assets at a point when the near-term upside is, at best, limited—in other words, when the risk-reward profile of the asset changes. And since that decision rests ultimately with the investor, active management is clearly required.

Most academic studies that have focused on capital-asset classes have suggested that clearly defined short-term trends are less the rule and more the exception. Therefore, most financial assets tend to move within a certain specified trading range.

The optimum strategy would thus be to buy at the bottom of the defined trading range and sell at the top of it. (Since most portfolio models are designed to display some negative correlation, when one asset is near the top of a trading band, another should be near the bottom of a range—or at best treading water.)

The next step, then, is to define a reasonable trading range. Just how aggressive you want to be depends on how much time you have to devote to the portfolio. More aggressive investors will use short-term trading ranges—and in some cases will change the parameters as circumstances dictate. Others, with less time, will probably establish a set of parameters at the outset and simply alter the weightings when those parameters are breached.

Obviously, you could simply estimate the reasonable trading range of each asset. And, depending on how well you can pick tops and bottoms, that may often be the best approach. You could also employ technical analysis, using it to either establish a trendline or to define a trading range using support and resistance points. In that case, you would physically sell as the asset hits upside resistance—and buy when it touches support.

Another approach is to let the marketplace dictate the trading range. The marketplace, in this instance, is the options market. Because professional options traders pay close attention to risk, option premiums imply a certain level of volatility. The higher the volatility, the wider the trading range—and vice versa.

The first question the balanced investor must ask is whether the options market is "efficient." In other words, how accurate are the assumptions that go into an option's price? If you assume that most professional options players are short-term traders, the marketplace should quickly reflect any change in the underlying security. And since most professional traders employ sophisticated computer programs to assist in controlling risk by pricing options effectively, you can assume that when inefficiencies occur, they are quickly corrected.

Given an efficient marketplace, you would then formulate a trading range based on the level of volatility implied by the options market. If, for example, the premiums on Standard & Poor's 500 Index options (traded on the Chicago Board Options Exchange) are implying a volatility of 20 percent, that generally means that, over the course of the next year, the options market feels there's a very high probability that the stock market will trade within a range approximately 20 percent above or below its current price.

Let's say the S&P 500 index is at about 780. Therefore, the options market is suggesting that the S&P 500 composite index could trade between 624 and 936. If either value is breached, that would be an opportune time to make a move.

As mentioned, this technique is for more aggressive investors and requires that you stay well-informed regarding the markets' movements. But if you qualify, you can enjoy exceptional returns on your investments.

Investing Retirement Assets

You've previously seen how asset allocation works (see chapter 7), but you can also use asset allocation as an action-planning tool. Let's see how just a slight modification in the makeup of a portfolio can lead to good things:

Suppose you start with the following mix: bonds, 50%; cash, 30%; growth and income stocks, 10%; and a balanced mutual fund, 10%.

From 1970 to Jan. 1, 1997, your average annual return would be 8.8 percent. If you then retired and began making withdrawals from your accumulated funds at a 6-percent rate, and assuming a 4.5-percent inflation rate during your retirement, you would exhaust your funds in 27 years.

But suppose you opt for a different portfolio mix—let's say 20% bonds, 10% cash, 10% growth stocks, 40% growth-and-income stocks, and 20% in a balanced fund. Your average annual return since 1970 would be 10.4 percent. Moreover, assuming all other conditions are the same (inflation, withdrawal rate), your nest egg would last 46 years.

Obviously, you would incur slightly greater risk, but this shows that action planning of this type will provide meaningful results.

Can You Employ These Action Plans?

As you've seen, the investment action plans described here can prove highly worthwhile. In your arsenal of investment techniques, they can allow you great flexibility and prevent you from taking unnecessary losses. Whether you sell short, use leverage, buy and sell options, dollar-cost average, or become a value investor, you've greatly improved your chances of investment success.

Chapter 9: Dividend Growth: A Consistent Winner

A cow for her milk,
A hen for her eggs,
And a stock, by heck,
For its dividends.

– Source unknown

More Than Just Income

Dividends have always been an important source of income for many investors. Dividends, the payout to shareholders from the profits of a company, can be much more than that, however. As you'll see in this chapter, they can not only add to your capital growth, but also serve as a indicator of whether a stock is a worthwhile investment.

The following strategies can be used by any type of investor, from the most conservative to the most aggressive, from the beginner to the experienced.

How Not to Outfox Yourself

So your stocks are treating you shabbily. Bears have always been rather brutal beasts, and when they invade the stock market, they tend to want to inflict damage on everything and everyone in sight, including you and your stock holdings.

But you know just what to do: SELL. SELL EVERY-

THING. After all, a fox like you is always more cunning than a stupid old bear. So you'll just outsmart him, keep your money in cash, and be ready when the bull returns.

Well, maybe you've outfoxed yourself this time, especially if you include in your investment portfolio a goodly supply of income-producing stocks—those that pay high dividends.

Therefore, before you act, consider some facts and figures for a moment.

From January 1946 through December 1992, less than 55 percent of the increase in stock-portfolio values was due to price appreciation. The remainder was a function of dividend payments and reinvestment.

In other words, the Dow Jones Industrial Average produced an annualized rate of return of 11.2 percent from 1946 through 1992 (assuming reinvestment of dividends). Of this 11.2-percent return, only 6.1 percent came from actual appreciation of stock prices. The remaining 5.1 percent came from dividends and the money earned through reinvestment of those dividends.

By the way, the Consumer Price Index, the government's measure of inflation, increased at a 4.5-percent annual rate during that period. That means that the money you made just from dividends alone outpaced the rate of inflation by a sizable margin. And keep in mind that those figures were of all stocks, including those that paid no dividends at all.

You've heard a lot about stock-dividend yield. But just how do you determine this important figure. Easy. Just divide the stock's annual dividend by the stock price and multiply by 100. This gives the dividend yield in percentage terms.

To this point, the discussion has focused on cash dividends. That is the type investors are most familiar with. Such dividends are paid out of profits and retained earnings and are normally set by the company's board of directors. Once a dividend is declared, the company must pay it—or risk legal default. And there's nothing that requires a company to pay a dividend—even if the company's earnings are sufficient to warrant one.

DO LOW DIVIDEND YIELDS STILL MEASURE THE MARKET?

Decades of analysts have convinced most experts that when the Standard & Poor's 500 stock index is yielding less than 3 percent, stock prices are considered as being far too high. The conclusion is that eventually the yield must rise, either because companies boost their dividends or stock prices will drop back to more reasonable levels.

Nowadays, with dividend yields at 2 percent or even under, we scoff at the notion of such an argument. In early 1993, however, conditions were different. Or so they seemed. The dividend yield had been flashing a danger signal for several months, and many people were very worried. Finally, with the S&P 500 rising to 448.93, the dividend yield stood at 2.79. And statistics showed that when the dividend yield drops below 2.85, the market immediately does a flip-flop and either corrects or begins a bearish movement.

But instead of an "accident" occurring, the market continued its rally, leading some analysts to declare that the dividend yield as a valuation tool was no longer reliable. For one thing, interest rates and inflation were low and stable in 1993. Moreover, the economy was in an early stage of recovery. And, finally, the nation's major corporations were expecting greater future profits so that investors felt stock prices would reflect those improving conditions.

In other words, investors were putting their money into stocks that would appreciate in value. They were apparently not that concerned about income because they realized that the alternatives—certificates of deposit, money-market funds, or even bonds—were no better.

That theory prevails four years later. But will the low-dividend indicator resurface at some future date to show that it was right all along? Most strategists say it won't so long as conditions remain as they have been so far in the 1990s. However, they add, once interest rates and inflation start rising, all bets are off.

Sometimes a company pays a *stock* dividend. As you can figure, a company pays these dividends in its shares rather than in cash. If, for example, a company declares a 6-percent stock dividend and you own 100 shares of the company's stock, you receive six additional shares.

Stock dividends of more than 25 percent are usually designated as "stock splits." That's when both the share prices and the dividends are split equally. Suppose, for example, that a stock trades at $60 a share, with a $3-a-share dividend. If the company then declares a two-for-one stock split, the stock price will be $30 and the new per-share dividend rate will be $1.50. The dividend yield remains the same.

WHY SPLIT A STOCK?

Why would a company split its stock and increase the number of shares available? For one reason, a large pool of shares available for trading increases the liquidity of the stock. Since a stock split also reduces the share price, it makes it easier for small investors to buy 100-share round lots. Moreover, many individual investors prefer stocks that carry prices under $60 a share.

For example, an investor who has $7,500 and wants to buy a stock selling for $300 a share could buy 25 shares, excluding commission costs. After a four-for-one split, however, the investor could buy 100 shares with the same $7,500. The dollar investment remains the same, but the perceived value is greater, since 100 shares appear to be worth more than 25 shares. And a broker's commission on orders for "odd lots," (that is, orders that are not 100 shares or multiples of 100 shares) usually carry a premium.

Finally, there's the *extra* dividend. Suppose a company sells an asset at a higher-than-expected price. That's an extraordinary profit that is also a nonrecurring event. The company is not required to declare a dividend to share the good fortune with shareholders. And in fact it could invest in expansion or reduce its outstanding equity. But it often declares on extra dividend.

Rules for Selection

So how do you pick those companies that will pay you high dividends—and offer a promise of capital gains (that is, stock-price increase) as well? That's not an easy question to answer. When a company pays a high dividend, it can mean that earnings are up and management wants to pass along those earnings to shareholders in hopes that demand for the stock will consequently increase. But a company that pays a high dividend may also be expecting slower growth and is paying out dividends rather than retaining them to finance future expansion or product research, both of which could mean an eventual drop is share price.

On the whole, however, steady increases in a company's dividend are a plus rather than a minus.

Take the ones listed in the following chart. They are companies that have maintained or raised dividends for 15 consecutive years or more. They all would be likely candidates for a portfolio that is heavy on dividend performance:

CHART 17

A DIVIDEND DREAM TEAM

The following NYSE-listed companies have outstanding dividend-paying records. For at least the past 15 consecutive years, all have either equalled or exceeded the dividend payout per share of the previous year.

Company	1996 Div.	Yield (%)
AMP Inc.	$1.00	2.7
Block, H&R	1.28	2.7
Bristol-Myers Squibb	3.00	2.3
Central & South West	1.74	7.1
Chubb	1.08	1.8
Clorox	2.22	1.9
Emerson Electric	2.01	2.2
General Electric	1.84	2.0
Kimberly-Clark	1.83	1.8
Masco	.77	2.3
May Department Stores	1.16	2.6
Morgan, J.P.	3.24	3.4
Pfizer	1.20	1.5
PPG Industries	1.26	2.4
Philip Morris	4.20	3.5
Quaker Oats	1.14	3.2
Tambrands	1.84	4.3
UST Inc.	1.48	5.2
V.F. Corp.	1.46	2.2

But this doesn't tell the entire story. As noted, most of the yields of these stocks are low even in today's market, where the average payout rate on a NYSE stock is a meager 1.9 percent. But keep in mind that stock prices are, for the most part, at record levels, and that fact tends to keep dividend yields low. For better-than-average dividend yields, look at banks, conglomerates, and utilities. A large portion of their total return come from dividends—which are reinvested, of course. (More on this later.) Still, you have to be selective. Fat payouts haven't been enough to produce good results in electric-type utilities or tobacco stocks, and certain stocks in the semiconductor and communications-technology industries have been leaders without much help from dividends.

PAYING DIVIDENDS—RECENTLY, THAT IS

Keep an eye out for companies that start paying dividends—and ones that resume paying them after a long pause. A recent study shows that such companies are great buys.

That study, conducted by Kent Womack, a professor of finance at Dartmouth University, shows that the stocks of companies that start or resume payouts get an initial price boost of about 3 percent, then continue to outperform the market by more than 20 percent in the next three years.

In contrast, the stocks of companies that eliminate their dividends tend to drop in price an average of 7 percent in the first two days, then underperform the market by more than 15 percent in the next three years.

So you begin your search by examining the leaders in the banking and utility industries. That's not as easy as it sounds. Nowadays, holding companies and conglomerates with non-bank- or nonutility-sounding names may avoid detection.

Let's consider utilities. The Dow Jones Utility Average is a composite of 15 companies, and their dividend payouts in 1996 are shown in Chart 18.

CHART 18

COMPONENTS OF THE DOW JONES UTILITY AVERAGE*

Company	1996 Dividend Yield (%)
Public Service Enterprise	7.9
Peco Energy	7.1
Consolidated Edison	7.1
Unicom	5.9
American Electric Power	5.8
PG&E	5.7
Southern Co.	5.6
Texas Utilities	5.2
Edison International	5.0
Duke Energy	4.6
Consolidated Natural Gas	3.5
Williams Companies	2.8
Enron	2.1
NorAm Energy	1.8
Columbia Gas	0.9

*These are the current components of the DJUA, which was reconfigured May 12, 1997.

With only a few exceptions, the companies included in the DJUA obviously pay generous dividends. In return, however, you must surrender any chance for high capital gains. For example, during the bull-market year of 1996, electric utilities as a whole achieved only a 2.5-percent price gain. And the three-year (1994-96) price-gain average was a paltry 4.6 percent (annualized).

From banks, you can expect less percentage income from dividends, but more capital gains. In fact, from the standpoint of price performance, banks have been one of the hottest segments of the stock market in recent years, and that means that dividend yields are historically low. For example, if a bank is paying a $2.50 dividend and its price is $50 a share, the yield is 5 percent ($2.50÷50 = 5%), but if the price rises to, say, $60 a share, the dividend yield drops to 4.2 percent (2.50÷60 = 4.16667).

With banks, however, although their sterling performance overall is attributed to their stock-price appreciation, dividend payout continues to be a major factor. Consider the following banks:

CHART 19

MONEY-CENTER BANKS 1996 PERFORMANCE		
Company	Total Return	Dividend Yield (%)
Bankers Trust NY	+36.5	4.4
J.P. Morgan & Co.	+26.3	3.4
First Chicago Corp.	+40.5	2.7
Chase Manhattan	+55.7	2.2
BankAmerica Corp.	+58.3	2.1
Republic NY Corp.	+34.4	2.0
Citicorp	+56.6	1.8

With very few exceptions, you can always count on the dividend yield of banks (or at least their holding companies) to be greater than that of most other companies.

Sources of Information

Barron's can be a big help in the dividend-paying selection process. This weekly financial newspaper provides information on current dividend yields. Usually, you can spot a utility or bank by the name. But if you aren't sure, check the listing in the most recent monthly issue of *Standard & Poor's Stock Guide*, which you can find at your public library (or which you can subscribe to for $145 a year; call 1-800-221-5277).

Once you have a list of companies that pay liberal dividends, you're ready to narrow them down to three or four that have the credentials you are looking for. Your evaluation process is only slightly different from that used for other companies. (See Chapter 12.) Here are the criteria suggested in the Hume High Yield Handbook *High-Dividend Stock Strategies:*

➤ A 4.8-percent or higher current annual dividend yield.

➤ The most recent earnings/price (e/p) ratio for the company within 80 percent of the yield on AAA-rated bonds. For example, if AAA-rated bonds are trading at an 8-percent yield to maturity, the minimum required e/p yield for entry would be 6.4 percent (0.80 x 0.08 = 0.064, or 6.4 percent). (The current average yield for AAA-rated bonds is listed weekly in the "Market Laboratory—Bonds" section of *Barron's* under "Best Grade Bonds.")

➤ A 10-percent or higher current return on equity (ROE). (Check at your public library for the most recent *Value Line Investment Survey*, which provides ROE information for companies you are considering.

➤ A medium-grade credit rating or better. In other words, the corporate bonds or other debt securities are rated at least BBB by Standard & Poor's or Baa by Moody's. (Check *Investor's Business Daily* for ratings of bonds that are actively traded.)

High-Dividend Stock Strategies also recommends holding, if possible, a minimum of three different high-dividend stocks to reduce the risk "of being right about using this strategy, but wrong about the actual stock chosen."

Dividend Reinvestment Plans: A Win–Win–Win Strategy

Dividend reinvestment plans, or DRIPs, provide a cost-saving way to increase the size and the value of your stock portfolio—even in down markets.

That sounds pretty good, doesn't it? Well, it *is* good. Many companies—especially the blue-chip firms—will allow stockholders to buy additional shares with their dividends. By taking advantage of this program, you can pyramid your holdings in a company over the years, even earning dividends on your reinvested dividends.

More than 1,000 companies now offer dividend-reinvestment plans. Shareholders can thus buy more shares by going directly to the firms, thereby bypassing the broker and commission fees. The cash dividends actually buy the stock. And most programs allow investors to make voluntary cash payments to purchase shares directly. Some companies even allow *partial* reinvestment of dividends.

Suppose you have 300 shares of MNO Company. The stock is selling for $30 a share and paying a dividend of $2.80 a year (a 9.3-percent yield). Every quarter, you could receive a check for $210 (70 cents x 300 shares). Or you could authorize the company to use your dividends to buy more shares and credit them to your account. Ideally, you would receive seven new shares for your first quarter's dividends. In some cases, however, you'll pay a small service fee (around 5 percent) or a prorated portion of the commission on the transaction (around 1 percent).

Some companies waive the brokerage commissions, and a few will even sell you the shares at a 5-percent discount from the market price. Your $210 will thus buy you 7.37 shares—in most cases, you will receive credit for fractional shares. Other companies will allow you to add funds to round off fractions. For example, you might be permitted to add $18 to bring the total up to eight shares or contribute even more to buy additional shares.

The next quarter, your dividend will be based on your new total number of shares. Assuming you received the fractional shares, you'd now have 307.37. You would receive $215 credit toward more shares of MNO. Applying the 5-percent discount (and assuming the price still is $30 a share), that means you'll get seven-and-a-half new shares. In six months, you've increased your holdings in MNO Company by almost 5 percent (14.87 shares) without paying a penny.

That's like free money. If, for example, a company's stock is selling for $50 a share on the NYSE, but you can buy 100 shares of it at a 5-percent discount, the company is giving you $250.

One caveat: You will pay federal income taxes on the dividends even though you don't receive the cash. And, if you buy the stock at a discount from its market price, the difference also is considered taxable income. However, the tax consequences, in most cases, are far outweighed by the opportunity to pyramid your stock holdings and put your dividends to constructive use.

DRIPs are such a good idea that if you are considering two companies that have similar good points and advantages, but one offers a DRIP and the other doesn't, always go with the one with the DRIP.

To start a dividend-reinvestment plan, purchase 100 shares of a company that has a plan in place. You may have to use a broker for this transaction, but it may be the last time you will need his or her services. Then ask the broker to register the shares in your name. The company will thereafter send information on its DRIP directly to you.

Fill out the forms you get and return them to the company. This process usually takes three or four weeks. When the next dividend is payable, you should receive a statement showing the amount of your dividend and the number of shares it bought. That statement from the company should also show how many shares you now own.

To sell your shares, write a letter to the company instructing it to cancel the DRIP and issue the shares in the plan to you. A certificate should arrive in three or four weeks. You'll get a check for the value of any fraction of a share in the plan.

You then simply take the shares to your broker or bank and give instructions to sell.

A source for information on DRIPs is available from a newsletter named, appropriately enough, *DRIP Investor*, published monthly by NorthStar Financial, Inc., 7412 Calumet Ave., Suite 200, Hammond, IN 46324 (219/931-6480). Subscription rate is $79 a year.

Every Dog Has Its Day

A dividend-type investment strategy that is simple, safe, and almost sure to produce above-average results is known as the Dow Dividend Plan, sometimes also called "The Dogs of the Dow" strategy. When you use this tactic, you concentrate on the 10 highest-yielding stocks of the 30 companies included in the Dow Jones Industrial Average. By doing so, you get not only the obvious good source of income from the dividends (which you reinvest, of course), but also, according to research, excellent capital gains. So your total return can be excellent.

But here's a pleasant paradox: Analysts have found that by limiting the Dow Dividend Plan to the five lowest-priced stocks within the top-10 highest-yielding category, you get even better investor returns. Brokerage firms call this the "Top-10/Low Five" strategy.

First, the Dow Dividend Plan. A couple of years ago, investment researchers discovered a startling fact: The 10 highest-yielding DJIA stocks have almost consistently outperformed the DJIA as a whole. That finding was based on figures from January 1972 through December 1993 and assumed that returns are reinvested at the beginning of each calendar year in equal dollar amounts. Results for those 22 years showed that the top-10 dividend payers were, in fact, far ahead of the entire DJIA: 15.9 percent compared to 11.7 percent. After 22 years, an investment of $10,000 in those 10 stocks would have multiplied to about $260,000.

But then the researchers found that the five lowest-yielding stocks of those 10-top dividend producers provided a total return of 20.5 percent for the 22-year period. So investors who put $10,000 in a Top-10/Low-Five portfolio in January 1972 would have more than $600,000 on December 1993. By comparison, an investor who would have simply invested in a stock index based on the DJIA and with no deviations would have only $110,000.

Moreover, the Top 10/Low Five were steady performers. They produced positive actual annual total returns in 20 of the 22 years. And in one year—1975—the five averaged a 67.3-percent return.

For 1996, the Dogs (top 10) returned 30.5 percent for investors, compared to 30.4 percent for the DJIA as a whole. But the Top 10/Low Five registered a 34.2-percent gain for the year.

Keep in mind, however, that because of the fewer number of stocks in which you would be investing, the Top-10/Low-Five strategy carries more risk. During 1990, for example, you would have suffered a 15.8-percent drop in the value of your holdings. But that's true of most investments: The more risk you incur, the greater your return potential.

On the other hand, out-of-favor stocks, like those in the Top 10 and the Top-10/Low Five, may decline less as a group during market declines than the DJIA. That's because their price weakness usually is already reflected in their higher dividend yields.

You may wonder why the Dow Dividend Plan (or Dog plan) and the Top-10/Low-Five strategies outperform the markets to such an extent. Prudential Securities studied the phenomenon, and here's its explanation:

"The answer involves investment philosophy as well as simple mathematics. Typically, the selected stocks attract investment dollars looking for both income as well as the potential for capital gains, By emphasizing both income and potential capital gains, [the DJIA dividend plan] enhances overall potential significantly.

"The mathematical explanation for some of the advantage is based on the fact that with prices held constant, higher-yielding stocks by definition will produce greater returns. Our studies show that at least 100 basis points of the improved return is due simply to the compounding effect of a higher-yielding portfolio."

Prudential also found that a higher percentage of underperforming stocks from within the top 10 are often found among the five lowest-yield stocks from that group. Notes Prudential:

CHART 20

FOR DOGGONE GOOD RETURNS

Company	Price ($)	Yield (%)
DJIA's Top 10 Based on Yield		
Philip Morris	114.25	4.80
J.P. Morgan	100.75	3.42
AT&T	38.38	3.40
Texaco	106.50	3.21
Chevron	68.50	3.15
Exxon	103.25	3.04
General Motors	60.63	2.66
Int'l Paper	42.63	2.36
Minnesota Mining	85.63	2.32
DuPont	108.75	2.13
Remaining 20 DJIA Companies		
Caterpillar	77.75	2.06
Goodyear	54.88	2.05
General Electric	101.50	2.02
Kodak	85.50	1.97
Merck	84.75	1.92
Sears Roebuck	49.13	1.89
Union Carbide	43.63	1.72
Procter & Gamble	111.63	1.65
United Technologies	67.25	1.64
American Express	58.50	1.53
AlliedSignal	70.38	1.29
Alcoa	71.63	1.27
Boeing	105.75	1.06
Westinghouse	19.38	1.03
Coca-Cola	57.63	0.88
IBM	165.50	0.85
McDonald's	44.63	0.67
Disney	68.88	0.64
Bethlehem Steel	9.00	–
Woolworth	21.00	–

"Overall, the top 10 stocks tend to consist of shares that have underperformed the remaining DJIA stocks, which is one of the reasons behind their relatively higher yields. However, considering the historical strength of many DJIA stocks, major restructuring could and has helped the DJIA laggards achieve potential upside reversals. As corporate fortunes change, improved investor perceptions may lead to higher prices. Since the Top-10/Low-Five portfolio emphasizes low prices, and statistically contains a higher percentage of DJIA laggards, the opportunity for capital appreciation is greater."

So which stocks are currently eligible for assignment to a Top-10/Low-Five portfolio? Obviously, this will change over time, but in early 1997, the candidates were as shown in Chart 20.

To implement the Top-10/Low-Five, assign 20 percent of the total funds available for investment to each of the indicated stocks. If AT&T closes at $38.38, and assuming a $30,000 overall investment, the $6,000 available for this stock means you purchase 156 shares. Follow the same procedure for the remaining four stocks. And make all your purchases at the same time.

To implement the Top-10 strategy, simply divide your purchases by 10, investing equal portions in each of those Dogs.

After 12 months, add your dividends and other cash distributions and determine the closing values of the stocks. Divide the total by five (or 10). That's how much is available for investing in your new portfolio.

Dogs for the Small Investor

You may be saying to yourself that you don't have the funds to take advantage of this strategy. In fact, to realize the full benefits, you would probably need at least $20,000 to start with. Plus, you are buying odd lots, and by doing so you pay higher brokerage fees.

But if you don't have that much money to spare, don't despair. To the rescue are a couple of mutual funds that are attune to these dividend-based strategies.

The first is the Payden & Rygel Growth and Income fund (800-572-9336). It invests 50 percent of its assets in the Dow's

Dogs, with the remainder positioned in stocks of the S&P 500. The fund is no-load, and annual expenses are set at 0.54 percent of assets. Initial investment is $5,000.

The second is the O'Shaughnessy Dogs of the Market fund (800/797-0773). It also puts 50 percent of its assets in the Dogs' stocks, but the remaining half is invested in stocks with similar characteristics to the Dow Dogs. And it is a no-load fund, but annual expenses are 1.7 percent, though that figure is expected to drop when assets increase. Initial investment minimum is $5,000, but only $500 if invested in an IRA.

Some of the large brokerage firms—namely, Merrill Lynch, PaineWebber, Prudential Securities, and Smith Barney—also offer unit investment trusts that employ the Dogs strategy. One, known as Select 10, has grown rapidly despite a unusually high sales charge (1 percent) and annual management fee (1.75 percent). Another is the Target 10, managed by Nike Securities and sold through regional brokers.

Unit investment trusts are unmanaged portfolios that investors buy shares of. The Tax Code is not kind to the trusts, however. They are self-liquidating regardless of whether the same stocks qualify for inclusion the following year, which means they are taxed heavily in good years like 1995 and 1996. Nevertheless, they are attracting thousands of investors who want to get the benefits of the Dogs of the Dow and have only a thousand dollars or so to commit. (Select 10 is available for as little as $1,000, or $250 for IRAs.)

Some investors even buy the Dogs on their own. In fact, perhaps as much as $1 billion has been invested in the Dogs by individuals.

Dogs Abroad

This strategy apparently works when applied to a U.S. stock index. So why wouldn't it do just as well using a foreign stock index? In fact, it does. In most case, extremely well.

Bloomberg L.P., which has brought us Bloomberg Business News, Bloomberg Financial Markets, *Bloomberg Personal* magazine, The Bloomberg Forum, Bloomberg Information, etc., recently asked Merrill Lynch to calculate the performance of $10,000 invested in the Dogs of the London, Tokyo, and

Hong Kong stock markets from January 1981 through September 1996. Merrill Lynch took on the project and carefully analyzed the underlying indexes of London's Financial Times Stock Exchange 30 Index, Japan's Nikkei 225 Index, and Hong Kong's Hang Seng Index.

The London Dogs performed best over this nearly 16-year period, providing a 22.3-percent average annualized return. A $10,000 investment thus would have been transformed into $237,268.

By comparison, the Financial Times index returned just $79,557 in that time, or 14.1 percent a year.

Merrill Lynch's analysis of the Tokyo market also disclosed remarkable gains from purchases of the Dogs. An investment of $10,000 in the Nikkei Dogs would have become $128,539 at the end of that period, for a 14.1-percent average annualized return. And if you've been following the Japanese stock market, you may recall that during the period analyzed by Merrill Lynch that a collapse occurred in 1990, and things haven't been exactly right since then. For example, $10,000 invested in the Nikkei 225 index produced a total of only $64,941 during the period analyzed. That's only about a 12.5-percent average annualized gain.

Moving on to the Hang Seng, $10,000 during that period would have grown to $134,369, for a 17.9-percent annualized gain. That was better than the average return for the Hang Seng's 33 stocks, but only by 2.2 percentage points.

So how did the U.S. mutts do when compared to those from abroad? Well, Dow's Dogs placed behind those of all three foreign indexes. Merrill Lynch figures show that $10,000 would have grown to $108,769 during the period analyzed, for a 16.4-percent annualized return.

This doesn't mean, however, that every foreign market is going to produce superior returns when you use the Dogs strategy. Make sure the market is mature before you plunge in, and even then do your research (or have a broker do it for you) to check the Dogs' performance over at least the past 10 years.

✳✳✳✳

In this chapter, you've seen how important dividends are to your investment philosophy. This is true whether you're simply investing for the dividend payout (reinvested, of course) or as a way to measure the market, such as with the Dogs of the Dow technique. In sum, consider the dividend as one of the best ways to reap the rewards of stock investing.

Chapter 10: Matching the Market

"Matches are made in heaven."

– Robert Burton

The Exciting World of the Mundane

Investors of all types of discovering the potential of a very humdrum type of investing. The potential lies not in trying to outsmart the market, but in simply staying in step with it. In other words, these investors make their money simply by targeting the performance of all the stocks traded on the New York Stock Exchange, the NASDAQ market—or both.

The following strategies can be used by anyone, of any means, and of any age. They are proven formulas that can work for you.

The Simple Logic of Index Investing

Recently, an article in *The Wall Street Journal* carried the somewhat cryptic headline "Fidelity, Dimming Flash, to Push Index Funds." You could probably figure that "Fidelity" is Fidelity Investments, one of the largest mutual-fund companies in the world. But who or what is "Dimming Flash"? Well, the explanation is simple enough, but a bit of translation is required. Fidelity, like any other fund manager, strives through its stock-selection process to outperform the market as a whole. If it can achieve that goal, it then can publicize the fact and entice investors who are hoping to achieve superior gains.

But in fact neither Fidelity nor any other investment company consistently outperforms the market as a whole. Some funds do, of course, but many fall short. Yet the funds keep touting the competency of their fund managers, many of whom have become household words (e.g., Peter Lynch and John Templeton). That's the "flash" referred to in *The Wall Street Journal* article.

So why is Fidelity *dimming* that flash? Well, obviously to push index funds. And that makes sense, because a stock-index fund has about as much flash as a black hole in outer space.

So just what is a stock-index fund anyway? In fact, what is a stock index?

Ever heard of the Dow Jones Industrial Average? Of course you have. That's a stock index. The Dow follows the fortunes of 30 blue-chip stocks that supposedly represent the market as a whole. They don't, of course, because often the smaller companies, not the blue chips, are where the real action is.

More representative is the Standard & Poor's 500, which like the Dow gives a reading of the movements of the stock market as a whole. As its name implies, the S&P 500 is a group of 500 stocks, and because of that fact it gives a more reliable picture of market performance. It is "market-value-weighted" for accuracy. That means that the 500 stocks included are not counted equally, but are measured in proportion to their total value. Thus, a $1 move by General Motors will affect the index much more than a $1 move by a much smaller company included in the index, say, Ryan's Family Steak Houses.

The S&P 500 also consists primarily of New York Stock Exchange-listed companies, though some American Exchange and over-the-counter stocks are included. In all, 400 industrial companies, 60 transportation and utility companies, and 40 financial companies are included and supposedly reflect about 80 percent of the market value of all issues traded on the NYSE.

Fun with Funds

All this brings us to stock-index *funds*. Those that track the S&P 500 are the most popular, but others track the Russell 2000 index and the Wilshire 5000. (The numbers in those indexes depict the total of companies included.) And some track international and sector indexes. Most investment companies offer at least one index fund.

Some such companies, however, actively manage the index portfolio. They frequently use options or futures in an effort to beat the market. As a result, they have a high expense ratio and a relatively high turnover of stocks in the fund. Big differences can exist in two funds based on the same stock index.

The "pure" stock-index fund, then, passively replicates the index. The manager has little to do except keep an eye on the index for changes in its makeup. The manager and the fund's investors could pull a Rip Van Winkle and probably fare quite well during their long nap.

This is not meant to malign index funds. It's just that they are dull—deadly dull. When you invest in an index fund, you are in a sense saying to yourself, "Hey, I am not clever. I can't outsmart anyone. I am scared to death of risk. I am plain vanilla."

Yet, you may be the smartest guy or gal around. Consider this: In 1996, the average return for diversified U.S. stock funds was 19.5 percent—a figure that the investment companies crowed about. But if an investor had the means to own the shares of companies included in the Dow Jones Industrial Average, he or she would have achieved a 26.01-percent gain for 1996. The Standard & Poor's Index during 1996 was up 20.26 percent, and the NASDAQ Composite Index was up 22.71 percent for the year.

Okay, you might say, but that was for *one* year. How about the last *five* years. Didn't the average stock fund do better than the indexes over that longer term? Well, no, as a matter of fact it didn't, as Chart 21 shows.

CHART 21

HOW STOCK INDEXES COMPARE WITH MUTUAL-FUND CATEGORIES (ANNUALIZED)	
Fund or Index	5-Year Performance
DJIA	+18.37
Russell 2000*	+16.25
S&P 500	+15.22
Small-Company	+14.97
Growth & Income	+14.00
Mid-Cap Stock	+13.80
Equity Income	+13.65
Growth	+13.23
Capital Appreciation	+13.13
High-Yield Taxable	+12.16
Global	+11.21
Stock/Bond Blend	+10.88

*As tracked by the Vanguard Group.

No other fund category realized an annualized return over five years in excess of 10 percent.

Okay, what about 10 years? Surely one type of fund did better than the indexes over the course of the past decade?

Sorry to disappoint:

Fund or Index	10-Year Performance
DJIA	+16.66
S&P 500	+15.29
Mid-Cap Stock	+14.66
Small-Company	+14.22
Growth	+13.55
Growth & Income	+13.30
Capital Appreciation	+12.76
Equity Income	+11.81
Global	+11.29
Stock/Bond Blend	+10.52

No other fund category realized an annualized return over 10 years in excess of 10 percent.

THE TAX BENEFITS OF INDEX FUNDS

Mutual-fund returns are calculated before taxes. And with most mutual funds, the capital-gains distribution portion of that return can present a tax problem for investors. But because index funds have a much lower portfolio turnover than actively managed funds, index funds tend to realize and distribute to shareholders only modest (if any) capital gains. (In fact, the average turnover rate for passively managed index funds investing in common stocks is roughly 35 percent; for actively managed funds, the average turnover rate is 75 percent.) And since the objective of most investors is to defer paying the tax on distributions as long as possible, the indexing strategy allows them to do just that.

But there's a potential downside involved here. The reason so many funds have trailed the S&P 500 benchmark may lie in corporate size. The largest companies have recently been the best performers in the stock market, and the S&P and DJIA comprise those stocks almost exclusively. In contrast, most actively managed stock funds hold a mix of large and smaller stock issues. What would happen if small-company stocks start outperforming the blue chips?

That's the chance you take. But that's not much of a chance, considering what has happened in recent history.

And some folks just as plain vanilla as you at Fidelity must agree. They have apparently figured out that index funds aren't such a bad idea. Indeed, Fidelity has devised a host of new products, services, and advertising campaigns to show its vanilla flavoring. For example, Fidelity's new top man, Paul J. Hondros, doubled (to six) the number of index funds Fidelity sells and has ordered that those funds be heavily advertised to potential customers. That's also an acknowledgement that many investors simply want to ride the market (upward, obviously) and not rely on a fund manager's ability to try to do better.

Borrr-ring.

Yes, no doubt. But that's okay. You never really intended to become a rock star, a political leader, or an all-star pro quarterback. Your goal is to avoid the limelight and just become wealthy. And a stock-index fund can certainly help you reach that goal.

Stock Indexes for the More Adventuresome

If stock-index funds seem too tame for you, you might find two investments based on stock indexes a bit more appealing. Consider either stock-index futures or stock-index options.

Stock-index futures are contracts based on the value of an index multiplied by a specific dollar amount. In the case of the S&P 500 and the New York Stock Exchange Composite Index (among others), the index value is multiplied by $500. If one of the indexes has a value of 200, the futures contract would be worth $100,000. You could in a sense buy the index from a commodities broker with an initial margin deposit of around $6,000. (Note: Margin requirements change regularly—rising when markets are volatile and falling when prices are relatively stable.) If the index rises, you make money; if the index falls, you lose money. You can also sell a contract. You do that if you think the market is headed for a downturn. When you sell, of course, a market rise means you lose money, and a market decline means you make money.

But unlike investing in the stock index itself, when you trade stock-index futures, you're betting that something will happen pretty soon. Contracts are for three months, six months, and nine months in the future. You can buy them for longer periods, but those are not actively traded. So you can't just sit on these contracts and forget about them.

But after buying a stock-index futures contract, don't worry about having to take delivery on 500 stocks at the contract's expiration date. If you hold a contract on the S&P 500 when it expires, you will settle for the cash value. The final settlement is tied to the closing value of each index on the last trading day, or the day before, depending on the individual index. Be absolutely sure to get the exact particulars on settlement from your broker or an exchange.

With stock-index options, you can immediately translate your analysis of the market into trading decisions. That cuts down on the delay involved in analyzing individual stocks. And stock-index options also help investors hedge an existing portfolio of shares of individual companies.

CHART 22

Index	Exchange	$ Value
Index Options		
S&P 100	CBOE	100 x Prem.
S&P 500	CBOE	100 x Prem.
Russell 2000	CBOE	100 x Prem.
Composite	NYSE	100 x Prem.
Major Market	AMEX	100 x Prem.
Computer Tech.	AMEX	100 x Prem.
Oil	AMEX	100 x Prem.
Institutional	AMEX	100 x Prem.
Gold/Silver	Phil.	100 x Prem.
National OTC	Phil.	100 x Prem.
Value Line	Phil.	100 x Prem.
Utilities	Phil.	100 x Prem.
Wilshire	Pacific	100 x Prem.
Index Futures		
S&P 500	CME	500 x Index
S&P OTC	CME	500 x Index
Major Market	CME	500 x Index
Value Line	KC	500 x Index
Russell 2000	CME	500 x Index
Composite	NYFE	500 x Index
NASDAQ 100	CME	100 x Index
Futures Options		
S&P 500	CBOT	500 x Prem.
NASDAQ 100	CME	100 x Prem.
Composite	NYSE	500 x Prem.

Abbreviations:
AMEX = American Stock Exchange
CBOE = Chicago Board Options Exchange
CME = Chicago Mercantile Exchange
KC = Kansas City Board of Trade
NYFE = New York Futures Exchange
NYSE = New York Stock Exchange
Pacific = Pacific Stock Exchange
Phil. = Philadelphia Stock Exchange

So if you've been right about stocks, but hurt by market reverses, or if you've been right about the market, but wrong when it comes to picking individual stocks, index options may be right for you.

Finally, there are options on futures. The growth of these options reflects the continual need to control risk in modern investing. And the good news is that even the smallest futures investor can use options for protection. Since options on futures can be traded independently, they've very quickly become a way for individual investors to speculate with a greater degree of safety on market movements.

Chart 22 gives a list of various index options, index futures, and futures options available to you, plus the exchanges they call home.

A Dull Person's Walk Down Wall Street

Let's look at some index funds to determine how you would have done had you invested in them.

The Vanguard Group is noted for its stock-index funds. At last count, it had 17, and they based their investments on indexes ranging from international to real-estate investment trust (REIT). But you're just interested in one that tracks the stock market as a whole. So you focus on a stock-index type named "500 Portfolio." You learn that it has performed well over the past five years. Returns, annualized, are 19.6 percent for the past three years and 15.1 percent for the past five years. Both beat the average of mutual funds as a group.

You order a prospectus from Vanguard, and it tells you quite a bit. You learn you have to pay $3,000 initially to buy shares. It's a no-load fund, so you don't have to pay an annual fee, and the expense ratio (the operating expenses as a percentage of average net assets) is 0.20 percent. In contrast, the expense ratio of the average general equity fund is 1.34 percent, according to Lipper Analytical Services.

WHY NOT SMALL-STOCK INDEXES?

The success of the more popular index-based mutual funds might lead an investor to think that all such funds are alike. Certainly, indexing has proven to be an excellent mutual-fund-investment technique—but with one noteworthy exception: the indexing of small stocks.

In fact, small-stock types have pretty much been index dawdlers. Those that try to mirror small-stock indexes like the Russell 2000 and Wilshire 5000 fall short of the performance of small-stock funds that actively try to beat the market.

The problem seems to lie with stock picking itself. As professional money managers explain, the small-stock arena is more amenable to skilled stock picking than that of large stocks. A company like Microsoft or Coca-Cola, for example, is scrutinized daily by thousands of analysts. But many small NASDAQ companies normally get little attention, and a skilled fund manager is more likely to find among them some undervalued gems that few investors have yet discovered.

Moreover, figures from Morningstar show that the average small-company fund has 18.5 percent of assets in technology stocks, compared with only about 13 percent in funds based on the Russell index. That emphasis on fast-growing technology stocks by small-company funds improves the potential for their better performance.

Another advantage for the small-stock funds: They usually select the companies that have the greatest capitalization. Some even include NYSE blue-chip types in their portfolios. In contrast, the Wilshire 5000 includes many small-capitalization companies that experience difficulties during certain periods of their existence, and their addition to the index (and the index funds) tends to reduce overall index performance.

Don't dismiss small-stock index funds totally, however. During some years—most notably 1988 and 1992—the Russell index outperformed the vast majority of actively run small-stock funds. And when risk is factored in, the performance of the two types of small-stock funds has been very close during the past five years.

The prospectus also tells you that the fund has net assets of more than 23 billion and has been in existence since 1976. No fly-by-night fund this one.

You also will obviously be investing in large companies, and that means you will get dividends (which you probably will want to reinvest). Nevertheless, you are exposed to risk—*market* risk. (See chapter 5.) There always is the possibility that stock prices overall will decline over short or even extended periods. Vanguard explains with the following chart showing the best, worst, and average total returns (dividend income plus change in market value) for the U.S. stock market over various periods as measured by the S&P 500 Index.

CHART 23

U.S. STOCK-MARKET RETURNS (1926-1995)*				
	1 Year	5 Years	10 Years	20 Years
Best	53.9%	23.9%	20.1%	16.9%
Worst	-43.3	-12.5	-0.9	3.1
Average	12.5	10.3	10.7	10.7

*Returns do not include the costs of buying and selling stocks or other expenses that an actual portfolio would incur.

Additionally, the 500 Portfolio, as well as other index types, is subject to "objective" risk. That is the possibility that returns from the S&P 500 will trail returns from the overall stock market. With the 500 Portfolio, however, that risk is marginal, at best.

The 500 Portfolio, you also determine, holds each stock found in its benchmark index in roughly the same proportions as represented in the index itself. So there are 500 stocks in the S&P 500, and there are 500 stocks in the 500 Portfolio. But of course some are held in greater proportion. Representing 18 percent of the portfolio's total net assets, the top 10 holdings for the 500 Portfolio as of June 30, 1996, were:

1. General Electric Co.
2. The Coca-Cola Co.
3. Exxon Corp.
4. AT&T Corp.
5. Philip Morris Cos., Inc.
6. Royal Dutch Petroleum Co.
7. Merck & Co., Inc.
8. Microsoft Corp.
9. Johnson & Johnson
10. Procter & Gamble Co.

The prospectus also tells you how the 500 Portfolio has done compared to the index that it is based on. Chart 23 displays the figures:

CHART 24

AVERAGE ANNUAL TOTAL RETURNS* FOR PERIODS ENDED 6/30/96				
	1 Year	5 Years	10 Years	20 Years
500 Portfolio	25.9%	15.6%	13.5%	13.9%**
S&P 500 Index	26.0	15.7	13.8	14.4**

*   Assumes that any distributions of capital gains and dividends were reinvested for the indicated periods.
**   Since 500 Portfolio's inception (Aug. 31, 1976).

So the index and fund figures are very close, indicating a faithful adherence to the index by the fund's manager, George Sauter, and his staff. But what about that small amount of difference? Why aren't the two *exactly* the same?

Well, get the prospectus and read on. And what you read may make you shudder. It states:

"Besides investing in stocks found in [the S&P 500 Index], the 500 Portfolio may follow a number of other investment policies to achieve its objectives. *The 500 Portfolio reserves the right to invest, to a limited extent, in stock futures and options contracts, warrants, convertible securities, and swap agreements, which are types of derivatives.*"

Derivatives?! Oh, no! Remember the derivative-induced bankruptcy of Orange, Calif.? And that's not all you learn:

"Losses (or gains) involving contracts can sometimes be substantial—in part because a relatively small price movement in a contract may result in an immediate and substantial loss (or gain) for a portfolio. Similar risks exist for warrants..., convertible securities..., and swap agreements...."

Wait. Before you deposit the prospectus in the trash can, read further: Only a limited percentage of the 500 Portfolio's assets—up to 5 percent if required for deposit and no more than

20 percent of total assets—may be committed to such contracts.

What a relief! Right.

In any case, you find that the fund uses derivatives to keep "cash" (that is, short-term interest-bearing securities that can be quickly converted to cash) on hand to meet shareholder redemptions or other needs. Also, derivatives reduce costs by buying futures (see above) rather than actual stocks when futures are cheaper.

Risk Reduction

So far we've learned what the fund does to *incur* risk. So what does it do to *reduce* risk?

Well, there are certain limitations imposed. For instance, the 500 Portfolio's manager will not invest more than 25 percent of its assets in any one industry. Nor will it borrow more than 15 percent of its assets. (In fact, if borrowing exceeds 5 percent, the fund will not make any additional investments.)

SPOTTING A TOP WITH INDEX FUNDS

There's some evidence that by watching the moves to and from stock-index funds, an investor can determine when a bull market is flattening out.

That evidence is based on the exaggerated popularity of the large-capitalization stocks that index funds buy for their portfolios. As more investors turn to the funds, the fund managers acquire more and more of those stocks, resulting in their prices reaching excessive levels. In other words, they are overvalued based on their fundamentals. And they can't sustain such heights for very long. Eventually, they reach a point where they have no place to go but down.

Such were the conditions in the early 1970s, when investors found refuge in the so-called "Nifty Fifty" blue-chip stocks. Those stocks shot up in price as demand increased, only to come crashing down during the subsequent bear market.

And in the late 1980s, big institutional investors also poured money into index funds, only to be kicked in the teeth when blue-chip stocks floundered in 1990.

Comments one investment analyst, "If too many people try to do it [invest in index funds], the stock market gets all screwy." He adds that "pretty soon" after the flight to index funds, the market typically takes a "not-so-nice" pounding.

So where do you start if you are interested in index funds? The following is a list of 10 of the more popular ones:

Fund	Telephone #
Dreyfus S&P 500 Index Fund	800-645-6561
Fidelity U.S. Equity Index Fund	800-544-8888
Gateway Index Plus Fund	800-354-6339
Schwab 1000 Fund	800-526-8600
Schwab S&P 500 Inv. Fund	800-526-8600
Smith Breeden Equity Plus Fund	800-221-3138
T. Rowe Price Equity Index Fund	800-638-5660
United Services All American Equity Fund	800-873-8637
Vanguard Balanced Index Fund	800-581-4999
Vanguard Index 500 Fund	800-581-4999

With regard to 75 percent of its assets, the fund will not invest more than 5 percent in the outstanding securities of any one company. Nor will it buy more than 10 percent of the outstanding voting securities of any company.

Are You a Candidate for the Indexing Strategy?

Now that you've learned about index funds and the strategies based on them, you may be ready to jump in. A few words of caution before you do:

First, don't think of this investment strategy in terms of making a quick buck. Your real benefits will come after several years. You might even consider indexing for an individual retirement account, 401(k), or 403(b) plan.

Second, if you are risk-averse, indexing is a good strategy for you. You get a high degree of relative predictability—that is, you can feel assured that you are not in a fund that is an underachiever. You may sleep better at night.

Third, if you're just starting your investment program, you have a steady, reliable building block. With an index fund, you then can select specific actively managed funds or other types of investments to help you achieve outstanding results.

Fourth, if you are looking for tax protection, index funds

offer much more of it than other types of funds. As mentioned, low-turnover index funds distribute far fewer capital gains compared to their actively managed counterparts.

Chapter 11: Real-Estate Investing for the Small Investor

"As you may or may not know, I am very heavy into real estate. In order to make money in that game, you buy for little and sell for a lot. Problem: how to make it more valuable between the time you buy it and the time you sell it.... We all have our faults, and this is California's [points on a map to the San Andreas Fault]. West of that line is the richest real estate in the world. To the east is hundreds and hundreds of miles of worthless desert land. Land owned by Lex Luthor Corp. Call me foolish, call me irresponsible, but it occurs to me that a 50-megaton bomb at the proper point here [pointing] would destroy California. Everything to the west would fall into the sea. Goodbye, California. Hello, new West Coast. MY West Coast."

– Lex Luthor (Gene Hackman),
from the movie "Superman"

America's Favorite Investment

Real estate is the nation's most-desired investment. Almost all of us want a piece of land and a house of our own. By comparison, securities and gold run a distant second and third to this type of investment. And as you'll see in this chapter, an investment it is. For even the most modest ownership share of real estate has the potential to yield an outstanding return in capital gains to the investor. You'll see how you can own real estate, not only in the form of personal property, but also through real-estate stocks and mutual funds.

REITs Make It Possible

Unlike Lex Luthor in the previous quotation, maybe you've ruled out real estate as part of your investment portfolio. If so, you probably based that decision either on the fact that you don't have a 50-megaton bomb handy or that you think real-estate investing takes big bucks. After all, even a modest home nowadays requires a down payment of $15,000-$20,000. And you may have to come up with as much as $50,000 for prime commercial real estate.

But before you dismiss real estate altogether, consider some alternatives to purchasing it directly. What if you could buy shares in a real-estate project—or several real-estate projects—just like you'd invest in shares of corporate stock. Well, you can. A type of security known as a real-estate investment trust, or REIT, makes it all possible. When you buy REIT stock, you're getting a piece of a portfolio of properties and mortgage loans. That means you can evaluate REITs using some of the standards for mutual-fund investing.

And their performance recently has been nothing to sneeze at. In the past 10 years, they've paid an average annual yield of 7.8 percent. That compares with a 7.7-percent yield on 10-year Treasury bonds and the average 6.95-percent yield for stocks that compose the Dow Jones Utility Average.

Moreover, the outlook for REITs is excellent. A study by AEW Capital Management LP of Boston in 1997 found that REITs should return an average of 10 percent to 12 percent a year over the next three to five years. Finally, for investors worried that the bull market in stocks is nearing its end, REITs are a great defensive play because they often behave differently from stocks and bonds. Over the past 10 years, for example, the returns on equity REITs have correlated with the performance of the S&P 500 only 65 percent of the time. And during a recent month when stocks took a drubbing, REITs were up 5 percent.

THE REIT INCOME TEST

If you buy shares of a REIT, you're investing in a "passive" investment. In other words, you aren't involved in the management and have little or no voice in management's decisions. But that doesn't mean REITs can do whatever they want with your money. They are under strict guidelines, with the income test being the most restrictive. That test consists of three parts, and each must stand an annual trial:

Part 1: 75 percent of a REIT's gross income must be derived from the following sources:

➤ Rents from real property.
➤ Interest on obligations secured by mortgages on real property.
➤ Gain from the sale or other disposition of real property other than deal-status property.
➤ Dividend distribution from other qualified REITs.
➤ Gain from the sale or other disposition of a real-estate asset that is not a prohibited transaction.
➤ Qualified temporary investment income.

Part 2: 95 percent of a REIT's gross income must be derived from the following sources:

➤ Income that qualifies under the 75-percent test.
➤ Interest and dividends.
➤ Gain from the sale or other disposition of stocks or securities.

Part 3: no more than 30 percent of a REIT's gross income may be derived from the sale or other disposition of the following types of assets:

➤ Short-term gain from stocks or securities.
➤ Property in a prohibited transaction.
➤ Real property held for less than four years.
➤ Interests in mortgages or real property held for less than four years.

REITs must also show that they are investing in real-estate assets. Seventy-five percent of the total value of a REIT's assets must consist of cash, real-estate holdings (including mortgages secured by real estate), governmental securities, and investments in other qualified REITs.

Because stocks and real estate are very different kinds of investments, however, REITs have quirks of their own. For example, depreciation is an important factor when you're investing in real property, but investors of course can't depreciate a portfolio of stocks. Taxes also make a difference. REITs pay no corporate taxes on their earnings, provided 70 percent or more of their revenue comes from real estate or mortgages on real estate. (They also must pay out 95 cents of every dollar earned to shareholders.) This allows REITs to avoid the double taxation of dividends, which are taxed once when the government takes its share of corporate earnings, then again after shareholders receive them.

Don't confuse REITs with real-estate limited partnerships, however. The latter invests in real estate, all right, but any losses, as well as any profits, are passed along to the investors—the limited partners. More about limited partnerships later.

Neither are REITs like publicly traded land-development-companies. Such companies are in the business of buying land, developing it, then selling it. When you buy shares of a land-development company, you're buying part of a company that has no favored tax status and pays out whatever earnings it chooses. Moreover, its properties are usually of the same kind and located in the same general area.

Most REITs get their revenue from rents on their properties and, as mentioned, distribute their earnings each year to shareholders. To keep the tax benefit, the REITs are prohibited from actually managing their properties.

A major advantage of a REIT is that it provides a means for investment in real estate by a large number of small investors. And that translates into reduced risk through a type of diversification. Moreover, a REIT provides limited liability to its investors and liquidity in the public markets. In fact, a REIT must have at least 100 shareholders during 335 days of a calendar year. And five or fewer individuals cannot own (directly or indirectly) more than 50 percent of the value of the outstanding shares.

REITs come in three flavors. The most popular is the equity REIT. If you invest in this type of REIT, you become part owner of the commercial or residential properties the REIT holds. The second type is the mortgage REIT. Instead of buying property, these REITs borrow money from banks and other commercial lenders and relend it to real-estate developers and contractors. They thus make their money on the spread between the interest paid and the interest received. The third type is the hybrid REIT, which combines both equity and mortgage investments.

Let's say you are interested in adding real estate to your investment portfolio. You learn from a friend that an equity REIT named Prime Properties has done well over the past few years, and she passes along to you a prospectus and other investment-related information.

Prime owns property throughout the Southeast. Its largest holding is one of the major shopping malls in Florida, but it also owns several apartment complexes and three strip shopping centers. If you buy Prime Properties shares, you'll receive dividends based on rents paid by the tenants of that shopping center, plus other commercial properties that Prime Properties' owns.

However, you want to receive both dividends and capital gains (the combination of which is the *total return*) that exceeds 10 percent annually. So how do you receive capital gains? That occurs when Prime Properties sells any of its holdings. For instance, suppose one of Prime Properties' shopping-center tenants wants to buy the center from the REIT. If the REIT decides to sell, a share of the proceeds goes to you in the form of a capital gain. That amount can be distributed separately to you and the other shareholders of Prime Properties. In fact, when investors buy shares of an equity REIT like Prime Properties, they're likely to be thinking of receiving more than just dividend income.

So the more owned property in a REIT's portfolio, the more you have to think in terms of total return instead of yield alone. REITs with a lot more "For Sale" signs on their shopping centers and garden apartments are attractive in terms of total return. Mortgage REITs can also get in on the total-return game if their loans guarantee a "participation" in the property, meaning a percentage of any gain on a sale.

Suppose Prime Properties sells an apartment complex and instead of using the proceeds to purchase another property distributes the gain to shareholders. If a REIT keeps on doing that, it will end up with all its profits distributed, but have no more property. And some REITs have just that plan in mind. They're called "finite-life" REITs, and an investor buying shares in one of these self-liquidating REITs gets a diminishing stream of dividends, plus a stream of capital gains. Usually the self-liquidation has a specific schedule, ranging from seven to 15 years and depending on how long a depreciation period tax rules permit.

REITs may also take advantage of leverage. Though some have virtually no debt financing, others use it extensively. The disadvantage is that when mortgages are in default, when contractor loans go unpaid, and when property can't be sold and begins to deteriorate, a highly leveraged REIT can get in big trouble.

CHART 25

A TYPICAL REIT'S SOURCES OF FUNDS AND INVESTMENTS

Some 50 percent of the funds used by a typical REIT are borrowed from a bank or savings institution. The balance is evenly divided among funds contributed by shareholders, mortgage borrowings, and miscellaneous debt. Also, approximately 50 percent of REITs invest in property. The balance of their investments is divided between first mortgages, junior mortgages, and cash and securities, with first mortgages being the largest areas of investment for REITs after real-estate properties.

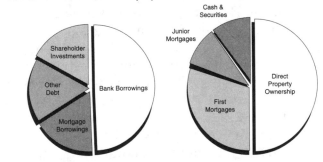

That's just what happened in the mid-1980s and to a lesser degree in 1990-91, when financial disaster struck REITs. Popular since their creation in 1960, REITs were increasingly attractive until the double whammy of inflated real estate and stock prices led to sharp declines that toppled overextended REITs nationwide. Today's REITs are much more careful, but investors have a long memory. The chief beneficiaries of the REIT rediscovery have been the safest, infinite-life equity REITs.

Choosing a Winning REIT

One indication of how the market views future performance is the percent REIT shares are selling over or under their appraised value. You can compare the appraised value per share. Take note of the sometimes considerable discrepancies between the appraised values and actual prices of the REIT shares.

Also, recall that a REIT must pay out 95 percent or more of its income to shareholders each year, so all you need to do is look at the dividend pattern. A trust that owns good, solid real estate and has made judicious loans will have a generally unbroken record of dividend payments that shows an upward trend over the years as the rents on properties are increased. The ability to maintain dividends through the recession of the early 1990s is a particularly good indication of a well-managed REIT.

But keep in mind that earnings per share isn't the key criterion for measuring REIT performance. Rather, most investors go by a REIT's "funds from operations" (FFO), which is net income excluding gains or losses from sales of property or debt restructuring, with depreciation added back in. To really evaluate a REIT properly, look at its FFO growth. And to get a valuation, instead of a price/earnings ratio, look at the price/FFO multiple.

Such multiples vary by property type. In early 1997, for example, hotel REITs had an average multiple of nine; apartment and health-care REITs, 11; and office REITs, 12. Generally, a lower multiple is more desirable.

In the typical case, you will not be able to evaluate the individual properties owned by the REIT nor the properties on which it has made loans. You will have to rely on the record to indicate the investment skill of the trust. One situation to avoid, however, is the trust that has a large portion of its assets in long-term, fixed-interest-rate mortgage loans. A trust of this type has relatively little opportunity to improve its income, so its dividend-paying ability is probably limited.

In addition, a seasoned trust should be slowly liquidating old property and buying new in order to improve the portfolio of real estate. By law REITs cannot buy and sell for quick appreciation, but they can occasionally sell, which is evidence of active management.

Certainly, as with any group investment, your success as an investor depends on the expertise of those in charge. Give high marks to the management of trusts that have come back after difficulties during the 1980s—and even higher marks to the managements of trusts that were able to make it through that difficult period with the least damage.

Keep in mind, for example, that during some recent periods, the shares of most equity REITs sold for quite a bit less than the book value of the real estate owned. The book value of the real estate shows you the actual cost of the acquisition, unless there is a notice to the effect that some other value is being reported, such as the current market value. Since book values represent the original cost of the property, they are usually much lower than current market values.

If a REIT's shares are selling at substantially less than the book value per share, it usually indicates that the trust is having trouble and the investing public is pessimistic about its future. But market pessimism is often an overreaction and the under-book-value shares sometimes represent an excellent buy.

Putting your money into REITs still means picking a trust that will pay off. So follow these 11 selection dos and don'ts:

➤ Do look for a REIT with a strong history of growth and increasing dividends. Since REIT dividends vary sharply with earnings, consistency can be more important than temporary high yields. A solid and carefully diversified REIT portfolio should produce steady gains.

➤ Do pick an equity REIT that wants to be more than a caretaker. A REIT that's worth investing in is one that adds value to the property it buys.

➤ Do be sure to investigate REITs that diversify into property other than apartment complexes and shopping centers. Successful REITs have done well by acquiring health-care properties, including nursing homes.

➤ Do check out REITs whose properties are close to your home. Visit shopping malls and apartments owned by a REIT you're evaluating.

➤ Do look at internal growth—"same-space" revenue growth on a year-to-year basis. Such growth indicates management's effectiveness at cutting costs and increasing rents and occupancy.

➤ Do check out management's stake. Those in charge of a REIT should have a sizable position in the operation. Beware if in reviewing a proxy statement you see that management once had a large portion of stock, then sold it.

➤ Don't overlook REITs that have been around for a while. Since their properties are established, they're more likely to be undervalued. Seasoned management with a well-known track record is another plus.

➤ Don't invest in new REITs whose properties have yet to be acquired. You won't enjoy the results if the REIT targets an overbuilt market or a depressed area.

➤ Don't pick a REIT with a fully financed portfolio. Upside potential will be limited if a REIT's portfolio is full of overleveraged properties.

➤ Don't forget that mortgage REITs that guarantee participation usually got part of a developer's equity when interest rates were high. Developers are less willing to make that sacrifice when rates decline. So these REITs may find fulfilling their guarantees much more costly.

➤ Don't overlook concealed leverage. The real-estate industry raises more and more cash in the stock and bond markets. And some REITs use both sources at once.

The REIT used in the previous example—Prime Properties—is hypothetical. But now let's look at a real and somewhat typical REIT to get an idea of how to evaluate one for investment purposes. The REIT we have selected is Tanger Factory Outlet Centers, Inc., a North Carolina-based company that develops, owns, and manages factory-outlet centers in more than 20 states.

The mode of operation of Tanger is to locate on busy highways, usually near tourist destinations. Each Tanger center has 40 to 65 stores operated by upscale manufacturers and designers. Examples of tenants are Lenox (china), Ann Taylor (women's apparel), and Timberland (footwear). Obviously, the Tanger sites are located away from shopping malls and central shopping districts so tenants won't be competing with their own products in full-price stores.

Expansion is the name of the game for Tanger, and in one recent year, its retail space grew 60 percent. Currently (1997), total space is more than 3.5 million square feet, yet it boasts of a 99-percent occupancy rate. An unusual innovation to increase security and enhance the marketability of its properties: The company now locates police substations in its shopping centers.

The company has been public only since 1993, and proceeds from the sale of stock were used to retire all debt. Since then, sales have increased from $30.3 million in 1993 to $46 million in 1994 to $68.6 million in 1995. But in 1996 that progression ended when sales dropped to $50 million.

Despite the decline in sales, however, this REIT is interesting, isn't it? So you investigate a bit further.

You learn from your online service (more about this later) that Tanger's headquarters are in North Carolina. So you write to the address (1400 W. Northwood St., Greensboro, NC 27408) and ask for an annual report. Once you get a copy of the report, you check the fundamentals, using chapter 12 for guidelines, and see that they are all in place. Here's a final checklist for evaluating a REIT such as Tanger:

➤ **Dividends:** The REIT should have a consistent record of dividend payments. Avoid any REIT that has recently cut its dividend.

➤ **Debt:** Debt should never exceed 30 percent of shareholder's equity.

➤ **Diversification:** The REIT should hold properties of various kinds and in various locations in the nation. If not, diversify by selecting more than one REIT.

➤ **Cash Flow:** The REIT's profits should derive from ongoing operations, not from the sale of properties.

➤ **Management:** The REIT's management team should have many years of experience—at least five and preferably 10.

You also learn that Tanger's sales drop results from a industry-wide shakeout. Retailers have apparently lost some of their enthusiasm for outlet centers. Nevertheless, Tanger has fared better than most REITs of this type and fully expects to rebound next year because of its strong position nationwide and its competent management.

If you're still satisfied with Tanger, you're ready to invest. That's all there is to it. In mid-1997, Tanger's stock was selling at about $29 a share, and you buy 100 shares, for a cash outlay of $2,900, plus broker commissions. Good luck.

REIT Mutual Funds

If you want to really diversify in real estate, then a REIT mutual fund may be more to your liking. Since the end of 1991, the number of funds has grown from six to more than 50 at last count (1997).

And there's good reason for this growth. Many REIT mutual funds have outperformed the average REIT itself by a substantial margin. Take CGM Realty Fund, for example. That REIT fund, which has been in existence only since May 1994, rose nearly 20 percent in 1995 and returned 19 percent for the first nine months of 1996. A sister fund, CGM Capital Development Fund has produced an average annual return of 21 percent over the past 20 years, and that's six percentage points better than the average U.S. growth fund.

Like any sector fund, which invests in a specific industry or industry segment, REIT funds tend to be growth-oriented.

They're also more risky than other types of mutual funds because they violate one of the principles of mutual funds, which is diversification. Drops in overall real-estate performance can result in a depressed earnings report. What's more, good past performance—never an assurance of future success—is even less meaningful in REIT funds than in broader-based funds. A rising REIT fund may merely reflect a "hot" market, not the expertise of the fund's managers. Conversely, the best manager may be powerless to maintain his portfolio's performance if the bottom drops out of his industry—as occurred with many real-estate ventures in the 1980s.

But with the bright future for real estate, such risks are minimal.

Here are the best-performing REIT funds based on performance in 1996:

Fund	1996 Return
CGM Realty	44.1
Longleaf Partners Realty	40.7
Van Kampen Am. Cap. Real Est. B	38.5
Cohen & Steers Realty Shares	38.5
Columbia Real Estate Equity	38.2
Heitman Real Estate Adv.	37.5
Davis Real Estate A	37.1
Pioneer Real Estate A	36.5
Invesco Adv. Real Estate C	36.3

Limited Partnerships—Minuses Outweigh Pluses

Not all group-type real-estate investments are alike. With REITs, you have the advantages of liquidity, diversification, limited risk, and a track record that will give a good indication of the security's performance. But with real-estate limited partnerships, a type of investment often confused with REITs, many of those qualities are missing.

First, what are limited partnerships?

A limited partnership is really nothing more than a group of individuals who invest in some type of hard asset, such as oil and gas, films, farm operations, or real estate. The most popular hard asset, of course, is real estate. And in a real-estate limited partnership, you can participate as a general partner or a limited partner. General partners are considered "active" partners because they are actively involved in making the investment and management decisions of the operation. Limited partners are considered "passive" because they have little influence on the management or decision-making process of the partnership.

An investor with who simply wants a small piece of the action becomes a limited partner by buying shares in the partnership. Your objective is to receive income—and perhaps a capital gain, if you're lucky—from the venture. The main advantage in being a limited partner is that in case a project fails, your potential liability to creditors and others is limited to the amount you actually invest. The general partners can lose quite a bit more, including, in some cases, their personal assets. But if you invest $10,000 to become a limited partner in a real-estate project or projects, the most you can lose is your $10,000.

A limited partnership can be offered either privately or publicly for subscription. The primary difference between the two is that public offerings are registered with the Securities & Exchange Commission, and each state has investor-eligibility requirements.

In private programs, the number of investors is usually smaller, the program is less regulated, and requirements are much higher. A public limited partnership may have thousands of investors. Each investor's contribution could be small, perhaps $1,000. The large number of participants enables the group to pool huge amounts of money to make investments in major pieces of property.

If the partnership shares are offered for public sale, federal and state governments closely regulate them. Among the regulations are those requiring the organizers to provide, in a prospectus, detailed information to potential investors. Each prospectus is reviewed by the Securities & Exchange Commission and must meet the same requirements as an issue of stock in a corporation. So technically, under federal and state securities laws, a real-estate limited partnership

A VERY LEAKY TAX SHELTER

At one time, an investor could expect substantial tax breaks from buying shares in a limited partnership. He or she could, for example, use any losses to reduce the amount of tax on income from salaries, wages, or investments. But no more. A little more than a decade ago, the tax laws changed, and today investors who suffer losses from a limited-partnership venture can offset only the income from that investment. Because of their limited role in the activities and management of the partnership, limited partners are considered "passive" investors and any money they receive from the venture is treated as passive income. Similarly, any losses of the partnership are passed along the limited partners as passive losses, which can only be used to offset passive income.

interest is treated as a security and is therefore subject to numerous disclosure and regulatory provisions for protecting the investor.

Now for the bad news. Most partnerships have a liquidation plan, but the exact time to sell is usually up to the general partner. If you want to get your money out before the properties are sold and the partnership is liquidated (usually seven to 12 years), you may find a buyer for your shares—and you may not. And if you do sell, it will probably be at a sizable discount.

One investor tells of buying two $1,000 units in a real-estate limited partnership in 1984. Over the course of the next 12 years, he received cash disbursements of only $918 per unit. That's less than a $5^1/_2$-percent annual return over those 12 years. The limited partnership was supposed to liquidate around the end of 1996 with a close-out disbursement of about $125 per unit. And the investor wasn't sure that he would get that amount and was entertaining bids for $90 per unit.

That's the risk of a real-estate limited partnership. You could be stuck in one that performs poorly, and that was the plight of many investors in the 1980s, when many general partners and financial planners pushed limited partnerships because of generous tax breaks. Those tax breaks are mostly gone, but investors still buy into limited partnerships, mostly on promises made by financial agents and limited-partnership management companies of high returns. There's little recourse if you get stuck in one. But if you do, you can try selling through a limited-partnership broker, such as Chicago Partnership Board (800-272-6273). If you do sell in this way, expect commissions and transfer fees to take a heavy toll.

Despite the risks, however, many investors buy shares in a limited partnership, and there is always the potential for a good return. If you learn of one that sounds too good to be true, it probably is. Nevertheless, spend sufficient time researching the prospectus. It will outline the risks involved. These disclosures protect the general partners as well as inform you of the various potential problems, such as high vacancy rates, unforeseen competition, a rise in property taxes, or special assessments. The general partnerships want to be sure that you won't later be able to claim that you were not fully informed about the investment risks. So they often tend to overstate them.

In fact, the disclosure section can be very discouraging reading. For example, a standard paragraph in a limited-partnership prospectus reads as follows:

"No assurance can be given that such occupancy rates will be achieved, that actual expenses will not exceed projections, or that competitive factors in the local market will not limit the ability of the Partnership to achieve such sale prices."

CHART 26

SIZING UP A REAL-ESTATE GROUP INVESTMENT

Key Questions	Public Limited Partnership	Private Limited Partnership	REIT
Minimum investment	$5,000 ($2,000 for IRAs)	$10,000+	$2,000– $10,000*
SEC registration	Yes	No	Yes
Liability limitation	Yes	Yes	Yes
Tax benefits	Some	Some	None
Number in group	Unlimited	35 or fewer	Unlimited
Risk level	Moderate	High	Low
Liquidity	Low	Very low	High
Diversification	Low	Low	Moderate

*Assumes a purchase of 100 shares.

Some of the risks mentioned may be matters of genuine concern, whereas others are included primarily for the sake of presenting a complete list of all the possible problems. It is up to you to decide which of the risks are worth worrying about and to evaluate the overall risk picture for the investment.

Limited-liability companies are a newcomer to the world of investing, and when properly structured can provide its members with the tax advantages of a partnership and the limited-liability protection of a corporation. And an LLC may avoid many of the disadvantages of a limited partnership or a corporation.

Real-Estate Stocks

Another type of real-estate opportunity aimed at small-scale investors is real-estate stocks. These stocks are of companies that are in the business of building, finishing, furnishing, or financing traditional houses, manufactured houses, commercial real estate, or apartment complexes. Hundreds of companies fall into this broad category, and they range from Home Depot and Masco Corp. (building and home-improvement products) to Georgia-Pacific and Weyerhaeuser (lumber and wood products) to Shaw Industries (carpet) and Maytag (home appliances) to Dime Bancorp and Golden West Financial (real-estate lenders). They also include developers, such as Rouse Co., Host Marriott Corp., and Newhall Land & Farming.

Your Home: Your Best Investment

Finally, don't overlook a home as a real-estate investment.

And again location is a key to eventually making a profit, whether from your home or from rental property you own. Here are the top 20 cities to buy residential property, based on the projected rise in value of the median-priced home in 1997:

City	Projected gain in 1997
San Francisco	5.5%
Portland, Ore.	5.2
Seattle	4.9
San Jose	4.9
Salt Lake City	4.9
Minneapolis/St.Paul	4.7
Miami	4.2
Orlando	4.2
Houston	4.2
Denver	4.2
Sacramento	4.1
Dallas	4.1
Oakland	4.1
Norfolk	4.0
Detroit	4.0
Orange County, Calif.	4.0
Phoenix	3.8
Fort Worth/Arlington	3.7
St. Louis	3.5
Cincinnati	3.4
Charlotte	3.4

Source: Regional Financial Associates

❋❋❋❋

This chapter has explored the various means of investing in real estate. You've seen how a person with only a couple of thousands of dollars can get started. Real-estate investment trusts assure that you will be investing in major commercial and residential properties—all for the cost of regular common-stock shares. Real-estate mutual funds and limited partnerships provide another low-cost means of investing in real estate. Both provide diversification and a chance to get a piece of the action.

Chapter 12: How to Know When You've Hit Pay Dirt

"An extensive knowledge is needful to thinking people—it takes away the heat and fever; and helps, by widening speculation, to ease the Burden of the Mystery."

–John Keats

A Matter of Technique

Now you're going to see what it takes for you to spot a stock that will make you wealthy. Of course you first must have a knowledge of what to look for. You must know how to analyze figures in an annual report or other financial statement. For without such knowledge, you will never be able to distinguish between a winner and a loser.

In the past, you may have been intimidated by the columns of facts, figures, and notes in published financial statements. Indeed, they can look daunting. But with just a few pointers, you can evaluate a company quickly and easily—just by the information contained in its annual report.

Later, you will see how a balance sheet and an income statement can be used in your personal financial planning. When analyzing the financial statements of a company, you simply apply the same rules and standards. Your investment analysis depends on your own objectives and constraints. An understanding of this subject will help you build a foundation for more reasoned—and thus more profitable—investment decisions.

You should have no difficulty getting all the information you need. All companies listed on public exchanges, as well as many that are not listed, are required by law to publish their financial statements annually. Your analysis of those financial statements will help you determine whether the company's stock price is overvalued or undervalued, and whether its bonds are secure. You'll thus be able to discover whether the company is being operated efficiently, whether profits are rising or falling, whether sales figures are acceptable, and whether performance matches projections. The answers to all such unknowns will form a part of your evaluation of the company, so it's important to understand how to use the information provided.

A copy of the annual report may help you study the various financial statements and analyses discussed here. If you own any stock, the firm must send you its annual report. If you don't, most companies are happy to supply a report on request. Some periodicals, such as *Forbes* and *Business Week*, carry advertisements for firms that distribute their reports. Or your broker can usually get you the annual reports you seek.

A Balancing Act

The balance sheet of a corporation is similar in content to the one you devise for your personal finances. It represents the financial position of the corporation on the date of the report. Simply, the balance sheet takes one of the following forms:

Assets	$1,000	Liabilities	$ 800
Less: Liabilities	800	Net Worth	200
Equals: Net Worth or Shareholders' Equity	$ 200		$1,000

Note that the asset side always equals the liabilities and shareholders' equity side for every company.

So what are the components of a good balance sheet? The answer to that question depends on the parts of the balance sheet and how they relate to one another. Let's consider the financial statements of a small, growth-oriented company named Farfex, whose stock trades over-the-counter. Let's start with the balance sheet:

Okay, we'll take this balance sheet apart and put it back together. First, you are already familiar with the meaning of the term "assets." Current assets are nothing more than cash and holdings that are likely to be converted into cash in the near future—usually within a year. The need for cash is obvious. Every company needs cash for its day-to-day operations, whether to pay employees, pay taxes, or meet other demands.

Marketable securities are merely short-term investments. These usually are highly liquid government or corporate bonds (or even stocks, for that matter) that the company can sell if there is a need for cash. Generally, these are valued at cost, with the market value in parentheses. Only if the market value declines substantially below cost will the company write the investment down from cost to market value.

Accounts receivable are also current assets. They represent amounts owed by customers. These payments are typically expected by the company within 30 days from the invoice date, but a 60-day or 90-day waiting period is not unusual.

Inventories are the company's assets that are eventually sold to its customers. Inventories can be raw materials, semi-finished goods, or final products. The amounts of each are important, since final products are more easily marketable. For example, in Farfex, there could be a significant difference, depending on whether the $25,000 of inventory comprises mostly raw materials or finished goods. Most companies, in valuing inventories, use the lesser of cost and market value. Cost valuation, however, is merely an artificial figure derived by one of many methods, including:

> **LIFO (last in, first out):** This means that the cost of the last goods purchased or made is the cost of the first goods sold.

> **FIFO (first in, first out):** This means that the cost of the

first goods purchased or made is the cost of the first goods sold.

➤ **Average cost:** This means that the cost of all goods is calculated at an average of purchasing cost.

➤ **Specific identification:** This means that the cost of each specific item is the standard the company uses.

The same inventory can thus have different values, depending upon which method a company chooses for inventory valuation. The choice of method usually depends on the firm's objective. For example, FIFO shows current values for inventory, while LIFO shows outdated values because the goods with the most recent prices are assumed to have been sold first. In time of inflation, LIFO tends to understate the inventory valuation of the balance sheet.

The final current assets are prepaid expenses. These are items the company has bought, but has not yet used, including prepaid rent, insurance, and supplies. They are current assets because the company plans to consume them in less than one year.

Getting a Fix on Assets

Fixed assets are tangible assets of a relatively long life and are used by the company in its day-to-day operations. These assets are generally not intended to be resold in the near future, and they include furniture, machinery, trucks, cars, buildings, and land. The proportion of fixed assets to total assets for a given company depends on the type of business it conducts. For example, a construction company has a large amount of fixed assets, but a bank may have relatively few.

Fixed assets are usually valued at historical cost, which is the price the company originally paid for them. Note that this figure does not reflect market value or replacement cost for the asset. This value cannot be left on the balance sheet forever unadjusted. With the exception of land, fixed assets, for tax purposes, undergo wear and tear as they are used, so they are subject to obsolescence.

CHART 27

FARFEX CORPORATION
BALANCE SHEET
FOR PREVIOUS FISCAL YEAR

Assets
Current Assets
Cash on hand and in bank	$ 45,000
Marketable securities at cost	
(market value $90,000)	50,000
Accounts receivable	20,000
Inventories	
(lower of cost and market)	25,000
Prepaid expenses, at cost	12,000
	$152,000

Fixed Assets
Equipment, at cost	$ 67,000	
Less accumulated		
depreciation	7,000	60,000
Buildings, at cost	70,000	
Less accumulated		
depreciation	17,000	53,000
Land, at cost		15,000
		$180,000
Total Assets		$280,000

Liabilities and Shareholders' Equity
Current Liabilities
Bank loan	$10,000	
Accounts payable	20,000	
Wages payable	500	
Taxes payable	60,000	
Dividends payable	9,500	$100,000

Long-term Liabilities
8% bonds payable 11/1/06	80,000
	$180,000

Shareholders' Equity
Capital stock -	
common stock, par value $9,	
authorized and issued	
10,000 shares	90,000
Retained earnings	
(as per statement)	10,000
	100,000

Total Liabilities and Shareholders' Equity	$280,000

To account for this reduction in value, a company records "depreciation." Each year, the amount of the fixed asset depreciated represents the expense of using that asset in earning income. Thus, the company reduces the asset recorded on the balance sheet by "accumulated depreciation," then enters the same amount on the income statement as the "depreciation expense" of doing business. By recording this entry each year, the company accounts for the cost of an asset over the course of its useful life.

Under the various tax-law changes in the past 10 years, depreciation has been simplified. Whereas in the past, useful lives of assets were often judgment calls and subject to a challenge by the IRS, the law now provides a schedule of useful lives. The "class lives" used for depreciation are three, five, seven, 10, 15, and 20 years. Nonresidential real property—plants, warehouses, and office buildings—has a depreciation life of 39 years and uses the "straight-line method." Residential property uses a $27^1/_2$-year straight-line method.

With a straight-line calculation, you simply use this formula:

$$\text{Depreciation} = \frac{\text{cost}}{\text{number of years to be used}}$$

The other method of depreciation is the "declining-balance" type, which allows for a greater charge for depreciation in earlier years and less charge in later years.

The following will give you an idea of the useful lives assigned to various types of property:

Three-year class life

Short-life tangible property. Autos and light trucks are included. A company can use the 200-percent declining-balance method.

Five-year class life

Autos, light trucks, computers, and research equipment are the usual components of this class. A company may recover cost using the 200-percent declining-balance method.

Seven-year class life

Single-purpose agricultural structures and railroad tracks

fit into this category. Again, a company may recover cost using the 200-percent declining-balance method.

10-year class life

This category includes railroad tank cars, certain public utility and mining equipment, manufactured homes, and amusement-park property. These assets must have an asset-depreciation-range (ADR) midpoint of 16 to 20 years. The 200-percent declining-balance method is allowed.

15-year class life

Telephone equipment, sewage plants. A company can use the 150-percent declining-balance method.

20-year class life

Such things as sewer pipe fit into this category. Again, a company can use the 150-percent declining-balance method.

In case you're confused at this point—and anytime tax issues are involved there's confusion—let's use an example with Farfex. Suppose Farfex buys a truck for $20,000. Its useful life would be five years. Farfex would record the truck on its balance sheet a year later as follows, using the above formula:

Truck, at cost	$20,000
less accumulated depreciation	4,000
	$16,000

On the income statement, depreciation expenses of $4,000 are recorded. The next year, Farfex would show the following:

Truck, at cost	$20,000
less accumulated depreciation	8,000
	$12,000

Again, on the income statement, depreciation is $4,000.

Finally, Final Assets

"Other assets" fit into a final category and include long-term investments, trademarks, goodwill, deferred charges, and other intangible items. Don't be too concerned with these, except for investments and other sizable amounts. If the amounts are large, find out what they represent.

Goodwill is the present value of expected future earnings exceeding the earnings normally realized in the industry. Such an asset may arise from superior management, favorable customer relations, manufacturing efficiency, a monopoly, or an excellent location. Goodwill occurs when a company is sold for more than the fair-market value of the other net assets, and thus is recorded only upon the company's sale. Because of this rule, many companies with considerable goodwill show no goodwill asset on their financial statements, simply because they never actually bought goodwill along with another company.

Deferred charges are expenditures (other than for fixed assets) that are not consumed completely for more than one year. They can be defined as long-term prepaid expenses. For example, suppose Farfex spends $5,000 repairing an office. The company expects to benefit from this repair for 20 years. So the $5,000 is a deferred charge. It is reduced each year over the 20 years the same as fixed assets. The reduction each year is an expense on the income statement.

A Matter of Liabilities

The liabilities of a company are those debts and obligations that are payable by the company. Current liabilities are those payable short term—usually up to a year from the date of the balance sheet. Included in current liabilities are bank loans, accounts payable to suppliers, and such accrued items as wages, taxes, and dividends. Also included as a current liability is the current portion of long-term debt—that part of the debt due within the year.

Current assets are the normal source of payment for current liabilities. The relationship between current assets and current liabilities is extremely important, and you'll thus return to this subject later.

Long-Term Debts and Other Liabilities

Long-term debts are a company's liabilities that become due in more than a year. They include bonds, debentures, long-term loans, mortgages, and long-term notes. In addition to the long-term and current classifications, just as with the other-assets classification, there are "other liabilities." This category consists primarily of deferred credits. An example is deferred taxes. Because of certain provisions in law, a corporation may be paying less tax than it shows on its income statement. This means that the corporation has deferred this year's taxes to future years, which results in the deferred-tax liability on the balance sheet.

The Interest of Shareholders

Shareholders' equity is the interest shareholders have in the company. The capital stock represents the total amount of money the original shareholders paid the company for no-par-value shares. (More on this in a moment.) Capital stock often consists of several classes. In our example, Farfex has only outstanding common stock. For each of the 10,000 shares, Farfex received $9, so that its capital stock was $90,000. When other companies issue various classes of preferred stock, the proceeds are treated on the balance sheet like common stock.

The significance of the par value is not very great. When a company first sells its shares, any amount paid in excess of the par value is recorded as "contributed surplus." This is a premium on issue of the stock and is not part of capital stock. For example, if 5,000 $10 par-value shares are each sold for $11, capital stock is recorded as $50,000 and the contributed surplus shows $5,000 (5,000 x $1).

Secondly, preferred-share dividend rates are often quoted as a percentage of par value. Thus, a 5-percent $100 par-value preferred stock receives $5 in dividends per share annually. Aside from those two uses, the par value means little to the investor and bears only a small relationship to the market price of the stock.

Reporting Retained Earnings

Retained earnings are the cumulative profits that the company has reinvested into the business after payment of dividends and taxes. Profit occurs only after the company pays or accounts for expenses, dividends, losses, provision for depreciation, income taxes, and other liabilities. This reinvestment can be in the form of cash, inventory, accounts receivable, or fixed assets.

Think of retained earnings and capital stock as an ultimate liability of the corporation to the owners. This liability becomes due only on dissolution of the company. Capital stock and retained earnings are not cash. The company has long since spent that money. Those two items merely represent a recording of past events. Cash is represented only by the cash item on the balance sheet.

And that's really all there is to a typical balance sheet. If you understand everything to this point, you should have no problem with that type of financial statement. So now you're ready for the next step: the income statement.

The Income Statement: Getting the Inside Scoop

The income statement, often called the "statement of profit and loss," presents a company's revenues and expenses for a specified period of time: monthly, quarterly, or annually. In its simplest form, it is nothing more than this:

Revenue	$ 1,000
Less expenses	- 800
Profit	$ 200

The income statement may be more informative to you as an investor because it presents details of the operations of the company for up to an entire year. The present-income statement, along with past-income statements, hint at what you may expect of a company in the future. Chart 28 shows the income statement of Farfex Corporation.

CHART 28

FARFEX CORPORATION INCOME STATEMENT (FOR PREVIOUS FISCAL YEAR, IN THOUSANDS)		
Net Sales		$19,600
less cost of goods sold		10,000
Gross Profit		$ 9,600
less selling and administrative expenses		
Wages	$3,000	
Depreciation	500	
Rent	1,000	
Utilities	200	$ 4,700
Net Operating Profit		$ 4,900
add other revenue		
Investment income earned	$2,000	
less other expenses		
Interest expense	900	$ 1,100
Net Profit Before Taxes		$ 6,000
Income Taxes (federal and state)		1,500
Net Profit After Taxes		$ 4,500

Revenues: The Heartbeat of a Company

Sales revenue represents the amount for which the company sold its product or rendered its services. This is usually expressed as "net sales"—that is, sales after accounting for those goods returned, discounts offered, excise taxes, and the like. Moreover, the company reports "other revenue" not related to its primary business. Often, this is shown after net sales. In the statement above, other revenue for Farfex Corporation appears after the net operating profit, signifying that it is not part of the normal operations of the business. This type of revenue includes dividends from investments, interest earned on investments, royalties on patents, and so on.

When you read the income statement, look for what accountants call "extraordinary items." If a company sells a plant, for example, profits might get a boost in the current year, but that income (or the plant) won't be around the next year.

Other companies may combine revenues. When this is done, you will find it difficult to obtain a true picture of the earning power of the various operations.

Expenses: Are They Under Control?

The cost of goods sold, which follows net sales on the income statement, is the cost that the company paid to its suppliers. A manufacturing company includes the direct costs of production, such as labor and utilities. When you deduct the cost of goods sold from net sales, you get the "gross operating profit." When compared with results of previous years, gross operating profit gives you some indication of the profitability of the main business of the company.

Next, you deduct the selling and administrative expenses, such as rent, depreciation, wages, supplies, and utilities. This leaves you with the "net operating profit." This very important figure indicates the company's reported profitability, before taxes, as generated from its main line of activity.

More Revenue, More Expenses

Following the net operating profit are the other revenues and expenses. You already know about other revenue. Similarly, other expenses include such items as interest owed on the company's debt. At this point, you are left with the company's "profit before taxes." In addition to federal income taxes, some states and even some cities levy income taxes. After deducting income taxes, you have arrived at the company's "net profit after taxes." This figure, also a very important one, represents the profitability of the company.

It's What You Keep That Counts

You know by now that profit increases assets. In the statement of retained earnings, you add to the profit any nonrecurring extraordinary prior-period adjustments, additions, or subtractions, then deduct any dividends declared during the year. Combine this with the old retained-earnings balance, then transfer the resulting year-end balance of retained earnings to the balance sheet. And voilà! You have a statement of retained earnings.

The form of the retained-earnings statements is usually very simple:

CHART 29

FARFEX CORPORATION STATEMENT OF RETAINED EARNINGS (AT THE END OF THE CURRENT FISCAL YEAR)	
Balance, at end of previous fiscal year	$ 15,000
Add Profit for the Year	4,500
	$19,500
Less Dividends	9,500
Balance, at end of current fiscal year	$10,000

As mentioned earlier, include such items as dividends and adjustments to prior-period statements in the retained-earnings statement. These items are not related in any way to the current period's operations.

Finally, One Last Statement

We're nearing the end, and the statement of source and application of funds completes the important financial information about a company. This statement is similar in design to your personal statement of funds. However, use of the word "funds" here means working capital, which is the excess of current assets over current liabilities. The statement of funds explains the change in working capital for the past year. If the change is positive, the sources of funds will exceed the application of funds.

The funds statement has six basic parts. Sources of funds may be from any—or all—of the following:

➤ Operations.
➤ Issue of securities.
➤ Sale of fixed assets.

Applications of funds may be for any—or all—of the following:

➤ Repayment of long-term debt.
➤ Additions to fixed assets
➤ Payment of dividends.

Here's what Farfex Corporation's statement looks like:

CHART 30

FARFEX CORPORATION STATEMENT OF SOURCE AND APPLICATION OF FUNDS (AT THE END OF THE PREVIOUS FISCAL YEAR)

Source of Funds		
From operations		
Income	$50,000	
Add back expenses that do not use funds (depreciation, for example)*	5,000	$55,000
New financing, shares		10,000
New financing, bonds		10,000
Sale of fixed assets		2,000
Total Sources		$77,000
Application of Funds		
Retirement of long-term debt		10,000
Purchase of trucks		15,000
Dividends - common stock		12,000
- preferred shares		12,000
Total Applications		$49,000
Net increase in working capital during year		$28,000

*This is a source of funds because it is an expense of the income statement, although it does not cause a cash outflow. Thus, to show the total funds provided by operations, you must add it back to the reported profit for the year.

The statement of source and application of funds is important because it helps explain changes in current assets and liabilities. For you as an investor, the statement thus aids you in analyzing managerial decisions and possible future managerial policy. For example, it might show why a company cannot pay cash dividends despite healthy earnings. Also, it can reveal a company's ability to repay short-term obligations.

Read the Footnotes, Too

To this point you have covered the four financial statements. In examining them for a company you're interested in, however, pay close attention to the accompanying footnotes, referenced to the appropriate items within the statements. The footnotes might seem like something trivial, maybe an afterthought put at the end by some accountant. But in some cases footnotes can explain a lot. They can tell you, for example, how the company accounted for depreciation or deferred taxes.

Also found in the footnotes are "contingent liabilities," items that are currently nonexistent, but that can be a future debt. Example: a lawsuit against a company could lead to a substantial cost in future years. Also look for any changes in the company's accounting methods. Such changes could shift earnings significantly.

The Independent Audit

In reading the financial statements, you have the assurance that they have been prepared in accordance with approved accounting practice. Toward the end of the financial statements, you should find a form letter known as "the auditor's report."

The auditor's report assures you that the financial statements have been prepared properly and that they show a fair view of the company's financial condition and of the results of that company's operations for the period. The confidence you can place on this report is founded on the independent role that the auditors play. The shareholders appoint them, and management cannot dismiss them without the shareholders' approval.

Sometimes, the auditor may not give an opinion of the statements or may give a "qualified opinion." Under such circumstances, be very wary of the company, its operations, and its management. Make sure you investigate the company more thoroughly than usual.

How to Dig Out the Information

So far, you have considered the purposes and contents of financial statements. Now on to the task of interpreting and analyzing them. To this end, a variety of financial ratios are your tools. They can help you dig out the information you seek so you can judge whether the company you're studying is a good investment or not.

The financial statements themselves may provide some of these ratios. Nevertheless, you would be wise to determine exactly what they signify and how much to rely on them. However, keep in mind that depending on your needs and goals, two people may rely on a given ratio in two distinct ways. An investor seeking growth prospects, for example, has different intentions for a stock than someone wanting safety and consistent income from investments.

In any case, no matter what your needs, the ratios used in financial analysis permit you to compare the performance of two or more companies. These ratios fall into four classes:

1. **Liquidity ratios**, which measure the company's ability to meet its short-term obligations—that is, its ability to remain solvent after paying current debts.

2. **Profitability ratios**, which measure, as the name indicates, the profitability of the firm.

3. **Financial ratios**, which measure the equity and debt contributions to the financing of the firm, plus the return to investors.

4. **Efficiency ratios**, which measure the productive use of assets in the operations of the firm.

Two warnings when using these ratios: First, one year's figures and ratios are generally inadequate. To gain a more representational picture of the earning power of a company, examine the date from a series of years. This irons out any short-term abnormal fluctuations. Second, in comparing ratios of two or more companies, make sure that the companies are similar enough in their operations for you to compare them.

And when you examine a company's ratio to a generally accepted industry standard, make sure the company's operations allow a *meaningful* comparison.

Before we get started, however, keep in mind that analysts use some ratios much more than others. From only four or five, they can determine whether a company merits further investigation—or not. So highlighted with an arrow (➤) are those that you can call on to help you with an initial investigation of a company. If those ratios tell you that the company has potential, then you can use the other ratios to finetune your analysis.

Liquidity Ratios

➤ The Current Ratio

You have already learned what working capital is, and a company should obviously have a comfortable amount. The current ratio, which provides a good indication of whether working capital is sufficient, is calculated as follows:

$$\text{Current ratio} \quad = \quad \frac{\text{current assets}}{\text{current liabilities}}$$

For Farfex Corporation, the current ratio would be 1.52 (152,000÷100,000 = 1.52). This means that the company has $1.52 of current assets for each $1 of current liabilities. You can compare this ratio with that of similar firms and also with the accepted standard. A 2-to-2 ratio is considered average for industrial companies, but that can vary depending on the firm and the industry. Be particularly concerned if this ratio changes dramatically within a short period.

Working capital allows the company to meet its obligations or be in a position to take advantage of opportunities as they arise. At times, however, working capital amounts are deceiving. For example, if current assets contain a large portion of inventories, a firm may not be as liquid as the current ratio suggests.

➤ The Quick-Asset Ratio

The quick-asset ratio (sometimes called the "quick ratio" or "acid-test ratio") involves the use of quick assets—cash, marketable securities, and accounts receivable. They are referred to as "quick" because they are readily converted into cash.

You can calculate the quick ratio as follows:

$$\text{Quick ratio} = \frac{\text{cash + marketable securities + accounts receivable}}{\text{current liabilities}}$$

For Farfex Corporation, this ratio is 1.15 (115,000÷100,000 = 1.15). The company has $11.5 of quick assets for each $1 of current liabilities. This ratio is useful in further assessing the liquidity of a firm. You can also use it to compare similar firms and against an industry standard. A quick ratio of 1-to-1 is generally considered adequate, although this is subject to modification because of the peculiar nature of a business and the industry of which it is a part.

The two liquidity ratios mentioned above serve as a guide in assessing the company's ability to meet its short-term obligations. The liquidity of a firm is also revealed by the composition of the current assets. If a large proportion of current assets are inventory and accounts receivable, the company may not be as liquid as the ratios indicate. Examine the turnover of inventory and the conversion period of accounts receivable.

Calculate the accounts-receivable conversion period as follows:

$$\text{Average of receivables} = \frac{\text{accounts receivable}}{\text{net sales}} \times 365, \text{ or } 365 \div \frac{\text{net sales}}{\text{accounts receivable}}$$

For example, Farfex Corporation might have a ratio calculated as 15,000÷100,000, or .15 x 365, with an answer of 54.75 days. That means that, on average, Farfex requires 54.75 days to collect its receivables. You now can compare that figure with the company's credit policy. If management allows a 60-day limit, its collections are probably problem free. However, if 30 days' credit is normal, the company's accounts receivable are not as liquid—and not as likely to be collected. Such a situation could point to poor management control.

Inventory-Turnover Ratio

Calculate the inventory-turnover ratio as follows:

$$\text{Inventory turnover} = \frac{\text{cost of goods sold}}{\text{average inventory for year}}$$

The average inventory for the year is calculated by adding opening and closing inventories and dividing by two. For a company that assumes that average inventory equals closing inventory, the turnover might be: $100,000 \div 5,000$, or 20. This can be translated into days as follows:

$$\frac{365}{20} = 18.25$$

This means that, on average, every $18\frac{1}{4}$ days the inventory is completely sold and new items replace the depleted stock. You can use this information to compare the efficiency of management to that of similar firms. It also provides a measure of the adequacy of the firm's inventory, given the volume of business being handled. If the turnover is low, the inventory could be outdated, overstated in value, or simply too large for efficient operations. Keep in mind, however, that inventory turnover is very much a function of the type of business in which the company is involved.

Profitability Ratios

The ability to make a profit is the most important objective of a company. A current level of profitability does not always furnish the entire story. You must also know about the historical trend of earnings of a company. In determining the earnings, ignore items that will not occur again. Don't count these "extraordinary," or "nonrecurring," items as part of the average earning power of a company. For example, a company's construction of a new manufacturing addition is not expected to occur each year.

Net-Operating-Margin Ratio

Calculate the net operating margin as follows:

$$\text{Net operating margin} = \frac{\text{net operating profit}}{\text{net sales}}$$

For Farfex Corporation, this ratio is 25 percent (4,900÷ 19,600 = .25, or 25 percent). This ratio indicates that, for every dollar of net sales, 25 cents remain as profit after the company deducts all operating costs. Compare this figure with that of previous years. If the five previous years recorded profits of, say, 22, 27, 31, 31, and 36 percent, then 25 percent is not good. You might also compare a company's net operating margin with that of similar businesses in the same year.

➤ Gross-Profit-Margin Ratio

You derive this ratio as follows:

$$\text{Gross-profit margin} = \frac{\text{gross profit}}{\text{net sales}}$$

Thus, for Farfex Corporation, the gross-profit margin is 49 percent (9,600÷19,600 = .49, or 49 percent). This ratio is useful in assessing profit potential. It indicates that for every $100 of sales, $49 are left after the deduction for the cost of goods sold. Therefore, for two companies having the same fixed expenses (such as property taxes, rent, or depreciation), the one with the higher gross margin usually has a better profit potential if sales expand.

A high gross-margin company is generally a low-volume sales company. An example is an auto dealership. A low gross-margin company is generally a high-volume operation, such as a supermarket.

➤ Net-Income Ratio

As an investor, you are concerned with the ultimate amount of profit a company earns. The net-income ratio indicates profit, and you calculate it as follows:

Net-income ratio $= \dfrac{\text{net income}}{\text{sales}}$

For Farfex Corporation, the ratio is 23 percent (4,500÷ 19,600 = .23, or 23 percent). That means that for every $1 in sales, the company earned 23 cents. That is an excellent figure for this type company.

➤ Earnings-Per-Share Ratio

The most meaningful (or at least the most widely used) ratio to an investor is earnings per share. The most used earnings-per-share figure is for common stock. Here's how you calculate the earnings-per-share ratio:

Earnings-per-share ratio $= \dfrac{\text{net income - preferred stock dividends}}{\text{number of common shares outstanding}}$

For Farfex Corporation, the figure is 45 cents per share ([4,500 - 0] ÷ 10,000 = 45). This indicates that after all obligations have been provided for, you as a common shareholder have 45 cents per share that "belongs" to you. Now you are in a position to see whether your ownership is a profitable one. For Farfex, the ratio indicates that ownership is profitable. Farfex has paid 95 cents (9,500 ÷ 10,000) per share in dividends this year. However, the company has earned only 45 cents per share, which means that the dividend is inadequately backed.

Times-Interest-Earned Ratio

This ratio tells you whether the company is adequately covering its fixed-interest expenses. Calculate the times-interest-earned ratio as follows:

Times interest earned $= \dfrac{\text{net income + taxes + bond interest}}{\text{annual bond interest charge}}$

The tax is added back because interest expense is deducted before taxes. And the interest is added back because the earnings available for interest are the earnings before bond interest. This ratio for Farfex Corporation is 7.7 ([4,500 + 1,500 + 900] ÷ 900 = 7.7). This tells you that Farfex is earning 7.7 times the interest expense it incurs. Generally, a safe investment should earn at least three to four times its bond-interest requirement.

Preferred-Dividend-Coverage Ratio

You can use a similar ratio for preferred-dividend coverage:

$$\text{Preferred-dividend coverage} = \frac{\text{net income after taxes}}{\text{preferred dividends}}$$

This ratio tells you the number of times the company has earned the preferred dividends it pays. The higher the ratio, the more certain the preferred shareholder is to receive the indicated preferred dividend.

Financial Ratios

These ratios disclose the financial position of a company. Some of these are concerned with the capitalization of the company. This is important because generally as the debt rises, so too does the financial risk associated with a company. This does not mean that risk is bad. Keep in mind that leverage is usually good business. By taking on debt, a company uses money from outside sources to make money for its shareholders.

See how much long-term debt the company must repay in the years ahead. The details are in a financial footnote labeled (naturally) "long-term debt." If profits are off, the debt may be hard to pay, or the company may have a hard time getting new loans. High interest rates also make new debt more expensive.

Stability and growth of income are prime factors in assessing the risk associated with the leverage effect.

Capitalization Ratio

The capitalization ratio highlights the proportion of each type of security issued by the company. For Farfex, the following capital structure exists:

	Amount	**Percentage**
Bonds	$ 80,000	44.5
Preferred Stock	–	–
Common Stock	90,000	50.0
Retained Earnings	10,000	5.5
	$180,000	100.0

This shows that bonds account for $44\frac{1}{2}$ percent of the capital structure. Since retained earnings, in a sense, belong to the common shareholders, the common stock and retained earnings are usually combined.

In analyzing the capital structure, assess what proportion of long-term debt is acceptable for the company. Generally, it is desirable for an industrial company to have no more than 25 percent of its capital structure in bonds, and for its common stock to equal bonds plus preferred shares.

Bonds and preferred stock represent fixed charges to a company, and fixed charges that become too great may impose serious stress. The more stable the profits, the higher the ratio of debt a company can safely have, and vice versa.

➤ Equity Ratios

Once you have examined a company's capitalization, you are in a position to determine its equity ratios. The following three ratios are measures of the long-term solvency of a corporation:

(1) $\dfrac{\text{total liabilities}}{\text{total assets}}$

(2) $\dfrac{\text{shareholders' equity}}{\text{total assets}}$

(3) $\dfrac{\text{shareholders' equity}}{\text{total liabilities}}$

A low ratio for (1) and a high ratio for (2) and (3) signal the same condition—that is, a large cushion of security to the creditors. For example, relatively few liabilities compared with assets reduce the charges placed on a company. It is in a position to easily meet the fixed demands and also to offer a favorable return to its shareholders. (Note that [1] + [2] = 100 percent.)

However, too small a ratio of liabilities to assets may mean that a company is not using its assets and borrowing power to enhance its growth and earnings prospects.

➤ Book Value

An investor should try to determine a company's net book value for a $1,000 bond, for a preferred share, or for a common share. Book values denote the assets backing these securities. Calculate as follows the net book value for bonds, preferred shares, and common shares:

For a $1,000 bond:

$$\frac{\text{total assets - intangible assets - current liabilities}}{\text{number of \$1,000 bonds}}$$

For Farfex Corporation, this value is $2,250 ([280,000 - 0 - 100,000] ÷ 80 = $2,250). This means assets worth $2,250 back each $1,000 bond in Farfex Corporation.

For a preferred share:

$$\frac{\text{total assets - intangible assets - total liabilities}}{\text{number of preferred shares}}$$

For a common share:

$$\frac{\text{total assets - intangible assets - liabilities - preferred stock}}{\text{number of common shares}}$$

Or alternatively:

$$\frac{\text{shareholders' equity}}{\text{number of common shares}}$$

For Farfex, the net book value per common share is $10 ([90,000 + 10,000] ÷ 10,000 = $10). This tells you that $10 worth of tangible assets are behind every common share out-standing. In other words, if a company is forced to liquidate its assets and pay off all its debts and preferred shareholders, $10 will remain for each common share at book value.

A word of caution: You can evaluate the book value of a security, but the book value bears little or no relationship to the market value of that security. The disparity is due to the market appraisal given a company by investors concerned more with profit potential than book value. Also, the book value of most assets is quite different from their replacement, or market, value. Example: Land at $10,000 on the books may have been purchased 20 years ago and may actually be worth $90,000 today.

Efficiency Ratios

Efficiency ratios gauge whether the firm is making productive use of its assets and whether those assets are at an optimum level.

Return-on-Investment Ratio

Calculate the return-on-investment ratio like this:

$$\frac{\text{net income} + \text{interest}}{\text{total assets}}$$

Interest is added back to remove the effect of borrowed funds. For Farfex Corporation, this ratio is 1.9 percent ([4,500 + 900] ÷ 280,000 = .019, or 1.9 percent), which is extremely low. This ratio indicates, to some extent, the efficiency of the assets used. Also, it lets you compare businesses with entirely different capital structures.

Miscellaneous Ratios

You now have examined the four sets of ratios. Also be aware of a few miscellaneous ratios in assessing a company. The first of these is the venerable price/earnings ratio.

➤ Price/Earnings Ratio

The market price and return to a security (usually common stock) depends on a number of factors. One factor is the relationship between the price of the security and its earnings per share. This ratio is:

$$\frac{\text{market price}}{\text{earnings per share}}$$

Thus, for Farfex, assuming its common is trading for $12, the price/earnings ratio is 12 ÷ .45, or 26.7 to 1. This means that Farfex's common stock is trading at 26.7 times earnings, a very high multiple.

To investors, the price/earnings ratio is a key to valuing common stock. A progressive, high-growth-potential security usually sells at a higher price/earnings ratio than a slower-growth company, such as a utility.

But keep in mind that the price/earnings ratio is not all that worthwhile for a relatively new company or for a company that has erratic or cyclical sales or profits.

Cash-Flow Ratio

Because a company pays its debts by cash rather than by accounts receivable, retained earnings, or profits, a cash-flow analysis can shed light on a company's profitability and liquidity. Cash flow is also a good indicator of a company's ability to pay dividends and to finance future expansion. You can also use cash flow to compare companies in the same industry.

Begin your analysis by considering the profit. However, first adjust the profit calculation for items, such as depreciation, that do not involve a cash flow. Add back noncash expenses in the profit calculation, and subtract noncash revenue items.

For Farfex, you are left with:

Profit, as calculated	$4,500
Add noncash expenses:	
Depreciation	500
Profit, on a cash basis	$5,000

Like earnings, this can be calculated on a per-share basis. For Farfex, cash flow per common share is 50 cents (5,000 ÷ 10,000 = 50). However, avoid using cash flow by itself. Also, examine the current ratio, quick ratio, and other items to get a more complete picture of the financial condition of the firm. This is in part handled for you in the statement of source and application of funds. Here, you see your sources and uses of funds and the excess of deficiency.

➢ Stock-Yield Ratio

Finally, consider the income aspect of an investment. With a bond, you know your exact interest income. For stocks, you need a figure that allows you to compare its yield to that of other investments. The stock-yield ratio is:

$$\frac{\text{dividend per share x 100}}{\text{share price}}$$

For Farfex, the current stock yield is 7.92 percent ([.95 ÷ 12] x 100 = 7.92, or 7.92 percent. Obviously this yield fluctuates with changes in market price and in dividends declared.

Dividend-Payout Ratio

To learn how you as a shareholder have shared in the earnings of a company, you must go beyond the stock yield. This ratio tells you the portion of earned funds that the company paid out. Calculate the dividend-payout ratio as follows:

$$\frac{\text{total dividends x 100}}{\text{net profit}}$$

For Farfex Corporation, this is 211 percent ([9,500 ÷ 4,500] x 100 = 211, or 211 percent). This would indicate that Farfex is overpaying on its dividends. Should earnings not rise, 95 cents per common share probably won't continue. In general, the dividend-payout ratio, if taken over a series of years, clearly indicates the dividend policy of the firm. Note that with preferred shares and preferred dividends, the payout ratio for common shares becomes the following:

<u>dividends (common)</u>
net income - preferred dividends

Putting the Ratios to Work

Ratios are only tools and should not make your decisions for you. They can, like any other tools, help you come to a conclusion only if you employ and interpret them with the correct perspective or analysis.

CHART 31

FARFEX CORPORATION INCOME STATEMENT (AT THE END OF THE PREVIOUS FISCAL YEAR)		
Net Sales	$19,600	100.00%
Cost of goods sold	10,000	51.02
Gross Profit	$ 9,600	48.98
Selling and administrative expenses	4,700	23.98
Net Operating Profit	$ 4,900	25.00
Other revenue	1,100	5.61
Net Profit Before Tax	$ 6,000	30.61
Income taxes	1,500	7.65
Net Profit After Tax	$ 4,500	22.96%

With the assistance of ratios, you can make use of two types of analyses. Using "horizontal" analysis, you can tabulate data over time, permitting you to recognize trends and potentially favorable and unfavorable developments. "Vertical" analysis, as the name implies, is an up-and-down process. In this type of computation, all balance-sheet items, for example, are presented as a percentage of total assets, and all income-statement items are stated as a percentage of sales. Chart 31 shows an example of this type of analysis.

Vertical analysis lets you examine the relationship of various parts of the statement to the whole. For example, the income statement shows you exactly where each sales dollar went. Also, vertical analysis more easily allows comparison of different companies' financial statements.

The ultimate in analysis is a combination of both vertical and horizontal methods. You can more easily see the trends of individual parts, then compare them. Perhaps they will reveal some very interesting information about the company.

This information shows many important trends: For example, you can see whether selling and administrative expenses have been rising faster than sales (as indicated by the continual rise of those expenses as a percentage of sales).

CHART 32

	Year 1		Year 2		Year 3		Year 4		Year 5	
	($)	(%)	($)	(%)	($)	(%)	($)	(%)	($)	(%)
Net sales	10,000	100	11,000	100	11,000	100	2,000	100	12,000	100
Cost of sales	2,000	20	2,200	20	2,200	20	2,400	20	2,400	20
Gross profit	8,000	80	8,800	80	8,800	80	9,600	80	9,600	80
Selling & administrative expenses	2,000	20	2,400	22	2,600	24	3,000	25	3,300	27.5
Net operating profit	6,000	60	6,400	58	6,200	56	6,600	55	6,300	52.5
Taxes	3,000	30	2,700	25	2,600	24	3,300	27.5	3,150	26
Net profit	3,000	30	3,700	34	3,600	33	3,300	27.5	3,150	26

FARFEX CORPORATION YEAR-BY-YEAR ANALYSIS

What to Beware Of

Keep in mind that many companies do not confine their activities to a single line of business. Some companies in fact conduct an assortment of activities through separate companies—that is, subsidiaries that they own in whole or in part. This creates problems in analysis. First, the parent company may report its activities on a consolidated basis, combining all activities into one set of statements. Thus, in analyzing the various ratios, you might not be able to determine the industry in which the firm is principally engaged or the products that contribute most to the company's profit. That means you cannot compare the ratios with those of other companies or with accepted industry standards. Simply be aware that various methods of statement consolidation exist and that each has a different impact on the financial statements.

Also, you have seen that the method of valuation of assets is the adjusted historical cost. Accountants have traditionally favored this method over others, and companies have generally concurred. In periods of rising prices, many assets valued in such a way on the balance sheet are greatly understated.

For example, a piece of land that a company bought 20 years ago at $150,000 could be worth as much as $2 million at present. If the company still states its land value at $150,000, it is understating its asset value by a considerable amount. Another company that recently bought a similar tract of land for $520,000 shows a higher ratio of assets to shareholders' equity. Inflation drastically distorts many financial ratios and destroys comparability among different companies, making it more difficult to compare a single company from year to year.

Watch for Differing Accounting Methods

Often, two similar companies will differ in their accounting techniques. For example, let's say a company's profit before depreciation is $10,000. The company has five $10,000 machines, each with a life expectancy of 10 years. Under the straight-line method, the depreciation per machine is $1,000 annually. Thus, the profit falls to $5,000 after depreciation. Under the 200-percent declining-balance method, the depreciation per machine would be $2,000 in the first year (assuming full-year use). Thus, the net profit would fall to zero. The difference is quite significant and becomes even more so when dealing with hundreds of thousands of dollars.

This is but one example of an accounting-method distortion. Different accounting methods also exist for inventory valuation, taxes, goodwill (which is amortized), leasing versus buying, consolidation, extraordinary gains, and other items.

Aside from the varying accounting methods, you will find many discretionary items or estimates on financial statements. For example, the allowance for doubtful accounts can vary substantially, depending on management's wishes. The same applies to depreciation, intangible assets, investments, and some other items. These accounting "aberrations" can damage your evaluations of companies. Even more, they make examination of the same company's successive statements somewhat unreliable. Should a company change a method of accounting from one year to the next, some otherwise meaningful comparisons may be lost.

Who's in Charge?

Conventional financial statements cannot represent all the factors that dictate the progress and growth of a company. Factors such as management competency, personnel quality, the state of the economy, and the actions of competition are clearly missing from financial statements. Management competency is a key to an investment, since you are placing your confidence in the leaders of a company.

Answers to the following questions can provide clues to management's ability:

➤ How does the company's top management compare with other companies?

➤ What are the financial policies of the company?

➤ What is the attitude of management toward the average shareholder?

➤ How are the products (services) of the company—and the company itself—promoted?

➤ Does management show an enlightened attitude toward public issues?

As well, consider other factors that influence the success of an investment. Examine the company's industry. Is this industry new, growing, maturing, or faltering? Investigate the major product(s) or service(s) of the company. Are they in demand and is that demand growing?

Such questions go beyond a mere study of financial statements and will be the subject of the next chapter of this book. Meanwhile, keep in mind that financial statements can help you gain an understanding of what a company is all about.

Liquidity ratios, the profitability ratios, and the efficiency ratios offer clues to the safety of an investment in a firm you are considering buying a part of. On the other hand, they can also indicate that your money is at risk—and whether the risk is justified by the potential.

Now let's see if you've been paying attention. Yes, that's right: a pop quiz.

Questions

1. Which reveals more about a company and its future prospects—the balance sheet or the income statement? Explain your answer.

2. You have the financial statements of ABC Company. You are considering investing in this company and have decided to do some preliminary analysis. From the statements that follow, construct the following ratios:

➤ Current ratio.

➤ Quick ratio.

➤ Net-operating-margin ratio.

➤ Net-income ratio.

➤ Earnings per share.

➤ Capitalization ratio.

➤ Equity ratios.

➤ Book value for a $1,000 bond and for common stock.

**ABC COMPANY BALANCE SHEET
(AT THE END OF THE CURRENT FISCAL YEAR)**

Assets		Liabilities	
Cash	$ 7,000	Accounts payable	$ 11,000
Accounts receivable	21,000	Notes payable	5,000
Inventory	50,000	Other current liabilities	6,000
Total current assets	78,000	Total current liabilities	22,000
Land and buildings		Mortgage bond	20,000
(net of depreciation)	100,000	Total liabilities	42,000
		Capital	
		10,000 common shares	
		P.V.: $5, issued: 5,000	25,000
		Retained earnings	111,000
Total Assets	$178,000	Liabilities & Capital	$178,000

Answers

1. The balance sheet reveals the financial condition of a company at a given time. The income statement shows the revenue a company receives and the expenses it incurs during a one-year period. Because the income statement explains past operations, it can also aid in making projections. The balance sheet, by itself, offers almost no aid in the way of growth analysis. Although the income statement hints at the earning power of a corporation, the balance sheet determines its financial strength. Most analysts consider the profitability to be the most important factor governing future prospects, and liquidity, as shown on the balance sheet, is extremely important, even for profitable companies.

2.
➤ Current ratio $= \dfrac{78,000}{22,000} = 3.5$

➤ Quick ratio $= \dfrac{28,000}{22,000} = 1.3$

➤ Net-operating-margin ratio $= \dfrac{7,000}{230,000} = 3.04\%$

➤ Net-income ratio $= \dfrac{1,500}{230,000} = 65\%$

➤ Earnings per share $= \dfrac{1,500}{5,000} = 30$ cents

➤ Capitalization ratio =

Mortgage bond	$ 20,000	12.8%
Common shares	25,000	16.0
Retained earnings	111,000	71.2 = 87.2
	$156,000	100.0

➤ Equity ratios $= \dfrac{42,000}{178,000} = .236$, or 23.6%

$\qquad\qquad\quad = \dfrac{136,000}{178,000} = .764$, or 76.4%

$\qquad\qquad\quad = \dfrac{136,000}{42,000} = 3.24$, or 324%

➤ Book value = $1,000 mortgage bond $= \dfrac{156,000}{20} = \$7,800$

$\qquad$ common share $= \dfrac{136,000}{5,000} = \$27.20$

ABC COMPANY INCOME STATEMENT
(AT THE END OF THE CURRENT FISCAL YEAR)

Net sales		$230,000
Cost of goods sold	$170,000	
Operating expenses	+ 53,000	223,000
		$ 7,000
Interest expense		4,000
Profit before taxes		3,000
Taxes		1,500
Profit after tax		$ 1,500

Well, how did you do? Okay, so you had to refer back to the material you had previously read. The important thing is that you know how to evaluate a company you are considering. If you can, you are well-equipped to handle financial analysis.

❋❋❋❋

Don't get the impression that financial statements provide complete answers to all your questions. Such records are only a part—though a very important part—of the overall picture you hope to view. But you have learned in this chapter how to analyze a company's balance sheet, income statement, statement of retained earnings, along with the ratios that help you decide whether that company is worthwhile as an investment.

Chapter 13: The Quest for Winners

"For the proverb saith that many small maken a great."
– Geoffrey Chaucer, from *The Parson's Tale*

Did Chaucer Invest?

Chaucer's quote has a lot of truth built in. And, except for the 600 or so years' difference in time, he could easily have been referring to the subject of modern investing. (And who knows? Maybe he was.) Though in some cases, only one or two, not necessarily many, smalls can maken a great—future for you, that is.

Here we're going to explore smalls that have the potential to be great for you. These smalls, of course, are small companies. For it's their stocks that can help you accumulate wealth in a way that, compared to all the other investments you have access to, could be the surest and the quickest—and perhaps even the safest.

How can that be? you may ask. And why doesn't everyone simply buy the stocks of small companies, then sit back and let the bucks roll in?

In answer to your first question, the stocks referred to can bring you secure prosperity because the possibilities almost always exist for a certain percentage of small companies to become immensely successful—and to do so swiftly and with little real risk to their investors. As for the second question, not everyone is equipped with the proper expertise, patience, and temperament to find, then hold, a stock that has the capacity to make them rich. That's the sad part, too, because stocks like that are commonplace in investing. That's right. Commonplace.

Maybe you wonder if you have the gumption to become a successful investor in small companies. As a test, ask yourself this question: Am I a follower or a leader? If you are always a follower, then you probably don't have what it takes. History shows that investors who always follow the pack don't do all that well. Consider these findings by Oppenheimer Management Corporation, which conducted a study of how different groups of investors fared during each quarter of a recent five-year period. The group that put its money into the type of investment—stocks, money markets, government bonds, junk bonds, etc.—that was attracting the most new money earned only 19 percent during the period. But those investors who bought stocks and held them for the full period earned more than 70 percent. In that case, by following the changing trends, an investor earned only a small fraction of what he or she would have earned through persistence and patience.

Such qualities are not inherent in us all, however. Some of us need to develop them. That doesn't mean you should take a course in leadership training or get a personality makeover. But it does mean changing certain attitudes and viewpoints that prevent you from generating confidence in your decisions.

The Search/Research Begins

Most investors look for bargains. They want an undervalued stock whose market price doesn't accurately reflect the true worth of a company's shares. That's fine. We're looking for pretty much the same thing. But with an exception. We want a company that hasn't been discovered by the market *at all*.

That's a tall order. Hundreds of thousands of people are trying to do this same thing at this same time. That means that quite often you are going to find what you think is a potential winner—only to learn that other investors have already "discovered" the stock and that its price has gone so high that it is no longer a bargain.

Still, that may not be a real deterrent if you think the stock may continue to appreciate. As investments expert Peter Lynch puts it, "Never assume you've missed the boat." Keep in mind that you'll always be preempted by some investors. If the company you are considering has any promise at all, its principals and their relatives and friends will know about it and have invested their money, too. But you will still be able to get in on the ground floor, if not the bargain basement. You are like other value investors: You not only have to seek a bargain, but it should be the *best* bargain.

That means searching among many markets for the companies selling for the smallest fraction of their true worth. The best bargains will be in stocks that are completely neglected— of companies that practically no one is even studying, either because they are new or because they are not currently in favor. Such investing is like looking for the needle in a haystack of some 30,000 stocks that are available to value investors. But of course that's why those who accomplish the task make so much money.

Finding a stock in a haystack requires knowing what you're looking for. When evaluating a company, put yourself in the position of the prospective owner of the business. Instead of asking whether a stock you're eyeing can make money for you, ask whether you would buy the company. Here are some characteristics of a company you would consider buying:

➢ It's in a business and/or industry that you understand.

➢ It makes money consistently and in its own special way.

➢ It shows consistent growth built more on earnings than debt.

➢ It wants your investment because its management is investor-oriented.

Right away, you can probably rule out any companies listed on the New York Stock Exchange or even the American Stock Exchange. To find an under-researched or undiscovered stock, you are obviously better off in the over-the-counter (OTC) market. So once you've spotted a company that interests you, check the NASDAQ National List and the Supplemental List, which is where you want the listing to be.

BEWARE OF THE SPECULATORS

Speculators are often the bane of long-term, value investors. Consider the following example:

In May 1996, a small company named Comparator Systems announced it had developed a device that almost instantaneously identifies a person by distinguishing his or her fingerprints from those of everyone else. Investors looking to catch a rising star and become a participant in this remarkable invention reacted by trying to buy some of Comparator's stock.

To that point Comparator was an obscure company with a nondescript past and only a few thousand dollars in cash. Its stock occasionally traded on the NASDAQ market (ticker symbol: IDID) for about five cents a share. With the announcement of the fingerprint system, however, Comparator's shares exploded in price, becoming NASDAQ's most actively traded stock ever. Daily volume on three consecutive days during the week after the announcement ranged from 123 million to 176 million shares, accounting for nearly a quarter of NASDAQ's total volume on each of those days.

What happened? Speculators had immediately spotted the potential of Comparator. From a nickel a share, they pushed Comparator's stock price to $1.88 before it settled after a rush of profit-taking to close at 88 cents. But many investors had gotten in at or near the peak and found themselves with immediate paper losses after the speculators had taken their profits. And that's not surprising. At that point, the market apparently recognized that the company's some 605 million shares outstanding were valued at a unsustainable half a billion dollars or more. In fact, the response to that valuation from a company executive: "That's ludicrous."

Indeed it was ludicrous. Especially since a lot of people were openly skeptical about the product developed by Comparator. Had true investors taken the time to check, they would have discovered that just prior to announcing the new fingerprint system, the Newport Beach, Calif., company had a mere 29 irregularly paid employees, including part-time consultants. It had no manufacturing plant and its only property was a leased 5,900-square-foot office in Newport Beach. As for the fingerprint system, called Biometric Identity Verificiation, the company did not even know exactly how to market it. Perhaps, company officials vaguely explained, it could be used by businesses and government agencies to verify IDs.

But investors must have been salivating over the possibilities of such a system checking fingerprints of people boarding airplanes, cashing checks, using credit cards, clearing immigration, getting money from ATMs, buying prescription drugs, and collecting welfare benefits. As for speculators, they had something else in mind: making a quick buck. They were not really interested in whether the Comparator product was revolutionary or a hoax. (In fact, others in the fingerprint ID business expressed doubts about Comparator's ability to become an important player in that relatively new industry.)

(Contuiued)

BEWARE OF THE SPECULATORS (continued)

Perhaps speculators sensed they could repeat the success they enjoyed in early 1993, when they made a killing on shares of a company known as Spectrum Information. Those shares had skied in price to $13.13 following the company's securing of several patents on technologies used to transmit data from wireless phones. But those investors in Spectrum stock hoping for a continuation of the stock-price runup quickly learned a lesson. A Spectrum contract with AT&T that supposedly was worth "hundreds of millions of dollars" turned out to involve only a small fraction of that amount. The stock price started falling as speculators started bailing out. Then as lawsuits, investigations into Spectrum activities, and Chapter 11 bankruptcy followed, long-term investors finally sold, most licking their wounds from substantial losses. In mid-1996, Spectrum stock was selling for about 35 cents a share. The speculators had made their money from the Spectrum debacle, and they were happy. As for the long-term investors. Well...

But back to Comparator. As of May 1997, the value of its shares stood at a fraction of a penny each.

First, however, you have to find investment prospects. And information about them can often come from unexpected places, as the following example demonstrates:

If you were around just after World War II and someone had said to you that someday you'd be able to put a document into a machine, press a button, and within five seconds out would come an exact duplicate, you'd probably have laughed in his face. But then again maybe you wouldn't have. Maybe you would have heard speculation about such machines, and maybe you were of the type who believes that anything is possible.

Keep in mind that just after the war, you could indeed make a reproduction of a document. Mimeograph machines, which could create multiple copies, were prevalent at that time. However, mimeographs required the creation of new master documents on special paper that were then attached to a machine that could roll off duplicates. The quality was limited, however, and the odor from the process was an annoyance.

Many companies also went for offset printing. This was an expensive proposition that again required the creation of a master document. Unfortunately, that also meant that copies were affordable only if a large number were involved.

Although there were some true photocopying pioneer efforts by a number of companies, their processes were all flawed in terms of cost, quality, and reliability. The need, however, was there, and a company that would eventually be named "Xerox" would eventually meet it.

Let's suppose you decided that photocopying was a trend of the future. You had read about the process in a publication called *Popular Science*. And you had a few hundred dollars to invest. Your research showed, however, that photocopying is amazingly complex. It is part chemical, electrical, and mechanical. Plenty of things can go wrong with machines that try to duplicate documents. But the company that was to be Xerox—Haloid Company of Rochester—seemed to be leading the way. And by 1949, its first commercial model was in fact ready for distribution. (By then, the name of the duplicating process had been changed to "xerography," which is Greek for "dry writing.") And you bought the stock of Haloid Company with what money you could afford.

You soon regretted that decision. The first xerography model was huge and had only limited appeal. In the decade that followed, Haloid continued to produce new machines, but none was very successful. Nevertheless, the company remained committed to developing a practical machine. Between 1947 and 1960, Haloid allocated $75 million to research and development.

Then, in 1960, the payoff began. The company entered the market in a big way with its 914 model. It too was enormous. In addition, production was limited. Even several months after its introduction, only a handful were in the market. Moreover, companies were reluctant to get around the idea that other types of copiers, competitive ones, were available for a few hundred dollars. Xerox nonetheless had found its meal ticket with the 914. Demand soon outstripped the company's ability to produce the machine. After 10 years of seeing only mediocre performance in your stock investment, suddenly you were watching your purchase take off.

When you reached retirement, you were set. The investment of a few hundreds dollars in Xerox had multiplied. You retired with a nest egg of close to $1 million.

A Look at Tomorrow

Ah, yes, sounds easy, doesn't it? But it's not, of course. For one thing, how do you know—how does anyone know—which company is a potential Xerox? How would even the most perceptive among investors in 1947 have anticipated that photocopying would become so universal, so much a part of our everyday lives? And how could anyone anticipate that Xerox would emerge as the leader in producing photocopying machines?

In answer to those questions, let's look at Xerox again. Recall that Xerox (Haloid) did not invent photocopying. The company merely perfected it. Other companies were working on the process at the same time, but Xerox was willing to spend big bucks on research. Had you read about photocopying at the time and used your imagination, you might have envisioned a time when every office—in fact, every department in every office—would have a photocopying machine.

So how would you have known where to read about photocopying? In this case, recall that *Popular Science* magazine had written articles about the subject. But maybe science isn't your bag. Well, that's okay, because many other periodicals and books publish information on trends and projections. Become familiar with them. Instead of spending your time on a novel or a homes-and-gardens magazine, read a book like *Megatrends* or a magazine like *The Futurist*. You may be surprised by all you learn about what tomorrow will bring.

Here is a list of some of the best books and magazines available for your purposes:

Books:

Burrus, Daniel (with Gittines, Roger). *Technotrends*. HarperCollins, 1993.

Clarke, Arthur C. *Profiles of the Future*. Rev. ed. Warner, 1985.

Diebold, John. *The Innovators: The Discoveries, Inventions, and Breakthroughs of Our Time*. Plume, 1990.

Drexler, K. Eric. *Engines of Creation*. Anchor Press, 1986.

Dychtwald, Ken, and Flower, Joe. *Age Wave: The Challenges and Opportunities of an Aging America*. Bantam, 1989.

Fisher, Jeffrey A. *Rx 2000: Breakthroughs in Health, Medicine, and Longevity*. Simon & Schuster, 1992.

Gilder, George. *Microcosm*. Simon & Schuster, 1989.

Leebaert, Derek. *Technology 2001: The Future of Computing and Communications*. MIT Press, 1991.

Naisbitt, John, and Aburdene, Patricia. *Megatrends 2000*. William Morrow and Company, 1990.

Strauss, William, and Howe, Neil. Generations: *The History of America's Future 1584 to 2069*. Quill/Morrow, 1991.

Toffler, Alvin. *The Third Wave*. William Morrow and Company, 1980.

Magazines and Newsletters:

Discover (monthly magazine)

The Futurist (bimonthly magazine)

John Naisbitt Trend Letter (biweekly newsletter)

Popular Science (monthly magazine)

Science (monthly magazine)

Science Digest (monthly magazine)

Scientific American (monthly magazine)

Popular Mechanics (monthly magazine)

Technology Review (bimonthly magazine)

Technotrends Newsletter (monthly newsletter)

A SOURCE WORTH TAPPING

Forbes magazine's list of the best small companies in America is published annually. Here is the top 20 as published in the Nov. 4, 1996, issue of the publication:

Company	Product/Service	5-Year Average Return on Equity
Safeskin	Disposable medical gloves	100+%
Metrotrans	Buses	100+
Apollo Group	Education programs	77.7
Employee Solutions	Employee-staffing	59.6
OnTrak Systems	Semiconductor equipment	57.5
Southern Energy Homes	Manufactured homes	54.2
Oakley	Sunglasses/goggles	53.2
Equity Marketing	Speciality merchandise	50.3
Miller Industries	Towing/wrecker equipment	46.6
Alternative Resources	Information technology	45.5
RTW	Insurance	44.6
APAC TeleServices	Telemarketing	42.7
NN Ball & Roller	Ball bearings & rollers	42.5
Chad Therapeutics	Home-health-care equipment	41.9
Medusa	Mining	40.8
Speedway Motorsports	Motorsport-venue operator	40.7
Game Financial Corp.	Financial services at casinos	40.0
Remedy	Applications software	39.0
McAfee Associates	Network software	38.7
Department 56	Collectibles and giftware	37.4

And there are others like the above. Read the business news published in the daily financial press regularly, not so much the big stories about well-known companies, but the smaller reports of management changes and new contracts. Your daily newspaper is another excellent source, for therein can lie information about small or startup companies that have not yet made the national news. And if you have access to the Internet, employ it in your search. (In fact, the company we're going to use in the example to come is from that source.)

All such sources can provide suggestions and directions, but most of their specific recommendations may be well-shopped already. You must be alert to every little tidbit of information available. For example, other investors who have discovered bargains like to boast. At a party or while traveling by plane, query those persons you think may have something to offer. Most people don't need much of an excuse to discuss their work, so question salespeople, repairmen (who usually know what works and what doesn't), suppliers, even former employees of companies. A good source is a company's customers. Visit trade shows, where at various booths you'll likely find salespersons who are eager to talk if they think you are a possible customer. Ask about competitors and their products and services.

Go to your public library to see what you can find. Soon you'll get a feel for trends, technological breakthroughs, and innovations in business and industry.

Here, for instance, is the type of book you should find useful: *Technotrends*, by Daniel Burrus. In it, Mr. Burrus features 24 technologies that he thinks will eventually revolutionize our lives. Here are a few:

➤ **Electronic Notepads:** A form of pen-based hand-held computer that can enter, store, and retrieve information. Look for future models with wireless keyboards and voice-recognition properties.

➤ **Totally Integrated Manufacturing:** Systems that allow a manufacturer's operations, from engineering and planning to production and distribution, to function as a fully controlled unit.

➤ **Personal Communication Networks:** Digital, ground-based networks of small ratio transmitters and receivers that allow the operation of telephones that are static free and relatively inexpensive.

➤ **Diamond-Hard Synthetics:** Mixtures of chemicals to produce ultra-thin films for industrial and manufacturing applications. Look for applications like scratch-proof eyeglasses and windows, faster computer chips, and longer-lasting razors, sandpaper, and cutting tools.

➤ **Advanced Compact Disks:** CDs that store, interact with, and retrieve large amounts of data in a relatively small space. Look for CDs that hold digital images from film-based photography and interface with television sets to allow users to interact with information without the need of a personal computer.

➤ **Endoscopic Technology:** A minimally invasive method for performing surgery and mechanical internal procedures by using a long hollow tube (endoscope) that carries a bright light and allows a tiny television camera to see inside the patient or other object.

➤ **"Fuzzy-Logic" Computer Software:** Programs that add a "maybe" to the standard "yes-no" operation of computers. Software can thereby operate at a higher level of abstraction and handle conflicting commands. No more jerky subway-train starts or automatic transmissions.

➤ **Antinoise Technology:** A digital sound-sampling process that counters high-decibel noise by generating a mirror-image, out-of-phase signal at the same volume.

➤ **Antisense Technology:** A method of blocking the actions of specific genes, thereby shutting off those that trigger such human illnesses as cancer.

Mr. Burrus' predictions are based on sound research, as are George Gilder's observations in *Microcosm*. Let's take a few excerpts from Mr. Gilder's book to see what we can discover. Like this one, for example:

"It is just a matter of time before the mechanical piano will go the way of the harpsichord, if not of the mechanical calculator."

Care to invest in the makers of grand pianos? Here's another excerpt from *Microcosm*:

"To eclipse television technology, the digital computer needs only a few more years of learning curve pricing and a means to deliver digital video signals to the computer. The learning curve is a sure thing. The digital channel awaits the widespread extension of fiber-optic cables to the home. Scores of thousands of times more capacious than copper cables, digitally switched fiber optics will permit a computer to send or receive high-definition video to or from any address accessible to phone lines anywhere in the world."

Not a very good sign for traditional cable-television companies, would you think?

Another excerpt:

"The U.S. semiconductor industry will disappear. It will become a different kind of business, dominated by design and systems. Semiconductor companies no longer are chiefly making components. In the future, components will be almost entirely part of the chip....Most important, U.S. companies can still dominate the computer industry and its software...."
Just the end of the beginning for most computer-chip makers.

Finally, this excerpt:

"The use of steel, coal, oil, and other materials is plummeting as a share of value added in the economy....A silicon chip is less than 2 percent raw materials. A few pounds of fiber-optic cable, also made essentially of sand, carries as much information as a ton of copper."

Beware of those mining stocks, too.

Do those excerpts start your mind racing? If so, you undoubtedly see opportunities and hazards, prospects for investment and industries/companies to avoid.
Now let's turn to a final book that should stimulate your thinking. That book is *Megatrends 2000*, by John Naisbitt and Patricia Aburdene. Here is an excerpt gleaned from that book:
"Little noticed has been the progress in photovoltaic energy. During the 1990s, the cost of photovoltaic cells, which convert sunlight directly into electricity, will drop to a point where they will be used commercially to generate electricity on a large scale. The average price could go down to $1.50 per watt by the year 2000. If that happens—and many experts think it will—the total production could increase more than a hundredfold, and world sales would soar to $7.5 billion a year. Direct solar power could become the world's main energy source in the 21st century."

Let's keep an eye on that average price.

And this excerpt:

"At the state and local level, the privatization [the trans-formation of public services to private enterprise] trend con-tinues strongly....Thirty-six percent of local governments hire private contractors to collect garbage and repair streets. One of the most recent manifestations is the contracting out of the management of prisons. At the national level, there is increas-ing talk of the United States privatizing the Postal Service and the Social Security system, or at least opening the doors to private-sector alternatives."

How many possibilities can you spot in that commentary?

Isn't this fun? Let's try one more excerpt from *Megatrends*:

"The information explosion may be more responsible [for the recent surge in book sales] than the renaissance. Nevertheless, one in five American adults buys at least one book a week. People 18 to 34 years old buy 2.6 books a week. And they read them. The number of people who read more than one book a month has increased, according to a report by the Book Industry Study Group."

Who said television and the Internet are displacing books as the principal means of acquiring information? Maybe that aggressive new book-publishing firm you have been consider-ing investing in is worth a second look after all.

Now let's see how the search/research process works in practice:

Clicking on the Internet

While perusing Web sites on the Internet one day, you come across the following information:

"A U.S. company is making giant strides in marketing a process it has developed for building structures from panels of molded polyvinyl chloride. The target market: China's billion-people population.

"The company, New World Homes Inc., fabricates panels of the polyvinyl chloride, which are then slipped together and filled with concrete. Houses built of the panels are thus cheap and easy to erect. Moreover, because wood products are not needed in the process, the adverse impact on the environment is virtually nonexistent.

"China was chosen as the market for the product because of its need for inexpensive, well-built homes. According to a spokesman for New World Homes, "We envision hundreds of thousands of Chinese people building their own housing. The labor component is nil.

"Already New World Homes has penetrated the Chinese market, having supplied the building materials for two apartment complexes in Shanghai...."

Now you have a lead. Next question: Is the company privately owned? If so, of course, the stock is not available. So you check *The Wall Street Journal* or *Barron's* for New World Homes in the exchange price quotes. You don't find it, so now you check the separate list of stocks that didn't trade the previous day—and there aren't many. Again, no New World Homes. You also strike out when searching the OTC lists. Even if you don't find anything at this point, however, don't give up. The more difficult a stock is to find, the more under-valued it's likely to be. Call your stockbroker and ask him or her to look for New World Homes in the "pink sheets"—a listing of infrequently traded OTC stocks. Many pink-sheet companies sell for prices far below their intrinsic value. So finding them, though challenging, is also highly rewarding.

In this case, however, your broker is able to give you the company's ticker symbol: NWHM. New World Homes, he reports, is too small for his firm to be bothered with. To you, that's great news because it means that it is publicly owned and investors may have overlooked this stock. So now you are really interested and consequently start the research process.

You have many sources at hand, either through your personal computer or your local public library. If you subscribe to an online service, such as America Online or CompuServe, you can probably get all the information you need. For example, with CompuServe, you have access to Disclosure II, which is a database compiled from the 10Ks and other reports that all publicly owned companies file with the Securities & Exchange Commission. Included are 10K management discussions, detailed financial statements, footnotes to financial statements, business-segment data, five-year financial summaries, and the company's address, names of its officers and directors, and names of owners who hold 5 percent or more of the company's stock. That information is updated every Sunday, with market prices updated every night.

If you don't have access to an online service, check your public library for some of these publications:

➤ **Standard & Poor's Corporation Records:** A good place to start. Includes information on corporations of all sizes and types. Here you'll find a discussion and summary of the current outlook for a firm and its stock, along with a chart of price action, sales, and earnings data in full, plus extensive coverage of finances and balance-sheet and income-statement data. But in our case, New World Homes is still too little-known to be found here.

➤ **Standard & Poor's Stock Reports:** You want the version that provides information on stocks traded on the NAS-DAQ and regional exchange systems. Here you'll get at least some basic information: interim earnings, full earnings for five years, details of capitalization and debt, current assets, liabilities, cash, dividends, and stock-price ranges. Here you'll probably find New World Homes.

➤ **The Security Traders Handbook:** Includes information on approximately 2,000 hard-to-find predominantly OTC stocks. Among the data are annual reports and financial statements. You'll probably find New World Homes here, but you also need more details for a real decision on whether to buy.

➤ **Moody's Industrial Manual:** Includes detailed information on OTC companies. Among the data are a complete history of the firm, lists of subsidiaries, products, plants, properties, managers and directors, annual meeting dates, numbers on stockholders and employees, debt coverage, operating facts, and seven years' worth of financial statements. Drawback: The information is published only once a year, so you sacrifice timeliness for thoroughness.

If the above sources aren't available, you still have a couple of other. The SEC can provide the following:

➤ **Form 10K:** Companies must provide this report to shareholders upon request, and some companies distribute them
with or in place of the annual report. Form 10Q is the
quarterly version of the 10K, and both must report all
details of the firm's financial situation, along with management's analysis of the state of the business and future
prospects.

➤ **Form 13D:** Companies must file this report when ownership of a public company's stock exceeds 5 percent. This
report must also reveal the extent, purpose, and funding
used when a stake of this size is acquired. News of a 13D
usually sends stock prices up because a large stake can be
a prelude to a takeover attempt, even if the form claims
the purchase was made for investment purposes only. As it
turns out, only the chairman owns more than 5 percent of
New World Homes, so no other major investors have discovered the company—yet.

From these sources, you should be able to get a comprehensive picture of New World Homes. If so, we can now get on
with the research:

The Pieces of a Picture Puzzle

From New World Homes' financial facts and figures, you
can determine a lot about the company and its prospects for
making you rich. First, however, compare all the information
you have so you can determine if there are any inconsisten-
cies. If the figures don't agree at all, take a careful look at all
sources to be sure the time periods and statement data are the
same. If you still can't resolve the problem, you may have run
into a case of duplicity. But in New World Homes' case, agreement in 100 percent. Now you can begin your analysis.

Obviously, you could study the financial statements of New
World Homes for months, but unless you have some standards
against which to compare the company's operations and activities, your analysis is useless. For example, you note that the
company has reported assets as follows:

	1997	1996
Current Assets		
Cash	$10,400,000	$ 9,260,000
Receivables	26,200,000	16,100,000
Inventories	1,800,000	3,000,000
Total Current Assets	$38,400,000	$28,360,000
Fixed Assets		
Land	1,550,000	1,550,000
Buildings	4,000,000	3,900,000
Equipment	3,725,000	3,505,000
Gross Fixed Assets	9,275,000	8,955,000
Less Depreciation	1,390,000	1,345,000
Net Fixed Assets	7,885,000	7,610,000
Other Assets	375,000	200,000
Total Assets	$46,660,000	$36,170,000

So total assets increased more than $10 million over the past year. So what?

Well, in fact at this point you don't have a lot of information, except that assets are used by management to produce income, and in the case of New World Homes, the value of its assets is obviously on the rise. But you still don't know a lot about the company. So let's look at New World Homes' liabilities:

	1997	1996
Current Liabilities		
Payables	$ 4,300,000	$ 2,950,000
Notes Payable	1,000,000	1,500,000
Taxes Payable	1,885,000	1,725,000
Total Current Liabilities	7,185,000	6,175,000
Long-Term Liabilities		
Bonds Due 2019	3,000,000	3,000,000
Shareholders' Equity		
Preferred Stock (100,000 shares)	1,000,000	1,000,000
Common Stock (550,000 shares)	1,100,000	1,100,000
Retained Earnings	34,375,000	24,895,000
Total Shareholders' Equity	36,475,000	26,995,000
Total Liabilities & Equity	$46,660,000	$36,170,000

Now we're getting a clearer picture of what New World Homes is all about. In fact, this is sort of like a picture puzzle: The more pieces you put into place, the more you are able to recognize the scene that the puzzle depicts.

For example, you know that retained earnings are accumulated past profits that have not been distributed in the form of cash dividends to shareholders. But these accumulated profits are not simply a pile of cash. New World Homes is sitting on a cash hoard of $10,400,000 for operating purposes. But the retained earnings, which are part of shareholder equity, represent an ownership claim against all the assets. So the company's obligation to its shareholders—their equity—far exceeds the par-value totals in the stock accounts. If equity by itself were the only factor in the price the stock market puts on a company's shares, the market price would equal the shareholders' equity on a per-share basis. A market price lower than the equity would mean you'd have a bargain. But you're not going to get the market price yet. Have patience.

For now, you can be pleased that in the year-to-year balance-sheet data both the assets and the equity of New World Homes are up sharply. That's a good sign. But you need more information—more pieces to fit into the picture puzzle. You need the profit-and-loss statement:

	1997	1996
Sales Revenue	$60,750,000	$49,525,000
Cost of Goods Sold	(44,920,000)	(35,850,000)
Gross Profit	15,830,000	13,675,000
Operating Expenses:		
Sales/Administration	(4,526,000)	4,130,000
Operating Profit	11,304,000	9,545,000
Other Income	466,000	225,000
Bond Interest	(750,000)	(750,000)
Income Taxes	(1,110,000)	(1,005,000)
Net Income	$ 9,910,000	$ 8,015,000
Common Shares Outstanding	550,000	550,000
Net Income Per Share	$ 18.02	$ 14.57
Earnings Per Share	$ 17.84	$ 14.39
Preferred Dividends (10%)	$ 100,000	$ 100,000
Common Dividends ($.60/1997; $.52/1996)	$ 330,000	$ 286,000

Suddenly, you have a wealth of information about New World Homes and its prospects. You're now ready to use the primary tools of fundamental analysis to determine if New World Homes is a buying opportunity for you. Using data from the company's financial statements, you'll compute 12 critical numbers to help with your analysis. You begin with the liquidity ratios, which tell you how solvent the company is—how easily it can pay its bills.

	1997	1996
Current Ratio	5.34	4.59
Quick Ratio	5.09	4.11
Debt-to-Equity	.279	.340

The current ratio matches current assets with short-term obligations. The quick ratio is, well, quicker than the current ratio because the latter omits inventories, which may be difficult to liquidate. When analysts speak of wanting a ratio of 2 or more here, they mean that liquid assets should be at least twice as great as current bills. Both the current and the quick ratios in our example tell you that New World Homes has five times more near cash than close bills, indicating a highly liquid position. The debt-to-equity ratio further confirms liquidity by showing you the proportion of a company's capital that has been borrowed. An industry standard of .613 (as indicated by Dun Analytical Services' Industry Norms & Key Business Ratios) shows us that New World Homes is, if anything, underleveraged and is becoming increasingly so.

The company's liquidity is therefore up and debt is down, meaning extremely conservative management is at work. From an investment point of view, New World Homes is cash rich and secure, making the probabilities of its venture in China that much more potentially successful.

Now let's turn to the operations ratios, which measure management efficiency by assigning dollars made by sales to assets:

	1997	1996
Asset Turnover	1.30	1.37
Inventory Turnover	18.72	11.20
Debt Margin	1.28	1.34

The underlying principle of operations ratios is that assets used well will produce as many dollars as possible. Because it takes more assets to make steel than to sell dresses, industry considerations play a large part in the evaluation of asset turnover—that is, when you see how many times assets go into (or are turned over) sales. But keep in mind that too few assets or too many assets indicate poor management. Duns Analytical Services gives an industry average of 2.39 for 617 residential-construction companies, which means New World Homes is less efficient than some competitors and probably requires high use or greater production facilities to stem a declining trend.

Confirming this picture are inventory utilization numbers. While high turnover is desirable, turnover that's too high means inventory shortages that lead to loss of future sales. Low turnover also hurts because excess inventory can lead to obsolescence. In New World Homes' case and in comparison to the 9.9 industry standard, the figures indicate an efficient producer turning into one that's running out of inventory, as demand sharply outstrips production.

New World Homes is not in a bind, however, because it has plenty of funds for expansion. But the upward trend in inventory turnover is severe and time is needed to expand production of the home-construction panels. Nevertheless, the situation casts some doubt on management's ability to see latent problems and its willingness to act on them.

The debt margin shows how proficient management is in using equity to acquire needed assets. Compared to industry standards, the New World Homes ratio is very low, indicating the use of too little leverage, or borrowed funds. So from an operating point of view, rapid sales growth is on the verge of creating problems requiring capital expansion. Yet management has an obvious distaste for leverage. Such a conflict might cause an investor to sense that trouble is brewing right in the midst of success. Let's continue by analyzing profitability ratios.

	1997	1996
Return on Equity	27.17%	29.69%
Return on Sales	16.31%	16.18%
Return on Investment	24.23%	26.39%

Note that the calculated return on sales (the ratio of net income to sales revenue) increased slightly from one year to the next. However, the return on investment (the ratio of operating profit to total assets) actually declined. This is exactly consistent with a picture of a company that lacks the assets needed to keep up with increasing sales. And from the shareholder's perspective, the return on equity (ROE), which indicates the rate of return management is earning on capital provided by its stockholders, while high by industry standards, is down and declining. Again, this is consistent with an underleveraged operation in which production is failing to keep pace with growing demand (which is generating high current sales revenue).

ROE is a critical component in determining the investment prospects of a company. Frank Cappiello, renowned investment manager and author of *Frank Cappiello's New Guide to Finding the Next Superstock*, awards ROE the highest criterion in the stock-selection scoreboard he has developed. And for good reason. As he explains, ROE is simply a measure of "management's productivity of capital," or "just how successful management has been with the stockholders' money." Well put.

High-growth firms use high leverage to drive up ROE, and in New World Homes' case, just the opposite is happening. Both debt margin and asset turnover are declining—even while return on sales is increasing. No wonder ROE is declining. New World Homes' earnings growth makes the company's stock a bargain! Nevertheless, the ROE is cause of some concern, as we'll learn from its investment ratios:

	1997	1996
Cash Flow Per Share	$20.55	$17.02
Book Value Per Share	$64.50	$47.26
Earnings Per Share	$17.84	$14.39

So far, you've learned quite a bit about the ability of New World Homes to make money for itself, now and in the future. But the major question is whether the company can make money for *you*. The investment ratios we've calculated should be the final pieces to the puzzle we've been working on.

First, the cash-flow-per-share figure: It tells you how much real income is behind each share. (Recall that it adds depreciation back into net income, since depreciation is a bookkeeping charge only.) This indicator in the case of New World Homes is appealing to an investor.

Even more "fine-tuned" as a measure of a winner is the earnings-per-share (EPS) figure. Moreover, it helps you determine the price/earnings ratio. Because earnings are so important as a determinant of performance, you have to make sure you get a correct figure. That means separating earnings from operations and those caused by asset sales, tax-loss carryforwards, and other special accounting events. But in New World Homes' case, with more than 95 percent of net income derived from operations, you avoid this problem.

One other factor to consider: You get an EPS figure when you divide earnings by the number of outstanding common shares plus the number of new common shares that would be created if holders of warrants, rights, and convertible preferred stock were to exercise their privilege to buy or convert their holdings into common shares. This figure is called the "fully diluted" earnings. The potential shares increase the number of shares going into earnings, which reduces or "dilutes" EPS.

The third key investment ratio is book value per share, which tells you what a share is worth in terms of common-shareholder equity, and investors often think of "book" as what a share would be worth if the company sold off or distributed all assets to shareholders. Keep in mind that a potential winner is a company with underestimated earnings prospects and undervalued assets, so you want to compute the rate of change of earnings per share and book value as a last step before share-price considerations.

Subtract the previous year's per-share figures from the past year's figures and divide the difference by the previous year's figures. This gives you an EPS change of 24 percent. Determining the book-value ratios for the previous year and the past year, we see an increase of 36 percent. The large difference reflects management's decision to grow the balance sheet with larger retained earnings rather than pay dividends. New World Homes doesn't want to borrow and doesn't want to pay out—so the possibility that its assets will exceed its market price is very high.

O Brave New World

Okay, now you've been through the difficult part of your analysis. The rest is a breeze, during which time you'll learn once and for all if your work has been in vain—or if you've discovered a gem in the rough. You also will ascertain whether the shares are worth the price the market has set for them.

You are of course seeking a bargain for now as well as a future winner. A strong firm with a high p/e ratio is likely to be fully priced. Value investing is worth the effort because the market sometimes assigns a low p/e ratio to the wrong stock. That's right. The wrong stock. If you turn the p/e ratio upside down and compute its reciprocal, the earnings yield (which tells you how much price goes into earnings on a percentage basis), you'll see that if price is kept steady, yield will go up or down with earnings. If earnings hold steady, yield will go down as stock prices go up—and vice versa.

You want earnings to rise and the stock price to fall. But that's unlikely because rising earnings make news, and good news drives prices up. In the early stages of earnings growth, however, and particularly with a company that few investors know about, earnings can be high and share prices can be low. That's the situation a value investor is trying to find. It means low price relative to earnings, which means a higher earnings yield (because you're dividing higher earnings with a lower price). It also means a low p/e ratio (because you're dividing the lower market price with higher earnings).

By definition, therefore, a stock with a low p/e ratio should be a high-yield stock. And that's what you seek: a low p/e. But keep in mind that the very high prices of growth stocks signify the market's expectation of great earnings growth—and very high p/e ratios. And therein lies some answers to your questions about New World Homes.

Is the company what some professionals call a "loaded laggard"? A company is loaded if it has underestimated potential earnings and undervalued assets. It's a laggard if the market price falls to reflect the company's true value. New World

Homes qualifies as having value because its earnings are in a breakthrough stage, leaping from $14.39 to $17.84 in a single year. Moreover, the company has retained a huge portion of those earnings on its balance sheet (more than $34 million). The only drawback to our ratio analysis is that plans and equipment are not keeping pace with sales demand.

So what's missing in our puzzle? The final piece is the stock's price. And your broker calls to tell you that 500 shares are available at $33.75 per share. To determine if New World Homes is in fact a laggard, we must calculate the stock's p/e ratio, and that turns out to be 1.9 ($33.75 ÷ $17.84 = 1.9). That's incredibly low. New World Homes is definitely a bargain.

This situation presents an opportunity. You know that stocks with low p/e ratios are more likely to rise significantly than those with high p/e ratios. That just makes sense. Because a p/e ratio can go from five to 10 more easily than from 15 to 30, low-p/e stocks have a better chance to achieve truly outstanding performance. A company that is selling at a current p/e ratio of five and that grows 20 percent a year for 10 years (thus doubling its p/e ratio) will sell for more than 12 times its earlier price.

The Dividend Factor

When you think of high growth in a company, you rarely think of income. The objective of investing in high growth is of course appreciation. Dividends seem secondary, if they are considered at all. After all, to achieve growth, a company must plow profits back into operations and new equipment. But that doesn't mean you should ignore dividends altogether. Both the dividend-payout ratio and dividend yield are very important concerns. Stocks with generous yields can protect you against market slumps.

In New World Homes' case, however, the annual dividend is a rather paltry 60 cents per share, which equals a payout ratio of slightly more than 3 percent. But a company with volatile earnings should play it safe in that regard. That's because payout tends to vary inversely with growth, risk, and earnings fluctuations. Most mature companies with steady earnings have a relatively high long-run payout ratio of as much as 50 percent. But New World Homes, where the payout is small but the earnings haven't been plowed back into expansion either, has been retaining its profits.

Obviously, yield is low, too. At $33.75 a share, New World Homes' yield is only .18 percent. Even during the mid- to late-1990s, when average yields have been historically low, that's below average. But in the case of New World Homes, a low yield is okay as far as we are concerned. Fat dividends can come in the distant future—after we have retired and seek income.

Decisions, Decisions

You've done your homework, and you think you're ready to buy New World Homes. But your job is not quite done. To assure that you are making a good move, you would like professional help. Well, how would you like two of the most skilled and successful investment advisers in history at your service?

The first is Frank Cappiello, whom we referred to earlier in this chapter. He is a eminent author, analyst, commentator, and president of McCullough, Andrews and Cappiello, an investment advisory firm with assets under management totaling more than $1 billion. In his book *Frank Cappiello's New Guide to Finding the Next Superstock*, he set forth the criteria for establishing whether a stock has the potential for superstock status. Let's see how New World Homes measures up under Mr. Cappiello's demanding standards:

❏ **Size:** Mr. Cappiello agrees with the small-is-beautiful concept, but he does not award any points in this category. He simply gives priority to a company with sales between $25 million and $500 million. New World Homes would qualify here.

❏ **Unit Sales Volume:** Mr. Cappiello awards 15 points to a company that, over the past three years, showed sales increases that exceeded (percentage-wise) the Consumer Price Index in the same period. (For each year the CPI out-

paced sales growth within the past three years, he deducts
five points.) A check of New World Homes' financial statements shows that the company's sales allow a 15-point
award.

☐ **Pretax Profit Margin:** Mr. Cappiello believes that a rising trend in pretax margins over the past five to 10 years
of a company's operation is a good sign. He awards 10
points in such a case, then adds five points if the pretax
margin current is above 10 percent (though he deducts
three points for each year within the past three years that
the pretax margin declined from the preceding year). We
reviewed the financial statements of New World Homes
over its seven years of existence, and the trend is indeed
rising. Give 15 points to the company.

☐ **Return on Stockholders' Equity:** As mentioned earlier,
Mr. Cappiello gives his highest marks to this criterion. He
would judge a company as to whether it has the potential,
within the next two years, to have an annual return of at
least 15 percent on average stockholders' equity. If the
answer is yes, he would award 25 points. If ROE is currently above 15 percent, he would add another five points.
(Incidentally, he would deduct 10 points if ROE has not
been in a rising trend over the past five to 10 years, taking
into account that any economic recession may have distort-
ed the figures during that period.) In New World Homes'
case, the maximum of 30 points is awarded.

☐ **Relative Earnings-Per-Share Growth:** Mr. Cappiello
awards 20 points to a company whose earnings per share,
over the past three years, advanced by a larger percentage
increase than that calculated for per-share earnings of the
Dow Industrials. (He cautions, however, that adjustments
or allowances for extraordinary events—"nonrecur-
rences"—should be taken into consideration.) New World
Homes achieves the maximum of 20 points.

☐ **Dividends:** Mr. Cappiello awards points to a company
only if it pays a dividend and if the dividend trend over the
past five years is rising. If the payout ratio is below 40 per-

cent, he adds five points; if the payout ratio is above 40 percent, he does not award the five points unless the "earned growth rate" is above 7.5 percent. (The earned growth rate is calculated by taking the earnings per share for the year ended, less the dividend paid to stockholders. The "plowback" of what's left of earnings is then divided by the book value at the beginning of the year to give an earned growth rate percentage.) New World Homes gets the maximum five points.

☐ **Debt Structure:** Mr. Cappiello awards 10 points to a company whose long-term debt is below 35 percent of stockholders' equity. If long-term debt is above 35 percent, but less than 50 percent, of stockholders' equity, he awards only five points. No points go to any company whose long-term debt is more than 50 percent of stockholders' equity (and if debt exceeds stockholders' equity, deduct 10 points). Give New World Homes 10 points.

☐ **Institutional Holdings:** Mr. Cappiello assigns five points if institutions (mutual funds, insurance companies, etc.) do not own more than 10 percent of the outstanding shares. If more than 10 percent, but less than 15 percent, he adds only two points. He does not award any points if institutional ownership exceeds 15 percent of the outstanding shares. New World Homes gets all five points here.

☐ **Price/Earnings Multiple:** Mr. Cappiello assigns no points to this criterion, but he points out that superstocks "will, by definition, outperform the overall market over the long term." Except for some temporary setbacks, he adds, a company's stock under consideration should therefore advance at least as well as the Dow Jones Industrial Average. Otherwise, he warns, "Beware!" With New World Homes, there's no worry in this regard.

So New World Homes scored a maximum of 100 points under Mr. Cappiello's rigorous system of analysis. And a score of 80 points or more, he explains, signifies that an investment has the characteristics of a future superstock. We seem to have stumbled on a winner.

Now let's turn to another professional for "advice." This time it's Ben Graham, whom we met earlier in this book. Recall his 10 criteria for selecting a bargain stock. Let's use those criteria now to determine how New World Homes stands.

1. Is the price of New World Homes less than two-thirds of net quick assets (current assets less total debt)? Yes. The company's current assets of $38.4 million, minus total debt ($10,185), gives net quick assets of $51.30 per share, and a two-thirds limit of $33.85, which is above New World's market price of $33.75.

2. Is the price less than two-thirds of tangible book value? Book value of $64.50 gives a limit of $43, far above New World Homes' price per share. And using the $72.50 per-share estimate of true book value increases the distance.

3. Are earnings per share greater than 20 percent of price (a p/e ratio of five or less)? The limit of five is above New World's p/e ratio of 1.9. New World's stock, then, satisfies this price criterion at a market price of $33.75 a share.

4. Is the p/e ratio no higher than 40 percent of its five-year high? Long-term data put the five-year p/e ratio at a high of nine, with a 40-percent restriction of 3.6, which is still above New World's current 1.9.

5. Is the dividend yield greater than two-thirds of the AAA bond yield? New World's stingy 1.7-percent dividend yield is nowhere near two-thirds of AAA bond yield, here assumed to be about 8 percent.

6. Is earnings yield greater than double the current AAA bond yield? With the assumed 8-percent AAA bond yield, New World's earnings yield is six times higher.

7. Does compound 10-year earnings growth exceed 7 percent, with two or fewer earnings declines under 5 percent in the period? Moody's makes it plain that only one of New World's earnings declines exceeded 5 percent in a 10-year period, while its 10-year growth rate also exceeds the 7-percent requirement, and its two-year rate of 24 percent is

superb. Therefore, the only earnings test New World can't pass is the dividend requirement. But that is less a matter of earnings power than of management priority.

8. Is the current ratio two or more? Its current ratio of 5.34 is more than double the minimum of two.

9. Is total debt less than tangible book value—a debt-equity ratio below one? New World's debt to equity, which we also calculated earlier, is .279, less than one—and declining.

10. Is total debt less than twice net liquidation value—net quick assets? Total debt ($10,185,000) is far less than twice net quick assets ($56,430,000). New World is underleveraged, not overextended!

So in terms of these 10 criteria, New World Homes stacks up well when it comes to being not only a bargain stock, but also one that will continue to appreciate far into the future. It's a keeper. Buy it, hold it, and reap the long-term rewards for your faith in it.

Unfortunately, I have to tell you now that New World Homes is a fictitious company. Actually, it's an amalgam of several companies. But this will give you a good idea of what you should look for and how you should analyze a company such as this one once you spot it.

Initial Public Offerings: Pros and Cons

You've probably heard about investors who have doubled their money in a short time by buying initial public offerings (IPOs). Unless they are inveterate liars, they were very likely telling the truth. Stories about IPO successes are many. Consider these examples:

➣ **Manhattan Bagel**, a 1994 IPO priced at $5 a share soared to a high of $29.50 within a short time.

➣ **Case Corp.**, another 1994 IPO priced at $19 a share reached a high of $56.25 within 18 months of its IPO offering price of $19.

- ➤ **PMI Group**, a mortgage insurer, jumped from its IPO of $34 on April 10, 1995, to $53.50 just a short time later that same year.

- ➤ **Fort Howard**, a sanitary-tissue manufacturer, in early 1995 doubled in price from its IPO of $12.

- ➤ **Globalstar Telecommunications**, a high-tech IPO priced at $20, was selling at $65.75 a few months later.

- ➤ **Gucci Group**, a manufacturer of high-priced apparel accessories, was sitting at $73 a share shortly after its IPO of $22. Investors who got a piece of that action more than tripled their money.

Before you call your broker to see if you can get in on the IPO action, however, let's consider some less prominent examples—those of IPO fizzles and flops:

Manhattan Bagel, the company mentioned above, saw its initial success quickly evaporate, as its stock more recently plummeted to $13.75 a share after company officials said they would lower first-quarter earnings results due to accounting irregularities at its West Coast unit.

Documentum, a producer of document-management software, went from $46.50 a share just after its initial public offering to $22.25 a share—all in a matter of days.

Forte Software, another high-tech company, dropped to $21 a share after reaching a peak of $81.75 after its initial public offering.

But those were extremes. To get a better picture, let's look at some of the larger IPOs that were offered in 1994, then see in Chart 33 how they were faring two years (or thereabouts) later, in mid-1996.

CHART 33

IPOS: THE GOOD, THE BAD, AND THE UGLY				
Issuer	Offering Date	Offering Price	8/15/96 Price	% Change
TeleDanmark	4/27/94	$23.53	$23.38	-0.6
British Sky Broadcasting	12/07/94	24.05	47.88	+99.1
OfficeMax	11/02/94	19.00	14.00	-26.3
TeleWest Communications	11/22/94	28.50	21.63	-24.1
SGS-Thomson Microelec.	12/07/94	22.25	37.38	+68.0
Nokia	7/01/94	40.38	40.13	-0.6
Vastar Resources	6/27/94	28.00	34.63	+23.7
Western National	2/08/94	12.00	17.75	+47.9
Mills Corp.	4/14/94	23.50	19.88	-15.4
Case Corp.	6/24/94	19.00	44.75	+135.5

As you saw, getting in on an IPO deal doesn't always guarantee big profits. And some successful investors simply ignore IPOs. For example, the Beardstown Ladies, whom we met earlier, avoid initial public offerings altogether. They simply prefer to invest based on a record of several years of earnings growth as a public company. Nevertheless, IPOs remain popular with investors, as Chart 34 shows.

CHART 34

TOTAL IPO ISSUANCES–1975-1995			
Year	No. Issues	Year	No. Issues
1975	6	1986	727
1976	40	1987	556
1977	32	1988	291
1978	38	1989	254
1979	62	1990	213
1980	149	1991	402
1981	348	1992	605
1982	122	1993	818
1983	686	1994	476
1984	357	1995	572
1985	355		

Source: Securities Data Co.

As seen, however, investing in IPOs can be risky. They require intensive research and a knowledge of the markets in which they are offered. Moreover, market corrections can take their toll on IPO performance, as the following shows:

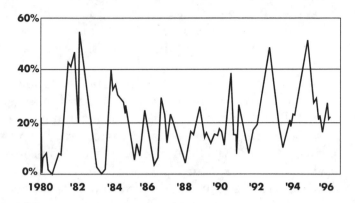

Sources: Smith Barney, Securities Data Co.

Moreover, the mood of an IPO market can change abruptly. In the summer of 1996, for example, a frenzied sellers' market turned to a much more sedate buyers' market. In a very short time, investors went from thankful to get a piece of a deal to picking and choosing what they wanted. Such a mood change was reflected in the slowing flows of cash into emerging growth funds. That, in turn, reduced the amount of money aimed at IPOs. Result: Investors expecting big returns from IPOs were sorely disappointed.

So what does an investor do at such times? Well, he or she could invest in IPOs of a different kind. One popular alternative is the REIT—the real-estate investment trust. During bull markets in real estate, such IPOs can offer very satisfying returns. And they are typically set up to lure long-term investors.

A REIT, as you learned earlier, is a sort of real-estate mutual fund. It invests in commercial and in some cases residential real estate, and if you buy shares, you receive a portion of the income from those properties. REIT shares are traded daily on the stock exchanges, and when first offered, they are IPOs. REITs could be taxed as corporations but for the fact that they pay out at least 90 percent of their incomes as dividends.

REITs go through the same cycles as does the real-estate market itself. And real-estate investment crazes have come and gone since 1961, when Congress enacted legislation permitting the existence of REITs. In the 1970s, REITs blossomed to $20 billion, then crashed. In the 1980s, some $70 billion of property partnerships were sold before tax laws changed and values collapsed. As a result, REITs lost support from investors, and that image has lingered for the most part till this day.

But especially when CDs and money-market funds are offering less than a 5-percent yield and the stock market is in the doldrums, REITs can be a safe and profitable haven. At such times, yield-hungry individual investors who don't know where to turn can buy REITs, usually at prices that offer cash-dividend yields of better than 7 percent.

Proving the growing popularity and new notions about REITS was the fact that by 1995 the estimated value of the market was $25 billion, up from $6 billion just three years earlier. And predictions of a $100-billion market seemed plausible.

You Take Your Chances

IPOs of course involve risk to one degree or another. To help you better understand and deal with IPO risks, we'll continue with our example of New World Homes. Let's say after reading the blurb about the company on the Internet, you find out that it is privately owned, but that a group of underwriters plans to issue new stock of the company in a couple of weeks. You learned about the IPO, incidentally, from the formal announcements of new issues—called "tombstone ads"—that appear in *The Wall Street Journal*. But those announcements are made only a day or so prior to the offerings, as Chart 35 shows.

CHART 35

SECURITIES OFFERING CALENDAR

The following U.S. Treasury, corporate and municipal offerings are tentatively scheduled for sale this week, according to Dow Jones Capital Markets Report and Dow Jones News Service:

TREASURY
Today
$25.0 billion three- and six-month bills.
CORPORATES
Today

Haynes International Inc. - $130 million senior notes due 2004, noncallable for four years, with a three-year equity call for 35%, via Merrill Lynch & Co, rated single-B3. Offers a yield of 11.5%. High-performance alloy concern in Kokomo, indiana.

Sprint Spectrum LP - $520 million (proceeds) of debt, comprising $270 million (proceeds) of 10-year senior discount notes and $250 million of 10-year senior notes, via Merrill Lynch & Co. and Lehman Brothers Inc. Offer is for a yield of 10¾% for the senior notes and 12¼% for the senior discount notes. B2/B+. Personal communications services in Kansas City, Mo.

One Day In The Week
Omnipoint Corp. - $150 million of senior notes due 2006, noncallable for five years, via Donaldson, Lufkin & Jenrette Securities Corp. Digital wireless technology in Arlington, Virginia.

Radio Mevil Digital Americas Inc. - $130 million Rule 144a senior notes due 2003 via Lehman Brothers Inc. Offer range is 13% to 13¼%. Caa/CCC+. Specialized mobile radio networks in South American countries.

United USN Inc. - $155 million Rule 144a eight-year senior notes with a three-year equity call via Smith Barney Inc. Local telephone service in Chicago, Illinois.

Wachovia Corp. - $300 million of 10-year debt via Smith Barney Inc. Winston-Salem based bank holding company.

Initial Public Offerings
Atria Communities Inc. - five million shares, via Alex. Brown & Sons Inc. Offer range is $12-$14 a share.

Beverly Bancorporation Inc. - one million shares, via Howe Barnes. Offer range $14-$16 a share.

Capstar Hotel Investors Inc. - 9.25 million shares, via Lehman Brothers Inc. Offer range $17-$20 a share.

Gradall Industries Inc. - 3.5 million shares, via Dillon Read & Co. Offer range $13-$15 a share.

Interaction Media Corp. - 1.25 million shares and 625,000 warrants, via Paragon Capital Corp. Offer range $4 a share.

Metro One Telecommunications Inc. - 2 million shares, via Black & Co. Offer range $8-$10 a share.

Pacific Coast Apparel Co. - 1.25 million units, via National Securities Corp. Offer range $4.50 a share.

R&G Financial Corp. - two million shares, via Friedman Billings Ramsey & Co. Offer range $13-$15 a share.

Stericycle Inc. - three million shares, via Dillon Read & Co. Offer range $11-$13 a share.

Transact Technologies Inc. - 1.15 million shares, via Cruttenden Roth Inc. Offer range $9.50-$11 a share.

XOX Corp. - 850,000 units, via Equity Securities Trading Co. Offer $7 a share.

Other Corporate Offerings
Nichols Research Corp. (NRES) - 1 million shares, via Robinson-Humphrey Co.

Oregon Metallurgical Corp. (OREM) - 3.5 million shares, via Salomon Brothers Inc.

Outdoor Systems Inc. (OSIA) - 7.7 million shares, via Alex.

That doesn't give you much time. And you need to act quickly, because your stockbroker isn't likely to call you to tell you about this new issue. Demand for leading IPOs is almost always intense, so unless you're a heavy trader (and you shouldn't be, of course), the broker is going to give only his or her major clients a shot at this opportunity.

So you initiate contact. You want a prospectus, and you should be able to get one. If need be, go to your broker's office and get one. Once you have a copy, you have a wealth of information at your fingertips. As you may know, a prospectus is an abbreviated form of registration statement that describes the issuer, its business, and the securities being offered. Included is data about the company's products or services, management, assets, liabilities, income, dividends, and similar facts and figures.

Many prospectuses offered in recent years have been upgraded from their traditionally gray, dull, and usually forbidding appearance by including color photographs. Still, a prospectus is basically a legal document—indeed, you can think of it as a "document of negatives"—and the typical prospectus can be difficult to read because it contains pages of ponderous, sometimes equivocal text, and, for the investing neophyte, confusing numbers. Here are some of the areas to focus on as you examine the prospectus:

➤ Management's discussion and analysis of financial conditions and operating results, all of which can give you a good handle on potential earnings and growth.

➤ A comparison of the book value per share *before* the offering with the book value per share *after* to determine dilution of ownership. In a fast-growing high-tech company, for example, dilution may be immaterial; in an established company in a mature industry, a great deal of dilution may be a warning signal.

➤ The company's accounting methods.

➤ The company's use of proceeds from the sale of stock. (To retire debt and pay for salary increases of corporate officers, or to invest in the business for future growth?)

➤ The experience of management.

➤ Footnotes, which can be excellent clues to real and latent troubles within a company.

❊❊❊❊

To sum up, the company or companies that will prove to be winners won't just tumble from the sky and land in your investment portfolio. You will need to diligently search for them. And they will likely turn up at the darnedest times and in the darnedest places. Maybe while reading a magazine in your doctor's waiting room. Or while leafing through a used book you bought for a dollar at a charity sale. The key is to be alert to and open-minded about new ideas and developments. Think of them in terms of what they can mean to you as an investment opportunity. Then follow up with sound and thorough research. Sooner or later, you will be rewarded for your efforts.

Chapter 14: Profiting from Turnarounds

"The smallest worm will turn, being trodden on."
– William Shakespeare

The Signs Are There

Even the best of companies can flounder. Some never recover and are either disassembled and sold piecemeal or become another bankruptcy statistic. But most companies will eventually rebound, and those investors able to distinguish between the ones that stage a comeback and the ones that don't can make big money. That's what this chapter is all about. It will show you how to spot a company in distress, how to recognize the recovery potential, and how to profit from that knowledge.

The Thick and the Thin

Let's say it's 1992, and you've got a few thousand dollars to invest. You read that Tandy Corp., the consumer-electronics retailer, has been suffering financially from market forces that seem beyond the company's ability to cope with them. You note that earnings per share are a dismal two cents, and the stock price has dropped to $22.25 a share. But you know a guy who works for Tandy, and he says his company has taken measures to turn things around. He then explains what those measures are. You are sold and buy as much Tandy stock as you can, then hold on through thick and thin.

Had you done that, you would have been amply rewarded. The company does in fact make an remarkable turnaround, so that by 1995, the earnings per share improve to $3.12, and the stock price increases to $64.25—nearly tripling your money in three years.

Or let's say it's again 1992 and you want to put some money into a computer manufacturer, then keep it there until retirement. You read that Compaq Computer Co. is struggling to keep pace with its many competitors in the industry. But you also learn that the company has put in place some very dynamic long-range plans that, if they pan out, will correct the problems that plague it. So you buy several thousand shares at the going price at that time: $7.38 a share. Then you watch, somewhat nervously, as Compaq begins to right itself. Eventually, your faith in the company starts to pay off—and so does your investment: By 1994, the stock price reaches $42.13 a share. Your retirement nest egg has suddenly grown in value by nearly 500 percent, and, better yet, the company seems destined to continue to carve out a larger and larger piece of the computer-industry sales pie.

Were you and others who invested like you just lucky? Did you simply throw a dart at the financial pages of the newspaper and accidentally hit Compaq or Tandy? Probably not. More likely in 1992 you dug into the records and reports on one or both of the companies and discovered that the prospects were good for a reversal of their fortunes. Then you invested, not for quick profits, but for long-term gains.

In this chapter we're going to investigate struggling companies and how they turned things around for themselves and for their investors. In other words, you're going to learn how failure or near-failure can be transformed into opportunity—for you. In that regard, you're going to see how the hope and the ability of managers and workers to regain control of their shattered companies can multiply the holdings of savvy investors. And you'll learn the important signals that mean the difference between a company's success and failure.

Unfortunately, not every troubled business turns itself around. And failures that lead to total destruction of a company are a terrible and enormous reality. Thousands of businesses die each year and many more flop around like a fish on land, hoping to somehow find their way back into water. In the process, investors suffer, sometimes greatly.

Even more meaningful as far as you're concerned is that investors can often see trouble coming—if they know what to look for. Failures and death struggles aren't limited to little-known companies that might have been too small, obscure, or adventurous for their own good. Rather, these problems are apparent everywhere, even affecting companies and products that are as familiar to us as our neighbors or local baseball teams. And the news media report all the grisly details to us. Later, we'll focus on one of the nation's premier companies to see how it floundered, then, in remarkable fashion, not only revived, but also prospered. Just an important, we'll see how many investors foresaw the turnaround and took advantage of it to the maximum.

First, consider just a few other companies that fell on hard times: Eastern Airlines, U.S. Steel, Caterpillar, Taco Bell, and Chase Manhattan Bank. They all made big headlines—often months or years before difficulties struck. Of course, some turned it around, but some didn't. And the list doesn't stop there. The cancer even worked its way into the heart of America—the auto industry—which is about as quintessentially American as you can get.

The Cancer That Spared No One

Cars and the freedom they provide have meshed nicely with the country's psyche since the first horseless carriages rolled off the Detroit assembly lines at the turn of the century. In fact, it seemed that whatever Detroit produced, with the exception of a few well-known duds (the Edsel, most notably), the public embraced. It was a love affair that for decades helped make the automobile industry a profit-spewing fixture of the American economy along with the likes of steel, machine tools, airlines, and computer chips.

Unfortunately love can be fickle. The American automobile industry discovered this painful reality in the mid-1970s and in so doing provided a classic example of how an industry nearly self-destructed. In a story that's been well-told,

Detroit's greatest fault may have been to lose touch with its customers. The landscape changed and the giant automakers just didn't keep pace. It wasn't a matter of a single misstep. Detroit's shocking collapse came about for many reasons: vanity, ignorance, laziness, short-sightedness, and greed.

Foreign competition certainly helped accelerate the disintegration. The growth of the Japanese auto industry from being a mere curiosity to a worldwide force gave U.S. consumers a new and attractive suitor. Its rise helped change the way consumers looked at new cars. New emphasis was placed on quality, affordability, style, and service. Beyond this, the Japanese realized that the rising cost of gasoline (thanks to Middle East politics) was making consumers more aware than ever of the gas mileage each car offered. Brand loyalty, so long a positive marketing bulwark for U.S. automakers, gave way to a growing consumer awareness of the need to buy what's best rather than what's traditional. In this case, what was best increasingly meant Japanese or European.

To make matters worse, the increased foreign competition was putting pressure on profit margins. This ultimately meant U.S. car makers couldn't limit their concerns to just what they made. They also had to be concerned with how they made it. In critical areas, such as development time, marketing, and production, Detroit was simply out of pace and no longer cost competitive.

The cancer that ate into Detroit spared no one. The "Big Three," General Motors, Ford, and Chrysler, were not just looking at some cyclical setbacks or a down quarter when profits fell a bit. By the beginning of the 1980s, they were simply looking to survive.

How bad was bad? Between 1978 and 1981, the U.S. auto industry would lose billions. In the decade that followed, tens of thousands of auto workers saw their jobs disappear, their plants close, and their communities suffer economically and spiritually.

Ford Motor Co. alone would lose $3.3 billion during this time, and the stock price would fall to an incredible $1.75 a share. Ford therefore became cash destitute, and, even worse, was saddled with high overhead and little in new models that would spur a turnaround. Beyond this, it had neither the financial backing of General Motors nor the government support of Chrysler, which came in the form of $1.5 billion in loan guarantees. All Ford had in 1981 was problems. In fact, the public didn't actually realize how close Ford came to going belly up, because Chrysler's battle to survive was stealing all the headlines.

Yet Ford managed to overcome its problems through a massive multibillion-dollar restructuring and an equally important change in corporate culture. In fact, in five years time (by 1986), it was recording record profits and even outstripping those of the larger General Motors, which along with Chrysler had also turned things around.

If the story of Ford's collapse is a prime case study on what can go wrong, then Ford's resurrection is an equally potent example of how to spot a company as an investment turnaround. If examined closely, the Ford rebound not only provides concrete examples of how to rebound from near extinction, but also offers hope that no matter how bad the situation appears, salvation may be possible.

To be sure, there is no such thing as a guarantee. No matter how hard company officials work, no matter how daring their strategy and clear their vision, no one can bank on a turnaround effort being successful. For one thing, situations differ from company to company, industry to industry, and country to country. And many times, the environment simply moves beyond the ability of a company to control its own fate.

Probably the only thing that is assured is that troubled companies will go under if their leaders do nothing or only pay lip service to righting their businesses. It may sound sophomoric, but the commitment to struggle to resolve problems— no matter how long it takes—is perhaps the most essential ingredient to any turnaround. If nothing else, remember that point when analyzing a company as a turnaround investment possibility.

Common Threads of Turnarounds

So what do you look for when considering whether a seemingly doomed company can turn things around. Well, first, consider that many things must go into a successful turnaround. And, of course, every strategy has to be tailored to a company's individual needs and resources, regardless of the problems it faces. Yet, common threads are woven through all successes, whether they come in the automotive industry or the women's apparel business. They almost all include new ideas, the creation of a unifying vision, the hunt for a company's core problems, a systematic examination of the company's advantages and drawbacks, and the development of a far-reaching and detailed plan of attack. Unfortunately for an investor looking for a pattern, these components don't always appear in the same order.

Something else to look for: Often, but not always, turn-around recipes involve bringing in a new top manager, be it a chairman or a chief executive officer, to engineer the rescue program. The reason for this is obvious. While new faces aren't essential, new ideas are. Too often, long-standing veteran managers are tied to the past, emotionally and intellectually. Having set the company's current operating structure in motion, the existing managers usually don't have the resolve to break the mold that has been cast.

Of course, there are always exceptions to the "new-top-dog" principle. A few years ago when Chase Manhattan Bank was reeling because of a series of bad foreign loans, Chairman David Rockefeller fought off attempts to remove him. But he understood changes needed to be made. So he brought in Alan Lafley, formerly from General Electric, to serve as executive vice president for human resources. What Lafley did was convince Rockefeller that Chase still needed more outside help, which led to the appointment of Frederick Hammer, who redesigned and revitalized Chase's retail operations. Again, at Chase the principle of new leaders with new ideas was central to its rebound, even though it didn't mean that David Rockefeller had to give up his post.

More often, however, catastrophe brings a lot of changes to the top spot. Business history is full of legendary chief executives who are brought in to save the day and rescue a company that would otherwise be headed for oblivion. There is Iacocca at Chrysler, Thomas Graham at Armco, and Richard Teerlink at Harley-Davidson, among others.

New leaders, approaches, and ideas are essential to saving

troubled companies. Yet it doesn't matter how good they are unless a company has correctly identified its core problems and developed a tightly focused plan to deal with them. The stumbling block here is that core problems aren't always that obvious. Often, it takes an enormous amount of work and time to peel back the layers of side issues and symptoms before a company—and its potential investor—discovers what's really gnawing away at it.

SPINOFFS CAN TURN PROFITS

Businesses that have been spun off by large corporations are worth a close look from investors, especially in light of recent findings by analysts.

As new publicly traded companies, spinoffs can offer excellent returns for investors willing to assume the risk of perhaps owning an unknown quantity. For in most cases an investor in the parent company has little knowledge of the subsidiaries, many of which may be in different industries from the parent.

But when a spinoff occurs, stockholders receiving shares in the new company shouldn't automatically sell. That's because spinoffs tend to be greatly undervalued during their first six months of trading. And if you're a value investor, you may have a diamond in the rough.

Consider, for example, that average annualized returns after two years of trading of spinoffs issued from 1990 to 1995 came to 29.2 percent. That compares with an average annualuzed return from the S&P 500 of 14.9 percent.

Here is a more recent example of what can happen to a subsidiary after a spinoff:

Cytec Industries is a 1993 spinoff from American Cyanamid. Afterwards, troubled by environmental and retiree liabilities, the stock dropped to $4.67 a share. But analysts soon took note of Cytec's successful effort to reduce the liabilities, and in mid-1997 the stock was trading at $38.75 a share.

And in 1996 the 31 spinoffs from corporations were worth nearly $200 million. By mid-1997, the worth of those spinoffs had grown to about $240 million.

Spotting the Sickness

The hunt should use a systematic approach. Otherwise, you're likely to hear the company simply declare the apparent when difficulties arise. "We've got a problem. Yes, we're losing money." Usually, that's only a symptom of some greater illness. The sickness may rest with the company's philosophy, management structure, facilities, or marketing—or any combination of these or other issues.

If the company should choose the wrong problem, the plan will be as effective as a Band-Aid on a gaping wound. What's worse, the company will only delay putting an effective remedy into place, propelling it into greater financial trouble, while allocating what limited resources are available for a cure. Even if it takes a bit more time, the effort you put into finding out what is really wrong with a company is crucial. Often you can start your research at the top.

For example, David Kearns, president and chief executive officer of Xerox, has been largely credited with that company's turnaround in the late 1980s in the face of all sorts of problems. Yet Kearns admits that even while he was overseeing a massive restructuring of Xerox, he often lost sight of the core problems he was attacking. It is a symptom too often seen in American managers. If the stricken company identifies the core problems, however, it can move on to the next step: developing a plan to provide a clear strategy for attacking a company's maladies over the short and long term.

Who Needs a Turnaround? More Companies Than You Think

Investors make a mistake when they become obsessed with the bottom line. But it is a great place to start if you're unsure whether the company you're interested in needs a turnaround effort. It is the most obvious barometer of a business's health. If the P&L statement is full of red ink (and has been for some time) without good reason (like a strategic writeoff or a massive investment needed for long-term health), the company is a prime candidate for some intensive care.

Sadly, however, turnaround efforts are all too often left to those companies that are already close to death. Yet lots of other companies, even those making a profit, would be well served by putting a plan in place. Certainly, businesses with limited or stagnant growth are strong candidates, as are many companies that are seemingly healthy.

In fact, look closely at many of the country's most successful companies and you'll discover that they are constantly remaking themselves, ever conscious of detecting fundamental shifts in the market or problems on the horizon. In these cases, some companies decide to make preemptive strikes. Such strikes reflect not only leadership, but also a substantial amount of courage.

Ultimately, it takes a keen eye to see that there's something fundamentally wrong with a company, especially if it is still making money. It also requires fortitude to stick with it while it launches a costly turnaround plan. It's a gamble. Should the chief executive get it wrong and hasten a company's decline, you, as an investor, will pay.

Problems, Problems, Problems

If solutions differ from company to company, so do problems. Some problems come from within, while others reflect changes in the market. Often they are connected, perhaps springing from the same core faults. Regardless, the same type of problems reoccur throughout business. Helping to identify these themes can make developing the solutions easier. Most companies, for example, are always faced with shifting market conditions or new and unforeseen external pressures.

Here are some warning signs that should cause you some serious doubts as to whether a turnaround is possible:

➤ Shifting consumer demands, such as an appetite for more fuel-efficient cars or low-cost personal computers. Style also plays a role. A shift in consumer whims can mean a whole new set of demands that might have little to do with the quality or efficiency of a product: Consider the growing demand for Internet-access products.

➤ Changing government attitudes. New or revised government regulations, such as more stringent environmental controls, worker-safety demands, or financial supports, can be major factors in the performance of a company. In contrast, companies operating in the vacuum of a regulated market can see their world turned upside down as a result of deregulation. The telecommunications and airlines industries suffered this fate.

➤ Tough times. Recessions like those of the late 1970s and early 1990s transform the business landscape, drying up consumer spending, drawing down sales, eating up profit margins, and squeezing a company's ability to put funding into research and development, marketing, advertising, and so on.

➤ Competition from overseas. There is the constant threat that foreign competition will invade a market traditionally supplied by domestic companies. The U.S. car industry's battle against the influx of Japanese imports is legendary. Lesser-known examples include battles against imports of textiles, steel, machine tools, microchips, and even photofilm.

➤ The rising costs of their raw materials. A sharp rise, or even fall, in the price of steel, oil, coal, silicon chips, or electricity can have a tremendous impact on companies. How quickly they respond to these changes, either through increased efficiency or alternative sources (or a combination of both), is vital to their survival.

➤ Unbalanced balance sheets. Companies have to make sure that they weigh the cost of expansion or modernization with the impact the increased debt burden will have on their operations. Even if there is a low debt-to-equity ratio, companies can still find themselves in trouble if they are insufficiently financed or have cash-flow problems that will hinder their ability to operate effectively.

➤ Mismanagement. Obviously, even if the financing and end product are sound, a company might have a lousy management structure that offsets other benefits. Problems usually arise because a company hasn't hit the right balance between providing enough review and oversight and being too bureaucratic and cumbersome.

➤ Inability to maintain a proactive labor force that is satisfied, productive, and feels included in the production process. The solution to this, of course, comes with wage levels that enable the company to remain competitive with both its domestic and foreign counterparts. Striking this balance has been a particularly daunting task for America's heavy industries, which in the last decade have been forced to rework labor agreements in the face of new challenges from abroad.

➤ Outdated facilities. Labor agreements aren't the only things that need to be revised. Plant facilities also have to be restructured to meet the latest market conditions. The steel and automotive industries, for example, were littered with overcapacity, antiquated, and inefficient plants. It is a legacy of decades of neglect fostered by a false sense of security.

With regard to this last symptom, consider the steel industry. Rather than driving their then still-enormous profits into new technologies in the 1950s, 1960s, and early 1970s that would make them more efficient and productive, U.S. steelmakers chose to put their earnings into the hands of their shareholders. The regrettable aspect of this, reflecting a true lack of vision, is that Japanese and European steel companies (and automakers, too, for that matter) weren't sitting on their hands. They were investing in anything that would make them strong and more efficient. The plan paid off, as they bit off large shares of the U.S. market, forcing many companies here either into ruin or severe restructuring.

Shortsightedness isn't limited to steel. It can be found anywhere—and often is. Sometimes companies go beyond just having a lack of vision to ignoring obvious problems. Solutions in these cases are either nonexistent or come under the quick-fix variety that might show a little black ink today at the cost of millions—perhaps billions—in red ink later on.

Moving to Action

The range of solutions and approaches to problems are as varied as the problems themselves. What is constant, as far as you as an investor are concerned, is that solutions should match the resources a company has at hand, whether that involves personnel or plant facilities. But as with problems, successful turnaround strategies generally have some common threads.

As noted earlier, before a plan is put into place, a company must identify what needs to be corrected. In simplest terms, that means effective trouble-shooting, creating a plan to find out what's at the center of the company's problem. In some cases, that means bringing in new faces with fresh perspectives. In other cases, it means recognizing that fundamental problems exist and creating a small group of dedicated company members to root out and analyze the ailments.

Beyond just the problems, companies must develop a clear vision of what they intend to be. Usually this is performed by the top executive, whose position allows him to create the unifying vision. Once a vision is established, the company then has to create a detailed supporting plan that's tied to a company's particular needs, whether it means reorganization, expansion, closures, layoffs, or new marketing schemes. The best plans are a curious mix. They not only have to be detailed and focused, but also have to be flexible enough to grow and adjust as a company's condition changes. Rigid adherence to any strategy can be almost as deadly as no plan at all.

Moreover, to understand how companies succeed, investors must understand how companies fail. No inquiry into turn-arounds is complete without looking at strategies that simply fell short and apart. Obviously lots of failures can be attributed to a company's waiting too long to act—or not acting at all. It is even more disturbing to see companies act decisively and still manage to collapse or at least make strategic mistakes that set them back. Some of the companies stumble so badly they now no longer exist. Others are still around, but paid dearly for their missteps.

We'll also take a detailed look at one company's effort to rebuild itself: Xerox, a giant in the business world that lost its edge, only to recapture it.

In virtually all cases, however, be it Ford, Xerox, or Eastman Kodak, success is a byproduct of determination—determination to find out what's really wrong with a company, determination to develop a strong and realistic plan to deal with the problems, and determination to carry the plan through.

Becoming a Turnaround Detective

In his work *The Super Chiefs*, Robert Heller offers a set of principles that any investor can use in detecting a turnaround in the making:

1. It decides to acquire the leading technology of product and process.

2. It invests effective power and clear responsibility in people.

3. It trains and educates its personnel.

4. It develops a "management collective" that works together.

5. It builds a "superstructure of success" by assigning the right roles to the right people.

6. It uses all information possible to develop an ambitious strategy.

7. It masters and uses hard and soft management techniques.

8. It ties status, rewards, and responsibility to results.

9. It pulls together the means to accomplish the "impossible."

10. It unifies organic strengths to win exemplary success.

But it takes more than hard judgments and common sense for a company to turn around. The company also must have the ability to look beyond the obvious and to understand the fundamental trends and shifts in the economy and culture that affect the way business is conducted.

Knowing when the end, or maybe a new beginning, is coming is just as important as what to do when it arrives. Stan Davis and Bill Davidson return to this theme constantly in their work *2020 Vision*. To them, the road to success is information—being able to use and provide it. "Today," they maintain, "information-based enhancements have become the main avenues to revitalize mature businesses and to transform them into new ones." They add that "in every economy, the core technology becomes the basis for revitalization and growth. Information technologies are the core for today's economy, and to survive, all businesses must informationalize."

Davis and Davidson point to professional sports teams as examples of mature businesses that "have spawned new generation, informationalized businesses, whose economic value outstrips that of the original sports. Sports teams once were thought of as a collection of money-losing tax shelters. Growth today can no longer come from simply playing more games, raising ticket prices, or enticing more people into the stadium." Now, they add, they are seen as a core element of a business, "around which much larger information businesses are wrapped."

They use the example of the National Basketball Association, which has seen phenomenal growth in the last few years, with franchise values growing faster than in any other professional sports: "The games remain the core business, but they are now almost overshadowed by retail licensing, home video, television production, event marketing, publishing, sponsorship, media sales, and other sports-generated businesses."

New Tricks Mature Companies Can Use

Companies and industries, like people, have distinct life cycles. Davis and Davidson explain: "In the life cycles of an economy, each technological breakthrough produces a subsequent quantum leap in business growth. When the particular technology matures, growth slows. Past mid-life, businesses rely more on marketing techniques and nominal product changes, such as style and colors, to keep their edge. Further advance is marginal, doing the same thing a little bit better. Aging has set in."

In the final phase—aging—returns diminish no matter how many resources are used. Yet, unlike people, the final phase of a company doesn't mean death, they assert, "It simply means death of dominance." They add that the company must learn to live on in the next economy as one of many no longer dominant competitors.

The need to adapt also isn't limited to one type of industry. "Organizations must be revitalized because continued dominance requires adaptation to changing market conditions. This need for transformation isn't limited to smokestack America. It includes many of the relatively new high-tech companies in Silicon Valley...," explain Noel M. Tichy and Mary Anne Devanna, authors of *The Transformational Leader*.

As for as investors are concerned, the question of whether the turnaround is real lies in the ability of the company's new management. Nowadays, the speed and degree of competition that industry and businesses now face call for a new group of leaders. Its members are called "transformational leaders": "These people take on the responsibility for revitalizing an organization. They define the need for change, create new visions, mobilize commitment to those visions, and ultimately transform an organization," Tichy and Devanna explain.

Against all this, they stress, there's the importance of an investor knowing the difference between various types of leaders. The entrepreneur, for example, works with a clean slate, creating what he likes. The transformational leader must deal with the mess that's already in place.

Regardless of the particulars, transformational leaders deal with some general themes. First, they need to recognize the need to revitalize; next, they must create a new vision; and finally they must institute the change. Each stage creates different challenges. There are also challenges to be met after the fundamental restructuring has occurred. Employees, for example, must be prepared for the frustration that accompanies failure as they replace thoroughly mastered routines with a new act. Tichy and Devanna warn that, ultimately, success depends on everything and everyone being rehearsed "so that the play can become again a seamless whole rather than a set of unintegrated scenes."

The 14 Steps to Heaven

Of all the turnaround gurus that have flooded the market, few people are as well-known and perhaps as influential as W. Edward Deming. In developing his theories of what was wrong with American industry, Deming didn't concentrate just on U.S. businesses. Instead, he went looking around Japan. What he found was surprising and troubling. Deming argues, for example, that, contrary to popular opinion, American businesses aren't in trouble because of Japan's low labor rates or its massive commitment to technology. In fact, he adds, U.S. industries have the potential to make up for these Japanese advantages.

Deming instead contends that the problems facing many U.S. businesses have gone beyond the obvious disadvantages of having lesser equipment, higher labor costs, and less government help. The trouble facing American businesses has been deeper and more fundamental, he says, and unlike the Japanese, U.S. businesses simply haven't taken a long-term view of their operations, and it has tended to crush them.

"To Deming," Andrea Gabor wrote in *The Man Who Discovered Quality*, "America's quality crisis is symptomatic of a fundamentally outdated management system that focuses on short-term results at the expense of the process." Ultimately, she explains, "Deming rejects the model of the modern American manager, who can 'manage anything' based on a company's balance sheet." It is an approach that is more concerned with short-term results at the cost of quality, customer satisfaction, and long-term health. "Instead, he advocates the creation of process-obsessed managements that are able to bring the best out of its employees while fine-tuning the entire organization to higher and higher standards of excellence and innovation," Gabor notes.

Deming's approach is built on a few fundamental elements that all come together in his well-known "14 Points." When accepted by management, they go beyond giving companies a quick-fix improvement. Rather, they offer a process that continually enhances the production and quality of a product. "The Deming-style manager learns to probe behind the numbers, knowing that numbers don't give you the answers, only the questions that need to be asked, and understanding that in the short term figures can be dressed up to suit almost any occasion." Lose touch with the process, Deming warns, and you lose touch with the customer. And that can signal a death knell for a company and industry.

As an investor, you really only need to know that the 14 points are, in effect, a set of commandments for managers. They can be boiled down even further, according to Gabor.

Ultimately, they center on quality being defined by customers: reducing variation in every process; a management having an unrelenting commitment to improvement; improvement as all-encompassing and including everyone in an organization; employee training and education for ongoing improvement; and elimination of performance-ranking schemes.

Taking a Hard Look

It doesn't take a genius to figure out something is wrong when a company is losing money. When millions of dollars are involved, it is pretty clear-cut that the problems are severe. Roger Smith was to discover this soon after his appointment as chairman of General Motors in 1980. Yet almost immediately after his appointment, Smith noted that General Motors would remain largely unchanged under his realm. "I'd be very surprised if there were any dramatic changes," he said at the time of the appointment.

Within months, GM and Smith would be forced to take a hard look at his first prediction, thanks to the company's reporting its first loss in 60 years, a setback of $763 million. Times were tough throughout the industry and many observers believed that Ford and Chrysler were even worse off. Yet General Motors had enough problems of its own. The auto industry was working its way through a fundamental change and GM was in the midst of a complicated and costly investment program designed to reassert the giant automaker as a technology leader.

The plan wouldn't go off easily, however, and the losses that underscored the company's growing problems wouldn't go away soon either. In fact, before GM could right itself, it would have to undertake one of the most massive restructuring plans in America's industrial history.

Initially, many in and out of GM thought the loss was a temporary setback, perhaps an aberration caused by some unforeseen glitch in demand or production. Smith, however, seemed to grasp that the loss reflected a more serious problem and one that wasn't going to go away soon. "We're up to our ass in trouble and we've got to start doing things differently. We're behind our foreign competition right now in quality, in technological design, in plants and facilities, and, yes, even in our own management.... In 1980, the little girl with the lemonade stand down the street made more profit than all of us—GM, Ford, Chrysler, and AMC together."

Consider what Smith went through as a bit of shock therapy. On the other hand, Thomas Graham didn't need any shock therapy when he was offered the chance to take over U.S. Steel. The mammoth steelmaker with billions of dollars in worldwide sales was already deeply in trouble when Graham was offered the job. Its foremost problem was easy to spot. It was losing an ocean of money for a variety of reasons. And it wasn't going to end any time soon, no matter what Graham did.

In Graham's first year, the steelmaker reported another $850 million loss. Yet as with Smith at GM, Graham first had to rouse the existing management into action—or at least instill a new way of thinking. There was no sense of impending doom. No one, in fact, could believe that U.S. Steel was a high-cost, ineffective steelmaker, despite the billions of dollars in losses. That was, in fact, U.S. Steel's central problem. Its upper management simply believed their company was the best—even when the bottom line told them otherwise. No matter how much money U.S. Steel pumped into rebuilding, its success would always be thwarted until this issue was resolved.

Beyond the Bottom Line

For investors, bottom lines can be deceiving, whether they are in the red or the black. Michael Blumenthal discovered this when he become head of Burroughs Corporation in Detroit. Ironically, Blumenthal thought he had found the perfect situation when Burroughs approached him. After all, after two years as Secretary of the Treasury under Jimmy Carter, he was ready for a new post, and Burroughs, with its excellent reputation, seemed to provide this.

It didn't take Blumenthal long to realize something was amiss. "I would say almost within the first week—I may exaggerate with the first week—but certainly within the first month, because I began to sense that the quality of the people that were there, that I was meeting and talking to, seemed oddly at variance with the performance of the company. They were very unimpressive. Not only that, they didn't know the numbers. They didn't know where their profits were coming from—where they were making profits. They didn't have data; they didn't collect data; they didn't use computers!"

Not surprisingly, the conditions at Burroughs were ripe for a shock and it came as soon as the company started reporting losses. Not only did this make an impact on the company's operations, it also affected the employees. Notes Blumenthal, "Here they thought they were working for a company that was forever moving upward. Suddenly they were reading one item of bad news after another about the company.... Some of them finally realized what they had suspected all along, that something was wrong with the company and that it badly needed fixing."

Quick Fixes and Long-Term Disasters

Keep in mind that short-term, quick-fix solutions to problems almost always fail. Usually their focus, whether it is directed strictly at the bottom line or on the production process, rarely takes into account the long-term impact of such decisions. What might seem like a solution today could actually turn into another problem a year or two down the line.

The easiest and perhaps most deadly quick fix is to juggle the bottom line, cook the books, fudge the numbers. That is done all the time, usually by companies in deep trouble looking to relieve a momentary pressure by hiding expenses or overstating one-time windfalls to make a company look healthier than it really is. Ultimately, managers know that the fiddler will come to call, and when she does the company could be in worse shape than when it started. Many of them assume they will be out of the picture by then, leaving it to someone else to deal with.

That type of situation occurred at Xerox. For several years, as Xerox's business was actually declining, many members of the sales force would fudge their sales by switching revenues from one quarter to the next. For a while, it seemed like these salespersons were pulling off miracles. Ultimately, the bottom fell out, and a bad scene was made even worse.

As one observer noted, "Instant gratification is part of the American culture. Managements are no exception. Over the years they have picked up and discarded hundreds of management hula hoops developed to solve fundamental organizational problems." What are examples of quick fixes? "Scientific" management, time-motion studies, human-relationship gimmicks, management by objectives, zero-based budgeting, quality circles, and Japanese management.

Also keep in mind that it is a big mistake for investors to limit the search for problems. Some come from within a company, like poor management, faulty marketing, out-of-date equipment. Others come from outside the structure: increased competition, deregulation and changes in consumer tastes. What all companies have in common is that their success in dealing with these challenges depends on how well they're able to identify what ails them. Success also depends on their sense of history. Have they, in effect, learned from their past mistakes and those of others?

Too Much Control, Too Little Guts

Philips Electronics, with sales of more than $30 billion annually, is an international giant based in Holland. In existence for decades and operating in a "well-defended base in Europe," the company could claim some incredible assets, the type that only come to companies with size and longevity, such as strong name-brand recognition and a well-established distribution network. Despite this, the company suffered mightily in the early '90s, sustaining a loss of $2.5 billion in 1990 and seeing its stock price drop to $11 a share.

One observer notes that with a company of Philips' size, all sorts of problems can come to the forefront: obsolete product(s), poor production, faulty marketing, and sales overextension. In many cases, a big company can overcome these types of problems. But Philips finally was overwhelmed. The reason: "There is only one possible answer: management. The weaknesses listed above haven't permeated the whole of Philips, but in some of its too many businesses, they became endemic."

In other cases, the business units just didn't live up to their potential. Robert Heller, in his book *The Super Chiefs,* attributes this largely to an overcentralized bureaucracy: "That overload not only had stifled the effect of operational managers to maximize their portfolio, but had imposed unstoppable strategic burdens on the whole corporation."

Heller cites Philips' muddled efforts to launch its V2000 model videocassette recorder as a classic example of what can go wrong in these circumstances. The company's North American operations, in fact, refused to take on the project, noting that Philips had simply waited too long. They argued correctly that the Beta and VHS formats were already too well established to give Philips any chance at successfully marketing its product.

Philips seemed to quickly recover, however, and many investors took advantage of the company's impressive turnaround in 1991, when restructuring (that is, closing or trimming unprofitable operations) occurred. By 1995, in fact, Philips seemed to have completely rebounded, with the stock price climbing to more than $53 a share at one point.

But Heller notes that the quick turnaround was probably misleading. It could, in fact, only reflect that Philips was so riddled with problems that the initial corrections were easy, he said. Soon, the company was indeed again nursing some wounds, and investors who were rejoicing in 1995 at their good fortune soon saw the value of their holdings decline, as the stock price fell to $34 a share in 1996.

Heller's insight on the quick financial turnaround should serve as a warning to an investor: Even if a company seems to have worked its way through a disastrous financial situation in short order, the key to the future lies less in stopping losses than in replacing ungotten gains—like the lost VCR market—with gotten ones. Philips' management problems were only highlighted by the saga of the V2000. As noted, flaws of all stripes permeated the company, and the losses registered in 1990 reflect this.

Technology, Technology, Technology

You can't stop progress no matter how big and rich you are. If you try, you can find yourself in big trouble. Gillette Co., in fact, was hurt by its own power. It felt that by supplying the best razor, it could easily monopolize blade sales and thus maintain a tight grip on both the consumer and distribution system. But Gillette's strategy floundered when it failed to move ahead of its competitors rather than merely concentrate on keeping them at bay.

In this case, Gillette wasn't necessarily complacent. The company was making money after all. The mistake Gillette made was assuming it was powerful enough to control progress and therefore didn't need to worry about its competitors. Big mistake. The company's strategic error was to delay developing stainless-steel technology for blades. Eventually, stainless-steel blades did come about, but Gillette's competitors got them first and in so doing grabbed a share of the market.

But Gillette rebounded once it saw the error of its ways. Its management quickly corrected its myopia and moved forward with new products and new marketing techniques. Astute investors who saw the turnaround in progress achieved excellent returns on their money—doubling, tripling—even quadrupling—their investment in a few years.

Interestingly, the American steel industry didn't try to block progress. Steel companies simply didn't seem to care a great deal about it one way or another. No doubt, making lots of money at the time probably dulled their senses. There was mismanagement in all forms, not to mention what many have described as a soft position with labor that led to a string of exceedingly expensive labor contracts. Yet with the world's major market right at its fingertips, the domestic steel industry stood back and watched profits during the 1950s, 1960s, and first half of the 1970s pour into its coffers.

At first glance, there seemed little reason to worry about smoke on the horizon. In contrast, foreign competitors in Japan, South Korea, Taiwan, and even Europe weren't as lax. In rebuilding their steel industries after World War II, they constantly upgraded their plants with the latest and most efficient machinery and methods available, including continuous-cast production, galvanizing lines, and robotics. The investments were made even at the expense of initial profits.

Ultimately, however, the U.S. industry picked up the tab for the investment that foreign companies were making. The smoke that U.S. producers saw on the overseas horizon in the late 1960s and early 1970s turned into a wildfire at home a decade later. Low-priced foreign imports flooded the United States, claiming as much as a quarter of the $40-billion market. With their own market under attack and the prospects for exports extremely limited at best, U.S. steelmakers couldn't compete. Their labor contracts and antiquated factories were a burden they no longer could bear. Losses quickly rolled up into the billions, and hundreds of thousands of workers lost their jobs as dozens of factory towns saw their No. 1 employers close their doors for good.

Too Much of a Good Thing

Complacency is probably the biggest reason foreign companies are able to move so successfully on U.S. markets. Too often, U.S. companies, usually longstanding and extremely secure in their home markets, lack the motivation necessary to keep pace with new consumer demands and production techniques. Some, however, are acutely aware of the ultimate danger—a market changed forever.

At a critical point in its history, Harley-Davidson replaced complacency with a vitality rarely seen in business and industry nowadays. As you may recall, Harley went from near extinction to become a roaring success—all in a decade's time. The company accomplished this in part with government help, successfully promoting both domestic and foreign sales, new labor contracts, more-efficient production facilities, and a change in consumer demand that saw older Americans buying motorcycles.

Yet, in an ironic twist, *Forbes* magazine noted in May 1993 that "Harley-Davidson, the Milwaukee-based motorcycle maker, is suffering from an acute case of success." Ultimately, the boom in business was actually causing problems. Delays of six months or longer in getting bikes to customers became commonplace. Dealers in turn worried that customers would start turning to competitors to meet their needs. A successful turnaround situation had turned into a problem for investors.

Since 1987, however, the company has more than doubled production, though dealers continue to report little if any inventory. But investors nevertheless enjoy the byproduct of the turnaround. Those who bought Harley stock in 1990 when it was selling for $3.38 a share actually saw their investment multiply in value in a remarkably short time. By 1997, for instance, the price per share of Harley reached $53. That's an increase in price of...well, figure it yourself.

Getting Started

As seen, saving a company on the edge of bankruptcy or pumping life into a corporation that is barely holding its own requires two fundamental things: (1) big moves (new leaders, visions, and broad strategies) and (2) the ability to put it all into place through competent management. One without the other is a sure recipe for disaster.

However, the big moves have to be in place before even the best-laid plans can be activated and begin chipping away the corporate rot. And that usually begins with new managers. As mentioned earlier, changing the top banana has always been a strategy for businesses looking to rebound. But the trend seems to be growing. Companies increasingly are looking outside their executive offices to find their new leader. In fact, a study by Michigan State University reported that of the Fortune 500 companies that recently changed CEOs, 31 percent secured their replacements from outside the company. That's the highest level since the school started keeping track in 1949.

Not all the outsiders succeed, of course. Some fail to comprehend the inherent strengths and culture of their new homes, making it extremely difficult to change a company for the better. Nonetheless, corporations are likely to continue looking outside their own ranks for help. Outsiders are simply more detached, which is a handy skill for any executive charged with turning a company around.

Lee Iacocca is perhaps a perfect example of the hired gun

brought in to save a company. A fixture at Ford for more than
a decade, Iacocca found himself out of work when he was fired
by Henry Ford II in 1978. What was open to him, however,
was a deeply crippled Chrysler. The story is well-worn. Within
a few years, Iacocca was able to resurrect the carmaker, seeking and getting federal-government loan guarantees, launch-
ing a $15-billion product-development line, and creating a
profit. In the process he became a legend to investors and the
general public alike.

Iacocca was able to accomplish this turnaround for two
reasons, points out Robert Heller. He took decisive action with
the support of his board (that is, $15 billion on a development
program), and he created a "cult of personality," in this case
his own. "The chairman himself was the Unique Selling
Proposition, the reason for buying a Chrysler rather than a
Ford or Chevrolet," Heller explains. "Appearing incessantly in
Chrysler commercials, Iacocca became a megastar; there was
serious talk of running him for President. And Chrysler was
saved, making the boss indecently rich in the process."

Iacocca went beyond just touting cars. He was able to
secure the attention of his staff. With annual losses in the billions, almost $4 billion in underfunded pension liabilities,
loads of debt, and a product line that just wasn't selling,
Iacocca was able to harness his company's resources. He did it
by hammering home the point that the company was not guaranteed to survive at any cost. "If you're not scared [by the condition of this company]," he reportedly told his senior managers at one critical point, "you're too stupid to work here."

Thomas Graham also knows about turning companies
around. During the toughest and most depressed time for the
steel industry, Graham ran U.S. Steel, J & L Steel, and
Washington Steel. His most-recent challenge was to bring
Armco Steel Co. back from the grave. One of the country's
largest integrated steel producers, Armco was also one of the
sickest. Special charges and unproductive operations in the
early 1990s were pushing losses to the hundreds of millions of
dollars a year. And the company seemed unable to save itself.
Worse, it almost seemed as if it were spinning out of control.

Armco responded by calling on the industry's fireman.
What Graham found when he arrived was a company that

wasn't so much in turmoil as it was seemingly resigned to suffer a gradual death. The management was so racked with doubt, Graham noted when he arrived, "that they would have taken direction from a street person. They'd lost their self-confidence and their zeal, and had become demoralized."

Only someone from the outside could have handled the situation. Graham, of course, had a plan in mind for restructuring the company. That plan called for layoffs, plants closures, investments, and more aggressive marketing. But he first had to lead. He didn't worry about creating a vision. Instead he offered a simple yet demanding directive: "Do Better!" And the company did do better. Much better. But it took more time than Graham had hoped. By 1996, the turnaround still was not complete, but all the proper ingredients were there, and time seemed to be on the side of the company.

The Components of a Turnaround Plan

Turnaround endeavors like that of Armco require all sorts of combinations. There are the general components, such as vision, leadership, determination, and flexibility. They're pretty much in all efforts. Yet they alone can't turn around a company unless they're matched with specific solutions that attack core problems. This may even mean a company's working with national leaders to resolve international trade issues or beating the halls of Congress in search of some legislative relief. These solutions are as varied as the problems they're designed to attack. And they're found in all sorts of locations: on a computer printout, a factory floor, or even a negotiating table.

Regardless of what's being applied, make sure the goal of the company you're considering is to fix what's wrong. The goal simply can't be to plug a leak for a week, month, or year. The true remedy lies in taking the company beyond a quick and flawed fix. Ultimately, when the solution is applied, whether it involves labor, plant, or financing problems, the company can't be satisfied with just not hurting. The solution means a transformation that takes a drawback and makes it an asset.

The required action depends on what's being repaired so

that the outcome is greater efficiency, higher production, lower financing costs, or more enthusiasm and creativity. What is constant in these specific solutions is that successful companies aggressively and creatively attack their problems— taking no half-measures even if it means attacking several of them at once.

Marketplace Knowledge

Inefficient and outdated plants, costly labor pacts, slow product development, tight financial constraints, poor distribution systems—these are just some of the reasons that a company can find itself in deep trouble. Yet the most efficient plants, competitive labor costs, and slickest distribution systems can only take a company so far if it is still basically out of touch with the market.

Investors in Ford Motor Co. discovered this in the early 1980s, when newly appointed Chairman Philip Caldwell took over from Henry Ford II, who was stepping down after 34 years at the helm. At the time, Ford was in a crisis that had, as mentioned earlier, brought the carmaker to the verge of total collapse. "Ford's close brush with extinction in the early 1980s was partly obscured from public knowledge because of the similar life-and-death struggle at Chrysler, which got all the headlines," Alton F. Doody and Ron Bingaham wrote in *Reinventing the Wheel*.

By declaring that "Quality is Job One," Ford publicly acknowledged that "growing numbers of Americans were switching to foreign-made cars, no longer so much because of price, or even for the sake of fuel efficiency, but increasingly and decidedly because of the superior overall quality," Doody and Bingaham report.

Detroit had run into a problem because of its definition of quality. In the past, Doody and Bingaham explain, that quality to a Detroit carmaker meant: high horse-powered engines, a big body, a plush interior, and "lots of chrome." The essential quality problem Detroit faced was that it thought of cars in terms of the strength of individual components.

Donald Petersen, chief financial officer, was put in charge of Ford's drive for quality and immediately realized that he had to take the "Quality is Job One" approach and expand on it. His goal was to make Ford "accepted as the manufacturer of the world's best-quality products...." He explained that it wasn't just the financial difficulties of the early 1980s that were driving this new approach. "We were experiencing a free-fall in market share. The nature of the automotive industry is cyclical, and we had suffered through bad times in the past. But this time we were not only losing large sums of money, our products were being rejected by customers."

Even before Ford knew exactly what it wanted to give its customers, the company knew it had to downsize its product line drastically. That was a difficult task, because, as Robert L. Shook points out in his book entitled *Turnaround*, "More than 50 years had passed since Ford was the trendsetter." Until the near catastrophe of the early 1980s, Ford had basically let General Motors lead the way in introducing radical designs, although even GM was certainly not breaking lots of new ground in that regard. Ford, as Petersen would later point out, had to come up with "a better way to listen to the customer, because what we were doing just wasn't working."

The carmaker turned to Martin Goldfarb, a Toronto consultant, who studied small groups of individuals to determine what Ford was doing right and what the company was doing wrong. Goldfarb took the unique approach. He not only analyzed how customers viewed Ford's message, but also what they thought about Ford's cars as they were being developed. This gave Ford a better chance of getting the car as defect-free as possible before it went into full production.

Goldfarb did this by asking drivers what they thought about comparable GM and foreign models. The approach used "pulse" groups, which are often made up of individuals, such as architects, designers, interior decorators, or others who might take a greater interest in how a car is made and what it has to offer.

The company also decided it was time to produce softer, more aerodynamically designed cars that are not only more gas efficient, but also more attractive than the big boxey cars of Detroit's past. The attempt, in 1983, first yielded the new Thunderbirds and Mercury Cougars, which "bore little outward resemblance to their popular predecessors." Next came the Ford Tempo, Mercury Topaz, and the Lincoln Continental Mark VII. With the public's acceptance of these cars, Ford had finally broken from its past.

The next break, however, was even greater, with a $5.1-billion investment to develop a totally new line of cars from the drawing room to the showrooms. The commitment, which also included $2 billion to modernize plants and upgrade other lines, resulted in the production of the Taurus and the Sable. Taurus would reflect what the Ford executives had learned, although the gamble was significant. Doody and Bingaham note that the $5.1-billion investment represented half of the company's net worth.

Many investors saw this move as an either/or situation. Either spend and remain competitive by offering models the public wanted, or get out of the car business altogether. How successful was Ford? Very. The Taurus paid off huge dividends. It was, after all, a car built for car owners rather than car designers.

...And Not Just the Big Boys

So far, we've covered some of the world's largest companies. But make no mistake: Small companies are big business. They account for a surprisingly large amount of the nation's manufacturing muscle and employment base. Unfortunately, their significance doesn't make them immune when it comes to problems. From an investor standpoint, there is little difference between the troubles facing big and small companies. They can all be plagued by poor management, changes in the market, increased competition, and financing difficulties.

In many respects, a company's size doesn't change the general approach to confronting its problems. All companies need strong leadership, vision, a game plan, and the will to carry it through to its conclusion. Despite the similarities, however, differences do exist between the big and the small. Small companies face their own set of distinct challenges, which require their own set of specific responses and remedies. Consider just a few:

By their nature, most small companies obviously don't have the resources of a large company. In good times or bad, a small company with annual sales of no more than $5 million isn't going to have the same research and development funds as does a big multinational concern. Nor will it have the same marketing reach, the depth of personnel, or the product diversity—not to mention the name recognition.

So because small companies lack the manufacturing muscle of their larger counterparts, they are at a disadvantage in negotiating lower raw-material purchasing costs, reducing unit manufacturing costs, and controlling inventory expenses. And the differences don't end on the factory floor. As a result of the limitations that small businesses face, both in terms of resources and production, banks are often reluctant to extend loans to them. Consequently, financing and credit lines, essential for survival and expansion, are usually difficult for these companies to secure. And when money is available, it is rarely provided at the same advantageous rates given to larger companies.

Ironically, crises often come to small companies just as they are growing successful. No one is arguing that companies should avoid being successful, but problems seem to surface as something akin to growing pains. What's particularly dangerous is that these pains don't go away naturally as a business matures. In fact, if left untreated, they can devastate a company—and its investors.

One reason small firms face problems is that they are often started by entrepreneurs who have good ideas, but who may not necessarily be good managers. Consultant Michael Gerber described this phenomenon as a "technician suffering from an entrepreneurial seizure." Simply put: "Too many people go into business believing that if they can do the work, they can successfully run a business that does the work." Ultimately, they cannot always do it.

Usually, however, managerial faults don't show up until the business begins to expand and the staff or structure can no longer meet the market's rising demands. Gerber notes some of the signs of trouble that investors can look for: "Jobs don't get delivered on time. Costs expand disproportionately to the actual time spend on the job. The company is plagued with any manner and form of chaotic events." The immediate response to this type of disintegration is to put all the key managers together and "pull the company apart," examining the faults and trying to restructure the operations to meet the changing needs.

Fortunately, investing in a small business isn't all bad news. Small companies have advantages that they can bring into play when there's a need to turn things around. The biggest advantage is that their size virtually guarantees that their operations are compact and less bureaucratic. That means fewer people at all levels and decisions that can be reached more quickly.

Such lean management also means that these companies are usually more flexible. They are quicker to respond and more willing to try new approaches to their problems. Moreover, the size of a company means that if success comes, the rewards are generally going to be greater for everyone involved, including investors. That helps keep morale high, the staff motivated, and investors happy. The best companies learn how to turn these factors to their advantage. Obviously, a lean management structure can sometimes hurt. One problem is that a company may become too dependent on a few key individuals. If one of them leaves, finding a replacement may be too much of a hurdle to clear.

The company's founder can also be detrimental to a company's health if he or she refuses to delegate decisions to subordinates. Carey Stacy, founder and president of Dialogos International Corp., a foreign-language services company based in Raleigh, N.C., discovered this fact as her company's business was starting to boom. Along with growth, Stacy found herself increasingly on the road. And that actually created problems, because in her absence decisions began to accumulate on her desk and opportunities began to slip away. Stacy acted quickly and started delegating authority to her staff. She recalls, "When I let go, we began to get jobs that we had lost before when they were piled up on my desk waiting for me to make a decision."

Another danger for small companies is the assumption that they don't need sophisticated planning. Ann Blakely, president of Earth Resources Corp., an environmental consulting and contracting firm in Ocoee, Fla., realized that she had to get a better feel for pending trends in order to keep her business running smoothly. Forecasting tools and planning sessions had to be developed to help her better prepare for upcoming slow and busy periods. Her first step was to set up weekly planning meetings with all departments.

Blakely notes, "Everything that exceeds a certain probability goes into the forecast log." And *Nation's Business* magazine reported that "by doing a 'quick and dirty' evaluation weekly and a full forecast model twice a month, Blakely can see—and correct—potential problems before they manifest themselves as poor service to the client."

Small companies may be able to choose their markets, but they can't choose their competitors. Eventually, they will come up against big companies that have more resources and muscle. Sometimes, smaller companies can compete effectively by clinging "tight" to their customers and keeping a close eye on quality and service. Unfortunately, that's not always the case.

Yet, small companies can get around the disadvantages of being small, sometimes by temporarily teaming with other small companies to develop a single product. PMF Industries of Williamsport, Pa., a producer of stainless-steel and heat-treatment products, took this tack in its efforts to compete for a German company's contract to manufacture microwave sterilizers (microclaves) that handle biomedical waste. PMF simply realized that while it had real expertise in developing all the related stainless-steel products, it lacked the skills needed to produce the circuit boards and other parts.

As a result, PMF joined with two other Pennsylvania companies, JPM Co. of Lewisburg and LSI Controls of Waynesboro, to bid for the manufacturing license. By combining to form a consortium, they all bring specific expertise to the products, thus making them more than simply competitive with larger concerns. Although the German firm has yet to grant anyone a license for its microclave, the actions by PMF and its other partners reflect a growing trend among small businesses to unite on specific projects, allowing them to compete more effectively in their own fields or expand into new ones.

Smaller companies, particularly manufacturers, are also forming cooperatives in response to shifts in demand from their traditional customers. Many of them, such as carmakers, are using fewer suppliers because they can demand better prices and higher quality. This has left smaller manufacturers scrambling to meet these new demands.

Opportunities Extend Overseas

For companies big and small—and in between—the key to a company's successful turnaround may lie overseas. If the company you're considering is not yet international in nature, then it's something it should explore. You don't know what it takes for a company to go international? Tom Peters' book *Thriving on Chaos* offers some pointers for the uninformed, the dubious, and the hesitant:

1. "Every $2-million firm, in service or manufacturing, has international potential." It should start thinking about it early. A company that is $25-million or larger and not doing 25 percent of its business overseas, and at least a bit in Japan, is avoiding today's realities and opportunities, and risking being out of touch in general.

2. "If [the company] is not prepared to spend six weeks a year overseas," there is no point in even starting. The first proposed product or service should be substantially tailored to meet the foreign market's needs. Packaging, colors, instruction manual, vagaries of distribution, let alone basic function are critical in that regard. Otherwise, the company is heading for a discouraging setback.

No Easy Solutions

Successful turnarounds are rarely simple. They are almost never merely a matter of cutting a few hundred workers, adjusting prices, or shutting down an antiquated factory. Companies usually get a kick-start as a byproduct of a multi-faceted strategy that carefully cuts across a whole range of business operations. Almost every company that has faced a loss—be it for a single quarter or a few years—has tried to engineer these across-the-board turnarounds. The success of their efforts varies. There are, however, some notable exceptions we have covered, such as Ford. These companies have all experienced great highs and some pretty frightening lows. What separates them from other companies isn't their desire to engineer a rebound, but the speed, degree, and complexity of the plans they put into place.

Don't feel despondent if the company you feel is turning things around continues to go through tough times. Consider this instead: Ronald Paul and James Taylor, in *The 101 Best-Performing Companies in America*, note that even some of the better-managed companies have had down years. Their findings may provide you some solace—and keep you in the right direction when your investment experiences tough times: "While it is usually impossible to tell with 100-percent accuracy from outside an organization exactly what has transpired within, some reasonably informed analysis suggests that the causes of these "down" years fall into six categories." Those categories are:

1. "The one-time event."

2. "The strong-dollar effect."

3. "Expansion/growth/R&D financing."

4. "Down markets."

5. "Fierce competition."

6. "Newly deregulated businesses."

Paul and Taylor advise: Regardless of the reason, the main goal of a company during lean years should be to limit the lows and raise the highs.

Image Is Almost Everything

A product's reputation is almost as important as its actual quality. After all, whether the customer is a corporation interested in buying billions of dollars in computers or airplanes or whether the consumer is a 12-year-old contemplating which video game to buy, the company's decision is often based on what the buyer thinks of a product. Obviously, reputations don't always equate with reality. Yet, reputation and reality are never far apart for long. Most retailers of all types are keenly aware of this—or at least the successful ones are—and they are the ones that can turn things around when times for them are tough. Such companies also know that it is often a lot tougher building a product's reputation than it is retaining it or returning it to public favor. Consider the mountain that American automakers had to overcome when they lost their edge to the Japanese; they succeeded in part because their name was established—though slightly tainted—among the consumers.

Nowhere is this fact more apparent than in the reputation-conscious fashion industry. Company officials at both AnnTaylor Stores and Liz Claiborne became painfully aware of reputation during the last few years as their profits tumbled and, in the case of AnnTaylor, disappeared altogether. Rebuilding their reputations and winning back customers became a wide-ranging effort that had to go far beyond marketing and advertising.

Liz Claiborne Inc., with sales in excess of $2 billion, is the country's largest maker of women's apparel. Yet, that popularity didn't stop a steep slide in profits in 1992. Finding answers for the decline isn't easy. Certainly observers of Claiborne's descent point to its 1980s' strategy of calling for expansion into all sorts of clothing lines: petite, full-figured, and men's. That move took it beyond its core business of providing stylish clothes for working women.

While there may be nothing wrong with a push in new directions, the company probably expanded too fast. And the move was somewhat half-hearted. There simply wasn't enough emphasis on its new products. They became a distraction, which drew company officials away from paying enough attention to its existing lines. What happened next? All the lines—formal, casual, and sportswear—lost their individual distinction.

Chairman Jerome Chazen decided to tackle the problem on several fronts. He planned to strengthen the image of the company's various lines, target specific markets, and improve quality. First, he reorganized the lines, making sure products didn't overlap. "It's up to us to make sure she [the consumer] sees the distinction and value in each brand," he explained. To do this, Chazen also brought in new managers to run the beleaguered divisions and pump up the styles. In line with rebuilding the customer base, Chazen also decided to hold prices basically in line across the board.

The company hoped to expand the market for some of its lower-priced lines by moving into Sears, J.C. Penney, and Montgomery Ward. Liz Claiborne also revamped its men's apparel by not only introducing a different range of styles, but also improving the quality of the products offered. In the past, company officials acknowledged that mediocre quality had pushed potential buyers away.

The results for investors who jumped onto the Liz Claiborne bandwagon early were impressive. From a price per share of about $15 in 1994, the company's stock rose to $48 a share in 1997.

At AnnTaylor, the need to rebuild was even greater. The company did rather well through the 1980s by positioning itself as a brand of women's clothes that were stylish, yet affordable. For a decade the company was closely in touch with its customers.

That changed markedly in the late 1980s after the chain was bought by Joseph Brooks and Merrill Lynch. As chief executive officer, Brooks decided that despite the company's ongoing success, he needed to start trimming costs. First, he exchanged the line's traditional materials of silk, linen, and wool with cheaper synthetics.

He also reportedly began squeezing suppliers by noting that he wanted to cut manufacturing costs by 25 percent. The suppliers responded. But they noted the reduction came at a cost. They simply could not turn over the same type of quality products for less money.

In an effort to reach a wider market, Brooks also decided to increase the chain's retail outlets from 139 to 200. The reaction was purely negative. The new lines with cheaper materials and lower quality no longer appealed to AnnTaylor's traditional customers, and the company didn't draw significant numbers of new clients.

The consequence was a nose-dive in sales and profits. By 1991, the company lost $15.8 million on $438 million in sales.

The board responded by replacing Brooks with Frame Kasaks, who had run the company in the early 1980s. She began to immediately reverse Brooks' strategy. It was almost as if her approach was to reverse everything Brooks had done.

Kasaks decided to upgrade the materials used in the clothes and start weaning away suppliers who couldn't deliver the quality she demanded. She banned, for example, companies that worked with silk in warm climates if their factories weren't air conditioned. Humidity, she noted, tended to make silk pucker, which was not acceptable. Serving as something of an one-person quality-control team, Kasaks began wearing AnnTaylor outfits almost exclusively to personally check out their durability and styling.

Information analysis also became a priority. As a result, in an effort to get closer to the market, Kasaks began to closely monitor chainwide sales on a weekly basis. By meeting with sales managers regularly, Kasaks and her senior managers were able to identify fast-moving items that needed to be pushed into the stores, while also being able to discover which outfits had sluggish sales and could be marked down to move them out more quickly.

The ability to monitor sales trends closely has provided an added bonus. It has allowed AnnTaylor to trim prices by about 15 percent, creating an additional lure to customers. The results came quickly. By 1992 the company was again in the black, recording a $7-million profit on $473 million in sales, which reflected a 7.4-percent increase from the previous year. Best of all for investors, stock values started to rise. In fact, at the start of 1996, the price of AnnTaylor stock was at about $9 a share; by June, that price had more than doubled, to $21 a share and has since reached $25 a share.

Meeting the Challenges

For the last decade, Johnson Controls and its investors have faced the type of challenges most experts would consider the components of a disaster. Johnson Controls is a diversified company holding leading positions in industries that were obviously more than just mature. Some investors might consider them decrepit. After all, not many groups are in car batteries, car seats, heating and cooling systems for offices and schools, and plastic beverage bottles. In many cases, these industries have received a double body blow in the last decade, suffering from the national recession that sharply reduced demand.

Beyond that, however, many of these activities were tied to industries that were in a decline that went well past recessions. For example, retail prices for car batteries remained stagnant for a decade, domestic car production suffered throughout the 1980s and early 1990s, general construction has been cyclical at best, and a natural limitation of materials has kept the market for plastic beverage containers constrained for decades.

Despite this, Johnson Controls has thrived. And it has done so by doing just the opposite of what many business strategists would have suggested. Company officials have been able to rebuild profits, having them reach record levels in the early 1990s by making their markets work. Despite the obvious handicaps, the company did this by gaining market share through acquisitions, increasing efficiency, and pushing new technologies that are providing breakthroughs in long-dormant industries.

One example of Johnson's strategy can be seen in its heating-and-cooling-system business. A few years ago the company decided to expand its position by buying Pan Am's World Services Division for about $170 million. The purchase reveals a shrewd and well-thought-out strategy, allowing Johnson Controls to move from just building heating and cooling systems to also servicing them in new and existing buildings. That has given Johnson Controls a powerful marketing position by permitting it to offer a money-saving package to consumers looking for customized system and operational services.

In the car-seat sector, Johnson Controls has been able to expand its business in two ways. It purchased Europe's leading seat manufacturer in 1989, gambling that European carmakers would follow their U.S. counterparts in increasingly outsourcing their production. That gamble worked. But even in the United States, Johnson was able to pump up profits by keeping costs in line and offering carmakers a unique bargain.

As one reported, "Johnson is able to completely integrate the design, development, and manufacture of seats." All the car-maker had to do was install them.

Of course, it helped that Johnson keeps its prices in check and its products attractive. The company accomplishes this through a fierce battle to maintain quality and improve efficiency, allowing profit margins to expand without raising prices.

The company has even managed to rebuild the car-battery business, perhaps the toughest challenge facing the group. To accomplish the feat, Johnson Controls cut the manufacturing time for lead-acid batteries by 40 percent. The savings recouped from trimming the manufacturing time and costs helped the company boost profits by 12 percent despite a drop in sales. In something of a slight divergence from its typical strategy, Johnson Controls is also seeking to move into something of a new market for batteries. The common strain with past actions, however, is that it hopes to use technology as a bridge. In this case, Johnson Controls has teamed up with W.R. Grace to develop a battery for electric cars, a market with enormous potential.

The company was able to again expand one of its key businesses, plastic beverage containers, by putting new technologies into action. In this case, it was able to develop a container that could handle fluids that are poured hot into bottles. In the past, glass held sole domain over this market because plastic containers would shrivel upon contact with a hot fluid. By finding a plastic that could take the heat, Johnson Controls significantly boosted its customer base.

The progress at Johnson Controls didn't come free of charge. Millions had be invested in research and technology, which put pressure on profits. It was a pressure that came in the late 1980s, when the company's mature markets seemed particularly weak. Yet Johnson Controls' long-term vision helped restore and recharge the operations. In fact, with the economy still soft in the early 1990s, Johnson Controls was moving to double-digit growth in sales and profits while other companies in stronger markets were being battered—an amazing achievement. Best of all for investors, the stock price was matching the remarkable turnaround of the company: from

$17.13 per share in 1990 to $75.13 in 1996.

Bleak Histories

Not all companies survive lean times. Some just shut down under the weight of losses, a shrinking market, high overhead, and the lack of will to keep fighting. Others have an almost perverse capacity to drag on endlessly, rolling up millions— even billions—of dollars in losses. Regardless of the problems a company faces, Corporate America rarely sees a member die without a fight. CEOs, chairmen, and presidents are forever devising turnaround strategies to resurrect their troubled companies.

Yet just trying doesn't guarantee success. The country's industrial landscape is littered with fallen companies that boasted all sorts of plans to cut losses, increase efficiency, improve quality, and restore health. Failure and success is often fickle. Sometimes luck plays a part, although no company can plan on unexpected windfalls. A company's future can also hinge on matters well beyond its control, as noted previously. Of course, the most successful companies—and those that rebound well—seem to have the innate or even systematic ability to not only respond to changes in the market, but also anticipate them.

Successful strategies also meet the very specific needs of a company. This means more than attacking core problems. It goes to developing a plan that uses a company's physical and financial resources without overextending them. It makes no sense, as Thomas Graham at Armco maintains, to pump millions of dollars into investments if the financial burden is too great for the company to bear.

The companies that falter generally fail to realize this. They often have good ideas, but they don't know how to apply them properly. There is, however, one benefit that can come out of failure. It can provide investors with an insight into why companies don't make it, even when those companies are trying desperately to succeed.

That Kodak Moment

By the end of the 1980s it became clear that Eastman Kodak was in deep trouble. Problems were rife, and many of them were self-inflicted. The company had divested out of control during the 1980s, overpaid for many of its purchases, and was strapped with an enormous debt burden. Even the company's core businesses, film and photography, were under threat from foreign producers, which were chipping away at Kodak's once seemingly invincible market share in the United States. These new competitors weren't limiting their attacks to this country; they were also pushing into foreign markets well ahead of Kodak.

Kodak's troubles, however, seemed to go much deeper. Although one of the great American industrial concerns, it had apparently lost its focus, its direction, its vision. Many observers and stockholders were complaining that neither the board nor management really knew what to do about the company's dilemmas or how to shape the future. The best the board seemed to be able to do was rotate executives. Yet all too often these new managers seemed to almost immediately isolate themselves after taking over, ultimately losing touch with the market and the company.

As one visitor of the company noted, executives work in an unhealthy isolation. "You get to the top of that building and there's only a handful of offices per floor. Unless they deliver the paycheck, you could die there and I don't think anyone would know." That certainly isn't the description of a company fighting to right itself. In fact, the best that Kodak seemed able to do was come up with herky-jerky plans and changes that would set the company moving in one direction, then, only a few months later, would send it in a different one.

Consider that in the past decade Kodak has launched five restructuring plans. With that type of planning, the best the company can hope for is to restructure, restructure, and restructure. Without a clear plan and the fortitude to carry it out, company officials were doing little more than just putting temporary patches on rupturing problems.

In fairness, the company's initial instincts that the market was changing were correct. In response, it moved to push into new markets. Its core film and camera business had made the company a giant, yet even a decade ago, it was obvious these industries were mature at best and faced with limited growth.

Nevertheless, rather than relying on plans to trim its core businesses, making them more efficient and the profit margins greater, Kodak went on a buying spree in the 1980s that pushed it into pharmaceuticals, electronics, chemicals, and copiers. Unfortunately, its diversification became more of a burden than a benefit as the decade wore on. In 1988, for example, the company paid $5.1 billion for Sterling Drugs, maker of Bayer aspirin. While the move into pharmaceuticals may have had merit in general, the price paid for Sterling was probably too high.

As part of this same plan, Kodak also tried investing in a promising field of technology that involves translating images into a language that computers can read and transmit electronically. That industry has great potential, but critics of Kodak argue that the company spent billions on R&D and purchases that were neither well-coordinated nor profitable.

In fact, along with the company's Sterling purchase, Kodak raised the company's debt to close to $10 billion. This type of burden, coupled with pressure to restructure, pushed the company heavily into the red in 1992 (a $1-billion loss) and 1993 ($1.5 billion in losses).

The company's plans suffered further damage through personnel disruptions, which undermined confidence both within and outside the company. In 1992, for example, then CEO Kay Whitmore brought in Christopher Steffen as chief financial officer. The move had the full support of the board, as Steffen was viewed as the perfect counterbalance to Whitmore. Coming from Honeywell, Steffen was seen as having both the vision and will to begin cutting the fat at Kodak and thereby righting the ship. His reputation was so powerful that within days of his arrival, Kodak share prices skyrocketed.

Yet Steffen's arrival soon became a huge embarrassment for the company. Within three months, Steffen walked out on Kodak, stunning Whitmore, the board, and the investment community. The company's share price plunged, and again Kodak was viewed as being in utter confusion. (While Steffen and Kodak officials wouldn't comment publicly on his departure, Steffen apparently left because the board was reluctant to endorse his plans to reduce debt by selling off assets, such as Sterling Drugs.) Again, rumors surfaced that the company lacked the resolve to effectively and decisively address its problems.

Within the year, the board fired Whitmore, bringing in George Fisher, formerly of Motorola. Fisher has brought along ideas that may help the company. But controversy has accompanied him, too. For example, some of his new managers have begun denting the company's debt load. And in an attempt to confront low-priced competitors that have been grabbing U.S. market share, Kodak has cut prices on its premium film and is now offering a low-priced alternative. Beyond this, the company appears ready to push further into overseas markets.

Like his predecessors, however, Fisher is also promising substantial growth by working to expand some of Kodak's more exotic holdings. Opponents claim that may just be another costly lark. They argue that the company should concentrate instead on expanding the film business in the United States and abroad, pumping up margins there through greater efficiency and dumping a lot of the company's ill-made purchases.

It is still too early to gauge Fisher's ultimate success. But the company, at least during the first year of his tenure, is holding the line and avoiding the trap of the past. Fisher is giving his plan the time to work. And for investors, their patience and perspicacity have been rewarded. From a low of about $40 in 1994, the price per share of Kodak stock moved up briskly to more than $94 more recently.

The Xerox Turnaround Story

When David T. Kearns took over as president of Xerox in 1977, he probably thought his good fortune was something of a dream come true. After all, Kearns had always yearned to run a major American company, and at the time he took over Xerox, it was seemingly one of the tops in the country.

Having started his career at IBM, another American giant, Kearns had been hired away in 1971 by Xerox. With the resignation of Archie McCardell, who left Xerox to head

International Harvester, Kearns was offered the presidency. His joy was short-lived. He soon realized something was terribly wrong at Xerox. While still profitable, the market was rapidly changing, and Xerox wasn't keeping pace.

"When I took over as president, I clearly did not understand the depth of the problems that plagued Xerox. It was perfectly plain that the company suffered from a confluence of problems, but I simply didn't appreciate their severity," he explained in his book, *Prophets in the Dark*. "They were slowly choking the life out of the company, just as surely as if an assailant's hands were around our throat. It would be awhile before I finally came to realize this."

The problems were everywhere—and growing in size and number. One of the biggest was Xerox's growth. The company had expanded so far and fast that it was somewhat out of control. Outside executives were brought in from the likes of Ford Motor Co. to provide some structure. In many respects, they did. Yet they also brought some problems. Their excessive control and dependence on analysis alienated many of the old-line Xerox employees, promoting internal conflicts, stifling creativity, and hindering productivity.

There were other problems: After years of virtually owning the photocopier industry, Xerox was beginning to feel the heat of competition. Domestic companies were suing to gain access to Xerox's technology. Foreign sources, particularly the Japanese, were gearing up to target Xerox's domestic market. In fact, even the company's long-standing philosophy of constantly "driving for growth" had actually begun to backfire. The company was pushing too hard to introduce and sell machines without spending enough time on quality and service. Customers were beginning to take notice.

But the major problem that afflicted the company was the contact it had lost with its customers. Moreover, the pricing of its products did not relate to quality. Several lawsuits were damaging, but the true challenges lay not in the courtroom, but in the growing competition from Japan. Yet Xerox's top management did not recognize the sources of the company's problems, but was instead drifting in a directionless sea of lethargy.

These problems didn't come about all at once. Kearns

points out that the problems that ripped Xerox apart in the 1970s and 1980s had their roots deep in the company's past: "It's often that people and institutions become prisoners of their pasts, and, in looking back, much of what happened to Xerox during the years I was there was dictated by what Xerox had once been. Misapprehensions about the past have a way of determining the future. As Xerox's size and reach swelled to almost unimaginable proportions, its former ways continued to tug at it."

Xerox also became involved in a series of lawsuits and countersuits from all sorts of companies claiming antitrust violations. The suits were eventually settled both in and out of court. Xerox even struck an agreement with the Federal Trade Commission by agreeing to give up its patent protection in return for licensing arrangements. The cat was out of the bag, however. In line with this, the FTC made Xerox also license the Japanese.

"Though it was not yet evident to us, something was going on over in Japan that was destined to have a profound impact on our future. Xerox was being identified as a 'targeted' company. That meant that the Japanese had decided that the copier business was an industry extremely important to Japan, and they were determined to marshall their collective resources to launch an all-out offensive against Xerox," Kearns observes.

That meant many things. Japanese producers stayed close to both their market and product. They were concerned with giving customers what they wanted and needed without sacrificing quality. At the same time, they also made lots of headway in keeping production costs down.

Xerox's obsession with "going for growth" was also laying the foundation for a disaster. Kearns points out that with a wonderful product, patent protection, and little competition, it was not surprising that Xerox was able to grow at amazing rates, producing profit after profit after profit. Managers, in fact, started assuming that the company's success was a result of their skills rather than the favorable circumstances.

How bad would it get? In 1970 Xerox held 95 percent of the American copier-installation market. By 1976 the number had slipped to 80 percent—still a commanding position. A little more than a decade later, the company's share had dropped to 13 percent, and a few years later it would fall to a low of 12 percent. The Japanese were largely responsible. While still profitable, Xerox's earnings were also taking a beating, although the bashing would be somewhat delayed. In 1981, in fact, the company recorded an operating profit of $1.5 billion, the best to date. A year later, however, profits would fall to $614 million.

Xerox's Solutions

Despite all the problems in marketing, pricing, production, quality, and customer service, Xerox officials had come to the conclusion that their core problem lay in their own arrogance. Even with all the evidence to the contrary from both home and abroad, Xerox employees simply believed they were the best at what they did. This fatal flaw, bred out of years of rising sales, undercut the intellectual and practical aggressiveness that Xerox needed to compete.

"Faced with this extremely disconcerting news, we conceived the idea of business effectiveness, a strategy to improve the basic competitiveness of the company," Kearns explains. "It embraced two underpinning thoughts: employee involvement and benchmarking."

While there would be lots of "hard remedies" taken that involved layoffs and plant closures, Xerox was careful to steer the company away from sheer cost-cutting of that type. The company didn't want cost-cutting to dominate the thinking, so it chose business effectiveness to describe its efforts.

(With regard to layoffs, Xerox has gained support in its policy from Geary A. Rummler, a specialist in reengineering and a partner at Rummler-Brach Group. Rummler maintains in a recent *Fortune* magazine article that layoffs are, in fact, "an easy way out for CEOs." He adds that calls for layoffs as the central point of a reorganization plan indicate management failure: "It is an admission that senior management (which initially overhired) has really screwed up. It shouldn't be a badge of honor."

The ultimate rescue plan would take time to evolve, but Xerox was now at least pointed in the right direction.

Employee involvement, which would later grow into a completely new and broader concept, received a big boost when workers at a Xerox wire-harness plant in Webster, N.Y., challenged Kearns to let them come up with a cost-cutting plan at the plant rather than face its shutdown. Kearns bought the idea and confirmed that employee involvement was for real.

To meet the high expectations top management knew were necessary, a new management process, attitude, and environment was required. That was difficult. Quality was discussed constantly in business, but the concept was nebulous. Often, managers thought that Xerox's initial efforts to define and develop a quality-conscious environment was a "top-management fantasy." To help move the matter along, Kearns appointed an 11-member committee to explore the issue.

In the meantime, Kearns made another strategic decision: "I realized that something else short-term had to be done to prop up the company. The chilly truth was that it was unlikely that the woes of the copier business were going to vanish anytime soon."

As a result, Xerox would again diversify to find a reliable source of profits and prop up the company while its new strategy was put into place. That decision led to the purchase of Crum & Forster, a casualty-insurance company, for $1.6 billion. This was the start of Xerox's financial-services group. The company also instituted massive layoffs of tens of thousands of workers and a broad restructuring that broke Xerox down into strategic business units.

The implementation of a quality-committed company wasn't expected to happen overnight. In fact, it was likely to be a five-year process, running from 1983-1987. Yet even with all the work, Xerox didn't come close to matching the timetable. Part of the problem lay in the faulty leadership chosen to head the critical transition team. Nonetheless, the company was moving forward on a number of fronts. Even the earlier efforts to improve business efficiency had begun to pay off, and with the introduction of the 10 Series copier line, Xerox was again putting itself in position to grow in the market instead of retreat.

The elements of a successful turnaround were in fact in place. As 1983 approached, Kearns felt the company needed some practical targets to hit. Profits had been running at a 7.5-percent return on assets. The target was 15 percent by 1988. Market share was to be significantly boosted, and customer satisfaction had to be raised.

Even with all the groundwork in place, the task was still enormous. At least four years were needed to retrain the company's 100,000 employees. Senior management had to be retrained first and with such thoroughness that the program would filter down through all the ranks. For if managers were not committed and familiar with the process, the workers below them would automatically revert to their old habits.

Improvements were visible everywhere. By 1990, however, Xerox's gains were being seen in real numbers. Revenues for the core copier business jumped from $8.7 billion in 1984 to $13.6 billion in 1990. Income nearly doubled, from $348 million to $599 million. Return on assets also grew, from 9 percent in 1987 to 10 percent in 1988 and to 12 percent in 1989. By 1990 the company was pushing its ROA target of 15 percent. Market share was also on the rise, having increased 7 percent to 19 percent of the overall market for installed copiers. Customer satisfaction rose by more than a third in the last four years.

The company was also starting to pick up quality awards around the world through its subsidiaries in Britain, The Netherlands, France, and even Japan. With this in mind and with the company making such substantial gains, Xerox officials decided it was time to have them measured from the outside. As a result, they applied for the Malcolm Baldridge National Quality Award, which was established by Congress and consists of a grueling process involving a detailed application covering all sorts of company activities. Those passing the written applications were subject to an on-site inspection of the company by panel members.

Xerox had indeed turned itself around, and many investors who spotted the turnaround situation in progress and bought Xerox stock when it was inexpensive became wealthy. How wealthy? Well, consider that if you had enough faith in Xerox when its price was around $27, that faith would have been amply rewarded when the price rose to $171 a short time later and the stock subsequently underwent a three-for-one split.

Key Points for Spotting a Turnaround Possibility

In this chapter, you've learned the techniques for discovering a company that is in trouble but has the capability of turning things around. Here are the key points covered for acting on that knowledge:

➤ Research all phases of a troubled company. That's the key to discovering a turnaround prospect.

➤ Keep in mind that problems can afflict small companies as well as large companies.

➤ Consider each company individually. Turnarounds must be tailored to each company's individual needs and resources.

➤ Use outside sources of information about a company. Many companies are unaware of problems that will eventually require turnaround efforts.

➤ Look for companies that have a vision. To effectively turn a situation around, a company must have the vision ingredient.

➤ Put yourself in the company's shoes. To understand success, an investor must first understand failure.

➤ Make sure the company you are interested in has these key elements: speed, detailed planning, and commitment of everyone involved—inside and outside the company.

➤ Be willing to take a risk. Sometimes the risk is necessary—and worthwhile to investors. A lot of risk is involved when a troubled company expands marketing lines, targets new markets, spends heavily on marketing, and cuts prices.

➤ Be aware that a company's reputation and reality are never far apart.

➤ Remember that internal controls alone won't solve a

company's problems.

➤ Make sure the company's product design, development, and manufacturing work closely for maximum productivity.

➤ And don't forget that some companies won't survive no matter which remedies are attempted.

Chapter 15: How to Tax Shelter Your Money

"The art of taxation consists of so plucking the goose as to obtain the largest amount of feathers with the least possible amount of hissing."

– J.B. Colbert

The Three-Fold Way to Tax Relief

Every adult person in the United States, almost without exception, can reduce his or her tax burden.

Yes, that is a bold statement. But it's true. From the 17-year-old part-time worker at a fast-food restaurant to the 75-year-old retiree living on Social Security and a pension, there's always something that can be done to cut taxes.

How about tax lawyers and CPAs? Surely they have taken all the tax breaks that are possible. Very unlikely. If you question them at length (and that's a grim prospect), you'll probably find that they too are paying more taxes than necessary—either because of indifference or oversight.

So how can the average person find ways to outwit the tax collector? Very simple. You avoid some taxes and delay others. That of course doesn't mean you *evade* taxes. Keep in mind that there's a big difference between tax avoidance and tax evasion. That difference, a wag once said, is about 10 years in the federal penitentiary.

No, you don't want to evade taxes. But you can adopt a plan of action that can prevent you from paying more than you should. And that's what this chapter is all about. Here, we'll explore three simple strategies that can play a major role in your tax-reduction efforts. Plus, you'll see how to get a return on investment that is totally free of taxes. And you'll cover how to take deductions and credits that you may never have known existed. Finally, you'll see how to take the greatest advantage of what some investment experts call "the million-dollar money machine." And you'll learn what the 1997 tax law means to you.

First, the three strategies that can help you reduce the tax bite. By careful planning, your goals are to:

1. Receive income that is not subject to taxes.

2. Take all the deductions and credits you are entitled to.

3. Postpone tax obligations with the idea in mind of paying less when they come due.

Let's consider these one at a time.

Tax-Free Income: Not a Fantasy

An aspiration of most Americans is to receive income that is not taxed. That is not as unheard of as you might imagine. Millions of your fellow citizens are doing that right now. And more will soon be able to as a result of the new Roth individual retirement account.

But first let's visit a traditional type of tax-free vehicle: municiple bonds. These fixed-rate, fixed-term debt instruments are issued by state and local government agencies, such as counties, cities, bridge authorities, airport authorities, water districts, and the like. Munibonds, as they are called, are sold through securities dealers, but for a real deal (that is, no sales charge) try to buy newly offered securities from an underwriting dealer.

Munibonds also trade in the secondary market. In that market, you can buy and sell bonds that have already been issued. In the secondary market, the sales commission varies, but is typically 2 or 3 percent of the purchase price.

Munibond denominations are typically $5,000, but some

issues have a face value of only $1,000. The actual price when initially offered may be more or less than par (which is the actual face value), depending on prevailing interest rates. Similarly, the value in the secondary market rises and falls inversely with interest rates. All munibonds are registered in the names of the owners, who receive interest payments every six months.

You can select from several kinds of municipal bonds. Some may be more suitable than others for your purposes.

The best part about them is their tax status. In most cases, the interest they pay is fully exempt from federal and state income taxes (if, of course, you have to pay state income taxes). That's because they are issued for "public purpose": the funding of schools, roads, bridges, public buildings, and the like. Income from bonds issued on behalf of charitable organizations, such as hospitals or religious and education organizations, are also usually tax exempt.

To receive interest income that is free of both state and federal taxes, you must be a resident of the state in which the bonds are issued. For example, if you are a resident of New York and you invest in New York state government bonds, the income is free from state and federal income taxes.

That means that if you are in the 28-percent tax bracket, a 5-percent fully exempt bond yields the taxable equivalent of 6.9 percent; a 6-percent bond, 8.3 percent; a 7-percent bond, 9.7 percent; and an 8-percent bond, 11.1 percent.

Chart 36 tells you the yields you would need to earn on taxable bonds to achieve the yields from tax-exempt bonds.

But a problem arises if you have too much income from private-purpose sources. A tax snare called the alternative minimum tax, or AMT, affects certain private-purpose bonds issued after August 7, 1986. They are exempt from the regular income tax, but are subject to the AMT (which has a ceiling of 28 percent). Private-purpose bonds are those used to finance industrial development, build public housing, and provide loans for students.

Moreover, there are taxable municipal bonds. Examples of taxable munibonds are those issued to finance the construction of sports stadiums, convention centers, and pollution-control facilities.

CHART 36

FEDERAL EQUIVALENT YIELDS TAX-FREE VS. TAXABLE BONDS			
Tax-Free Yields(%)	Taxable Yield Equivalents (%)		
Tax Brackets:	15%	28%	31%
3.5	4.12	4.86	5.07
4.0	4.71	5.56	5.80
4.5	5.29	6.25	6.52
5.0	5.88	6.94	7.25
5.5	6.47	7.64	7.97
6.0	7.06	8.33	8.70
6.5	7.65	9.03	9.42
7.0	8.24	9.72	10.14
7.5	8.82	10.42	10.87
8.0	9.41	11.11	11.59
8.5	10.00	11.81	12.32
9.0	10.59	12.50	13.04
9.5	11.18	13.19	13.77
10.0	11.76	13.89	14.49

Naturally, the fully exempt bonds tend to carry a lower interest rate than the AMT bonds, which in turn have a lower rate than the fully taxable bonds. Always ask your broker if a particular bond is tax exempt, because there are many exceptions to the above guidelines. When in doubt, examine the prospectus or call the finance office of the issuing authority.

One variation on municipal bonds is so-called "stripped munis." This type separates interest and principal payments. They don't pay interest until maturity, but they do sell at a deep discount from their face values. One drawback: Stripped munis frequently come due in from one to 12 years. Their gains are tax exempt so long as the overall yield isn't more than the muni's yield at the time it originally was offered.

They're also exceptionally safe: most stripped munis aren't subject to call (wherein the issuing company can repurchase the bonds at a set price after a specified time prior to maturity). And you'll lock in a good rate of return if interest rates fall. If you think interest rates will rise, though, you'll be better off in a tax-exempt mutual fund, which can reinvest its yield at the new, higher rates.

Yields on stripped munis are comparable to those of other high-grade municipal securities. Stripped munis are a good choice if you're saving now for a child's education, since you can time your purchase to pay off when you'll need the money most.

Tax-Exempt Funds

You can also diversify your munibond holdings with a bond mutual fund. Bond funds are a convenient way to buy into a bond portfolio. Most have $1,000 minimum investments, and they're ideal if you are investing less than $50,000, even though returns are slightly lower than for some individual bonds. That's because, as with any mutual fund, your risk is diversified over the entire bond portfolio.

Moreover, bond funds fluctuate in value less than individual issues. A fund may comprise 100 or even 200 issues, each with a different coupon and maturity and with a range of credit ratings. If interest rates drop, the net asset value of a bond fund won't rise as quickly as the market value of munibonds because only a portion of its holdings are long term. The balance are intermediate and short term. For the same reason, if interest rates rise, the net asset value of a bond fund won't decline as much as the market value of long-term bonds.

Some munibond funds enhance their yields by selling call options against their portfolios. Premium income from writing these options varies. It may boost current yield, but could also cause a fund to sacrifice much of its upside potential.

If you are a conservative investor or you have only a small amount to invest in bonds, mutual funds probably are the best way to enter this world. You'll be far less vulnerable than if you invest in one or two munibond issues on your own. A diversified bond fund of any type can help mitigate such losses.

Before you invest in a tax-exempt bond fund, however, keep in mind that fund yields are influenced by a long list of factors. And in order to choose your fund wisely, you'll need to sort the good from the bad. Following are questions to get answers to when examining the prospectus or when calling the fund's customer-service department:

➤ *What is the fund's total return?*

This goes for the previous year, five years, and 10 years. "Total return" means the amount by which fund shares appreciate with all interest (or dividends, in the case of stocks) reinvested. Note that a high yield doesn't necessarily translate into high asset value. A fund may offer high yields, but if its principal is losing value, the total return will be dragged down.

➤ *What are the fund's total net assets?*

With bond funds, bigger is better. Funds need at least $100 million to diversify adequately and to reduce their trading costs significantly.

➤ *What is the average maturity of the fund's holdings?*

Longer maturities generally mean higher yields—and more interest-rate risk. When interest rates move up or down, longer-term funds swing more wildly in value than shorter-term ones.

➤ *What does the fund do to enhance its yields?*

One method, as mentioned, is by writing options, a fairly risky practice. By writing a call option on some of its bonds, a munibond fund in effect assigns the right to those securities to someone else. The option buyer has a specific period of time in which to utilize the option, at a specific price. In turn, the buyer pays a fee to the bond fund.

No problem in doing that—provided that bond prices stay level or fall. But some funds figure the option income into the yields they quote to you and other customers. Should bond prices rise, the option owner will take advantage of his or her right to buy the securities below market prices. That sale will cut a chunk from the fund's principal, lowering its asset value.

Option income funds use the same technique. They sell calls on stocks or stock-market indexes. You're again paying for added yield while managers risk the fund's assets.

➤ *Does the fund charge a front-end or back-end sales load?*

Once you've become a savvy investor, you can choose a fund without your broker's help. Without paying commissions, you'll have that much more in your account from the start. Also be on the lookout for "12b-1" fees, which use the fund's assets for advertising. Such fees do nothing to enhance your return—and in fact diminish it.

➤ *What are annual expenses per $100 of assets?*

Munibond funds average a ratio of nine cents per $100. Ideally, you'll be able to find a fund with a lower ratio—including its 12b-1 fee, if any.

➤ *Does the fund invest in anything other than investment-grade munibonds?*

High-yield bonds—those from questionable government or agency sources—pay at least 3 percent more than those buying only investment-grade securities. But you run a higher risk that some bond issuers will default, thus dragging down the fund's total return.

➤ *How diversified is the fund?*

Broadly based funds invest in at least 40 different securities. No more than 10 percent of these should come from a single area or single type of government.

When you're ready to select a tax-exempt bond fund, you can refer to Chart 37, which lists recent returns covering one year, three years, five years, and 10 years.

Other tax-free income sources exist, of course, and here is a rundown on them:

➤ **The Roth IRA:** (More on this later in this chapter.)

➤ **Gifts:** Unlimited for the donor. Recipient is not taxed. Individuals may give up to $10,000 per year per person to any number of people ($20,000 if the gift is from a couple) without the donor incurring any tax liability.

➤ **Child Support:** Unlimited. The recipient is not taxed for support payments.

CHART 37

MUNIBOND FUND WINNERS
(AS OF JAN. 1, 1997)

One-Year Performance

Fund Name	Return (%)
United Municipal High-Income A	6.9
American High-Income Muni Bond	6.5
Voyageur Nat'l High-Yield Muni	6.2
Franklin High Yield TF Income I	6.2
Van Kampen Am. Cap. HY Muni A	5.8

Five-Year Performance

Fund Name	Return (%)
Smith Barney Managed Munis A	9.0
Executive Investors Ins. TE	9.0
Excelsior Long-Term Tax-Exempt	8.9
United Municipal High-Income A	8.6
Franklin High Yield TF Income I	8.2

Three-Year Performance

Fund Name	Return (%)
Smith Barney Managed Munis A	6.6
United Municipal High-Income A	6.5
Van Kampen Am. Cap. HY Muni A	6.5
Excelsior Long-Term Tax-Exempt	6.4
Franklin High Yield TF Income I	6.4

10-Year Performance

Fund Name	Return (%)
Excelsior Long-Term Tax-Exempt	9.8
Franklin High Yield TF Income I	8.7
Smith Barney Managed Munis A	8.6
United Municipal High-Income A	8.2
United Municipal Bond A	8.2

Source: Morningstar

➤ **Life-Insurance Dividends:** Considered return of premium. If dividends exceed premiums paid, however, the death benefit may become taxable.

➤ **Life-Insurance Proceeds:** With the exception mentioned above, death benefits are not taxable. However, under some conditions they may be included in the estate calculations for determining estate or gift taxes.

➤ **Inheritances:** Not taxed at the federal level.

➤ **Profits on Sale of Home:** Receipts must be rolled over into a new home within two years.

➤ **Scholarships and Fellowships:** Funds used for tuition or supplies usually are not taxable.

➤ **Social Security Benefits:** Unless your income from all sources exceeds certain limits.

➤ **Health and Accident Benefits:** Proceeds from insurance.

➤ **Worker's Compensation Benefits:** For injuries or illnesses.

➤ **Damages:** Tax free if collected as part of a judgment—unless they represent replacement of lost income.

➤ **Fringe Benefits:** The costs of health insurance, group life insurance up to $50,000, child care, educational reimbursement, automobile for business use, stock options, use of a company-owned vacation resort—all or part may be tax free.

The Seduction of a Deduction

Deductions are not as beneficial as some other types of tax breaks. But they are better than nothing. They reduce your income by a certain percentage, depending on which tax bracket you're in. Credits are better. They offset income dollar for dollar. So they are more difficult to come by. First, let's see how deductions can help you.

The most common way for an individual to reduce his or her taxable income is through the use of deductions. In a higher tax bracket, a deduction is worth more. But before you can take a deduction, you should have enough to exceed the standard deduction. And since the standard deduction now is at a high level ($6,700 for a married couple filing a joint return), your deductions must add up to at least that amount before they do you any good.

Millions of people do, however, have enough deductible expenditures to exceed the standard deduction. And you may have so many that you too need to start keeping track of them (if you haven't already). Keep in mind that for every $1,000 of extra deductions you find over the standard-deduction amount, you save anywhere from $150 to $396.

Here is a sort of laundry list of the allowable deductions for 1997:

➤ **Medical Expenses:** Prescription medicines and drugs, insulin, physicians, dentists, nurses, hospitals, medical-insurance premiums, transportation to and from doctors' offices or hospitals, hearing aids, dentures, eyeglasses. Total must exceed 7.5 percent of adjusted gross income. Only that portion that exceeds 7.5 percent of AGI is deductible.

➤ **"Other" Taxes (besides *income* taxes, that is):** State and local income taxes, real-estate taxes, personal-property taxes, portion of car-registration fee based on value. Not deductible: Federal income and excise taxes, Social Security taxes, federal estate or gift taxes, state or local sales and gasoline taxes, car-inspection fees, special assessments, license fees.

➤ **Interest Expenses:** Interest on first and second mortgages and equity-credit lines (within limits), investment interest that does not exceed investment income (so long as the investment is not a "passive" type; example: a limited partnership). Not deductible: interest on loans used to buy municipal bonds or other tax-exempt investments.

➤ **Charitable Gifts:** One-hundred percent of actual gifts (cash or property) to recognized charities, up to 30 percent of your adjusted gross income if the gift is cash or 20 percent of your AGI if the gift is appreciated property. Also, out-of-pocket expenses as a volunteer, including mileage to and from the charity's location or events. Not deductible: the value of your time.

➤ **Losses:** Losses resulting from theft, vandalism, fire, storm, or accidents, provided the property is not used to generate income (as for example, rental property or a truck used in business). The amount of each loss must be more than $100 and the total of all losses in a year must be more than 10 percent of your adjusted gross income. Also deductible: appraisals, etc., to prove the cost of your loss.

➤ **Moving Expenses:** If you take a new job that is more than 50 miles farther from home than your old job, you may deduct some moving expenses if you move closer to the new location.

➤ **Miscellaneous and Job Expenses:** Union dues, safety

equipment, uniforms required by your employer that can't be used for street wear, dues to professional organizations, subscriptions to professional journals, fees to employment agencies, tax-preparation fees, safe-deposit-box rental fees, some legal and accounting fees, clerical fees, job-related educational expenses that are not paid by your employer. The total of all these categories must be more than 2 percent of your adjusted gross income. Only that portion that exceeds 2 percent of AGI is deductible. Gambling losses (up to the amount of your reported winnings), some estate taxes, and specialized job expenses due to a physical handicap are not subject to the 2-percent limit.

COMPARE YOUR DEDUCTIONS WITH THOSE OF OTHERS

From tax returns for 1996, here are the amounts deducted by your average fellow taxpayer:

Adjusted Gross Income	Medical Expenses	Taxes	Interest	Charitable Gifts
$20,000-$25,000	$ 4,913	$2,049	$4,655	$1,171
$25,000-$30,000	3,223	2,374	5,478	1,259
$30,000-$40,000	3,147	2,717	5,546	1,217
$40,000-$50,000	4,123	3,287	6,020	1,688
$50,000-$75,000	6,003	4,424	6,437	1,685
$75,000-$100,000	10,116	6,312	8,079	2,142
$100,000-$200,000	17,500	9,772	11,349	4,017
Over $200,000	100,600	36,379	21,997	12,175

Spending the time to compute your out-of-pocket costs in these areas is worth your while. But when you compute your deductions, read the instructions carefully. For example, a family with an adjusted gross income of $25,000 has to have more than $1,875 worth of medical expenses before claiming that deduction—and then only the part that exceeds $1,875 can be deducted.

On the other hand, if your health-insurance premiums are $200 a month, you will have $525 to claim immediately ($200 x 12 = $2,400; $2,400 - $1,875 = $525). Other costs, such as transportation to and from a doctor's office or hospital, can be added to that. If your insurance plan requires you to pay a deductible or a prescription fee, you can add those costs to the total.

The most controversial deductions may involve interest expenses. At one time, you could deduct virtually all of your interest payments. In recent years, however, the deduction for personal interest, such as that paid on credit cards, was reduced over the course of a few years and is now only a fond remembrance. The lack of a deduction for consumer-interest expenses is one more incentive for you to eliminate your debt load.

One strategy for many people is to use a home-equity line of credit to consolidate their debts. Interest is still deductible on such credit. But while this may be a good short-term solution to the interest problem, it could saddle you with a large debt that would take 10 or 15 years to pay off. If you do use a home-equity loan, don't abuse it. Missed payments or default could result in loss of your home.

As mentioned, tax credits are more helpful than tax deductions. But they are rarer. For individuals, the most important credits are:

➤ **A full credit each year** for the first $1,000 in college expenses (except for room and board) the first two years of college: Parents also get a credit equal to 50 percent of the next $1,000 of expenses (except for room and board).

➤ **An earned-income credit:** This allows low-income taxpayers with children to claim credits against income.

➤ **A child-and dependent-care credit:** This provides a limited benefit to working parents and others who incur expenses for help in tending their children and other dependents.

➤ **A credit for the elderly and disabled:** This is another limited benefit. Eligible are senior citizens and permanently and totally disabled persons with incomes below $17,500 for single taxpayers or $20,000 or $25,000 for married taxpayers and Social Security benefits of less than $5,000 or $7,000.

Other credits are available, but relate primarily to business situations. One that you may be able to use, however, is a 20-percent credit for rehabilitation of certified historic structures and a 10-percent credit for rehabilitation of buildings originally placed in service before 1936.

The Last Truly Great Tax Shelter

Once upon a time, wealthy taxpayers had an array of tax-shelter choices. No more. Congress whittled away at them during the past decade or so until they now are practically nonexistent. But one type has survived. The retirement-savings tax shelter has endured unscathed. In fact, Washington lawmakers have refined it to some degree.

We're talking here about such wondrous investment plans as individual retirement accounts, 401(k)s, and the like. They can benefit you in two ways. First, some postpone the day when the tax collector takes his or her toll. That usually means less tax liability because when the tax bill comes due, the taxpayer is usually retired and in a lower tax bracket. Second, some allow taxpayers to reduce their tax on income they are earning during their working years. One such plan can also eliminate the tax on investment earnings altogether.

Consider the individual retirement account, or IRA. The superlatives flow when discussing it. This most marvelous device has *the most incredible* potential.

Some people call it the million-dollar money machine. That's because it can, machine-like, turn a $2,000-a-year investment into a million dollars. Of course, it takes time, and you have to invest the money properly. In other words, you won't automatically make a million dollars with an IRA. You have to work at it. But if becoming a millionaire is your goal, an IRA certainly makes it possible.

If you haven't opened an IRA account yet, set one up—now. As you go through the year without an account, perhaps waiting until next April before you make a decision, *you are losing money*. The earlier you open an account and begin making contributions, the more time your money has to grow, multiplying at tax-favored rates. An IRA allows you to defer or eliminate taxes not only on any interest the account may earn, but, with the standard IRA, on your contributions to it.

IRAs have been around since 1975, but many people were not eligible to participate in them. Now, however, almost everyone under the age of $70^1/_2$ can set up an IRA. And even those who can't (because of reasons explained in a moment) can benefit from an IRA's tax advantages.

You probably see a multitude of ads about retirement accounts. The message is in newspapers, on billboards, and on television. And they assure you that you can become rich by investing in an IRA. The ads are often so numerous (especially just before the April 15 deadline for tax-return filing) that many people become too confused to confidently make an investment decision at all. Should they put their money into an IRA? If so, which kind is best for them? And because an IRA is a long-term commitment, what if they change their mind? Can they get their money back before retirement?

As mentioned, the beauty of an IRA is that not only do you forego or eliminate paying taxes on any interest, dividends, or capital gains the account may earn, but with a standard IRA you may be able to deduct the contributions directly from your gross income. If you earn $30,000 after adjustments in 1997 and contribute $2,000 to a standard IRA, you would pay tax on only $28,000.

One taxpayer who had been eligible to invest in an IRA all along, but who had never done so, made a pleasant discovery in early 1997 while filling out his 1040 form for 1996. He found that he was getting a tax refund of $91. But then he picked up his pocket calculator and did some figuring. He found that if he would simply open an IRA and invest $500 in it, his refund would grow from $91 to $291. If he should put $1,000 in the IRA, the refund would be $491. And if he would contribute the maximum for 1996 of $2,000, he would get back an altogether gratifying $852.

This seemed to him like "free money," which in a way it was, because he would be getting the refund as a type of reward for *contributing to his own retirement fund.*

In fact, the snowballing effects of the standard IRA's tax deferment are an even better benefit. Take the case of two imaginary taxpayers, Fred and Kelly. For the sake of contrast, let's pretend that Fred has decided not to invest in an IRA, but Kelly has opened an account. Assume further that Fred and Kelly have the same income and expenses and are therefore in the same tax bracket: 30 percent (federal and state combined).

Fred wants to invest $2,000 of his income for the year in corporate bonds drawing 10-percent interest compounded quarterly. Since Fred has no IRA benefits, he first has to pay the 30-percent tax on that $2,000, leaving him only $1,400 to invest. In one year Fred's $1,400 investment earns $145.34 interest. However, he now has to pay a 30-percent tax on the amount, reducing it to $101.74. When that is added to Fred's original investment of $1,400, he has a total of $1,501.74.

Kelly wants to invest $2,000 in the same kind of bonds. Since she gets IRA benefits, she can invest the entire $2,000. And right here is the important point: The IRA rules allow Kelly to invest *pre-tax dollars*, giving her more investing power.

In one year the 10-percent bonds (compounded quarterly) earn Kelly interest of $207.63. She pays no tax on that interest, so she now has a total of $2,207.63, compared to Fred's $1,501.74.

Let's take it one more year. Kelly invests $2,000 additional pre-tax dollars, and Fred invests $1,400 after-tax dollars. Fred pays 30-percent tax on the new interest earned, while Kelly pays no tax on her interest. At the end of the second year, these are the assets:

Kelly:	$4,644.44
Fred:	$3,112.61
Difference:	$1,531.83

And remember that this gap has grown in only two years. Year by year the chasm will get wider until Kelly will leave Fred behind in the dust. After 10 years, Kelly's IRA assets will total $41,759; Fred's, $24,043.

Fred does have one advantage, however. When the bonds mature, he can withdraw his money without penalty, while Kelly cannot unless she is at least $59\frac{1}{2}$ years old. This situation will become clear during a later discussion of penalties. Incidentally, these bonds would probably mature in a few years, but ignore that fact to simplify the arithmetic.

Now what about those ads and commercials telling you that an IRA can make you rich. Can it? For some people, it certainly can. Here's what that can mean for you.

Look at Chart 38. It shows how an investor's assets can snowball in an IRA at different interest rates (compounded annually) by age 65. Notice that a person who starts contributing at age 30 and averages 13 percent a year will have more than $1.2 million at 65. Even a person who doesn't open an IRA until he or she is 45 can accumulate more than $182,000 by 65. And keep in mind that if both you and your spouse have IRAs, you could have double the amount at retirement.

CHART 38

ACCUMULATION IN AN IRA BY AGE 65

Age at Which You Open IRA	Total Contributions at $2,000 Per Year	Total Amount at Retirement Ave. Annual Interest Rate:		
		9%	11%	13%
30	$70,000	$470,250	$758,329	$1,235,500
35	60,000	297,150	441,826	662,630
40	50,000	184,648	253,998	351,760
45	40,000	118,530	142,530	182,940
50	30,000	64,006	76,380	91,344
55	20,000	33,120	37,123	41,628
60	10,000	13,047	13,826	14,646

Note: These calculations are for one yearly contribution made on the first day of each tax year. Interest is compounded annually. (The totals will be higher if compounding is more frequent.) The totals shown here are approximate.

The IRA Newcomer

And then there's the new Roth IRA (named after the U.S. Senator who was a guiding force in developing it). A product of the 1997 tax law, the Roth IRA is sort of a reverse of the standard IRA. Contributions to the Roth version aren't tax deductible, but earnings are tax free after five years. Because the eligibility levels are much higher (under $150,000 income on joint returns and $95,000 on individual returns), the Roth gives many more investors a chance to put $2,000 a year into stock funds or other investments and avoid all federal tax so long as the money is used for retirement or other qualifying purposes (such as the purchase of a first home or education expenses).

That raises the question: Which is better for those persons eligible for both the standard IRA or the Roth IRA? Tax experts seem to agree that you should choose the Roth. Figures show that putting $2,000 in a Roth IRA produces a bigger sum, after tax, than opening a tax-deductible IRA and investing the tax savings on the side. (This assumes 10-percent annual earnings, 28-percent tax on withdrawal from the deductible IRA, and 20-percent tax annually on the side account.)

The point is clear: Start your IRA retirement program now!

Okay, maybe you're partly convinced of the value of an IRA. But you may be wondering how you can achieve a 13-percent-a-year return. After all, interest paid on bank CDs and Treasury bills is currently in the single digits. That's true, of course, but savvy investors achieve much higher average returns than 5 or 6 percent—or even 8 percent.

Take a look at the following comparison of annualized returns over a recent 10-year period, during which investments in stocks, bonds, and Old Masters would have exceeded 13 percent:

Investment	10-Year Annualized Performance
Stocks	18.4
Bonds	15.2
Old Masters	13.3
Chinese Ceramics	8.5
Treasury Bills	7.6
Diamonds	6.4
Home Prices	4.0
Inflation Rate	3.8
Gold	0.6

Reprinted by permission of Salomon Brothers Inc.

Though this may not have been a typical 10-year period, imagine for a moment what would happen to your IRA funds if you *could* achieve a consistent 18-percent compounded return: For a 30-year-old person, contributing only $2,000 per year, the total at his or her retirement would be more than *$4 million.*

Getting the Most from Your IRA

Don't think of an IRA as a particular kind of account. It isn't. Rather, it is a *method* of sheltering a portion of your money from taxes. It's true that some new accounts have been created especially to be IRAs, but most traditional investment vehicles can be designated IRAs. For example, you can put your IRA money in a certificate of deposit at a bank or invest it in a stock-brokerage account, mutual fund, or insurance annuity plan (though why should you?).

And what makes these accounts IRAs? Simple. The organizations offering them have been approved by the Internal Revenue Service as IRA sponsors. When you open an account, the sponsor will give you special forms to fill out. And just like that you have an IRA. Moreover, it functions just like any other account...with the important difference that you receive tax protection.

Not everyone is eligible to take full benefits, however. If you or your spouse is covered by an employer retirement plan at any time during the year, your allowable IRA deduction may be diminished. The following sums up whether you can take a full deduction, a partial deduction, or no deduction:

➤ If you are eligible to participate in an employer-sponsored retirement plan, your contributions still are fully deductible if you're single and have an adjusted gross income of less than $25,000. If you're married and filing a return jointly with your spouse, the limit jumps to $40,000.

➤ Under the new law, the income limits will rise by $10,000 for couples and $5,000 for single filers in 1998, 2002, 2003, and 2004, when the income limits will be $80,000 for joint filers, $50,000 for single filers.

➤ Your contribution to an IRA isn't deductible at all if you're covered by an employer's plan, single, and have an adjusted gross income of at least $35,000. The same applies if you're married (filing jointly) and have an AGI of $50,000. However, those limits will also be adjusted in future years.

➤ But a portion of your contributions is deductible between these upper and lower limits: that is, if you're single and have an AGI between $25,000 and $35,000, or married with an AGI between $40,000 and $50,000, you're still allowed a partial deduction. Again, these will be adjusted later.

➤ Here's how the phase-out works for 1997: For every $1,000 of income above the $25,000 level (if you're single) or $40,000 level (if you're married and filing jointly), your $2,000 IRA taxable income deduction drops by $200. Suppose you're a single taxpayer with an AGI of $30,000 and make a $2,000 IRA contribution. That's $5,000 above the specified level ($30,000 - $25,000 = $5,000), or five $1,000s. You can deduct $1,000 (5 x $200 = $1,000, $2,000 - $1,000).

What if your contributions aren't deductible any longer? You still may be able to contribute up to $2,000 annually to a Roth IRA. While your contributions are not tax deductible for the year in which you make them, taxes on any earnings from your contributions are eliminated.

HOW MANY IRAS DO YOU NEED?

Some investors set up IRAs with several different sponsors. Is that wise? Probably not, most experts agree. They advise having only one or two accounts.

So if you have more than two IRAs, combine them. Decide which has the lowest fees, the most convenient services, and the highest returns. This is the IRA you want to retain.

To transfer the money from your other IRAs to this account, contact the sponsor of the account you want to close and ask the personnel there to send you the forms for a custodian-to-custodian transfer. When you get the forms, fill them out and send them back. A couple of weeks later, check to make sure the money was transferred and the account was closed.

With a standard IRA, you save every statement you get from your IRA custodian, which usually will be a bank or mutual-fund sponsor. As each statement arrives, make a note on the back stating how much of your contribution is deductible and how much isn't. Or consider setting up two accounts: one for your deductible and one for your nondeductible contributions.

About the only things you are not allowed to invest your IRA money in are certain tangibles, such as coins, stamps, art, antiques, diamonds, and the like. (Your IRA can, however, invest in one-ounce, one-half-ounce, one-quarter-ounce, or one-tenth-ounce U.S. gold coins or one-ounce silver coins minted by the U.S. Treasury Department.)

You can set up and make contributions to an IRA if you received taxable compensation during the year and have not reached age $70\frac{1}{2}$ by the end of the year. You may also be eligible to set up and contribute up to $2,000 a year to an IRA for your spouse, whether or not he or she received compensation.

You can set up an IRA at any time during a year or by the due date of your return for that year (but not including extensions). For most people, that means contributing by April 15 for the previous tax year.

When you reach $59\frac{1}{2}$, you can start withdrawing money from your IRA without penalty. You can draw it out in a lump sum or you can take out portions every month or every year or at any other intervals. If you have a standard IRA, the tax collector, who has been such a decent sort in staying away all this time, now appears to make a claim.

Does that mean you have built up a huge tax liability in your IRA that you now have to pay off? No, not at all. Whatever you remove from your IRA simply becomes part of your gross income for that year and you pay ordinary income taxes on it.

If you earn $20,000 when you are 60 and withdraw $10,000 from your IRA, you are taxed on $30,000. And remember that when you are retired or semiretired, you will no doubt be in a lower tax bracket. Therefore, chances are that you never will pay as much tax on the money as you would have paid without the IRA benefit.

Although you are allowed to withdraw your IRA money without penalty at $59\frac{1}{2}$, you are not required to. In fact, you can still contribute to the account.

However, during the year in which you become $70\frac{1}{2}$, you must begin making withdrawals and at a set rate each year. At that time the amount in your IRA is divided by the number of years in your life expectancy (based on an actuarial table), and you are required to withdraw the resulting amount each year. The purpose of this rule is to force you to empty the account—and pay the taxes on it—by the time you die.

Suppose you have built up a nice fund in your IRA and before you become $59\frac{1}{2}$ you get a hankering to take it out and pay education expenses or buy your first house. No problem. That is okay. Otherwise, the IRS will hit you with a 10-percent penalty on the amount withdrawn. If you withdraw $5,000 prematurely, for example, you will pay a penalty of $500. In addition, the full $5,000 will be added to your gross income for that year, and you will pay normal income tax on it.

But there are many cases in which the tax-free growth of your investment will allow you to make an early withdrawal, pay the 10-percent penalty and *still come out ahead*. This would depend on your tax bracket, the amount of interest your account has earned, and the number of years involved. If you can leave your money in an IRA for only four or five years, it would probably still be worthwhile to set up an account. If you like to play around with a calculator, you can figure different possibilities.

Is there any way your money can be withdrawn early without incurring the IRS penalty? Yes, three ways. First, if a person dies, the beneficiary designated when the account was opened will receive the money without penalty. Second, there is no penalty if a person becomes disabled or is otherwise unable to work for a living. Third, there's no penalty for withdrawals that are used to pay medical expenses, education expenses, or buy a first home.

If you put more money than the law allows into an IRA, you must pay a 6-percent penalty, as well as income tax, on the excess amount. For example, if you invest $2,200 in an individual IRA in one year, you will be charged a $12 penalty.

As mentioned, you are required to withdraw your IRA assets in specified amounts after you become $70\frac{1}{2}$. In the event that you fail to draw out the required amount, the IRS will exact a crushing penalty of 50 percent of the underwithdrawal. If you are required to withdraw $50,000 and you withdraw only $40,000, your penalty is half of the $10,000 you failed to withdraw.

One other federal restriction: You cannot use IRA funds as collateral for a loan. If you do, your money is considered distributed and the 10-percent penalty is triggered.

Transfers and Rollovers

As far as the IRS is concerned, you can move your IRA money from one account to another as often as you like without penalty.

For example, suppose you want to take your IRA dollars out of a money-market fund and put them in a credit-union savings certificate. You open an account at the credit union and have the money-market fund transfer your money directly to the credit union. You never take possession of the money, and the IRS is not notified. Your investment remains tax sheltered. However, remember that as you move your money around, you may be paying early-withdrawal penalties or fees to the institutions involved.

If you close an IRA and take possession of the funds, you have 60 days in which to reinvest them in an IRA. If you do, the transaction is classified as a "rollover" and there is no penalty. You are allowed only one rollover per year.

A special kind of rollover is available to some taxpayers. In the event that you receive a lump sum from a company pension or profit-sharing plan, either because you left the company or because the company dropped the plan, you can roll the entire amount over into an IRA and keep it tax sheltered. There is no limit on the dollar amount of a rollover.

Other Tax-Protected Retirement Programs

Keoghs and Simplified Employee Pensions

If you're a businessperson operating as a sole proprietorship or a partnership (but not a partner), you can set up a Keogh, or HR-10, plan. This type of pension plan can be exclusively yours, although if you have employees, you can include them as well.

The limits differ, depending on the type of Keogh plan you have. If your plan is a "defined-contribution" plan, the limit for each employee (and you are of course an employee) generally is the lesser of $30,000 or...

1. 15 percent of the employee's taxable compensation, if your plan is a "profit-sharing" type, or...

2. 25 percent of the employee's taxable compensation, if your plan is a "money-purchase" type.

WATCH THOSE FEES

You want to make certain that you're not paying more than you need to in IRA fees. As a rule of thumb, mutual funds usually charge between $10 and $30 for IRA accounts. Banks and brokerage firms charge between $30 and $50.

If you find your fees are excessive, ask your IRA sponsor to lower them, and if that doesn't work, move your account (if you can do so without having to pay a penalty).

Keep in mind, however, that you can deduct the fees (as a miscellaneous expense) you pay a sponsor. Don't allow your custodian to deduct the fee from your IRA contributions. Pay your annual fee separately so you keep all your IRA money working for you.

A defined-contribution plan can be one of three kinds: (1) profit-sharing, (2) stock-bonus, or (3) money-purchase.

A profit-sharing plan lets you and your employees or their beneficiaries share in the profits of your business. The plan must have a definite formula for allocating the contributions to the plan among the participating employees and for distributing the funds in the plan.

A stock-bonus plan is similar to a profit-sharing plan except that the benefits are payable in the form of the company's stock. Only a corporation can set up a stock-bonus plan.

A money-purchase plan provides benefits at a stated amount or is based on a stated formula that is not subject to your discretion, such as 10 percent of each participating employee's compensation. Your contributions to the plan are not based on your profits.

The deduction limit for contributions to a "defined-benefit" plan may be greater than for the defined-contribution plan.

A defined-benefit plan generally provides for set benefits. Your contributions are based on actuarial assumptions, and you will probably need professional help to have such a plan.

The Benefits Provided

Obviously, with a Keogh plan, you have greater opportunities. Instead of the $2,000 limit that you have with an IRA, you can set aside many times that amount with a Keogh (plus you can still set up an IRA even if you have a Keogh). So you will be able to reach your retirement goals much sooner in life.

Let's see how you can benefit from a Keogh.

Suppose you are self-employed and have set up a Keogh. Over the course of 10 years, you are able to contribute $15,000 a year, which you put into an investment yielding 7 percent in monthly increments of $1,250. At the end of 10 years, you would have accumulated $216,250.

But suppose you were able to contribute $15,000 a year over the course of 25 years. In such a case, you would achieve your goal of a million dollars. It would be your million-dollar money machine.

A Simplified Employee Pension (SEP) is a plan that allows you (if you're self-employed) or your employer to make contributions toward your retirement without becoming involved in more complex retirement plans.

The contributions go to an IRA (SEP-IRA) and can be as much annually as $30,000 or 15 percent (whichever is less) of your compensation.

SEP-IRAs require only an initial application with an IRA sponsor, and as with other IRAs, you can make contributions as late as April 15 of the following year. As a result, they're ideal for sole proprietorships, small businesses, and anyone who works on a freelance or consulting basis.

Like standard IRAs, SEP-IRAs are very flexible. You can put in little or nothing during slow years, making them a good choice if your income fluctuates from one year to the next. What's more, the eligibility rules governing SEP-IRAs are somewhat more inclusive than those for Keoghs and other plans. As an employee, you need only be 21 years old or older, have worked for a company during three of the past five years, and have earned at least $300 per year to be covered.

If you're an employee whose company offers a SEP-IRA plan, you also can make pretax contributions to the account from your pay. However, these contributions are limited to about $10,000 per year. And you can still make a $2,000 contribution to a standard IRA each year if you maintain a SEP-IRA account. But the IRS will consider you to be an active participant in a qualified plan. As a result, part of all of your regular IRA contributions may be taxable, depending on your income. Earnings on your standard IRA, as well as your SEP-IRA, will, however, accumulate tax-free until you begin withdrawals.

As with standard IRAs, you'll be subject to a 10-percent premature distribution penalty and to ordinary income tax if you withdraw your funds before age 59$\frac{1}{2}$. But unlike standard IRAs, you or your employer can continue making contributions to a SEP-IRA even after you turn 70$\frac{1}{2}$; essentially, contributions then become concurrent with distributions. Nor are SEP-IRA distributions eligible for five-year averaging, a form of favorable tax treatment, as are Keoghs and other forms of retirement plans.

Social Security

Financial planners suggest that persons contemplating retirement should count on Social Security benefits to provide about a third of the income they will need. Despite the pessimism that prevails about Social Security and its future, you should not dismiss this important tax-protected source of retirement funds. Our lawmakers seem intent on doing everything possible to ensure that all Americans receive the benefits they are entitled to. So Social Security can be an essential part of your retirement program.

Your benefits from Social Security will be based on the Social Security Administration's records of what you have earned over your lifetime of working. To make sure you're getting all the money you're due, request a written statement of all the earnings credited to your account. Ideally, do this every three or four years while you are still working. It's imperative that you do it shortly before you retire.

To find out how much the Social Security Administration says you have earned, call 1-800-772-1213 and ask for a Request for Earnings and Benefit Estimate Statement. In a week or so, you will receive a form that you will fill in to mail back. After doing so, you will receive a statement of your earnings record, along with an estimate of what your monthly benefits will be at the time of your retirement.

Contact the Social Security office if you think the statement is incorrect. Provide the clerk with as much evidence as possible, including the name and address of your past employers, the dates you worked there, and the wages you received. Stubs from payroll checks are particularly useful, as are copies of W-2 forms and past tax returns.

You are eligible to collect benefits if you are at least 62 years old and have contributed to the Social Security fund for a certain number of years (a number determined largely by your birth date).

Working spouses who have paid into the system are eligible for their own benefits; nonworking spouses 62 or older may qualify for a monthly check equal to half of what their retired spouses receive. Benefits are also payable to the divorced spouse of a worker, so long as the spouse was married to the worker for at least 10 years. Children under 18 (or 19, if they are in elementary or secondary school) may qualify for benefits if at least one of their parents is eligible. If you are seriously disabled and cannot work, you may be eligible for benefit payments regardless of your age.

When you are ready to apply for Social Security benefits, here's what to do:

➤ Contact your nearest Social Security office to make an appointment.

➤ On your appointment date, take along a copy of your Social Security card or a record of your number.

➤ Be prepared to show your W-2 form stating your earnings for the previous year. (If you've been self-employed, you'll need a copy of your most recent federal income-tax return.)

➤ Have a record of proof of age. (A birth certificate is best, but a driver's license will probably suffice.)

➤ If married, carry your marriage certificate if marital status is related to your claim.

Company Pensions and Salary-Reduction Plans

The same financial planners who maintain you should count on Social Security to provide a third of your retirement income also say a company pension should represent the second third (with the final third provided by an IRA).

The term "pension plan" is broad. But there's one arrangement that can benefit you no matter what type you have. A salary-reduction, or 401(k), plan makes sense for just about everyone. And currently, more than 90 percent of all major corporations offer a 401(k) to their employees. (The equivalent of a 401(k) for government workers is known as the 403(b), but it essentially offers the same benefits as a 401(k).)

Under a 401(k), your employer makes a nontaxable contribution on your behalf, thus, in the process, reducing your salary by the same amount. If you make contributions that reduce your taxable wage, called "after-tax contributions," you'll be able to recover them after you retire. A portion of your distributions then will be tax free.

Recent tax-law changes have eroded part of the attraction of 401(k)s. The maximum allowable contribution was reduced from $30,000 to $7,000 (though thanks to indexing, that figure has grown to nearly $10,000). Yet, 401(k)s are more popular than ever. That's because many middle-income and upper-income employees can't deduct their IRA contributions any longer. In that case, it makes sense to contribute to a 401(k) first.

If your company offers the 401(k) option, contribute as much as you can this year. You can go up to the limit, but be careful not to lock away money you may need before you retire. If you do, you'll have to pay a 10-percent penalty plus regular taxes on any early withdrawals. The law also bars you from taking earnings or company-matching contributions from your account before you turn $59\frac{1}{2}$.

Chart 39 may give you a better idea of why it pays to save with a 401(k) before you pay Uncle Sam.

A WHO'S WHO OF 401(K) PROVIDERS

The following companies are the major sponsors of 401(k) plans:

Company	Defined-Contribution Assets
Fidelity Investments	$80.7 billion
The Vanguard Group	40.3 billion
Bankers Trust	39.0 billion
State Street Bank & Trust	37.7 billion
Prudential Defined Contribution Service	33.0 billion
Wells Fargo Defined Contribution	22.8 billion
T. Rowe Price Associates	21.6 billion
Invesco	17.8 billion
Merrill Lynch	17.7 billion
Cigna Retirement & Investment Services	17.4 billion

Source: *SmartMoney* magazine

CHART 39

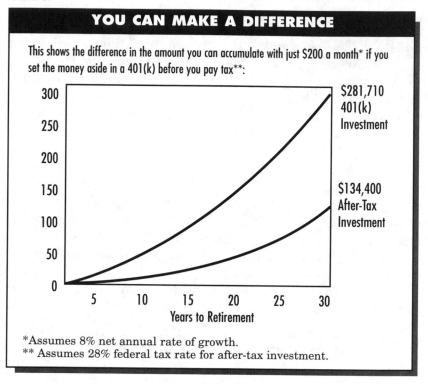

YOU CAN MAKE A DIFFERENCE

This shows the difference in the amount you can accumulate with just $200 a month* if you set the money aside in a 401(k) before you pay tax**:

$281,710
401(k)
Investment

$134,400
After-Tax
Investment

Years to Retirement

*Assumes 8% net annual rate of growth.
** Assumes 28% federal tax rate for after-tax investment.

Your 401(k) contribution may entitle you to an IRA tax deduction you couldn't otherwise take. As you recall, in 1997, married couples earning more than $50,000 and singles earning more than $35,000 can't write off any of their IRA contributions if they are covered by company-sponsored plans. But couples earning $40,000 or less and singles earning $25,000 or less still can, and people in both categories are entitled to partial write-offs.

Because 401(k) contributions reduce your total income, they may lower your earnings enough to let you claim an IRA deduction—or to increase the one you're already taking.

For instance, suppose you and your spouse earn $52,000 annually. Under the law, you're not eligible for an IRA deduction. But if you put $7,600 into a 401(k), your income will fall to $44,400. That means you'll be able to deduct half of any IRA contributions you make.

Show Me the Dough

If you are like most people who are retiring, you will have a choice of how you receive distributions from your various retirement plans. Most retirees opt for a monthly distribution. By spreading your benefits over several years instead of taking a lump-sum payment, you can reduce your overall tax burden, and the monthly check can go a long way toward supplementing the money you'll get from Social Security and other sources.

Still, taking payment in a lump sum has its advantages. It gives you total control over your investment choices, so your money will grow quickly if you invest wisely. You can also reduce your tax bite by taking advantage of an averaging formula that lets you account for the lump sum over several years instead of one. Remember, though, that retirees who take a lump sum and then lose the money through bad investments will have gambled away a large piece of their retirement nest egg.

If you have money in your company's pension, you can take the cash in a lump sum and put part or all of it into an IRA, where the money will grow tax-free until you begin withdrawals. This so-called "rollover" must be performed within 60 days of the date you get your lump-sum distribution. You can pull the money out of your IRA without penalty when you reach 59½. Withdrawals are, as mentioned, mandatory when you reach 70½. The rollover account must be established and maintained by you, additional contributions will not be allowed, and the assets cannot be used to buy a life-insurance policy.

Making the Decision

By now, you are probably convinced that you want to create your own retirement plan. If so, there are several factors to consider. First, make sure you have an emergency cash reserve, say, the equivalent of two months' take-home pay— and keep those funds liquid. Don't tie up all your savings in an IRA, for example, no matter how tempting it may be.

And you don't want to contribute money that you will have

to use in a couple of years—for a new home or to buy a business, for example. But after five or more years of compounding without being taxed, your earnings may more than make up for any penalty you will incur.

Having read this far, you know the options and should be able to match your goals with them. If you are only a few years from retirement, you will probably want a guaranteed yield, say, from a financial institution CD or an annuity plan. If you have a lot of years to go before retirement, you may want to invest in something that offers potential for higher growth although it has the possibility of loss, like a stock-brokerage account or a mutual fund. Of course, as the years go by, you may have investments in two or three different kinds of retirement plans.

Once you know what you want, there won't be any trouble finding sponsors glad to take your money. Chances are they have already found you. If not, look at the ads of financial institutions in your local newspaper or inquire where you bank. For ads by brokerage firms and mutual funds, flip through a few issues of *The Wall Street Journal* or look in the Yellow Pages. If you are interested in an annuity deal and haven't seen any advertising on one, call a couple of insurance companies and ask about their plans.

Tax Preparation by Computer

Owners of personal computers can prepare their income taxes using one of the tax-preparation software packages. And they can help you protect your money from the tax collector. But keep in mind the limitations of such programs. If you have a complicated tax situation, such software may help very little.

If you do decide you need such help, the software you select should be well-designed, inexpensive, and come in a version that is compatible with your computer. For most people, the right software can be a tremendous aid in navigating through the maze of bewildering forms created by the Internal Revenue Service. It can prompt you to use the right forms and handle the math calculations accurately.

IS AN ANNUITY FOR YOU? PROBABLY NOT

You buy annuities from a life-insurance company, either in one payment (called a "single-premium deferred annuity") or several payments over a period of time. The annuity, which is a legal contract, supplies you with regular income for a period you establish. Earnings on the annuity accrue tax free until the date you begin receiving your payments.

Payments may be based on either a fixed period or your life expectancy. In both cases, you can recover the amount you paid for the annuity tax free on a prorated basis during the period you receive your distributions. As with other retirement investments, you'll pay a 10-percent penalty on withdrawals before age $59^1/_2$.

With fixed annuities, which offer a specified rate for a period such as one year, the rate subsequently will change with market conditions. But it won't fall below a guaranteed minimum, typically about 4 percent.

Variable annuities invest your money in a fund chosen by you or your insurance company. Your return depends entirely on the performance of the fund.

As with other insurance policies, annuity fees, rates, and terms vary widely. You probably should consider a tax-deferred annuity only if you intend to keep it for the entire term. Otherwise, sales and administrative fees and early-withdrawal penalties can decimate your investment funds.

However, tax-sheltered annuities (TSAs), which are available to employees of public-school systems and tax-exempt organizations, can be among the most flexible and advantageous retirement investment you make if you're eligible. Typically, you can contribute up to 20 percent of your taxable income annually. Taxes on contributions and their earnings are deferred, subject to some limitations, until you begin drawing your retirement benefits.

Here are the top-performing players in the variable-annuity game:

Annuity	Telephone #
Aetna Map V Lowest (Q)	800-232-5422
American Skandia Advisors Choice	800-752-6342
Ameritas Overture II	800-634-8353
Best of America IV Nationwide	800-243-6295
Diversified Investors Var Q	914-697-8000
Fidelity Retirement Reserves	800-544-2442
Franklin Valuemark	800-542-5427
Life of Virginia Commonwealth	800-521-8884
MONYMaster	800-800-3219

Source: Morningstar Variable Annuity/Life Performance Report

But it won't necessarily save you money. It will probably spare you from making those math errors, but that also includes those errors that may have resulted in your paying less. It may remind you of deductions or credits you might have otherwise overlooked, but it may also remind you to declare some kinds of income you also may have overlooked.

So which of the leading tax preparation packages should you buy? With either Intuit's TurboTax/MacInTax, Kiplinger's TaxCut, or Parsons' Personal Tax Edge, you would have chosen well. TaxCut has not only a Windows version, but also a Macintosh version. All three are also available on multimedia CD-ROMs.

Intuit has now moved in on TaxCut's biggest specialty: its "interview" feature. This spares the taxpayer from filling out the form directly and instead prepares the return by asking a series of specific questions and offering tips and explanations to help the user answer.

Both TurboTax and TaxCut are available at most computer-software stores. Personal Tax Edge is available by direct mail only (888/883-0791).

The Road to Tax Relief

In this chapter you've seen how you can take effective action to reduce your taxes. With Roth IRAs and municipal bonds, for example, you can actually avoid paying a tax on your return. Deductions and credits also provide some tax-reduction assistance. And with plans such as standard IRAs and 401(k)s, you can delay the payment of taxes until such time as you want to pay them, meanwhile enjoying the compounding benefits of a tax-free investment status.

Chapter 16: Protecting Your Assets

"Heaven, they say, protects children, sailors, and drunken men."

– Thomas Hughes

But For the Rest of Us...

To the above quotation, Thomas Hughes might have added that for those of us who are not children, sailors, or drunken men, we'd better be well-insured. And that's what this chapter is all about. Here you'll learn the ins and outs of the various forms of insurance and see why most people need an overall plan—not only to protect them against disaster or death, but also to keep their insurance premiums to a minimum.

Getting Out of Harm's Way

Since you most likely are not routinely protected by heaven, that leaves you only one real alternative: insurance.

Nobody has to sell you on the concept of insurance. You know its value in the overall scheme of things. With insurance you protect yourself and others you choose from the daily hazards of life. You prevent the loss of your savings, your investments, your possessions—everything you own.

Before you can begin accumulating sizable wealth, therefore, you must make sure you have adequate insurance coverage. Note the word "adequate." It means that you have enough, but not too much. You want to avoid spending money for protection you don't need almost as much as you want to assure that you don't underinsure.

Moreover, you need to determine which types of insurance you need. Health insurance is invaluable. And if you have small children, life insurance is a must. But what about disability insurance? Statistics show that 30 percent of Americans between the ages of 35 and 60 will suffer a disability that will keep them out of work for more than 90 days. Statistics also show that during any year of your life, you are far more likely to become permanently disabled than to die, yet only 6 percent of American adults own individual long-term disability insurance to protect their earning power.

Obviously, you can't insure yourself and your possessions against all potential harm. If you try, you'd soon find yourself impoverished. To preserve your lifestyle and your wealth-accumulation plans, you should protect your biggest assets. They are:

➤ Earning power

➤ Life

➤ Health

➤ Property (especially your home)

➤ Exposure to lawsuit

As to which takes priority, you'll have to decide that for yourself. As mentioned, a family with children would probably value life insurance more than property insurance. If you're retired, you may not even need life insurance, but health insurance becomes essential.

To spread a safety net under yourself and your assets, you should establish an insurance program with policies for disability, life, health, and property protection, including liability. Start by checking the group life and health policies provided by your employer. In some cases, only a small gap may exist between your benefits and your comfort level. Keep in mind also that the purpose of insurance is to make you feel secure.

Let's take a look at some of the key areas to consider, especially if you are just beginning your financial-planning efforts and are still in the early stages of building wealth.

Life Insurance

When you mention "life insurance," most people think of whole life, which provides a fixed death benefit from the time it is purchased until the death of the individual (or the surrender of the policy). Whole-life policies also generate "cash value," based on the investment income of the issuing company. This cash value, in turn, can earn interest or be withdrawn from the policy for the use of the policyholder. It even can be used as collateral for a loan, or simply borrowed from the policy at a low rate of interest.

Whole-life insurance has a number of drawbacks, however. The cash value you build in such a policy is not a good investment when compared to the likes of stocks and bonds—or even certificates of deposit. Its main benefit is that the premium never varies for the life of the policy, and the insurance company can never cancel.

Because of the poor investment quality of whole-life insurance, many people choose term insurance. In fact, with the increased financial awareness of the last decade, term insurance has become a preferred means of providing protection for many investors.

Unlike cash-value insurance, term policies provide protection alone, with no cash accumulation, and only for a specified period of time. If you want to renew a term policy, your premiums may increase as you get older, and when you cancel or surrender the policy, there is no residual cash returned to you.

Behind term's popularity is the recognition that you can get greater returns on your money by investing the difference between the cost of protection and the higher premiums charged for cash-value policies.

A typical term policy may cost as little as a third of the price of a cash-value policy. If you were to invest the difference in a money-market mutual fund, you easily could wind up with several times as much yield as you would get from the cash accumulation in a traditional policy. Or you could use the difference to purchase additional coverage. The key, of course, is to use the savings, either for other investments or for more protection.

You'll find two principal types of term insurance:

➤ **Level term**, which provides the same amount of protection for the life of the policy. For example, if you are concerned with assuring your children of money for education, you might consider a 20-year term policy that would pay $100,000 if you die. Presumably at the end of that time, the education costs would have been paid from other sources, and you no longer would need the protection.

➤ **Decreasing term**, which drops in value over the life of the policy. The amount of the decrease and the rate at which it occurs vary depending on the company and the policy, but in most cases the premium amount remains constant. A decreasing-term policy can be useful if you want to be sure your family will have enough money to pay off a large debt, such as the mortgage on your house. As the size of the debt declines, the benefit decreases as well.

You can buy either type of term insurance with renewal or convertible riders. The first allows you to continue the policy for another term; the second permits you to exchange the policy for another type of coverage.

Two newer types of life insurance, created in response to demands from consumer groups, are variable life and universal life. With variable life you can purchase a degree of protection along with the risks of the stock market. Universal life, a more conservative product, allows you to tie your insurance fortune to the ups and downs of the money market.

Both variable life and universal life are designed to combine basic protection with higher rates of return. For those reasons, they may be an attractive way of supplementing your basic life-insurance program—provided you understand the risks. With universal, your premium payments are credited to a savings-account-like fund, which earns interest based on money-market indexes. The costs of protection and the company's overhead are deducted from the fund monthly, and the remainder of the fund continues to accrue interest.

Depending on the amount of money in the fund, you can increase or decrease both your premium payments and your death benefits during the life of the policy, so long as the balance in the account and the death benefit stay within a federally mandated ratio. To get the most from universal life, you're better off making your payments quarterly or even annually. That increases the size of the pool earning interest and the rate at which cash values accumulate.

Variable life is a hybrid of an insurance policy and a mutual fund. Part of your monthly premium goes for protection and part of it is deposited in an investment account. The earnings from the investment account can be used to increase the amount of your coverage. But if the investment account shows a loss for one quarter, that deficit must be made up in later quarters before any further gains are credited to your protection account.

When you buy the variable policy, you can select the type of investment fund your money will be credited to: growth, conservative, bond, money market, etc. Or you can add your funds to a mutual fund directed by the company. The risk, of course, is that the investment funds will perform badly and have a negative impact on your basic protection. While the protection amount can't fall below the policy minimum, it can fluctuate in lock step with the market. And cash-value withdrawals reduce the possibility of increased protection.

Through "riders," you can get an assortment of bells and whistles added to basic policies. Some riders have clear merit. Example: A family-income rider that assures your family, if you die while your children are still young, a decreasing minimum monthly income for a specified number of years, plus a lump-sum payment. But other riders seem almost ludicrous. Example: A rider that covers a young child.

How much life insurance should you buy? Chart 40 can help you answer that question.

CHART 40

CALCULATING YOUR LIFE-INSURANCE NEEDS

When buying life insurance, you need to identify what your family's cash needs will be in the future. First, multiply your annual take-home pay by the number of years your family will need that income. From that, subtract a number that represents annual income from your surviving spouse (if any) and payments from investments and Social Security multiplied by the number of years of need. That's how much life insurance you should buy.

For example:

Step 1: $ 30,000   annual take-home pay
        x 25   years
      $750,000   total amount of income needed

Step 2: $ 15,000   investment and Social Security income
        x 25   years
      $375,000   anticipated income

Step 3: $750,000   amount of income needed
       375,000   anticipated income
      $375,000   the amount of insurance you need today

Five years from now, the number will likely change because you may be earning more (or less) money, but your investments will probably have higher value and your years of need will have declined. For example:

Step 1: $ 45,000   annual take-home pay
        x 20   years
      $900,000   total amount of income needed

Step 2: $ 30,000   investment and Social Security income
        x 20   years
      $600,000   anticipated income

Step 3: $900,000   total amount of income needed
       600,000   anticipated income
      $300,000   the amount of insurance you need today

Another and quicker way to judge your life-insurance needs is to multiply your annual income by five and buy a policy for that amount. Though simplistic, that method has been endorsed by the National Insurance Consumer Organization (NICO), a nonprofit public-interest organization. NICO claims this rule applies to families with two young children and a primary provider who is eligible for Social Security and has an employer group life policy worth one year's salary. For example, if you earn $30,000 and have met the other criteria, buy a $150,000 policy.

CALCULATING YOUR LIFE-INSURANCE NEEDS
(continued)

But none of these two methods takes cost-of-living differences into account. Obviously, if you live in San Francisco, you will need more than if you live in Pascagoula Miss. With that in mind, the National Association of Insurance Commissioners (whose members are state insurance regulators), suggests that consumers comparison shop for insurance by using a special cost index. This index, called the "interest-adjusted net cost index," provides an accurate measure of relative prices of comparable policies for given periods of time. The calculations that go into determining the index numbers of policies are complex, difficult to explain easily, and really unnecessary for you to know. What you should know is that the smaller the number, the better the buy. Insurance agents will provide the cost index for each policy you are considering. You may have to be assertive in getting the number. If an agent won't provide it, go elsewhere.

In any case, follow these three steps:

1. Make cost comparisons between similar plans.
2. Compare index numbers for your age and the amount of insurance you plan to purchase.
3. Note small differences in policy features and company service that may affect index numbers.
4. Use the index for comparisons of new policies, not for replacements to your current policy.

Disability Insurance

As mentioned, disability insurance is as important—and often more important—than life insurance. Yet most people overlook or ignore disability coverage. And if you think about that situation, it makes little sense. Many people consciously decide to forgo life insurance on the belief that it is more important to earn money and build an estate in this life before creating a second one that materializes after their death. But then they neglect to insure their income streams. Should disaster strike, the mechanisms for estate building grind to a halt and the base that does exist will deteriorate.

In like manner, the vast majority of people who own life insurance fail to buy disability insurance. This means that most of us are better prepared to die than to be disabled by accident or illness. The purpose of disability insurance is to provide you and your family with an income if you can't work. It allows you to pay your bills without having to liquidate your assets.

Compared to life insurance, disability insurance is a complex product. With life insurance, while you're alive, you make premium payments. When you're no longer here, your beneficiaries collect money. It's that simple. Triggering the payment of disability income is not a cut-and-dried matter. For example, a banker who loses some fingers would most likely be able to perform his job, while a dentist with such an injury would not be able to work at all. Some arbiters of disability-funds disbursement could decide to pay neither under the rules of a particular system.

Disability policies are fraught with qualifications and technicalities. But one rule is certain. Even if you have protected yourself with disability insurance from your employer, the U.S. government and private sources, you will not receive more money than you earned at the time disaster struck. Just as you try to make certain in your life-insurance plans that your beneficiaries do not profit enormously from your death, the disability-insurance industry makes equally certain that you are motivated to continue working.

HOW TO FIND A DISABILITY INSURER

When buying a disability policy, make sure the company offering it has strong financial ratings. You don't want to have coverage, then learn that your company has gone down the tubes.

Go to your public library and ask the reference desk for publications by A.M. Best, S&P, Weiss, or Duff & Phelps. Then make sure the company or companies you are considering get a top rating from one or two of those sources.

The leading insurers that provide disability coverage (and they account for more than 50 percent of the market in disability-insurance sales) are:

> Provident Life & Accident Insurance Co., based in Chattanooga.
> Northwestern Mutual Life Insurance Co., based in Milwaukee.
> Unum Life Insurance Co., based in Portland, Maine.

Most likely you need disability insurance. In fact, everyone who works for a living and depends on a paycheck should investigate his or her sources of disability income. That suggestion also applies to people who have no dependents, in contrast to the case made for candidates for life insurance. As for the amount of income you should have, as a rule of thumb, establish a disability-income plan that will provide 60 percent or more of your predisability, after-tax earnings.

When evaluating disability-insurance products, check out these features:

➤ The length of benefit period. Each policy sets a maximum period of time in which you will receive benefit payments. It is expressed in numbers of weeks or months, or it extends to a specific age for the recipient or until the disability disappears. Obviously, the longer the benefit period, the better the coverage and the higher the premium.

➤ The elimination or waiting period. Beginning with the date of your illness or injury, this is the length of time that you must wait before you begin to receive benefit payments. Some plans begin making immediate payments under certain circumstances; others feature a waiting period of months. Once payments begin, however, they are not retroactive to the start of your incapacitation.

➤ The definition of disability. This provision sets the rules regarding your status for collecting benefits. Three common definitions are:

1. "Any occupational type," which means your disability is so severe that you are incapable of holding any paying job. This is the strictest definition for recipients. Insurers usually phrase the definition as "the complete inability of the insured to engage in any gainful occupation for which he or she is or becomes reasonably fitted by education, training, or experience." Under this definition, the dentist with the missing fingers—if he has a policy with this strict clause—might be expected to find work as a teacher, administrator, or lobbyist.

2. "Own occupation type" means you are considered disabled

when you are "prevented by such disability from performing any and every duty pertaining to your occupation." This, the most liberal definition from your viewpoint, would apply to the dentist.

3. "Split definition" combines elements of the two definitions. It applies the "own-occupation" requirement but qualifies it by setting a finite collection period that later changes the definition to "any occupation." The wording might be as follows:

    Total disability is defined as the complete inability of the insured to engage in any gainful occupation for which he or she is reasonably prepared by education, training, or experience. During the first 24 months of any period of disability, the insured will deem the insured to be totally disabled if he or she is completely unable to engage in his or her regular occupation and is not engaged in any form of gainful employment.

    Your goal, with this type of policy, is to find the maximum length of "own-occupation" coverage. It will vary by company and by circumstances. The "own-occupation" time frame generally lasts two to five years. Depending on the circumstances, it could last for 10 years. Some policies continue paying benefits until the recipient reaches age 65. Insurers, fond of attaching qualification clauses, have been known to require "house confinement" to their definition of total disability. If you encounter a clause of this type, consider it a "prison" clause and look for another policy, if possible.

4. "Perils covered" refers to either "accident alone" or "accident and sickness." The best bet is to get coverage for accident and sickness and avoid limitations of the accident-only policies.

5. "Renewal provisions" allow you to extend coverage. A "guaranteed-renewable" policy is in your best interest. That means that you will be assured that your coverage will continue as long as you pay the premiums until you

reach a specified age, usually 65. A "noncancelable" policy is also a guaranteed renewable and, additionally, the premium is guaranteed not to increase. Some policies permit you to continue coverage beyond age 65 so long as you are employed. They can be offered either on a guaranteed-renewable basis or at the option of the insurance company. Some policies may have a "terminal" age, such as 70, when coverage is automatically discontinued.

You may already have disability coverage without contracting privately for insurance. Social Security can be considered the base layer of protection if you become disabled. This federal-government program annually provides more than $20 billion in disability benefits to more than three million covered workers and more than two million of their dependents. Nearly 90 percent of the U.S. work force qualifies for Social Security. To be eligible for benefits, you must have worked in a Social Security qualified job for five of the 10 years prior to your disability if you are at least 31 years old (the requirement is less if you are younger), but you don't have to be the primary breadwinner in your household to qualify for benefits. In fact, you do not even have to be employed at the time of your illness or injury to collect.

Social Security benefits for disability don't come easily, however. To be considered disabled and eligible for benefits, you must have a "medically determinable" physical or mental impairment that is so severe you cannot hold "any substantially gainful" job. This disability must last five months before benefits can begin. You receive benefits only if your disability is expected to last at least 12 months or to result in your death. Such rules essentially limit Social Security payments to people with total and severe long-term disabilities.

The basis for the amount of money a disabled worker and his or her dependents can receive is the worker's wages that are subject to Social Security tax. This is the same approach the government uses to calculate retirement and survivor benefits. Your local Social Security office will calculate benefits for each applicant. The factors that go into the government's formula are so diverse that a standard chart of benefits doesn't exist. However, you can come up with a close estimate. Use Chart 41:

CHART 41

ESTIMATING YOUR SOCIAL SECURITY DISABILITY BENEFITS

1. Subtract the year you became 27 years old from the year you became disabled. The result is the number of years you will use to calculate average earnings.

2. List all your earning years until the year you became disabled. The maximum amount of earnings you may list are:

1959-65	$ 4,800	1979	$ 22,900	1989	$ 48,000
1966-67	6,600	1980	25,900	1990	51,300
1968-71	7,800	1981	29,700	1991	53,400
1972	9,000	1982	32,400	1992	55,500
1973	10,800	1983	35,700	1993	
1974	13,200	1984	37,900	1994	
1975	14,100	1985	39,600	1995	
1976	15,300	1986	42,000	1996	
1977	16,500	1987	43,800		
1978	17,700	1988	45,000		

3. Eliminate the low-earning years until the number of remaining years equals your answer in Step 1.

4. Calculate your average earnings for the remaining years.

5. Use the following table to estimate your Social Security benefits. Note that the averages depend on your age at the time your disability occurred and other entitlement factors.

MONTHLY SOCIAL SECURITY PAYMENTS TO BENEFICIARIES					
Average Earnings (from Step 4)					
Recipient(s)	$8,000	$9,000	$10,000	$12,000	$13,000
Disabled worker	$606	$641	$ 672	$731	$759
Disabled worker, non-working spouse, and child	$909	$962	$1,008	$1,097	$1,130

Health Insurance

Health insurance is essential to protecting your assets. You've worked hard to accumulate wealth, but a serious illness or injury can play havoc with your goals. Medical costs resulting from just a few weeks in the hospital can reach into the hundreds of thousands of dollars. Worse, those costs are escalating. So it's no wonder that financial planners advise that if you can afford only one type of insurance, you should buy health coverage. They know that many people think they can go without such protection, betting that their savings and investments can see them through a crisis. But that a bad bet, one you're almost sure to lose.

You may be covered with a group health plan at work. In fact, health insurance is today's most common employee benefit. And if you have access to one, by all means take advantage of it. Nevertheless, you need to make sure that it is adequate for your requirements, so the following should help—whether you have group insurance or you're self-employed and seeking it on your own.

First, calculate your medical insurance needs, and that's not so simple. There's more guesswork involved than with life, property, liability, and even disability insurance because you have no way of knowing when you will suffer illness or injury and you don't have an idea of what the cost will be for recovery. For that reason, medical insurance is structured by the type of expenses you might incur.

Your goal then is to have comprehensive health-insurance coverage designed to protect you and your family from the ruinous effects of a major illness or accident and provide some reimbursement for routine care or prevention. Any comprehensive plan should typically consist of...

1. **Basic protection.** This is the first level of coverage and is composed of hospitalization and physician expenses.

2. **Hospitalization coverage.** This insurance will pay for 80 to 100 percent of daily room and board and regular nursing services while you are in a hospital, plus certain hospi-

tal services and supplies, such as X-rays, lab tests, drugs, and medication. Surgeon's expenses should be covered as well. And a complete package will also include private-duty nursing.

3. **Physician-expenses coverage.** This insurance is less common than hospitalization and covers visits to the doctors' offices when you're ill or injured. This type of coverage normally does not include visits to the doctor for routine preventive care, such as an annual physical, nor does it pay surgeon's expenses.

Keep in mind that basic protection alone has limitations. Many types of important medical expenses might not be covered, and maximum benefits might be low compared to the high expense of medical care. Moreover, with medical costs rising so rapidly, your plan could easily become outdated.

That's why you need a second level of coverage called "major medical," whose purpose is to pay the expenses of long-term illness or injury after basic benefits run out. Major medical pays for a fixed percentage of all expenses rather than setting limits for each category. Because coverage is so high—$1 million is not uncommon—the deductible is also high: $5,000 or more. In addition to paying the deductible, you are also responsible for paying 10-20 percent of all the eligible expenses in excess of the deductible amounts.

For example, your policy pays 80 percent of all costs over the $1,000 initial deductible and your costs total $2,000. You must pay 20 percent of $1,000 ($200) plus the $1,000 deductible, for a total of $1,200. Insurers structure policies with this "coinsurance" feature to encourage you to keep costs to a minimum. Fortunately, most major-medical plans include a "stop-loss" provision that puts a cap on your participation. After your costs reach that level, the insurer picks up 100 percent of the charges.

The deductible and coinsurance features represent your out-of-pocket expenses under a health-insurance policy—in addition, of course, to the premiums you pay. Another feature that can result in cash outlay is the "reasonable and customary fee limitation." This is a charge that represents the general-area rate for identical or similar medical services. Thus, after you pay the deductible, your policy pays the 80-percent coinsurance charge up to the reasonable and customary fee. If your charges exceed that amount, you are expected to pay the balance.

You can avoid unpleasant surprises after you receive medical care by asking your doctor the charges for the procedure in question before you consent to treatment. Then you can determine your insurer's maximum payment. If your doctor's fee is beyond the range of your insurer, perhaps your doctor will lower his or her fee. Or perhaps the insurer will extend its payment range. Or maybe you should seek another opinion with another estimate.

Keep in mind that you always have the option of reducing your major-medical premium costs by raising the deductible. You might consider using your emergency reserve fund for this purpose, especially if you and your family members are healthy and your leisure activities are not dangerous. Or by using this "self-insurance," you can buy higher maximum coverage with the premium dollars you save.

One more thing about health insurance: When you evaluate policies, be aware of provisions that affect coverage. If you're covered by a group plan, you don't have to worry about these things. Otherwise, however, check these provisions:

➤ **Renewal or continuance.** These provisions validate your right to continue coverage from one policy period to the next.

➤ **Optional renewal.** These allow the insurance company to refuse to carry you as a customer as of any premium due date or policy anniversary. Some states have passed laws to restrict this type of activity, however. Under this provision, an insurer may also raise your premiums and/or attach restrictive clauses, such as demanding that you cease sky diving.

➤ **Guaranteed renewable.** These allow you to renew your coverage for a specified period of time, such as when you turn 65 and are eligible for Medicare coverage. The insurance company cannot make major changes in your policy or premium rates unless the company makes a wholesale change in rates for an entire class of participants.

➤ **Noncancelable.** These allow you to keep your policy in force by merely making your premium payments. The insurance company cannot change the payment rate by manipulations of any sort. As you might guess, the premium for this very liberal policy is higher than for a comparable benefits policy of the latter two types.

➤ **Pre-existing conditions.** You may get coverage for losses that begin with your policy period. Illnesses or injuries sustained before your policy is in force are not covered.

➤ **Time limit on certain defenses.** This provision stipulates that after you've had a policy for two or three years, you cannot be denied coverage of an ailment on the grounds that it existed prior to the start of your contract. Some policies contain provisions that specifically exclude coverage of certain conditions. All policies will void the time-limit provision if the insurer discovers you made fraudulent statements on your application concerning your state of health.

Following is a shopping list you can use when you buy health insurance:

CHART 42

CHECKLIST FOR BUYING HEALTH INSURANCE

Comprehensive Medical
- ☐ Deductible
- ☐ Benefit maximum
- ☐ Mental illness
- ☐ Stop loss
- ☐ Continuation of plan after conversion to individual coverage
- ☐ Medical supplemental for employees with continuation provision

Disability
- ☐ Short-term benefits (# of weeks _____)
- ☐ Long-term benefits (# of weeks, months, years _____)
- ☐ Elimination period _____
- ☐ Average monthly benefit to age 65 _____

Supplementary Major Medical
- ☐ Deductible
- ☐ Benefit maximum
- ☐ Mental illness
- ☐ Stop loss

Basic Expense
- ☐ Semiprivate hospital room
- ☐ Miscellaneous hospital charges
- ☐ Basic surgical costs
- ☐ In-hospital private physician
- ☐ Diagnostic X-ray and lab

Intensive Care
- ☐ Hospital room and board

Home Health Care
- ☐ Provided

Cost-Containment Benefits
- ☐ Generic-drug prescriptions
- ☐ Second opinions on nonemergency surgery
- ☐ Outpatient surgery
- ☐ Preadmission testing
- ☐ Paramedical services

Continuation and Conversion
- ☐ Provision for continuation at retirement or upon termination other than retirement

Property Insurance

The purpose of property insurance is to have a third party—an insurer—accept the risk of having to replace your property if it is damaged or destroyed by some unpreventable calamity.

For many people, their home and its contents represent their biggest investment. While mortgage lenders nowadays require a fire-insurance policy when you buy your home, many homeowners stop there. But what if your home burns to the ground? Would you have enough cash or assets to liquidate so you can replace everything involved? Even if you do, is that how you want to spend your money? Needless to say, the thought of having your home go up in flames should cause you to restructure your financial plans.

Renters also face the possibility of suffering severe financial loss from a fire. Do you really want to go on a major shopping trip with the money that you've accumulated for your financial future?

For those reasons, you will want to insure your property for its replacement cost rather than its market value. In fact, insurance companies require that you insure your home and other structures, such as garages and tool sheds, for their replacement value. Your home is likely to appreciate in value, but there is no booming market for old garages or tool sheds.

Replacement value relates primarily to construction costs. To value your home or other structures, multiply the number of square feet in your house by the local construction costs per square foot. These numbers vary by region, the quality of materials, and the architectural design you choose. Check with a local insurance agent for an estimate of current construction costs in your area or neighborhood. You might even check it against your neighbor's estimate. For example, if your standard wood-frame home is 1,700 square feet and local construction costs are $80 per square foot, your replacement cost is $136,000.

Reevaluate your home's replacement-cost estimate every few years to account for the effects of inflation on construction materials and labor costs. Some insurers offer an "inflation-guard endorsement" that automatically increases policy limits each year for that purpose. You may be tempted to call your local real-estate agent to get an estimate on the value of your home. Resist the temptation. The agent will tell you the market value of your home, including the land. In some cases, the land may be worth more than the house. Using the market value of your home to calculate your insurance needs will result in your being overinsured.

Be aware of the "coinsurance clause" when you calculate your protection needs. This is a provision that insurance companies use to reward you for properly insuring your home or to penalize you for underinsuring it. Under this clause, when you buy insurance equal to or in excess of 80-percent of your home's replacement-cost value, you will be reimbursed for losses up to the value of the loss, not to exceed the value of your policy.

For example, let's say you buy an $80,000 policy on your $100,000 home. You suffer a total loss. the insurer pays you $80,000. If your loss totals $60,000, your insurer would pay you $60,000. But if you insure your home for less than 80-percent replacement-cost value, you may not receive the entire amount of your policy in the event of a loss. Insurance companies use a formula:

$$\frac{\text{Amount of insurance coverage}}{80\% \text{ of the replacement cost}} \quad \times \quad \text{the amount of the loss}$$

This coinsurance clause goes into effect when both the amount of insurance you carry and the amount of the loss fall below 80 percent of the replacement cost. For example, suppose you buy $70,000 worth of insurance on your $100,000 home. You suffer an $80,000 loss. The insurer pays you $70,000. But if you buy $70,000 worth of insurance on your $100,000 home and you suffer a $60,000 loss, the insurer pays you only $52,500 ($70,000 ÷ $80,000 [80% of replacement cost] = 0.875; 0.875 x $60,000 = $52,500).

As for your personal property, begin by taking inventory of everything you own. If a tornado rips through your home, depositing your worldly goods over a two-mile radius, how many items would you be able to list as missing or destroyed? At present, can you name everything in the attic of your home?

Insurance companies prefer to work with lists compiled before disasters strike rather than lists recreated from memory after the roof has caved in or blown away. In fact, your insurance agent will even provide you with forms for taking inventory of your property. These can be updated as you acquire and eliminate items. Keep one copy for yourself and put another copy someplace away from the premises, such as a bank safe-deposit box.

With the inventory form in hand, go from room to room in your home and make a list of all the major items. Describe important possessions by serial number or distinguishing features. Include sales slips in your records. Take photographs of your property. You might even videotape a home tour with lingering shots of valuable items. Supplement the video portion with an audio chronicle of each important item with the price and date of purchase. If you don't own a video camera, you can rent one for the day from a video store.

Your personal inventory will determine the existence of your property rather than simply establish the value of any specific item. That's because you'll want to buy "replacement-cost coverage" rather than market-value coverage for your personal property as well as your home. As a rule of thumb, your personal-property insurance will have a value of 50 percent of your dwelling insurance. If you insure your home for $100,000, you'll get $50,000 worth of insurance on the contents. The insurance companies are actually doing you a favor by preventing you from underestimating the value of your property. Can you name the current cost of every item in your house, from the pillows on your bed to the love seat in the living room?

The replacement-cost endorsement on your property-insurance policy usually adds 10-15 percent to the premium costs for a homeowner and 20-40 percent for a renter or condo owner, but that's money well spent. Keep in mind, however, that the replacement-cost endorsement does not mean you automatically increase the dollar amount of your property insurance to, say, 70 percent of the dwelling value—although some insurers will do this.

Of course, such extra protection does not mean that the insurance company will automatically write you a check for

50-70 percent of the value of your home when fire destroys its contents. Instead, your insurer will make sure you use replacement money to actually replace your property by paying you the market or depreciated value of your property. When or if you actually buy the replacement items, you will then get the difference. So you can't transform your antique clock into a vacation to Europe. By the same token, insurance companies cap your coverage so you can't buy a $1,000 CD system to replace the five-track player you bought in college. Having that detailed inventory of your property supposedly keeps everyone honest and happy.

You may, however, have some items of value that require special treatment for insurance purposes. Still other items may be subject to certain limitations. Insurance companies offer two basic approaches to insuring property. They are:

1. Specific-perils coverage, which protects you against the specific causes of loss named in your policy, such as fire and theft. You are of course not protected against unnamed perils.

2. All-risk coverage, which protects you against all the risks or perils that may cause loss to the covered property except those that are specifically excluded, such as floods and earthquakes. This coverage, because it is broader, usually costs more than specific-perils coverage.

You have six options when shopping for homeowners (HO) policies. Each is a package deal that provides coverage for your home, such structures as garage and tool shed, and personal property. Some policies provide living expenses if you must stay in a hotel or rent a home while your house is being repaired or rebuilt; others provide personal-liability coverage in case someone sues you for an accident that occurred on your property. Chart 43 offers a brief description of the six policies and the coverage that each provides.

CHART 43

HOMEOWNERS INSURANCE

HO-1 Basic Form

Covers only a limited range and nature of perils, though there might be exclusions for each peril:

Fire or lightning
Smoke
Windstorm or hail
Explosion
Riots or civil turmoil
Damage by aircraft
Damage by vehicles
Vandalism or malicious mischief
Breakage of glass
Theft

HO-2 Broad Form

Expands the coverage of HO-1 to include:

Sudden and accidental damage from smoke
Falling objects, weight of ice, snow, or sleet
Collapse of buildings
Sudden and accidental rupture of steam or hot-water system
Accidental discharge or overflow of water or steam from plumbing
Freezing of plumbing, heating, air-conditioning and domestic appliances
Sudden and accidental injury from electrical currents artificially generated

HO-3 Special Form

This most popular policy expands coverage of HO-2 to include:

All perils except flood, earthquake, war, nuclear accident, and others as specified. Examples of exclusions in the "all-perils" category are: water backing up through sewers or drains, wear and tear, marring and scratching, rust, mold, wet or dry rot, smog, birds, bugs, acts of government

HO-4 Contents Broad Form for Renters

As a broad form, this policy covers the same range of perils as HO-2 for the contents of an apartment.

HO-5 Comprehensive Form

This broadest of all coverage available extends all-risk protection to personal property, home, and unattached structures, and premium costs are generally twice as high as for any other policy.

HO-6 Condominium Owner's Form

This coverage is similar to that of the renter's policy (HO-4), but fills the gaps between the condominium association's policy and the individual's need for protection. Policies vary in that some are written for market value, others for replacement-cost coverage.

Some homeowners may want additional coverage if they have a prized collection of stamps, works of art, or valuable jewelry. A "floater" may thus be necessary. It will provide you all-risk protection for the specified classes of personal property at home or wherever you may take your possessions. The cost of such coverage varies by item, by region, and even by city. You'll find it more expensive in urban, high-crime areas than rural areas.

If you live in a flood-prone area, you can get coverage at special rates, thanks to a joint effort by the insurance industry and the federal government. To qualify for flood insurance, you must live in one of the 20,000 communities that has agreed to plan and carry out land-use control measures to reduce future flooding.

Earthquake insurance is usually written as an addition to fire or homeowners coverage. Not surprisingly, Californians, who live in an earthquake-prone geographical area, account for about two-thirds of all earthquake insurance written in the United States.

Comprehensive Personal-Liability Insurance

Your chances of getting sued in your lifetime are one in 20. Some unfortunate people seem more susceptible to lawsuits than others. If, for example, you are a bad driver or you fail to make your residence a safe place for visitors, you may find yourself in court more than once in your life. We obviously live in a litigious society, and that means that to protect your assets, you need insurance.

Liability insurance can cover you and the members of your household from claims arising from bodily injury and property damage to others. Automobile insurance, which is mandatory in nearly all states today, includes a provision for liability, when you, in your car, cause damage or injury to others.

With comprehensive personal-liability insurance, you draw a protective shield around you for out-of-automobile legal encounters. This type of insurance, like most others, furnishes you with the security of knowing that your financial plans cannot be disrupted by a third party bent on using the judicial system to enhance his or her own financial future.

The insurer will pay, on your behalf, an amount of money to the policy limit that you are required to pay as damages. The insurer will also defend you in court in any lawsuit covered in your policy. Insurers protect themselves with a list of exclusions, such as the following:

➤ Business or professional pursuits (which requires separate insurance).

➤ Use of automobiles, large watercraft and aircraft (which also require their own specialized policies).

➤ Injury or damage that you intentionally cause.

➤ Benefits payable under worker's compensation.

➤ Injury or damage resulting from war, revolution, or nuclear energy.

➤ Damage to property you rent, except for property damage caused by fire, smoke, or explosion.

You may become liable through negligence. The law requires that we take reasonable care to avoid injury to others and their possessions. To set a standard for reasonable care, the court looks at what a prudent person would do under the circumstances. You must live up to that norm. Thus, a lawsuit based on negligence can result from an act on your part or a failure to act if either case can be cited as a direct cause of a predictable injury to a person or property. That means, for example, that you must put a fence around your swimming pool, and you must restrain your dog to prevent it from biting someone or destroying someone else's property.

Another type of liability occurs when you are responsible for the conditions or activities that lead to injury or property loss. This is known as absolute liability, and negligence doesn't matter in such cases. For example, your guest plugged in your electric fan and was electrocuted because the cord was frayed, so you are liable. Similarly, if your maid suffers third-degree burns while tending to her kitchen chores, you, as her employer, may be sued for bodily injury.

In such a lawsuit, you can exonerate yourself if you can prove that you (1) exercised reasonable care to prevent the accident and (2) you explained the risks of an activity to the injured party, who understood those risks, and voluntarily accepted them.

HOW TO CUT YOUR PROPERTY-INSURANCE COSTS

The following are suggestions on ways to reduce the cost of property insurance:

➤ Pay premiums computed on a three-year basis instead of a one-year basis.

➤ Increase your deductible.

➤ Install smoke detectors and fire extinguishers throughout your house.

➤ Inscribe your valuable property with a personal identification number, such as your Social Security or driver's license number.

➤ Buy a package policy rather than individual policies.

Of course, that still may not prevent your having to go through the aggravation and loss of time and money involved in a lawsuit. But with the following types of liability insurance, you may escape payment if a judgment goes against you:

➤ **General liability.** Homeowners policies include general liability coverage for activities in and around your home and away from home. Exclusions are situations involving slander, libel, and activities involving your automobile. The policy's "jacket provisions" list all the insurance company's commitments to you. If you are sued, your insurer will usually pay expenses for investigating your claim and defending you, court and bail bonds, and reasonable expenses, such as a minimum sum for missed salary. You are obligated to inform the insurer in writing of any occurrence that might lead to a damage claim; the insurer has the right to inspect your property any time during the coverage period.

Coverage provisions list the members of the household who are protected by the policy, namely, all relatives living with you and anyone under age 21 living in your care. You are protected from circumstances resulting in injury or damage that occurs on your property by guests, visitors, employees, or delivery people; at hotels or other temporary dwellings; by members of your family using sports or recreation equipment or borrowed property. Your policy will pay medical expenses up to $500 per person per incident for anyone injured on your property, regardless of who is to blame.

➤ **Umbrella liability.** This type of policy, once available only to doctors, lawyers, and other professionals, extends your liability coverage and broadens the definition of exposure. With this type of policy, you are protected in personal-liability claims, such as libel or slander. You can purchase umbrella-liability limits on your auto-insurance policy and your comprehensive coverage of your homeowners policy, which automatically includes a relatively small amount of comprehensive personal-liability coverage.

HOW TO CALCULATE YOUR PERSONAL-LIABILITY INSURANCE NEEDS

One of these simple formulas may help you determine your needs for this type of insurance coverage:

➤ Buy enough insurance to equal your present net worth and the aggregate value of your future earnings.

➤ Protect your current net worth and assume your future will be unencumbered.

Fortunately, the insurance industry apparently doesn't think your chances of being sued are too good. For that reason, personal-liability coverage is relatively inexpensive. In most areas of the nation, you can get several hundred thousand dollars worth of coverage for a few dollars a year. Of course, the cost of protection is chiefly determined by the number and uses of properties you own or use.

In Summary...

Insurance is a necessity of life. It allows us to manage risk and prevent the loss of our assets and purchasing power. In this chapter, you've seen how to select the appropriate life, health, disability, and liability insurance. By being a wise shopper, you can get the exact coverage you need—at the lowest cost.

Chapter 17: Some Guidelines to Get You Where You're Going

"Not in the clamor of the crowded street,
Not in the shouts and plaudits of the throng.
But in ourselves, are triumph and defeat."
— Henry Wadsworth Longfellow

Comparing Notes

You're still not quite through. In this chapter, you'll compare your situation with others who are also trying to accumulate wealth. Like you, they may be wondering if they are on the right path. So let's take a look at three typical investors, ages 25, 40, and 55. Even if you fall between those ages, perhaps in some way you can identify and learn from their examples.

Walter is 25 and works as a sales representative at a retail computer store, earning $28,000 a year. He is not married, but expects to be before he's 30. Meanwhile, he rents a two-bedroom apartment and drives a two-year-old car. He realizes the importance of investing, however, and has set aside for that purpose an inheritance of $10,000 he received from his grandfather when he died. Moreover, he takes $200 each month from his salary to add to his investment portfolio. Plus, he has a 401(k) plan where he works, and it invests an additional $200 a month in a high-growth equity mutual fund. Walter wants to retire at age 55 "with all the money I'll ever need."

Phyllis is 40 years old and is married (second time) to a

high-school football coach. She works as a copy writer for an
advertising agency, and she and her husband together earn
$60,000 a year. They have two children, ages 10 and 13, and
live in a home they bought 10 years ago. Phyllis handles the
money for the couple, and she makes sure to invest at least
$500 a month in a diversified portfolio whose market value is
$25,000. Her husband is a member of his state's teacher-
retirement plan, which invests $300 a month in a growth
mutual fund. She has a 401(k) plan where she works, and in it
she invests $250 a month, also in a growth mutual fund.

Doris and Bill are a married couple, are both 55 years old,
and empty nesters. He is a senior vice president at a bank,
and she works part-time at a local retail store. Together, they
earn $80,000. They have almost paid off the mortgage on their
home, but are just now starting to really plan toward retirement. They have accumulated only $20,000 in personal invest-
ments for retirement, but they can now set aside $3,000 a
month for that purpose. Moreover, Bill has a 401(k) plan at his
bank, and he has built that up to the point where its value
now exceeds $40,000. He is unsure, however, about the invest-
ments to select to assure that he and Doris will have enough
for retirement.

Before we visit them individually, however, let's first examine their general status.

The Three Preretirement 'Ages' of Investing

The three situations briefly described above represent critical "ages" of Americans.

At 25, you usually have feelings of immortality, indestruc-
tibility, and indifference about the distant future. You are generally far more concerned about the present. If you are married and have a family to support, your disposable income is
limited and your expenses are high.

To protect available investment capital, you would choose
some conservative investments. Time is on the side of people
in this age group. They can benefit from the amazing power of
compounding. (See Chapter 20.) So their investments should
emphasize top-quality stocks, bank certificates of deposit,

some bonds, high-quality preferred shares, and Treasury and government-agency securities. But they can also afford to be aggressive, and a large portion of their portfolio should also consist of growth stocks and mutual funds.

Obviously, if you are a single person like Walter or a two-income couple without children, you can take an even more aggressive stance. While still maintaining a solid base of low-risk assets, you can diversify into higher-risk investments, such as high-growth common shares, high-yield bonds, precious metals—and even options and managed-futures accounts. The rationale is that even if your portfolio slides a bit, you have plenty of high-earning years ahead of you.

At 40, you should be earning at near the peak of your lifetime. But if you have children, they probably will be in high school or college and will be financially reliant on you for the next few years. Again, you're going to be more concerned with paying the bills for their well-being than setting aside money for your retirement.

Investments at this age should be in blue-chip stocks (reinvesting the dividends), quality bonds, and real estate. A portion of your portfolio should also consist of growth stocks or growth mutual funds.

At 55, your children probably will have left home and won't be as financially dependent on you as they were when they were living with you or away at school. You'll have had the opportunity to save and to gain some experience at investing. You likely will have more capital available for investment purposes. And you'll be freer to travel and enjoy the fruits of your hard work. You can begin serious planning for your retirement.

Having consolidated your holdings on a solid base of low-risk investments, you now can look for higher returns by adding a few more growth-oriented investments. As you near retirement, however, you need to protect your investment nest egg by cutting back on your riskier investments in favor of those that will protect your capital and provide good income.

Keep in mind that when you retire, you no longer have a

paycheck or fees coming in. You must rely solely on your pension and/or Social Security, the accumulation in your individual retirement account or Keogh plan, and the income generated from stocks and bonds and perhaps real estate. You must consider your health and that of your spouse; medical care can get expensive. That's the downside.

On the bright side, even if you reach that point without a nest egg, you can take certain steps, as outlined in this book, to rectify that dilemma.

Targeting Your Objectives

Knowing your needs for investment safety, income, and growth is the key to your future investing success—and comfort. Determine as honestly as you can where your investment emphasis is: on safety, income, or growth. Emphasizing one does not exclude the others, but your portfolio weighting must reflect your investment objectives.

Chart 44 can help a person get his or her priorities in focus.

CHART 44

WHAT IS YOUR INVESTMENT 'PERSONALITY'?

To determine the type of investor you are, respond to the following statements:

I'm a compulsive risk taker.	❐ Yes	❐ No
I have a good sense of balance, but will take calculated risk.	❐ Yes	❐ No
I'm cautious. My first concern is protection of capital.	❐ Yes	❐ No
I'm ultraconservative. To be comfortable, I must stick with the safest investments.	❐ Yes	❐ No

Now, based on what you've learned in this book so far, determine your best means for wealth accumulation—and keep those means in mind when you consider straying for any reason.

Although you may be wondering why you are going back to square one, it's a fact that most investors make mistakes at the beginning of their investment experience. They pick the wrong category of investment vehicles. They overemphasize securities that are too risky, or they are too conservative when they're in a position to take on more risk. By regularly reviewing your investment personality and objectives, you'll avoid this major mistake.

The following shows sample portfolios for the persons whom we met earlier. And for our purposes, we are going to state that all three of these investors fall into the second category: They have a good sense of balance, but will take calculated risks. Obviously, since there are an almost infinite number of combinations of family situations, risk preferences, and objectives, you probably don't have a sample design that perfectly matches your situation. But unless your case is highly unusual, it should come reasonably close to at least one of the samples shown.

WALTER'S PORTFOLIO
(Moderately Aggressive)

Component	Target % of Portfolio	Purpose
Low-risk assets (Savings Bonds, bank CDs, etc.)	20	Income, preservation of capital, interest-compounding
High-quality stocks	10	Capital gains
High-yield bonds (Rating: A or lower)	10	Income, interest compounding
Diversified selection of high-growth stocks or a high-growth mutual fund	40	Capital gains
Gold/silver coins/bullion	20	Inflation/crisis hedge

PHYLLIS' PORTFOLIO
(Moderately Conservative)

Component	Target % of Portfolio	Purpose
Low-risk assets (Savings Bonds, banks CDs, etc.)	40	Income, preservation of capital, interest compounding
Medium-grade bonds (Rating: AA)	20	Income, interest compounding
Diversified selection of growth stocks or a growth mutual fund	20	Capital gains
Gold/silver coins/bullion	10	Inflation/crisis hedge
Real estate (REITs, limited partnerships)	10	Income, capital gains

DORIS' AND BILL'S PORTFOLIO
(Moderately Aggressive)

Component	Target % of Portfolio	Purpose
Low-risk assets (Savings Bonds, bank CDs, etc.)	25	Income, preservation of capital
High-yield bonds	20	Income
Diversified selection of growth stocks or a growth mutual fund	45	Capital gains
Gold/silver coins/bullion	10	Inflation/crisis hedge

Note two things about these investment portfolios:

First, they offer protection of a large portion of the investor's assets. Second, they leave room for the investor to take advantage of the high growth that he or she can get from stocks that may become the next superstars of Wall Street.

Now let's run the years forward to see what happened to these investors before they finally reached age 65 (or 55 in Walter's case) and retirement:

Walter's Portfolio

In keeping with his age as he grew older, Walter emphasized the low-risk assets in his portfolio. As mentioned earlier, he had time on his side, and after he married (at age 28) and he and his wife had two sons, he gradually shifted more of his investments into bank CDs, blue-chip stocks, and bond and money-market funds. At age 55, however, after his children had completed college and he found himself with additional income he could use for investment purposes, he was able to put more of it into equity-type investments.

By that time, however, the amazing power of compounding had made Walter wealthy—just on the low-risk assets in which he had invested. Here's how:

Recall that he had $10,000 to invest with to start. That alone, if invested at 8 percent over 30 years, would provide him with a nest egg of $109,357 at age 55. But he was also able to put $200 a month into an investment program, and at 8 percent compounded monthly, he would have accumulated nearly $300,000 by age 55.

But that's not all. Other than those investments, he had a 401(k) plan where he worked. It invested his funds, matched by his employer's contributions ($100 from Walter and $100 from his company) in a high-growth (aggressive) equity fund. That fund grew by 14 percent annually on average over the 30 years. So by the time Walter reached 55, he was sitting on an investment valued at—are you ready for this?—more than one million dollars.

Oh, yes, and Walter also bought a gold or silver coin from time to time, and by the time he retired, he had accumulated precious metals that exceeded $25,000 in value.

At 55, Walter thus had an investment portfolio of nearly $1.5 million. And he did it without undue stress and sacrifices. Obviously, he had to pay income taxes on his profits, but he was able to do that from his discretionary income. (Walter received regular raises from his employers during his career, so his salary when he retired was $65,000.)

Apparently, Walter's portfolio, which he changed very little during the 30-year period prior to his reaching 55, was nearly perfect. And there was nothing magic about it. He simply bought and held blue-chip stocks, and at the bank he did business with, he bought certificates of deposit. The CDs he selected were also long term (five years to maturity). He opened an account with a money-market mutual fund—in his case the Strong Money Market Fund—and it performed well. But currently (1997), about 300 money-market funds exist, and he could have chosen from those in Chart 45 and achieved equal or even greater success.

CHART 45

SELECTING A MONEY-MARKET MUTUAL FUND

These were the top-yielding money-market mutual funds on April 15, 1997:

Name	30-Day Yield	Telephone #
E-Fund	5.33%	800-223-7010
Kiewit	5.29	800-254-3948
Lake Forest	5.28	800-592-7722
Aetna A	5.28	800-367-7732
Fremont	5.22	800-548-4539

Source: IBC's Money Fund Report.

Walter also chose a mutual fund for his bond investments. As was the case with money-market funds, he had hundreds from which to select. He decided on the Kemper High-Yield A, and that was a good choice. But he could have selected from any of the following in Chart 47 and achieved above-average, steady returns over the years:

CHART 46

SELECTING A BOND FUND

These were the top-performing investment grade (BBB or better) corporate bond funds as of April 21, 1997:

Fund	One-Year Total Return	Telephone #
Loomis Sayles Bond	12.1%	800-633-3330
Dreyfus Invest Grade Intmed	11.9	800-645-6561
Alliance Corporate Bond A	11.1	800-221-5672
AIM Income A	10.4	800-347-1919
Phoenix Multi Sector Short A	10.3	800-243-4361

Finally, he chose a high-growth mutual fund for his 401(k) contributions. It was the Putnam Voyager A, which for 10 years achieved an annualized return that exceeded 16 percent. But then after marrying and having children, he switched from the Putnam fund to the more conservative growth fund, Putnam Investors A, where his annualized total return fell just short of 14 percent. Once he and his wife became empty nesters, he decided to diversify his funds and chose the Putnam Natural Resources A and the Putnam OTC Emerging Growth. The former was a specialty fund that averaged an annual return of about 10 percent, and the latter yielded on average about 19 percent. As mentioned, he averaged an annualized return from his equity mutual funds of 14 percent during the 30 years of investing.

Some Alternatives for Walter

Walter was a millionaire at 55. And you could say that he chose the perfect mix for his portfolio. But that isn't necessarily the case. He obviously could have achieved even greater success if he had chosen a different mix. In fact, he could have taken on more risk and been even more aggressive than he was. Let's say, for example, that instead of Putnam equity funds, he chose an index fund. As you learned in Chapter 10, index funds invest in a portfolio of stocks that tracks a particular market index, such as the Standard & Poor's 500, the Russell 2000, or the Wilshire 5000. The objective is to match the index's performance.

So how would Walter have done with an index fund that matches the S&P 500 over 30 years? Well consider that during the past 10 years, no type of equity mutual fund matched the 14.9-percent annualized gain of the S&P 500. Not the diversified type, not the specialty type, not the capital-growth type, not the total-return type, not even the aggressive type. Obviously, some funds within those types surpassed the 14.9-percent return of the S&P 500, but some did more poorly, too, and we're talking *averages* here.

This is not to say that Walter would achieve a nearly 15-percent return over 30 years with an index fund, but chances are good that the past 10 years is a good indicator of what can happen over a longer period, especially with the market performing the way it currently is.

So with a 15-percent annualized total return instead of a 14-percent return, Walter would have been richer by several hundred thousand dollars at age 55. And all because he chose a dull, boring index fund. Smart guy.

Now let's turn to Phyllis.

Phyllis' Portfolio

Before reaching 65, Phyllis had a tougher job accumulating wealth than did Walter—simply because she had less time. But as it turned out, she achieved results that were even more impressive. Her low-risk assets—Savings Bonds, bank CDs, and U.S. Treasury bonds—yielded an average of 7 percent. Her $10,000 (40% of the $25,000 portfolio) that she put into those investments multiplied to nearly $60,000. But it was her $500 a month that she invested in the medium-grade bonds and growth stocks that helped her accumulate the wealth she had hoped for. She selected the Fidelity Investment Grade Bond fund for the bond investment, and its annualized return over the 25 years was nearly 10 percent. The value of her holdings in the Fidelity fund at age 65: $330,000.

As for the growth stocks, she chose the 20th Century Ultra Investors, which during the time she invested provided an annualized return to investors of 19 percent. Over the 25 years she contributed her $250 a month (the other $250 went into the bond fund), she increased her holdings to an incredible $1.7 million dollars. In all, she had a portfolio valued at nearly $2 million when she and her husband retired at age 65. And her husband's pension added monthly income to the couple of $2,000.

Some Alternatives for Phyllis

Like Walter, Phyllis did fine on her own. She didn't have any special training or experience for investing. She read about the different types of investments and put together a portfolio that seemed likely to work for her. That portfolio wasn't complicated, nor did it need a lot of change over the years. She did "fine-tune" it once when she switched from CDs to Treasury bonds. Otherwise, she (as well as Walter) took advantage of two important principles: dollar-cost averaging and diversification. If the nation had experienced a series of recessions—or maybe even a depression—she would have survived quite well.

But let's say that the stock market was in a period of flux, and she wanted to switch to something else that would provide her with an alternative to her stock-fund holdings. Let's also suppose that she had read something about real-estate investment trusts and decided that they would make a good substitute for the stock fund in which she had invested.

As you learned in Chapter 11, real estate goes through cycles, and during good economic times they can outperform stocks—and are less subject to the frenetic changes that stocks sometimes experience. Moreover, as you also learned, REITs—as real-estate investment trusts are known—pay as much income as bonds, and they are as liquid as stocks and bonds. (Such liquidity is not the case, by the way, with such real-estate investments as limited partnerships.) REITs, as you recall, are publicly traded companies that own, operate, buy, and develop commercial properties. And anyone who wants an alternative to either bonds or stocks may want to select a REIT, especially when the real-estate market appears headed for bullish times—that is, when rents and occupancy rates are rising and interest rates are low.

Recall that REITs come in several forms, and there are even REIT mutual funds and REITs that concentrate on a particular part of the country. Besides equity REITs, there are mortgage REITs, which make loans backed by real estate, and hybrid REITs, which both own property and make loans. However, Phyllis chose an equity REIT fund known as the Vanguard Special REIT Index, which invests only in those REITs listed in the Morgan Stanley REIT Index. That index is a collection of the largest and most frequently traded equity REITs. By buying shares in the Vanguard fund, Phyllis was buying shares in a diversified group of more than 90 equity REITs. In other words, she was in essence buying the ownership and operation of many types of properties, from shopping centers and apartment complexes to office buildings and commercial developments.

Soon after buying the shares, she began getting income from her investment in the form of rents that tenants paid and that flowed back through to her and other shareholders. She asked Vanguard, however, to simply reinvest any return of capital, which offered her some tax advantages (though she still was subject to taxes on the income she received).

Phyllis chose the Vanguard REIT mutual fund, but she could just as easily have picked any of those listed earlier in Chapter 11 of this book.

Doris' and Bill's Portfolio

Because Doris and Bill started their investment program so late in life, they had to be more aggressive than they would have liked. Nevertheless, they devoted a fourth of their portfolio to low-risk assets. And their expenses were so modest that they could put $36,000 a year into an investment program.

At this point they have $60,000 in tax-deferred investments—an IRA and a 401(k) plan. During the next 10 years, that amount nearly tripled, to $165,000. And with 45 percent of the $3,000 a month they invest going into growth mutual funds, they enjoyed an average return of 12 percent, which, with dividends reinvested, provided them with an additional nest egg of $320,000. And the high-yield bonds, even after taxes, added another $110,000.

So with the precious-metals coins and the bank CDs, Bill and Doris will have about $700,000 in investment funds at retirement. That amount, along with the value of their house and other assets, will make them millionaires, too.

Anyone Can Do It

You've seen how four people, all of whom had average income and average intelligence, were able to achieve millionaire status. And note in particular that only Walter inherited any money, and his $10,000 was meager compared to what he was able to achieve through other means.

One thing that set these four people apart from many other people is that they had a plan and a goal. And they "paid themselves" before they paid for any luxuries. No fancy cars, no extravagant houses, no lavish vacations. Yet none were exactly tightwads, either. They enjoyed life *all* their life—and not just during the years of their maximum earning power.

Chapter 18: Launching into Investor Cyberspace

"The Net is your key to financial independence."
— Paul B. Farrell, author,
Investor's Guide to the Net

The Information Highway

Crucial to your making rewarding investment decisions is information. Simply put, the more facts and figures you have, the more intelligent your decisions will be. If you live in a large city, you probably have access to a well-stocked public library. And there you can roam the aisles, search the computerized resource data, and probably find almost anything you want.

As great as some public libraries are, however, one may not be close to you. You may live in a small town or a remote area of the country. Or your schedule may not permit you to get to a library during its hours of operation. Or maybe you just prefer to conduct your investment research in the privacy of your home, where, if you like, you can do so in your pajamas or nightgown.

You can probably guess what this is leading up to: Yes, that's right, you can use a home computer for investing and money management. If you are hooked up so that you're "online" to the vast resources that are available, you can find what you are looking for (and, unfortunately, a lot of stuff you *aren't* looking for). And with practice, you can sift through all these data and determine exactly which investments and financial plan are right for you.

In this chapter, we're going to start with the assumption that you have never used your home computer with an investing objective in mind. Then we're going to cover how, armed with the proper computer and software, you can find investment-related information, surf the Net for investment news, and even place trading orders.

Booting Up

Let's say you've used a computer only for keeping personal records, balancing your checking account, filing your income taxes, storing your favorite recipes, writing résumés, and so forth. Maybe you have even used your computer for tracking the performance of your investments. You bought several software packages, and you installed them yourself. If that is the case, you shouldn't have any trouble using your computer for investing purposes. You have enough computer "savvy" to go the next step upward.

Before you commit, however, keep in mind that going online and using the Internet and its most famous and usable feature—the World Wide Web—can be expensive, especially if you don't know your way around. You pay for that time you access the various services, and sometimes the bill may make you squirm when you get it.

Now let's get started. First, you need to know if your computer is powerful and quick enough to go online. Unless you bought it within the past five years, it probably isn't. Go to a couple of computer stores you trust, tell them about your computer and what you want it to do. If your computer doesn't have the capability, you may need a new one. But first ask if you can upgrade the one you have. If so, you'll probably save a lot of bucks.

Once you have your computer ready for action and your modem connected to a telephone jack (standard equipment in this regard currently includes the 28.8 kilobits per second v.34 fax-modem and high-speed serial port), you're set.

Next, consider an online computer network, such as CompuServe, America Online, Prodigy, or the up-and-coming

Microsoft Network. You may ask why you should pay $9.95 or so a month in basic fees (as well as additional charges to visit some sites) when the Internet allows you to download free information about stocks, bonds, and mutual funds. The answer is that the online networks provide easy access to timely, helpful financial information assembled by reliable firms. On the Internet, you often are confronted by questionable companies promoting investment products and services of dubious quality and usefulness.

Let's look at the online computer networks to see how they can help you:

Suppose you decide to use CompuServe, a subsidiary of H&R Block Co. You simply call 1-800-492-1849 and ask for free software. Usually, CompuServe will allow new subscribers several free hours of online time. (When this was written, CompuServe offered a service known as Money Personal Finance Center for one month free. This gave you financial support from *Money* magazine, plus free access to more than 3,000 other services on CompuServe, including news, weather, sports, shopping, electronic mail, reference libraries, the Internet, and the World Wide Web.)

HOW MUCH COMPUTER DO YOU NEED?

For investment-research purposes, your computer may not be adequate. To go online or use the Internet, or for both, you need a computer and peripherals with some of the following credentials:

➤ At least a 486 processor, but preferably a Pentium chip.
➤ At least a 500-megabyte (MB) hard drive and preferably a gigabyte (1,000 MB) hard drive.
➤ Operational speed of at least 66 megahertz (MHz).
➤ At least 8 MB of RAM (and 16 MB is better).
➤ A laser printer.
➤ A high-speed modem that can send and receive data at a rate of 28.8 kilobits per second.
➤ A CD-ROM drive that can run at 6X or 8X speed.

Some points of advice in this regard: Bigger is better. Power is good. More is preferable. In two years, you will be happy that you paid a little extra now to get the most capacity, speed, and power available.

ONLINE NEWSPAPER BUSINESS SECTIONS

If you feel that you need investment information from an assortment of news sources, an online service can meet your needs. Here, for example, are just some of the offerings of the three major networks:

CompuServe
Associated Press Newswire
Detroit Free Press
Deutsche Presse-Agentur
Reuters Newswire
U.K. News/Sports
United Press International
USA Today
Washington Post
500 industry newsletters
50 broker/investment-firm reports
125 regional business publications

America Online
Business Week Online

(America Online Continued)
Investor's Business Daily
Knight-Ridder/Tribune Business
New York Times
Orlando Sentinel Business
Reuters Newswire
PBS's Nightly Business Report
San Jose Mercury Business

Prodigy
Atlanta Journal/Constitution
Los Angeles Times/TimeLink
News Day
Richmond Times-Dispatch
Tampa Bay Tribune

Of special interest to investors is the business and financial information available to subscribers. You can analyze a company's historical data. You can get predictions on the performance of securities. You can place buy and sell orders. (More on this later.) You can access pricing trends. You can monitor foreign-exchange rates. And you can read abstracts on practical and theoretical management and marketing. In "chat" sessions, you can even discuss strategy and news with other investors. And you can do all this at any hour of the day or night, from anywhere in the world.

America Online also has a number of attractions for investors, though not near so many as CompuServe. The Personal Finance section serves hundreds of thousands of subscribers, and if you are the average investor, the information you can get there is probably all you'll need. And the price is reasonable.

Prodigy has even less in the way of financial services, but investment information is not what this network is all about.

Nevertheless, its Business/Financial section is adequate for most investors. And its upgraded Investment Center provides excellent business and financial news, stock and fund quotes, online trading, and a host of forums. For your purposes, all you may need are Prodigy's Stock Hunter, Strategic Investor, Wall Street Edge (a financial-newsletter service), and Kiplinger's reports.

And what if you want to do basic research on a company that you are interested in? If you have America Online or CompuServe, simply visit Hoover's Company Profiles, which offers descriptions of more than 1,750 publicly traded firms and up to 10 years' worth of statistics. Each profile has links that can lead you to the company's Web site or to financial disclosures the firm must file with the Securities & Exchange Commission. Prodigy has its Strategic Investor, which, for $14.95 extra a month, provides detailed information on more than 10,000 companies and also allows you to select stocks that meet specific criteria.

If you simply want to stay abreast of the news on companies and the markets, CompuServe's News and America Online's Company News sites give you reports from the Associated Press, Reuters, and other news services on companies as well as about the latest developments in the markets. Also, CompuServe's Business Database Plus has a five-year inventory of articles from 500 publications, though the cost to access this information may be prohibitive at 25 cents a minute plus $1.50 for each article you view or download.

No discussion of online services would be complete without mentioning the Dow Jones information network. The Dow database and its analytical tools are immense in size and scope. But the Dow market is different from the other online services, in that it is aimed primarily at institutional investors, brokers, and full-time traders. But Dow publishes *The Wall Street Journal* electronically and provides other modestly priced services. Here are some of the services the company offers the small investor:

➢ **Personal Journal.** Think of this as an electronic version of *The Wall Street Journal.* You can pick the companies, stocks, mutual funds, and *Journal* columns that interest you. You can also get the news you want, plus business and worldwide news summaries delivered direct to your computer. Plus, you get late-breaking news on your companies, and stock quotes are available to you throughout the day.

> **News/Retrieval.** You get the full text of *The Wall Street Journal, The New York Times, The Washington Post, The Los Angeles Times, The Financial Times* (of London), *Business Week, Time, Forbes, Fortune, The Economist*, as well as 1,500 other publications. And you get them hours before the print-version deliveries. Plus, you can use the CustomClip service to scan and send you selected articles.

> **WSJ Interactive Edition.** You can get the most important stories in business, technology, marketing, and the law—all continually updated 24 hours a day on the World Wide Web. Plus, you can get unlimited access to thousands of corporate reports, a personal clipping service, your own portfolio, and exclusive U.S. and international markets reports from the world-wide resources of *The Wall Street Journal*. "JournalLinks" provides added background on stories appearing in the print edition.

> **Market Monitor (aka DJN/R Private Investor Edition.** You can get securities and funds data, corporate reports, earnings estimates, market quotes, all sorts of historical data, market-making news, research reports, and national and international articles and columns. All this comes with screening applications to help you spot investment opportunities.

The above doesn't include another important Dow Jones service for investors hooked to cyberspace. We'll cover that later. For now, let's look at some other online networks that investors may find useful:

Dialog

"Immense" is a good word to describe Dialog. "Overwhelming" is another. Offered by Knight-Ridder, which acquired it rather than developed it, Dialog is recognized as one of the most powerful and useful research sources available. And for investors, it has great value.

At last count, Dialog had nearly 500 databases containing

more than 350 million articles, abstracts, and citations. You name a subject, Dialog can almost certainly find information about it. Operating through an adaptable search language, Dialog can network all those databases into a single database. You then have access to all the material on your subject through a single research function.

ProSearch

For information more directly related to specific securities, ProSearch is worth considering. Offered by Telescan, ProSearch allows you to customize your search using 207 technical, fundamental, and forecasting screens. If, for example, you decide you want to look at stocks with a price/earnings ratio below 11 and earnings growth exceeding 15 percent a year, this service can find those that match your criteria.

Lexis-Nexis

This online service includes extensive news and other general-subject research, which if you add the Nexis news service, boasts of a database with more than 400 million documents. And the service just keeps growing, adding some two million new documents per week. Among the business and financial information you can get from this source are corporate annual reports, investment banking and research reports, SEC filings, quotes on stocks, and news on acquisitions and mergers.

Playing With the Big Boys

If you were a really, really active investment trader (and you're not, of course, but if you *were*), the investment information you can get from the Internet's "Big Four" is almost inexhaustible. For select information, however, you'll pay a stiff price: $1,000 to $2,500 a month. These premium services are:

➤ **Dow Jones Telerate:** Supplies real-time information to market professionals in 85 nations. Covered are all major exchanges, markets, and all 150,000 securities. The Telerate Trading Room Systems and work stations provide comprehensive analytical and decision-making data.

- **Reuters:** Has three primary services: (1) media services, with news, photos, and graphics on a host of business and general subjects; (2) information services, with real-time information, historical databases, and analytical software technology covering 217 international exchanges and OTC markets; and Instinet, which is a private market for professional traders linked to the Reuters Crossing Network and operating as an information exchange and trading system for international equity transactions.

- **Knight-Ridder Financial:** Furnishes data and analytical tools to active traders and institutional investors. This service covers money markets, government and corporate debt, foreign currencies, commodities, futures, options, and other derivatives. This service is great—probably the greatest—if you trade futures, but is maybe not on a par with the other services as a supplier of information on companies and related data.

- **Bloomberg:** Covers all major global securities markets, including equities, money markets, currencies, all types of debt securities, and commodities. Many experts consider this the best of the four services aimed at professional traders. The good news is that Bloomberg seems intent on marketing some of its services—at a lower price, of course—to the small investor.

Other Internet services exist, but none can touch these four for the depth and dispatch of and easy access to information provided to customers.

Getting from Here to There

Let's back up a moment—we may be getting ahead of ourselves. We discuss services on the Internet, but you haven't learned how to get access to the Internet and the World Wide Web. If you subscribe to one of the three major online networks, you can connect through its "browser," which is the term used for the special graphical interface that allows you to see the subject matter on the Internet and Web. But you will probably find it cheaper to use a separate connection. For that, you'll need a different browser. You'll still have to pay for the service, of course, but maybe only a small fraction of the cost of the alternative.

Let's look at a few of the Web browsers you can use:

➤ **Netscape's Navigator:** An excellent browser. A newcomer to the Internet should find it easy to use. Features include easy downloading (that is, creating your own file of the information you receive from Internet sources) and bookmarking (that is, marking Web sites for quick access later). Navigator also has a convenient "View History," which helps you remember the locations of sources from around the world. Finally, you can use this browser on any Internet server, so that you can select, find, and change servers if you like. Netscape and IBM have recently teamed up to offer a version of Netscape's browser software for IBM's OS/2 Warp 4 operating system. That came on the heels of a similar pact with Apple Computer. In all, 17 operating systems support Netscape's browser.

➤ **Netcom's NetCruiser:** Also a very useful multipurpose browser. Though not quite as popular as Netscape's Navigator (which claims more than half of the 15 million or so browsers in operation), Netcom should see sales grow as a result of its major network of local access numbers to allow you to hook on with simply a local call from any-where in the nation. Plus, Netcom offers unlimited e-mail at no extra cost.

➤ **Microsoft Internet Explorer:** A challenger for the No. 1 spot. In fact, every new copy of Windows 95 now ships with a copy of Internet Explorer. The newest version includes advanced security options and a keyboard interface that allows you to move through a Web page without using a mouse. For beginners, the interface uses toolbars with but-tons that change color when you move the pointer over them, thus allowing you to know the buttons are active. You can also access through "shortcuts" your favorite Web sites.

➤ **NCSA Mosaic:** Much improved over earlier versions of Mosaic. Now you can have a one-stop system for exploring the Web online or on-disk. In addition to the standard browser window, you get a built-in news reader, mail client, and real-time collaboration feature.

➤ **Spyglass Enhanced Mosaic:** Reliable, but not as versatile as its competitors. The latest version is near the level of more advanced browsers, though it still falls short. But if you want the most bug-free and crashproof of all Web browsers, this may be your choice. To get it, however, you'll need to visit third-party Internet suites and applications. It's not available otherwise.

Then there are the Internet Service Providers, which offer access to the Internet, but lack the other features that online services offer. ISPs, as they are called, usually furnish at least e-mail accounts, a Web browser, and access to a news server through a UseNet. Some even include features like storage space for hosting your own Web page. The principal ISPs and their telephone numbers are:

AT&T WorldNet (800/967-5363)
EarthLink Network (800/395-8425)
IBM Internet Connection (800/344-7979)
InternetMCI (800/955-5210)
PSINet (800/453-7473)

Ready to Travel on the Web?

Once you've gained access to the Internet, you're ready to start exploring that thing you've probably heard so much about: the World Wide Web. Click away with your mouse at the proper icons until you link to the Web and can start moving around on it. (And by the way you don't necessarily have to connect to the Internet to explore the Web.)

Go to the Web address (which is also known as the Uniform Resource Locator, or URL) of any currently displayed Web document. If you're using Microsoft Internet Explorer, you'll see in the center of the program window a document. It will have several pictures, and all of them contain links. If you point to one, the mouse pointer changes to a tiny hand with only the index finger extended.

On MSN, the links serve as good starting points. You can go to another document by using the big picture in the middle: the **Explore the Internet**, **Searches**, **Links** and **Tools**. When you get to another document, you will find links to places that will help in your search for a particular subject.

But before you leave on any journey, you want to be sure you know how to get back home. The same principle holds true with the World Wide Web. Before you go off into cyberspace, it's a good idea to remember some landmarks to find your way back. Well, here they are, and you might want to commit them to memory:

➤ You can return to a previous page by clicking the **Back** button. Or you can select **View**, **Back**, or press **Backspace**.

➤ You can go all the way back to the start page by clicking the **Open Start Page** button or by selecting **File**, **Open Start Page**.

➤ You can open the File menu and pick one of the documents shown at the bottom of the History menu.

Note that the text links sometimes change from bright blue to purple. The purple links are those you've used, so you know where you've been and where you still need to go.

Okay, now double-click The Internet icon after turning on your computer and going through all the preliminaries. Select **Start, Programs, Accessories, Internet Tools, and Internet Explorer**. Next, select **Start, Run**, then you can type a Web address (URL), after which you will click **OK**.

THE NET IN 20 EASY STEPS

If you have recently bought a new computer, it probably comes equipped with the Windows 95 operating system. And nowadays, Windows 95 includes access to the Internet. (There's an easy way to determine if you have it: Icons, those cute little symbols that you click with your mouse to perform tasks, will be labeled "The Microsoft Network" and "The Internet.") If you decide to use Microsoft (MSN) as your service provider, here are the steps to take to get on the Internet:

1. Double-click The Microsoft Network icon (or click **Start**, **Programs**, and **The Microsoft Network**.) Soon The Microsoft Network dialog box will appear.

2. Click **OK**, and the dialog box will ask for your area or city code and the first three digits of your phone number. (The area code may already be listed because of the information you gave during your Windows 95 setup.)

3. After entering the telephone information, click **OK**, and a message box appears, telling you that the program is connecting to MSN.

4. Click the **Connect** button, and you will dial into The Microsoft Network to locate an MSN telephone number in your area.

5. Soon, the program logs off MSN, and you'll see a dialog box with three large buttons in the middle and several more at the bottom.

6. Click **Price** to see information about current MSN prices and free trials.

7. Click the **Close** button to return to the previous dialog box.

8. Click the **Details** button to display a short description of MSN.

9. Click the **Close** button to return to the previous dialog box.

10. Click the **Tell us your name and address** button, then fill in the requested information.

11. Click **OK** to return to the previous dialog box.

12. Click the **Next**, **select a way to pay** button, and enter your credit-card information.

13. Click **OK** to return to the previous dialog box.

14. Click the **Then**, **please read the rules button**, and if the rules seem satisfactory to you, click the **I Agree** button.

15. Click the **Join Now** button. If either the primary number or backup number are in your area code, click **OK**. If they are not, click **Change**.

16. Click the **Connect** button when the next message box appears. You will then dial into MSN and transfer the information you have entered.

17. Soon, you'll be able to enter your username (your MSN e-mail address), in a text box labeled **Member ID**.

18. In the **Password** box, enter a password you have selected.

19. Click **OK**.

20. Click the **Finish** button.

Now when you want to use the Internet and the World Wide Web, all you have to do is double-click **The Internet** button.

Now try moving around a bit. Click a few links, each of which is underlined and colored blue, and see where you go. You don't have to have any special destination in mind. You might start by picking **A sampler of links** from the big Explore picture in the middle. Or you might choose **Microsoft's Top Ten links** in the document that appears.

Once you feel comfortable moving around, try searching for investment information.

Let's say you know the URL of PC Quote. This is a free service that gives you all the information necessary for you to keep up with the stock market. The quotes are delayed 20 minutes, but you aren't a trader in any case, so that doesn't really matter. Type **http://www.pcquote.com** and then press Enter to go to the PC Quote Web site. You can also click the **Open** button or select **File, Open**. Then type the URL and choose **OK**.

By the way, if the URL doesn't work, either you don't have the right address or you typed it wrong. In either case, try removing the portion to the far right. For example, if you try **http://www.hume.com/author/rdavis** and that doesn't work, try **http://www.hume.com/author**. If that still doesn't work (and it won't, believe me), try **http://www.hume.com/**. Also, your Web browser will add the **http://** if you forget. Just be sure that http:// is indeed part of the URL and not something else.

So far, so good. Now let's go to some Web sites for other information. Try these:

➤ **Hoover's Online:** This Web site provides you with a wealth of information about companies you may be interested in. You can search using the MasterList Plus Database, link to the company Web site of the day, or survey the Hoover's List of Lists of businesses. Hoover's Online address: www.hoovers.com.

➤ **FinanceNet:** This alliance of federal, state, and municipal governments provides information on government assets, forums, mailing lists, training, and asset-sales opportunities. Plus it maintains a list of links to related organizations. FinanceNet address: www.financenet.gov.

➤ **Commerce Business Daily:** You may already be familiar with this publication. It has quite a bit of information and news that you can use. Many people visit this Web site just for the information on government contracts. *Commerce Business Daily* address: cos.gdb.org/repos/cdb/cbc-intro.html.

➤ **Internal Revenue Service:** No, wait. Come back here. This is a fun Web site. You can get not only downloadable forms, plenty of advice, and online filing, but also the latest tax information. One publication calls it "a great piece of work." IRS address: www.irs.ustreas.gov.

➤ **The 100 Best Business Web Sites:** From the editors of *Interactive Age* magazine. You can find plenty of information about potential investments. Address: techweb.cmp.com/ia/features/hot100.html.

There are many, many more. Each time you spot an interesting site in a magazine or on television, jot down the address, then store it where you have access to it later. Soon, you'll accumulate a library of references that you can use to stay on the cutting edge of investing.

Trading in Cyberspace

Now that you know how to flex your muscles in cyberspace, you're ready for the final use of this amazing development: stock trading. No longer do you need to call a stockbroker when you're ready to buy those 100 shares that will one day mean financial independence for you. All you have to do is go online to a broker and place your order. In fact, if you know what you want, there's no need to use the services of a full-service broker. A discount broker will do just fine—and save you a lot of money. How much? Well, on a typical trade, you may pay $100 or more to a full-service broker, but a deep-discount broker will cut that fee to less than $20.

So setting up an account online has great potential. But at the moment few investors know of its merits. In fact, online stock trading currently (1997) represents only about 3 percent of the total transactions handled by brokers. But stock brokers themselves estimate that by the year 2000, half of the stock transactions will be conducted by the computer.

At the moment, full-service brokerage firms are avoiding giving you access to them online. Their thinking is that investors are still going to want investment advice and help, and that's not possible through a computer setup. So any stock trading you do with your computer is going to have to be with a discount broker. Here are some of the companies now offering online stock trading:

Aufhauser & Co.
800-645-9486
http://www.aufhauser.com

Ceres Securities
800-669-3900
http://www.ceres.com

EBroker
800-553-9513
http://www.ebroker.com

Fidelity Investments
800-544-0246
http://www.fif-inv.com

Lombard
800-688-6896
http://www.lombard.com

Pacific Brokerage Services
800-342-8497
http://www.tradepbs.com

Quick & Reilly
800-837-7220
http://www.quickreilly.com

Schwab
800-540-0667
http://www.schwab.com

BANKING ONLINE

Online or Internet banking has finally arrived. Despite their previous reluctance to give up their paper checks and receipts, bank customers seem at last convinced that electronic transactions are an alternative to direct contact with bank personnel and ATMs.

Currently, more than half of households with personel computer say their PCs help them manage their personal finances. And most of them have a direct link to their bank. Under development: a compatible system that will give users access to their bank through a Web browser, a commercial online service, or a touch-tone phone.

Predicts one bank president: "Every one of the top 200 banks in the country will have some kind of online banking by the end of this year [1997]."

Moreover, the costs of online-banking services are falling. Customers generally pay $5 to $10 a month for the transactions they make. And some banks offer such services free.

Call several of these, inquire about rates and access, then choose the one you want to set up an account with. You'll need to fill in some forms. After that, you're ready to begin investing the cyberspace way.

You're Ready for a Cyberspace Visit

In this chapter, you've seen how to put your computer to work for your betterment as an investor. With the proper software—and the skills to use it—you can get valuable investment data. And as you've also seen, you can tap into sources that can offer advice and suggestions. Finally, you've covered how to use your online access to make investment trades. The potential is even greater, as technology improvements continue almost daily in cyberspace for investment decision makers.

Chapter 19: How to Recession-Proof Your Investments

"Thou'ldst shun a bear;
But if thy flight lay toward the raging sea,
Thou'ldst meet the bear i' the mouth."

— William Shakespeare

"Who's afraid of the big bad wolf?"
— Song lyrics from Walt Disney's "Three Little Pigs"

The Lessons of History

If you want to successfully deal with a recession, you have to have a starting point. And there's no better place to start than by defining exactly what you're dealing with. After all, you don't go shopping for, say, a camcorder until you know what one looks like and what purpose you want it to serve. By the same token, you don't want to try to contend with a recession until you find out what it does and how it affects you personally. That's what this chapter is about. It will show you how to recognize a coming recession so that you can prepare for its impact on you and your investments.

Maybe your definition of recession is a period when jobs are tough to come by, investment returns barely keep pace with inflation, and the economy is in a state of lethargy.

If that's your definition, you're not far off the mark. Most economists agree that we are in a recession when economic activity slows appreciably. At such a time, they add, financial-

ly weak firms may fail, and even the financially strong ones
may suffer from dismal or diminishing earnings. Layoffs
result, and consumers lose confidence in the present and
future. So they spend less, and sales slow or drop. During it
all, stock prices lose their momentum—and may even decline.

By consensus, a recession is defined as two consecutive
quarters of shrinking Gross Domestic Product (with GDP
being the output of goods and services in the United States),
as determined by the National Bureau of Economic Research
in Washington, D.C. Such a contraction occurs toward the end
of the business cycle, when inventories pile up and consumer
spending and business investment slow.

Some economists say that recessions are inevitable, that
they are part of a cycle that is inescapable, and that just as
surely as we enter a period of prosperity and its excesses, we
are doomed to an eventual recession and its hardships.

But is recession really a certainty? Does it result from our
excesses? Is it part of some immutable universal law that we
must endure.

In this chapter you'll address those questions and seek
solutions to the problems that come raining down on us when
our economy slides into a recession. Because even if a recession is predestined, we still need to be able to cope with it.
And successful confrontation is indeed possible—if you know
how to react and do the right things.

One other thing: The next few pages are going to explain
what happens before, during, and after a recession. You may
find some of the information—especially that regarding the
economy and the government's role—a bit demanding and perhaps even tedious. But an understanding of this subject
requires that you know how to detect what the economy is
doing. In that way, you can properly react—and ultimately
prosper.

How Recession Affects Investors

As mentioned, during recession, all aspects of the economy
feel the force. Investments—especially equity types like stocks
and real estate—usually take a drubbing. In the past 100
years, we have had 21 recessions and one depression. (A

depression, of course, is when the bottom falls out of the economy and recovery may take years or even decades. But don't worry. The chances of our having another depression are almost nonexistent.) At that rate, we are having two recessions every decade. And that's just about what has actually happened. We had two in the 1980s, two in the 1970s, only one in the 1960s, but two in the 1950s and two in the 1940s. The 1930s were no fun at all: a recession and The Great Depression. And the 1920s gave us three recessions.

So if we follow this pattern in the 1990s, which has already experienced one recession (1990-91), we are due for another within the next couple or three years. Will history repeat? Well, the odds are better than average that it will. And not just because of the pattern of the past, but because of certain events that are occurring as you are reading this.

To get a better understanding of what's happening, you need to know a few things about the economy and how it operates.

Business Cycles: Their Meaning and Impact

The bad news about recessions is that we don't get a lot of warning before they strike. Economists call such recessionary downturns "troughs." And they call prosperous times "peaks." If we examine a few leading economic indicators, for example, we find that the notice we get for peaks is in fact significantly different from the notice we get for troughs. Generally, the notice prior to peaks is quite long, but the warning prior to troughs is very short, which means that it is very easy to miss a turnaround to the downside, but on the upswing, you can be more patient waiting for confirmation from other indicators.

Take a look at the Chart 46, which shows the performance record of 13 leading indicators over a recent 20-year period:

CHART 47

Indicator	Mean Lead Time Peaks (Months)	Mean Lead Time Troughs (Months)
Ave. workweek (mfg.)	11	2
Ave. weekly unemployment claims	15	1
New building permits (housing)	16	7
New business formations	15	2
New durable goods orders	7	3
Plant, equipment orders	6	2
Mfg. inventories change in book value	6	1
Industrial materials prices	12	4
500 common-stock prices	9	5
Corp. profits (after-tax)	9	2
Ratio, price-to-unit labor cost, mfg.	14	0
Change in consumer installment debt	13	3
Composite index, reverse trend adjusted	5	4

You don't have to be an economist to figure out what all this means: A recession gives little warning. Even if you decide to judge an economic-downturn trend by one indicator alone—new building permits for housing—you have only seven months, on average, to prepare for the recession. And if you wait for the next confirming sign (stock-price decline), you have a scant five months to act on that knowledge.

What Goes Wrong—And Why

Seeing the signs of recession still doesn't explain what happens when we experience one. We know that overall conditions change and that we have to tighten our belts. But few of us know what goes on during those critical weeks before we enter recession.

Again, let's look at the history of recessions. During the past 50 years, recessions have lasted, on average, about 11 months. During the preceding 50 years, the average recession lasted 18 months, whereas in the two 50-year periods before that, the averages were 25 and 26 months.

So recessions seem to be getting shorter. The other good news is that the length of the expansions has been increasing through the years. During the past 50 years, the average expansion lasted 53 months, more than twice the 25-month average for the preceding 50 years. In the two 50-year periods before that, the averages were 31 and 30 months, nearly the same as the average recession.

Recall that the last major expansion ran for 92 months, from November 1982 till July 1990. A 16-month recession preceded and followed that boom.

So how do economists account for this trend of shorter recessions and longer expansions? For one thing, they credit a more service-oriented economy that is less dominated by the production of agricultural and manufactured goods (whose suppliers and industries are subject to wider and more frequent ups and downs).

Moreover, the government now plays a greater role in maintaining incomes and supporting business and consumer confidence during recessions. A hundred years ago, there were no unemployment insurance, welfare payments, and bank-deposit insurance. And the Federal Reserve Board, which influences interest rates and credit stability with varying degrees of success, was not created until 1914.

Don't believe for a minute, however, that recessions will ever go the way of the dinosaur. So long as we have an economy that is driven by supply-and-demand factors, investment markets, and consumer whims, we'll have business cycles. In fact, if economists can agree on anything, it is that we'll continue to have to endure occasional recessions.

Maybe if we review a couple of recent recessions, we'll get a better idea of just what sets the stage for them.

The 1981-83 Recession

One economist aptly declares that recessions "creep in on little cat feet." And that is exactly what happened during the early 1980s. Just before that, we experienced a high level of prosperity. Few of us thought about an economic crisis or crash. Large numbers of investors and corporate leaders bet their fortunes and the future of their companies on "more of the same." The overwhelming majority of investment advisers and economists proclaimed that there would be no recession, or that it would not come before "next year."

By late 1980, the rate of growth in sales and the stock-market averages reached an altitude they could not sustain. Explained one observer, "The economy was like an airplane that, while climbing, suddenly stalled in vertical flight."

A leading indicator of economic growth or contraction is the money-supply measure. Declines in the rate of growth of the money supply preceded business contraction by an average of several months in the past 100 years. Increasing the money supply led business-cycle upturns by an average of eight months in the same period. And the money-supply indicator has been found to lead stock prices in all major studies of indicator effectiveness. By showing a slowing in the growth of the money supply, this indicator warned of the 1981-83 recession, which the stock market failed to foreshadow, by many months. In fact, this indicator was ahead by more than twice the three-month average lead time for all leading indicators.

That was a big change from previous recessions. Before the 1957-58 downturn, the leading indicators warned a full 23 months beforehand that we were headed for tough times.

As for the stock market, it lulled investors into thinking that recession was impossible. The heady pre-recession years of 1977 to 1981 brought an unusually long bull market. In fact, in 1981, the news media hailed the investment markets for their "outstanding achievements." But then the market faltered, and to those monitoring the Dow Jones Industrial Average during 1981-82, it appeared that investors—especially those who were newcomers to equities—were in deep trouble.

Also during this period, the economy was suffering from double-digit inflation—that is, inflation of 10 percent or more a year. From January 1979 through December 1981, for example, prices rose 39 percent. In response, the price of gold during that period peaked at an all-time high of $843 an ounce. But then price increases slowed dramatically in a process called "disinflation." And inflation became less of a threat.

The 1990-91 Recession

The 1990-91 recession was unusual in that it seemed to respond to economic policy-making. The nation experienced a massive debt "overhang," caused by sustained deficit spending. That in turn inhibited fiscal "pump priming." As a result, this recession was termed "double-dip" because a second two-quarter contraction preceded recovery.

Also, that recession followed close on the heels of a 92-month expansion of the economy. And when the federal government finally detected that a recession was under way, it failed to act with major new spending programs because of a reluctance to increase the deficit. The government's thinking was that inappropriate measures might precipitate a much more severe recession—or even a depression.

It didn't have a chance to reach that point, however. But in both the 1981-83 and 1990-91 recessions, the economy reached a point that could have resulted in a depression. A few years ago, for example, the Connecticut-based firm of Bridgewater and Associates published an analysis that suggested that the final stage of a conventional recession is not unlike the third stage of a full-scale depression. The four stages of depression, according to analysts who have studied them, are these:

Stage 1: The economy becomes burdened by more debt than it can absorb and becomes susceptible to depression.

Stage 2: Since money is increasingly difficult or expensive to come by, business can get money only by borrowing or reducing inventories. Typically, they do both in their anxiety to stay liquid, keeping interest rates high.

Stage 3: The effort to stay liquid flounders, and business failures increase dramatically.

Stage 4: The demand for money drops sharply as the economy stagnates. Interest rates drop precipitously, but fail to attract new borrowers. The ratio of inventory to sales becomes extremely low and remains so until the reduced level of debt and low interest rates spark an eventual economic recovery.

Result: A combination of massive business failures and loan defaults, which evolves from an unsustainable debt position at too-high interest rates. Businesses that have previously borrowed to survive suddenly fail.

There is evidence that the United States in fact entered Stage 3 in the early 1980s and again in the early 1990s.

Government's Role

As mentioned, the economy usually rides its cyclical waves with fairly predictable patterns. During normal times, supply and demand stay in check, with neither gaining dominance. When the cycle breaks from its pattern, however, or when supply or demand experiences excesses, the government steps in to try to restore normalcy.

Using a variety of devices, government will either attempt to promote economic growth or slow it down. The attempt to regulate growth involves setting policy in three key sectors of the economy: monetary, fiscal, and trade.

Keep in mind that when we speak of "government," we're not just talking about the Administration or Congress or the Federal Reserve Board. We're talking about all of them. All may do a little pushing and shoving, and sometimes they work at cross-purposes, causing more harm than good.

Let's see how the different governmental forces influence the economy:

The Fed

By law the Federal Reserve Board, usually called simply "The Fed," is independent of direct control by any branch of government. But there are occasional attempts at influencing the Fed's actions. Whether those attempts are successful or not depends on the makeup of the Board. If Board members are strong and impartial and their Chairman is not swayed by political pressures, the Fed can be a powerful force in shaping the economy.

At the Fed's disposal are three tools, all of which can be used to control the money supply.

The first is the reserve requirement. Banks use their deposits to lend to borrowers, but some cash is retained to cover typical daily withdrawals. The Fed uses the reserve ratio to set the amount a bank must keep on hand. The lower the ratio, the higher the amount of loans a typical bank can make. Those loans eventually get redeposited, so that the same money can get borrowed again. The only check on this "multiplier effect," as economists call it, is the reserve ratio. The reserve ratio regulates the multiplied flow of credit from the banking system to the economy, where the credit will stimulate economic growth.

But what happens if the Fed doesn't want to *stimulate* growth? What if the objective is to *slow* growth? Then the Fed increases the reserve requirement so that banks don't have as much money to lend. Obviously, the Fed must be careful in taking such action: Too much stimulation of the economy can cause inflationary problems. Too much restraint of the economy can cause recession.

The second tool the Fed has is the authority to adjust the discount rate. Banks earn their profits by lending. Since their loans are restricted by the reserve ratio, banks may borrow reserves from the Fed in order to increase their lending and profit. If they pay a lower rate on the borrowed reserves than the interest paid on them on a loan, they'll come out ahead. The rate the Fed charges banks borrowing additional reserves is the discount rate. Since banks are willing to borrow less at higher rates, the Fed can tighten up on the money supply by raising the discount rate. Or the Fed can expand borrowing— and thus the money supply—by dropping the discount rate.

Changes in the discount rate usually precede changes in the prime rate, the rate banks charge their biggest and soundest borrowers. And although the discount rate isn't changed on a daily basis, it helps determine the overall level of daily rates. Even the federal-funds rate, which is the rate paid by banks borrowing reserves in the financial marketplace, is influenced by the discount rate. So changes in the discount rate make a distinct impression on the aggregate supply of money.

The third tool of the Fed is the ability to manipulate the open market. From 1914 until 1936, the discount rate was the only tool the Fed had to influence the money supply. The power to set reserve requirements was added after the Great Depression's wave of bank failures. But with the growth of the U.S. economy, the need for daily regulation of the money supply increased. The Fed now uses the open market and its operation as its primary agent to regulate, on a daily basis, the supply of money.

Such activities in the open market help to fine-tune the broad monetary policy signaled by the discount rate. Fed open-market operations consist of the purchase or sale of billions of dollars worth of U.S. Treasury bonds and bills. When the Fed buys U.S. securities, it pumps cash into the banking system. When it sells those securities from its reserves, it drains money from the system. These operations affect the federal-funds rate, which moves higher as the Fed pulls money out of the system. So open-market operations make cash reserves easy or dear, which curtails or encourages bank lending and relending on a daily basis.

The Fed in Action

Every successful investor needs to follow the actions of the Fed. If you haven't done this in the past, maybe it's because you don't know what to look for. Start by making a weekly check of the listings under "Money Supply," "Federal Reserve Data Bank," and "Money Rates." You'll find all three published in the Market Lab section of the financial publication *Barron's*. Also keep an eye on the discount rate and the balance sheet of Fed open-market operations. They're in *Barron's*, too.

By comparing current and past numbers, you can get a clear picture of the direction of Fed policy. If the Fed is expanding the money supply, as signaled by a declining discount rate, increased bond buying, and an opening of its bank-reserve window, then you can bet this stimulation will push the business cycle higher and lift economic growth. When the reverse is happening, the Fed is contracting, the business cycle is reversing, and growth will likely slump.

Fed tightening can cause a lot of trouble for investors who don't pay attention to money-supply signals. Recall that the stock market's October 1987 meltdown followed closely a Fed discount-rate hike. Investors who spotted the Fed's signal got an important warning sign to switch into cash for the short run and shop for investments that would profit most from a change in economic conditions.

How the Federal Government Uses and Abuses Fiscal Policy

The U.S. Treasury Department is the government's business arm, handling the spending and collecting of money from taxpayers. The government is the nation's biggest spender, consumer of goods and services, and employer. Fiscal policy is largely supported by tax revenues. Taxes have ranged from 18 percent to 22 percent of Gross Domestic Product, though they have been as high as 30 percent of GDP.

Since taxes come out of business earnings and consumer pockets, high taxes cut back on profits and consumer demand. Reduced profits mean that business will spend less on reinvestment in new plants and equipment. Consumers forced to pay higher taxes will buy fewer goods and services—and save less. Lower spending by consumers and business pushes down economic growth. So tax cuts are stimulative, and tax increases lead to economic contraction.

Big-government spending means an expansionary economic policy is in place. Higher taxes indicate that the government is pulling back from rampant economic growth.

The Foreign Factor

If the balance of trade between two countries is equal, then the rate of exchange between the currencies of those two countries will also be the same. That's how the dollar shapes up when all things are equal. But things are never equal, and that means you have to think about the shape the dollar's in when you're trying to stay ahead of economic trends.

The problem is that the United States is the world's largest debtor nation. If we export more than we import, our trade account has a surplus. But because we import much more than we export, we have a yearly trade deficit. And it's huge: more than $100 billion during most years.

The more we import, the more foreign currency we have to buy to pay for it. Since we need more foreign currency, and our trading partners need less dollars (because they have fewer U.S. imports to pay for), demand for dollars is less than demand for, say, yen and marks. That means a strong yen and mark—but a weak dollar.

How does that affect you? By monitoring dollar strength, you can often predict the direction of economic growth and the level of future inflation. Keep in mind that growth and inflation are the keys to choosing the most profitable investments. When the level of dollar strength is working to aid growth or hold inflation in check, successful investors can bet on positive business-cycle trends. But when dollar strength is working at cross-purposes, by hampering growth or fostering inflation, investors need to be wary of future change.

A weaker dollar is inflationary, exerting further upward pressure on interest rates. And a dollar that's expected to go lower will reduce foreign investment in the bonds that prop up our deficit. That's because overseas investors will demand a better price.

So the needs of the budget deficit also put upward pressure on U.S. rates. That's just what happened in 1994, when the dollar weakened and the Fed raised the discount rate to 3.5 percent. And since the interest on the deficit is a large part of the deficit, rising rates work to make the deficit worse.

"Declining currencies do not provide for extra flexibility in the conduct of monetary policies," was how one former Fed Chairman put it. The stock-market decline meant that investors expected the Fed to raise rates and risk a recession, or let inflation return, In either case, stocks would suffer. The bull market entered a state of lethargy that didn't change until 1995 and 1996.

History shows that the budget deficit worsens during

recessions. That's because slow growth cuts down the tax take and ups the cost of government-relief programs. In the past, the trade deficit has shown some improvement in recessionary periods.

The difference means that the flexibility of government economic policy is constrained. The government can't solve the budget deficit and the trade deficit at the same time. And that's precisely what the course of interest rates tells us. The path of interest rates is more important than the direction of either deficit, no matter how big, because interest rates reflect the actual progress of the business cycle.

That's cause-and-effect logic. For one, the trade deficit puts increasing pressure on the dollar. And the weakening dollar puts upward pressure on interest rates because high rates are necessary to finance the budget deficit. If those high rates lead to another recession, the Fed responds by trying to ease the problem. But an easy money policy, coupled with a weak dollar, is a sure recipe for inflation. The pressure of the business cycle is inescapable. The choice is slow growth or inflation, and the business cycle opts for the former.

The Road Ahead

As mentioned, some of the preceding explanation of how the economy works may be a little difficult at first. But learning to recognize the onset of a recession is the most important skill you can learn as an investor. Why are those skills so significant? Simply put, more fortunes are lost in the periods of violent transition from good times to tough than at any other point in a market cycle. That is the time when the general public is investing so heavily in stocks, bonds, and real estate.

In other words, you want to see signs that the bull market of prosperity is turning into the bear market of recession. Here are 10 signals that a bull market has lasted too long and could well turn into a recession-induced bear market:

1. Advances in volume and price seem never-ending.
2. The investment markets are jammed with small investors, desperate for a piece of the action.
3. Investors, and even professionals, are all wearing rose-col-

ored glasses, and no one is talking about an end to the boom.

4. The new-issues market in stocks is hot; real-estate prices become inflated.

5. Investors flock to risky stocks or real estate.

6. Investors desert once-favored stocks or real estate.

7. With stocks, more and more splits occur.

8. Good economic news leaves the market cold.

9. With stocks, price/earnings ratios rise to unusually high levels.

10. Dividend and other investment yields sink.

GUIDELINES YOU CAN RELY ON

When the economy is in a boom period, ask yourself these questions:

1. Is the boom more than 35 months old? Check such publications as *Business Week, Forbes, Barron's,* and *The Wall Street Journal* for historical data.

☐ Yes ☐ No

2. Are new investment products and services flooding the market? (With stocks, for example, are new issues abundant?) Check *The Wall Street Journal* for this information.

☐ Yes ☐ No

3. Are stock price/earnings ratios unusually high? Most daily newspapers and *The Wall Street Journal* carry such information.

☐ Yes ☐ No

4. Are many of the investments of smaller, riskier companies at new highs? (With stocks, for example, are NASDAQ stocks selling at inflated prices?)

☐ Yes ☐ No

5. Is a major industry group or investment type showing signs of collapsing over a 10-day period?

☐ Yes ☐ No

6. Are yields from income-producing investments suffering? (Are dividend yields of stocks, for example, falling—perhaps to the 3-percent level?) *The Wall Street Journal* is a good source for information to help you answer the last three questions.

☐ Yes ☐ No

Because the return of a bear market can suddenly wipe out your gains, you can use this period as a time of reflection and stern self-discipline. An error some investors make is that of trying to ride out a dying bull. Success depends on your ability to bail out of a market—even if you must sacrifice a bit of gain—to position yourself to take advantage of opportunities in the next. More on this in a moment.

Keep in mind that there are no absolutes. If one or two guidelines point toward a market reverse, it may be too soon to take action. But if four, five, or especially six combine to send you the same message, you definitely should take action.

Measuring Our Strengths and Weaknesses

So when a recession approaches, the signs are there—if you can interpret them. And suppose you do decide from what you read that an economic downturn is imminent. If you've made and acted upon your prophecy, you are in good shape to profit. But don't go looking for bargains at the start of a recession. The end is almost always farther off than you think.

You may think that this is a good time to go bottom fishing for stocks. But forget about the opportunities that seem irresistible. Usually, that stock you have in mind will be cheaper a month later. Aggressive market players can start selling short now or purchase long-term put options. Keep in mind that the average bear-market loss is 36 percent from peak to trough. Your best bet is to put your money into high-yield ultrasafe investments. From that point, you can simply wait until you see signs that a bottom has been reached. (More on specific strategies on this type later.)

So what do you look for? For starters, easier money, low interest rates, cheaper gold, and indicator upturns. To get a better idea, look at an example from recent history:

Judson Carr did not panic when in October 1987 the market sank into a bear phase. In bemused disbelief, the 44-year-old management-information-systems director watched his friends unload their stocks in a frantic attempt to cut their losses. Judson saw no point in fighting the bear market. After all, he reasoned, bull markets don't last forever. And with the cyclical nature of the stock market, there would be plenty of other bulls to ride.

Of course, he was able to assume that attitude because he'd already acted to protect his own investments. Mindful of the old Wall Street adage, "No one ever went broke taking profits," he had converted some of his handsome paper profits into actual capital gains. And he prepared himself to watch for the inevitable bear-market upturn known as a "secondary rally." As experienced investors know, money can be made in a bear market—if you play by the bear's rules. Consider these time-tested strategies to help you weather the rigors of a recession and accompanying bear market:

1. Just Do It: Sell

You must respond to signals that warn of reversals in broad market trends. As explained earlier, the markets will offer you plenty of clues that a recession is on its way. Once you're convinced that the storm signals are authentic, take action.

First, before the markets break out—actually make the turn from bull to bear—sell off your more speculative investments. They are the last to benefit from prosperity's momentum, but they'll also be among the first to tumble beneath the bear market of recession.

In other words, follow the wisdom of Judson Carr and take your profits while you can. The bull market will not continue forever. And what happens if you get out before the bull market's peak? Obviously, you'll lose a bit of profit. But that's much better than selling off your portfolio at a drastic loss or being forced to sit it out with your falling investments until the next upturn arrives.

2. Sell Short

You obviously know how to buy investments "long." You do so with the objective that they will appreciate in value. But when investment prices are falling, you can sell investments "short." After all, the principle involved—selling investments you don't own with a view to making a profit when the price goes down—is little different from buying. You simply reverse the process.

By selling short, you use one of the most dynamic techniques available to an investor for offsetting the severity of a recession. Let's review how this technique works with stocks, though you can also apply it to a host of investment types, including commodities, bonds, and, yes, even real estate.

As discussed in Chapter 8, when you sell short, you sell something you don't own—yet. Eventually you do have to buy the item and make delivery. The goal, of course, is to sell it at a higher price, then buy it at a lower price—and pocket the difference.

For most investments this procedure is easy. If you sell stocks short, for example, you borrow the shares of your choice, usually from a broker—someone who's in a position to maintain a short position indefinitely. The broker also borrows those shares. Typically, the broker gets them from other clients who have bought on margin and are not entitled to have the shares registered in their names, from the brokerage house's own portfolio, or from another brokerage house.

Of course, you must be satisfied that the shares are set to decline in price. Then you should ensure that the "float" of shares (the number of outstanding shares of a company) available to borrow on the open market is sufficient. If the shorted stock is in great demand, your broker may have to pay a premium, usually $1 for every 100 shares borrowed per business day.

Suppose that you have been closely watching all the signs and trends previously discussed, and you believe the price of BellSouth stock is about to decline from its level of $50 a share. You don't own any of the shares, but you call your broker and tell her you want to sell 100 shares of BellSouth short. Keep in mind that you must declare your intentions to short from the start.

Your broker arranges to borrow shares for you from another of her clients. Then she sells the 100 shares of BellSouth in the market. The buyer does not necessarily know that she's purchasing them from a short seller.

At this point, the transaction is treated just like any other sale. After paying the broker $5,000 ($50 x 100), plus commission, the buyer is entitled to take possession of the shares.

After the sale, you, the seller, ordinarily would be entitled to the proceeds of the transaction. Since you don't own those shares, however, your broker won't allow you to pocket this cash. Instead, it will be credited to your brokerage account. This offsets your broker's liability until you make good on your end of the bargain—that is, your delivery of the borrowed shares to the broker.

You're actually making a credit transaction when you sell short. So you must show your broker that you're a good credit risk. You do this by opening a margin account, which allows you to finance a fixed portion of your stock purchases through your broker. The amount you personally give the broker can range from 100 to 150 percent of the market value of the shares sold short.

Let's say that in shorting BellSouth, you find that the margin on 100 shares at $50 a share is $7,500 (150 percent of $5,000). Since your account has already been credited with $5,000 from the proceeds of the sale, you write your broker a check for $2,500 (plus commission). You now have $7,500 on account, or 150 percent of the market value of the shares.

Now let's say the share price of BellSouth rises to $55. That puts you in a losing position. Soon your broker will call to ask you to increase your margin with an additional $750 (that is, a total of 150 percent of $5,500. At this point, you can "close out" your position by buying back the shares you owe and taking a loss of $500 (before commissions). But let's say you are convinced that the stock price will eventually fall. So you "cover" your short sale by sending your broker a check for $750.

The recession eventually takes it toll, and BellSouth stock suddenly drops to $45 a share. The current market for those shares now is $4,500. You therefore can buy back those 100 shares for less than the selling price on your short sale, and you decide to close out your position. You then pocket $500, as the following shows:

Sell 100 shares of BellSouth @ $50 a share	$5,000
Send broker $2,500	2,500
Total in your account	$7,500
Cover position when share price rises to $55	750
Total in your account	$8,250
Buy 100 shares when price drops to $45	4,500
Total in your account	$3,750
Minus total margin	3,250
Total profit (before commissions)	$ 500

Not bad for a few days of patience.

3. Become a Contrarian

An investment theory that has a surprising number of adherents is "contrarianism." In fact, many highly successful traders have the contrarian trait in common—that is, to sell when everyone else is buying and buy when everyone else is selling. They buck the trend. They are perceptive analyzers of markets, and they often rack up sizable profits from taking such actions. They include the value investors and those who seek turnaround situations.

But adopting a contrarian philosophy takes nerve and an emotional detachment that many people don't have. In investing, the herd instinct seems to prevail. And investors generally are mindless members of that herd. Here is an example, using commodities, of how that herd instinct works:

Let's say the price of heating oil rises as a result of a mild shortage of the commodity. News stories and brokerage houses report the shortage, and traders begin buying in earnest. Speculators then enter the market and force the price of heating oil to unsustainable levels. At that point, the price peaks, then drops. Buyers then become sellers, and many speculators are cleaned out.

In fact, the shortage remains the same as it was before all the trading flurry. And had someone with a contrarian philosophy been involved, he or she would have made a bundle, buying when the price was low, then selling at or near the price peak. In this case, the market for heating oil became "over-heated" (no pun intended) and factors other than supply and demand were involved.

The considerations the contrarian must deal with are psychological. First, he or she must determine what the consensus is—and that's not easy. For example, suppose a contrarian is reviewing the commodities markets to determine who is buying and who is selling. Typically, he relies on the published research of several brokerage houses and advisory services. And from those sources, he compiles a list of commodities that interest him.

Using "weighted" figures for each source, he then arrives at a bullish reading for each commodity. If, for example, nine of 10 brokerage firms and advisory services favor buying gold, he gives gold a 90-percent rating. The premise he uses is that most speculators base their trades on broker and adviser recommendations. So the higher the rating, the more demand there will be for gold.

The contrarian's strategy is to take a position contrary to the percentage rating. By doing so, he or she will move against the herd, which, history shows, tends to be wrong at key points in a market trend. So gold gets a 90-percent bullish rating. That means that almost all speculators are buying gold, anticipating a continued rise in the price. But all that buying leaves little room for further price increases. Gold peaks, and there is only one way for the price to move. Down.

As the price levels out and further bullish news fails to stimulate new buying, the general mood changes. The news and advisory sources suddenly begin reporting bearish outlooks for gold. There's a mad scramble to close out long positions, and those who delay taking action lose their shirts.

For contrarians, however, they were selling gold short when everyone else was buying. In other words, when they spotted a bullish trend, they knew that a bearish position was best. Thus, they did what every investor dreams of: They bought low and sold high—except in this case they reversed the process.

The contrarian will typically decide that a consensus is strong and the time for action is ripe when an opinion is widely held and publicized. The contrarian's analysis is strengthened if the reasons supporting the biased opinion have already been discounted in the market or if the opinion is generated by widely accepted belief—not fact.

Contrarianism is a valuable technical tool when used with extensive analysis and precise timing. It can help prevent the user from being carried away by exuberant markets and can, in fact, help him or her unearth new information about a given security, industry, or commodity.

4. Reduce the Risk Factor

Only the foolhardy puts all his or her eggs in one basket. The primary point of investing is to lessen the odds against you and try to make them work in your favor. Take a game of chance like roulette, for example. If you took all your worldly belongings, liquidated them, and put the money on your favorite number, say, 21, you'd have one chance in 36 of that little ball coming to rest in your chosen compartment. But if you divided your money into four parts and covered the numbers 12, 18, and 36, as well as 21, the odds of your winning are reduced to one chance in nine.

Obviously, your winnings would be four times as great if you bet only on 21 and that number came up. But the risk of losing everything also would be four times as great. By spreading your bet across four numbers, you would be diversifying. You'd net less if you hit, but the odds would be considerably more in your favor.

The same principle holds true for the investments you purchase. Let's consider the stock market. Stocks are not static like numbers. They don't all perform the same way. Some securities, like those of gold-mining companies, oil-and-gas operations, and international firms, move up and down according to political pronouncements and events on the other side of the world. Other shares, like those of utilities, communications companies, and financial-services firms, usually plod onward, providing unspectacular but reliable returns.

In between is the mass of companies whose fortunes are governed not only by economic factors, but also by the quality of their management and the steadiness of their earnings record. And each share you buy for your portfolio has its own intrinsic, or "built-in," risk.

Risk is defined as "the chance or possibility of injury, damage, or loss." Risk focuses on the future and our ability to forecast that future. In turn, our ability to predict the future is largely dependent on what we've learned from the past. The best we can do is study the record and draw on experience— our own and that of others.

During recessionary times, the relationship between risk and return seems straightforward. In general, you will find that risk and return move in the same direction. In other words, if you accept a higher risk, you can expect to achieve higher returns. High-risk investments almost invariably promise a high return.

But equally important, where it is possible to win big, you can lose big. And the odds are always with the "house" (the provider of the risk/return). If all it took to create instant wealth was assuming high risks, you could assure yourself of millionaire status simply by going to the race track every day and betting all your money on the long shots.

But, as explained in Chapter 5, risk comes in several forms. For most investors during hard times, financial risk is the most immediate concern. It centers on the simple question, "If I put my money into this investment, will I at least get my money back?" Your best protection against financial risk is to explore any investment to the point where you understand the risk and can secure your principal. When you buy a common stock, for example, the financial risk is tied to the credit and operating history of the company issuing the stock.

So it's important to try to anticipate how a company will cope with recession. That means analyzing the firm's financial capacity (the ability to generate income). A firm that can't pay its debt or has a history of near-insolvency has a low financial capacity and a comparatively high financial risk. A company with earnings high enough to pay fixed costs many times over is thought to pose a lower financial risk.

Generally, certificates of deposit, commercial short-term paper, U.S. Savings Bonds, and Treasury securities are considered of low financial risk.

Another risk that you will encounter during a recessionary

period is market risk. This risk results from the uncertainty of future prices of an investment due to changed investor attitudes or other influences. "Investor psychology" plays an important role in determining security prices. Those attitudes toward particular markets are commonly reflected in such a phenomenon as a "soaring" or "plunging" Dow Jones Industrial Average.

Government bonds, high-grade corporate bonds, and securities with low financial risk are less vulnerable to investor whims than real estate or common stock. Usually, the better an investment withstands shifts in investor psychology (that is, the lower the market risk), the lower the financial risk on it.

Finally, there's interest-rate risk. During a recessionary period, interest rates can undergo a rapid dip, creating a confusing pattern in the market for investments with fixed-interest returns. If you buy a 10-percent bond and interest rates drop to 7 percent, the value of that bond rises. That's why you don't want to own a bond that is maturing just as the recession gets into full swing. You'll have to begin shopping for a replacement in a market where rates might have bottomed. Then the value of your bond would begin to drop as rates rise.

Rising-market interest rates drive down the price of bonds or other debt securities. Conversely, falling rates cause those prices to rise. Recessionary times call for safe, liquid, fixed-rate investments.

5. Revise Your Portfolio

If you're a knowledgeable investor, then, you hold a diversity of assets. In other words, you don't have just stocks or bonds or real estate or Treasury securities, but a combination of them. You also may have money in a bank savings account, some gold, some collectibles, and a bank certificate of deposit.

During a recession, however, some of your holdings may suffer more than others. So how do you know which are more "risk heavy" than others. Chart 47 should help. The assets are listed in ascending order of risk, beginning with Treasury securities. If more than 30 percent of your capital is invested in items in the lower half of this chart, that portion is risk heavy.

When a recession is imminent, you obviously want to reduce your risk as much as possible. Holdings you have in stocks could be reduced, for example, because stocks generally will not fare well during a prolonged economic downturn. The objective then is to move your assets up the above list as much as possible. As mentioned, you want to be as liquid as possible at such a time. And you want to be sure that your return on investment will remain at a level that will provide you with a meaningful return. You do that so you can not only weather the storm, but also be ready to take advantage of opportunities when you see a break in that storm.

CHART 48

A DESCENT INTO RISK

Asset	Current Value ($)
Treasury securities	
U.S. Savings Bonds	
Personal residence	
Government-agency bonds	
Bank savings accounts	
Money-market funds	
Bond mutual funds	
Equity mutual funds	
Bank certificates of deposit	
Municipal bonds	
Corporate bonds (high-quality)	
Preferred shares (high quality)	
Common shares (blue chip)	
Precious metals	
Investment real estate	
Junk bonds	
Common shares (high-growth, penny, etc.)	
Options	
Collectibles	
Foreign currencies	
Commodity futures	

Recession and Your Investments
Stocks

During recessionary times, your presence in the stock market must be minimal. In fact, no more than 25 percent of your portfolio should be in equities of any type. That's because most companies (though certainly not all) will suffer from declining earnings and lower stock prices. But judge each company on its individual merits. You can find exceptions. But as a general rule, the period just before a recession is the time to unload many of your equities.

Which ones? Keep in mind, that since unemployment rises during a recession, the government may try to create jobs by providing additional contracts to companies in aircraft, shipbuilding, and electronics, or firms that are located in areas that are particularly hard hit by unemployment. These companies may outperform the rest of the stock market until the economy recovers.

Blue-chip companies—well-established corporations with a long history of sound financial management—are good defensive investments during recessionary times. Aggressive young companies, which perform well in periods of low inflation, may not have the financial resources to weather the storm.

While past performance is no guarantee of future profitability, companies with good historical track records tend to remain viable. Put such firms high on your list of investment choices during a recession.

Bonds

Most corporate bonds do quite well during recessionary times. Just make sure you buy them while interest rates are high. Then, as rates drop, the value of your bonds will increase. The time to sell them, of course, is when interest rates bottom. Once rates are on the rise again, bond values drop.

Cash

The word "cash" doesn't necessarily mean dollar bills. In an investment sense, cash is any type of asset that is totally liquid and free from market movements. So cash could be a government security or a bank savings account or a money-market mutual fund. You want access to your money during recessionary times so you don't get clobbered by falling investment values—and so you can quickly take advantage of bargains once you feel that economic conditions are improving.

Real Estate

Real-estate prices normally drop during recessionary times. Home buying falls off, so supply usually exceeds demand. Houses that were previously selling at inflated prices suddenly don't sell. Commercial properties eventually suffer the same fate. Businesses stop expanding, so demand for office buildings and retail space nosedives.

Yet real estate, especially residential real estate, is often the first sector of the economy to recover at the end of a recessionary period. That's primarily because of political attitudes. No government can let too many homeowners endure deprivation for long periods. As a result, they are on the receiving end of tax benefits, special interest rates, and lender priorities.

As with stock investors, real-estate investors should have cash available to take advantage of bargains. The latter stage of a recession is ideal for the purchase of distressed properties and discounted commercial real estate.

Precious Metals

Gold and silver are havens for investors during inflationary times, but prices skid when a recession comes to town. The explanation for this situation is simple: Investors seek a hedge against the lost purchasing power of their paper money during a period of inflation, but they prefer cash when interest rates and the rate of inflation are falling. Again, supply and demand are the keys. Supply of gold exceeds demand, so gold prices fall. Chart 49 shows how gold has fared during periods of recession.

CHART 49

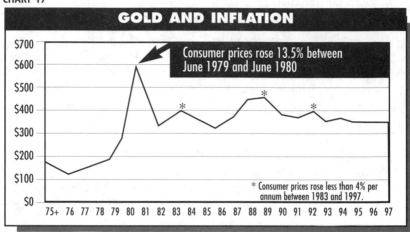

GOLD AND INFLATION

Consumer prices rose 13.5% between June 1979 and June 1980

* Consumer prices rose less than 4% per annum between 1983 and 1997.

A Matter of Timing?

As you have probably discerned by now, timing is critical to success when the economy takes a turn for the worse. Even if you could predict that a recession is in store, you must know when you should act to escape injury and profit from the bargains that will be available.

Examples of poor timing are widespread, and one school of investment professionals says that exact timing is impossible. Indeed, history is replete with examples of those who shun this investment device. Many investors who foresaw the 1987 stock-market crash did nothing. Many investors who felt that real-estate prices in California during the 1980s could not continue to escalate kept buying. And investors in 1997 who are aware that stock prices are overvalued continue to stay fully invested in the stock market.

Efforts at individual timing is therefore essential in every investment, and each investment must have its timing judged individually. But there is another form of timing that affects investing. It's known as "general" timing.

General timing is determined by economic circumstances. It tells you both the type of investment that makes sense and also whether you should invest at all. Some investment vehicles are independent of general timing; profits can be made in options, currencies, interest-rate futures, and commodities regardless of the prevailing economic climate. But most of the remainder of the investment types are at their best in an expansive economy.

Since late 1991 we have had such an expansive economy. This period has been, during most years, fueled by easy money, huge government deficits, and interest rates near or even below the rate of inflation. Under such conditions, leverage has worked wonderfully, and borrowed money has been used to buy almost any equity asset (stocks, precious metals, collectibles) that would increase in value far faster than the borrowed money would cost in interest payments. This has been an investor's/speculator's dream period, and many people have made fortunes during these times.

But the concept of business cycles dictates that change is inevitable. And the key to successful investing during changing times is recognizing when the economy is in a state of flux.

Can You Predict a Recession?

Maybe you can't predict a recession with total precision. Nobody can. But by now you know that you can detect certain economic changes that are in the wind—and subsequently cash in on that knowledge. The following chart should help in that regard. Starting now and at quarter-year intervals, you can evaluate the state of the economy, using the 13 economic indicators listed below. Many daily newspapers or *The Wall Street Journal* can be used as a source of such information. Start by entering under "Now" the current level for each of the indicators. For example, if the prime rate is, say, 8 percent at the latest reporting, enter that figure. Then at the next quarter, make note of the change with an arrow in the boxes, like so:

If the trend is up: ↑
If the trend is down: ↓
If there's little or no change: ↔

Then, after you have noted the indicators, at the bottom write in your conclusion about the general trend. Remember, you can win in periods of change. It's largely a matter of detecting and acting on trends.

CHART 50

	Now	Next Quarter	Next Quarter	Next Quarter	Next Quarter
Gross National Product					
Consumer Price Index					
Unemployment Rate					
Bank Prime Rate					
Gold Prices					
T-Bill Yield					
T-Bond Yield					
M-3 Money Supply					
U.S. Dollar Vs. Yen					
Housing Starts					
Retail Trade					
New-Car Sales					
The General Trend Is:					

A Model Investment Portfolio

The ultimate composition of your portfolio during a recessionary period will obviously reflect all such factors as personal wealth, projected income, family size and plans, objectives, and age. However, there are other basic principles of portfolio design to follow during such times.

For example, have a foundation of risk-free or near-risk-free investments. This base should be, except for the more aggressive types, a minimum of 50 percent of your portfolio. In case worse comes to worse (a prolonged recession, for instance), you add crisis investments as a hedge. For most people, the maximum crisis portion of a well-balanced investment will be 10 percent and should probably be about 5 percent.

From there, you would add your other components. With a solid base of fixed-income investments, gold (or silver), and perhaps foreign-currency-denominated assets for income and protection, you can include equities. The strategy you will adopt will, of course, reflect your risk preferences and your objectives. But don't forget the basic principles developed throughout this program.

As discussed, a portfolio of common stocks should be diversified and heavy with companies or industries that suffer little or none during hard times. If you cannot maintain the shares of at least three companies in your portfolio, you can buy instant diversification through mutual funds. You might even diversify your holdings of mutual funds as well.

As for speculative types of investments, have a strategy that ensures that you can lose no more than the portion of your portfolio allocated to high-risk selections. If you have the means to maintain a commodities account, for example, never commit more than, say, $2,000 and confine your trading to a maximum of three positions, preferably two. Your best bet in this regard may be a managed account, which diversifies your trades.

You are now ready to complete your tough-times portfolio design. Following are four sample portfolios. Since there are almost an infinite number of combinations of family situations, risk preferences, and objectives, none of these four will be ideal for your situation and circumstances. But unless your case is very unusual, one should come reasonably close and can thus provide some guidelines for you.

Note that real estate is not included in any of these suggested portfolios. As mentioned previously, however, real estate can be added once the economy starts showing signs of improving. Bargains should exist at that time, and the cash you have in the risk-free category can be converted to take advantage of those bargains.

CHART 51

SAMPLE PORTFOLIO—INCOME AND PROTECTION
Risk Level: Normally very conservative
Age: 55-65, no dependents
Major objective: Comfortable retirement

Component	Percent of Portfolio	Purpose
Risk-free assets (short-term CDs, money-market acct./fund, Treasury securities, etc.)	30	Income; preservation of capital
Corporate bonds (top-grade)	20	Income; interest-rate protection
Diversified selection of quality common shares or mutual funds	40	Capital gains, income
Preferred shares	5	Income, capital gains
Gold/silver	5	Crisis hedge

CHART 52

SAMPLE PORTFOLIO—CAPITAL GAINS
Risk level: Normally aggressive
Age: 40-55, one dependent
Major objectives: Retirement and specific purposes

Component	Percent of Portfolio	Purpose
Risk-free assets (short-term CDs, money-market acct./fund, Treasury securities, etc.)	20	Income; preservation of capital
Corporate bonds (medium- to top-grade)	20	Income; interest-rate protection
Diversified selection of common shares or mutual funds	50	Capital gains, income
Preferred shares	5	Income, capital gains
Gold/silver	5	Crisis hedge

CHART 53

SAMPLE PORTFOLIO—BALANCED
Risk level: Normally moderately conservative
Age: 35-45, three dependents
Major objectives: Education of children, comfortable retirement

Component	Percent of Portfolio	Purpose
Risk-free assets (short-term CDs, money-market acct./fund, Treasury securities, etc.)	25	Income; preservation of capital
Corporate bonds (medium- to top-grade)	20	Income; interest-rate protection
Diversified selection of common shares or mutual funds	45	Capital gains, income
Preferred shares	5	Income; capital gains
Gold/silver	5	Crisis hedge

CHART 54

SAMPLE PORTFOLIO—HIGH GROWTH
Risk level: Normally superaggressive
Age: 35-45, no dependents
Major objectives: Capital gains

Component	Percent of Portfolio	Purpose
Risk-free assets (short-term CDs, money-market acct./fund, Treasury securities, etc.)	15	Income; preservation of capital
Corporate bonds (medium-grade)	10	Income, interest-rate protection
Diversified selection of common shares or mutual funds	50	Capital gains
Foreign-currency-denominated securities	20	Income; capital gains
Gold/silver	5	Crisis hedge

Getting Well

So far, you've considered recession in view of how to detect one approaching, how to prepare for it, and how to deal with it. But you may ask whether you can actually profit from a recession.

You've explored some ways: thinking like a contrarian, seeking bargains, and investing in value. As you know by now, the best time for investors to buy is when the business cycle has reached its zenith (or in the case of a recession, its nadir).

At the bottom of a bear stock market, ordinary investors will be frantically selling their way down. That's the psychology that causes mainstream investors to miss the turning point at which a long-run trend finally changes direction.

No single indicator can identify an exact turning point. Normally, the bottom will be reached while you're still expecting it. But being late at the bottom is not a bad thing. Typically, investors overestimate the life of a boom and underestimate the extent of a recession. That's only human nature.

All investors want the good times to last and the pain to be short. So you've got to resist the temptation to underestimate the extent of a slump. At the same time, don't get so caught up in it that you miss the turning point. That's not easy, but by using the full range of indicators that are available, you'll be able to spot a turning point early enough.

If you remember no other point than this one about investing during a recession, you should have few problems. The point is that it's better to be a little late than too early. Once a business cycle changes direction, you'll be locking your money into specific investments and waiting for them to appreciate in value. Successful investing takes patience, and part of the patience is waiting to be certain that a trend has changed before you act—even if that means you don't get the lowest possible price. Better safe than sorry is the second most important investing rule of all.

That's why you want to watch the largest economic picture possible. Not just to get in early, but to get an overall confirmation of a changing trend. Since money supply is the key determinant, you will be trying to spot a shift to Fed pump priming. At the same time, keep the big picture in mind so that you don't confuse short-run Fed behavior with the implementation of long-run change. The Fed can vary the money supply on short notice. But changes in the discount rate are infrequent. The combination of successive discount-rate cuts and a swiftly growing money supply is a better indicator of an upward move from the bottom than either is alone.

As mentioned, cash is good to have at the bottom, and investors concerned with safety and access usually keep some cash on hand. Best of all is to have locked in a high-interest-paying investment at the top of the boom, timed to mature just before you need the cash to buy bargains. For example, let's say you bought high-interest bonds during boom times. As the level of interest rates declines during the various stages of recession, your high-interest-paying bonds will become desirable to other investors. They'll even pay you a premium to buy them.

Also keep in mind that the best place to buy on credit is at the bottom. Using leverage is always risky, but it's less risky at the bottom. At that point, you start to get as fully invested as possible. So stock investors who win big are usually margined at the bottom of a bear market and completely unmargined at a bull-market top. Other investors will put home-equity loans in place now while interest rates are low to make the most capital possible available for investing. At the bottom, you want the most buying power you can muster.

Summary: Be Prepared

Recession is a real part of the business cycle. The economy, as measured by Gross Domestic Product, does expand, but it also contracts. Predicting just when a downturn has started isn't easy. But successful investors know that recession inevitably follows boom times. Trees and stock prices grow, but they don't reach the sky, declares an old stock-market adage. That means that every bull market is followed by a bear market. That's what the most profitable market players never forget. But in the surges of a long bull market, ordinary investors often get so caught up in buying their way to the top that they forget about the business cycle.

In a long bull market, stocks seems to have a life of their

own, and the only direction seems to be up. That's just when a crash is most likely, for the business cycle will have already turned down, and only investors who didn't underestimate its power will have acted in time.

The same is true of other investors. At one time gold reached a price of $800 an ounce, but it was difficult to remember that fact a few years later, when gold was selling for less than $300 an ounce.

Only investors who understand how the business cycle leads to inflation and how gold reacts to that inflation could guess that the price would climb back to $500 an ounce in a very short time. Investors have to know where the highest current return is to be found.

Protection of your holdings means diversifying them. By doing so, you greatly reduce risk. No successful investor ever forgot the warning not to put all his or her eggs in one basket. But some baskets can contain many more eggs (rewards) than others. A lot depends on timing.

Here are a couple of rules to remember when the economy turns sour:

First, no matter how stable the economy, business moves in cycles. Second, never underestimate the actual power of the business cycle. The business cycle influences not only our investments, but also our lives. Moreover, that influence can be much greater than we imagine.

Government economists continue to seek a way to perpetuate the expansion phase of the business cycle and eliminate recessions. But GDP growth is never a straight line. The business cycle continues to exert itself, and the economy will ebb and flow. Making matters worse is that no two upturns or downturns are exactly alike, even though the National Bureau of Economic Research has tracked 30 full cycles in 100 years of data.

Finally...

As you've seen in this chapter, the persistence of the business cycle is an indication of its ability to overwhelm government economic control. You've learned to chart economy policy signals, from which you can gain an advantage over those who sit idly by when recession comes. You've also seen how the cycle can resist government intervention. The cycle of economic growth is stronger than the Fed and the Treasury Department combined. And when you have to make an investment decision, you now know that government monetary and fiscal policy may be successful in the short run. But the business cycle still rules in the long run.

Chapter 20: The Amazing Power of Compounding

"I have planted, Apollos watered, but God gave the increase."

I Corinthians

Adding Artillery

When you add compounding to your arsenal for accumulating wealth, you have at your command one of the most potent weapons that exist. Here, we're going to spend some time exploring this amazing weapon. You'll see what compounding can do and how it can turn small, consistent investments into huge fortunes. Through examples, you'll go to financial heights that are dizzying. First, however, let's look at some of the basics of the subject.

From the Commonplace to the Extraordinary

Compounding heightens the act of investing from something commonplace into something extraordinary. It can singly transform a modest return on investment into millions of dollars.

Let's look at some examples:

Suppose you are 25 years old and have saved a thousand dollars. Let's also assume you can save $50 a month and can obtain a 15-percent yield on your investments. Here's what you can accomplish with this amount and enough time:

Age	$1,000 + $50 a Month
25	$ 1,000
30	8,663
35	18,054
40	40,967
45	87,054
50	179,745
55	466,185
60	741,183
65	1,495,435

Of course, income taxes would normally take a huge portion of your accumulation if you haven't invested in something that is tax-free. But we're assuming that you have invested through an individual retirement account, which does provide you with tax protection.

Now let's assume that you're 30 years old. You'll need a slightly larger stake to begin with: $10,000. But this time, you're just going to let the initial amount earn its own way (at 15 percent) without adding anything more. As you can see, the results you'll get from compounding are just about as good.

Age	$10,000 + Nothing a Month
30	$ 10,000
35	20,113
40	40,456
45	81,371
50	163,670
55	329,190
60	662,120
65	1,331,800

Next, suppose you open an IRA. You put in $145 a month for 20 years. That's a total of $34,800. The contributions to the IRA do well, yielding 10 percent compounded annually. How much do you think you will have accumulated over the 20 years?

❑ $50,000   ❑ $75,000   ❑ $104,000

The answer is $104,000, give or take a few dollars. If you kept this up for another five years, incidentally, the total would increase to $178,967.

Finally, if you had an opportunity to invest $5,000 per year for 10 years, how much do you think you would accumulate at the end of that time if your money earned 12 percent compounded annually? (Leave taxes out of your calculation.)

❏ $51,200   ❏ $76,512   ❏ $87,744

The correct answer is $87,744. And if you continued the same process for another 10 years, you'd have $360,262!

Little wonder that interest has always been one of the major concerns of investors. And as you have seen in the previous examples, interest rates are the pulse of investing. Mastering the concept of interest in its various calculations is consequently fundamental to understanding much of what goes on in money and portfolio management. So let's take some time to fully understand what compounding is all about.

As you probably know, interest is expressed in terms of an annual rate of percentage upon a principal amount. Thus, if $12 is paid for the annual use of $100, the rate is 12 percent. The annual rate is also 12 percent, for example, if $1 is paid for one month's use of $100. Interest is often payable at shorter intervals than one year, but rarely at longer intervals. Three factors are involved in interest calculations:

1. Principal.

2. Time.

3. Rate.

The principal is the sum of money on which the interest is paid—the amount lent, borrowed, or invested. The time is the number of periods for which the interest is paid—that is, day, month, three months, six months, one year. The rate is the percentage per period of the principal that is paid as interest and is usually expressed as a certain percentage per year.

If the interest is calculated on the original principal only, it is called "simple" interest. But compound interest is something far different. Compounding occurs if at the end of the first period—a day, a month, etc.—the interest for that period is added to the principal so that the interest for the second period is subsequently calculated on this amount. That process then continues for a given number of periods—in other words it "compounds."

The calculations for simple interest and compound interest are each distinctive. As mentioned, simple interest is calculated on the principal without reference to the interest period, on the assumption that 1/365th of a year's interest accrues each day. The formula for computing annual simple interest is:

$$I = PR$$

where P is the principal and R is the rate of interest per year. For example, if principal of $1,000 is invested at a 12-percent annual rate of interest, the dollar interest per year (assuming that the interest is not reinvested) is:

$$I = \$1,000 \,(.12)$$

$$I = \$120$$

To determine the dollar amount of interest for principal invested for less than one year (365-day year; 366 in leap years), the formula is:

$$I = (PR)(D \div 365)$$

where D is the number of days for which the principal is invested. For example, if principal of $1,000 is invested for 31 days at an annual rate of interest of 12 percent, the dollar interest for the 31-day period is:

$$I = 1,000 \,(.12)(31 \div 365)$$

$$I = 120 \,(.0849315)$$

$$I = 10.1918$$

Compound interest is calculated on the principal plus the interest that has accrued and is payable on the compounded amount daily (sometimes called "continuous"), monthly, quarterly, semiannually, or annually. When interest is compounded more frequently than once a year, it produces an "effective" rate in excess of the nominal, or quoted, rate.

For example, if the nominal interest rate on a $1,000 bond is 12 percent, payable annually, the effective interest rate is the same—that is, 12 percent; if payable semiannually, 12.36 percent; if payable quarterly, 12.55 percent; if payable monthly, 12.68 percent, and if payable daily, 12.74 percent. The interest on a $1,000 12-percent bond compounded annually is therefore $120; $123.60 if compounded semiannually; $125.50 if compounded quarterly; $126.80 if compounded monthly; and $127.40 if compounded daily. More on this phenomenon in a moment.

The difference between simple interest and compound interest may be further illustrated by the following example:

Assume a 10-percent $100 investment for three years. If calculated on the basis of simple interest:

Simple interest   = 3 x .10($100)
                  = $30

If calculated on the basis of compound interest:

$ 100.00
   x .10
$ 10.00 interest first year
+$100.00
$110.00
   x .10
$ 11.00 interest second year
+$110.00
$121.00
   x .10
$ 12.10 interest third year

$ 10.00 interest first year
 11.00 interest second year
 12.10 interest third year
$ 33.10 total compound interest

Since compound interest is computed on the basis of successively larger amounts, interest computed on a compound basis will result in a greater total value than interest paid on a simple-interest basis.

The above calculation for compound interest for three years (or three periods of any duration) is obviously cumbersome. A computation for compound interest over a longer period of time or a larger number of time periods, say, 10 years or 14 months or 57 days, using the same method, would be even more tedious. So mathematicians have devised the following formula for computing compound interest more easily:

$$CA = P(1 + R)n$$

where

CA is compound interest (principal plus compound interest).
P is original principal or present value.
R is rate of interest per period.
n is total number of periods or intervals at which interest is compounded.

If the figures in the above example are substituted in this formula, we get

$$CA = 100(1 + .10)3$$

But even if you use this formula, computations are still labored and monotonous. And you need to use interest-rate tables constructed to show the amount of interest that will accrue on a given sum at different rates of interest for various intervals of time, thus negating separate and independent computations for each interest transaction. Fortunately, interest-rate tables are available from most book stores. Such tables are prepared in many different forms, with varying degrees of detail and refinement for calculating decimal places, interest rates, and time intervals, and to meet a wide variety of uses.

But now let's consider another type of compounding-type calculation. Sometimes you may encounter problems in ascertaining the "present value" of an investment maturing in the future. For example, how would you find the present value of a five-year $10,000 debt instrument bearing interest at 4.50

percent (compounded annually) if the interest rate currently is 6 percent (compounded annually)? From the formula we used previously (CA = P[1 + R]n), you can calculate the compounded amount CA:

$$R = 4.5\%$$

$$\frac{4.5\% \text{ p.a.}}{1 \text{ period p.a.}} = 4.5\% \text{ per period}$$

m = 5 (five years compounded once a year)

(1 + R)n = 1.246181194 (from compound interest tables)

CA = $12,461.819, or $10,000 x 1.24618194

To find the present value of this CA, you must find present value (PV), and you can do that by dividing both sides of the equation by (1 + R)n:

$$\frac{CA}{(1 + R)n} \qquad \frac{PV(1 + R)n}{(1 + R)n}$$

Since each (1 + R)n cancels the other, you get:

$$\frac{CA}{(1 + R)n} = PV$$

The value of (1 + R)n is again given in compound interest tables on the amount of 1 at various compound interest rates and periods. Hence you can compute present value as follows:

$$PV = \frac{CA}{(1 + R)n}$$

$$PV = CA \times \frac{1}{1 + R(n)}$$

Thus, if we substitute the applicable figures, we get:

PV = $9,312.20, or (12,461.819 x .74725817)

where

$$\frac{1}{(1 + R)n} = .74725817$$

and

CA = $12,461.819

Therefore, the present value of the obligation is $9,312.20.

Now let's return to the subject of frequency of compounding. The frequency is vital to producing the best results. In other words, the more frequent the compounding, the more you earn in interest.

For example, if you invest your $1,000 compounded monthly for one year at 10 percent in a financial institution, which in turn invests this sum for the same length of time and rate of interest daily, the financial institution would make an extra 50 cents on your money. Keep in mind that a financial institution may receive thousands of $1,000 deposits, and each basis point (.01 percent) of yield has a value of $1,000 per $10 million invested per annum alone.

Although you would normally consult interest-rate tables for this calculation, Chart 55 shows the most frequently used calculations on effective annual yield at selected nominal rates and time intervals.

For example, on a $1,000 term deposit paying 14 percent per year on a quarterly compound basis, you would receive at the end of one year $147.50.

Another example: Jim and Jack each had amassed $5,000 in their IRA. They both invested those funds in five-year 9½-percent certificates of deposit. Jim's CD compounded semiannually; Jack's CD compounded annually. At the end of the five-years, Jim had accumulated $7,952.61 ($5,000 plus $2,952.61 interest), while Jack had only $7,871.19 ($5,000 plus $2,871.19 interest). In the same time period, using the same basic investment instrument, with no difference whatsoever in the degree of safety, Jim pulled in $81.42 more than Jack. The difference developed because of the difference between the *nominal* interest rate and the *effective* interest rate.

Keep in mind, however, that we are not discussing "guarantees" here. You're simply seeing a visual account of what compounding accomplishes over a period of time if you are able to maintain a certain average return and receive interest at a certain frequency. No one can accurately predict what our future economy will be like. Of one thing you can be sure, however: You will never reach your goal of accumulating great wealth using "guaranteed" dollars—that is, bank savings, certificates of deposit, and other fixed-return investments—that you hold to maturity.

If you hope to reach your goal, you must invest your money aggressively and intelligently in well-managed and strategically positioned U. S. companies that are in the right industry at the right time, real estate expertly selected and intelligently leveraged, and natural resources that are in critical demand. Of course, such investments offer no guarantees that they will make your capital grow, but you will have provided your money with the opportunity to work as hard for you as you had to work to get it. The working dollar is an absolute necessity if your goal is to become wealthy.

Another point related to compounding: Never regard any income, capital appreciation, or equity buildup as spendable during the period you are building toward your wealth-accumulation goals. Instead, think of each as returns that are to be reinvested to increase your nest egg. In other words, don't eat your children. Let them produce more children. And before long you'll have an entire family of dollars working for you.

CHART 55

EFFECTIVE YIELD AT SELECTED NOMINAL RATES AND COMPOUNDING FREQUENCY

Nominal Rate(%) p.a.	Daily (%)	Monthly (%)	Quarterly (%)	Semiannually (%)
10	10.52	10.47	10.38	10.25
11	11.63	11.57	11.46	11.30
12	12.74	12.68	12.55	12.36
13	13.88	13.80	13.65	13.42
14	15.02	14.93	14.75	14.49
15	16.18	16.08	15.87	15.56
16	17.34	17.23	16.98	16.64

Dumfounding Compounding

Benjamin Franklin had this to say about compounding: "Money is of a prolific, generating nature. Money can beget money, and its offspring can beget more." Franklin was probably merely agreeing with one of his contemporaries, Baron Rothschild, who called compound interest the "eighth wonder of the world." Here, you've seen why those two notables of history were correct. You've seen through example how to use compounding to your benefit. You've taken the formulas and determined the results, which in most cases have been incredible.

Key Terms and Phrases Used in This Book

Adjusted Gross Income: An interim figure used to arrive at one's tax liability. Total (gross) income is obtained by getting the sum of income from all sources (wages, interest, dividends, royalties, capital gains, alimony, rents, etc.). Adjusted gross income is total income less allowed adjustments, which include such items as moving expenses, IRA contributions, and employee business expenses. Taxable income then results from subtracting deductions and the allowance for exemptions from adjusted gross income.

After-tax return: The rate of return an investor will receive after adjusting for inflation. Thus a 10-percent before-tax return corresponds to a 7.2-percent after-tax return for a taxpayer in the 28-percent marginal tax bracket.

AMEX or American Stock Exchange: The second largest stock exchange (after the New York Stock Exchange), listing firms that tend to be medium-sized compared with the larger NYSE companies.

Annual Percentage Rate: The yield to maturity on a fixed-income investment or the interest rate charged on a loan; computed using a compounding factor reflecting the balance due.

Annuity: An asset that usually promises to pay a fixed amount periodically for a pre-determined period. Some annuities, however, pay a sum for an individual's lifetime, and certain annuities' values are variable, depending upon the issuer's investment experience. Most annuities are sold by insurance companies.

Appreciation: The increase in the value of an investment over time.

ARM, or Adjustable Rate Mortgage: A type of mortgage in which the interest rate is periodically adjusted as market rates change.

Asset: Any item of value; often income-producing; appears on left of balance sheet.

Balanced Fund: A mutual fund that invests in both stocks and bonds.

Balance Sheet: A financial statement providing an instant picture of a firm's or individual's financial position; lists assets, liabilities, and net worth.

Bear: One who expects a declining market.

Bear Market: A declining market.

Bills: Government debt securities issued on a discount basis by the U.S. Treasury for periods of less than one year.

Blue-Chip Stock: Shares of a large, mature company with a steady record of profits and dividends and a high probability of continued growth in earnings.

Bond: A debt obligation (usually long term) in which the borrower promises to pay a set coupon rate until the issue matures, at which time the principal is repaid. Some bond issues are secured by a mortgage on a specific property, plant, or piece of equipment.

Bond Rating: An estimated index of a bond's quality/default risk.

Broker: An employee of a financial intermediary who acts as an agent in the buying and selling of securities.

Bull: One who expects a rising market.

Bull Market: A rising market.

Bullion: Gold, silver, or other precious metals in the form of bars, plates, or certain coins minted to contain a specific unit or weight.

Call: An option to buy stock or some other asset at a prespecified price over a prespecified period.

Capital Gains (Losses): The difference between the price paid for an asset and its current market value.

Cash Surrender Value: The accumulated savings element of a life insurance policy that can be recovered by canceling the policy, or borrowed against at a specified interest rate.

CD or Certificate of Deposit: Special redeemable debt obligations issued by banks and other depository institutions.

Commissions: Fees charged by brokers for handling securities trades.

Commodity: In general, any article of commerce; in investment terminology, any of a select group of items, such as wheat, corn, live hogs, or gold, traded on one of the commodity exchanges.

Common Stock: An asset representing proportional ownership of an incorporated enterprise.

Compound Interest: An amount derived from the reinvesting of returns and the interest earned, so that interest is gained at a multiplying rate.

Credit Union: A cooperative association where the members' pooled savings are available for loans to the membership.

Currency: Any form of money accepted by a government and in actual use within that country as a medium of exchange.

Deduction: In tax computation, an amount that may be subtracted from adjusted gross income to determine taxable income.

Default: Failure to live up to any of the terms in a bond indenture or other credit agreement.

Discount Broker: A broker who charges below-retail commission rates but usually coupled with more limited investment services.

Dividends: Payments made by companies to their stockholders; usually financed from profits.

Dividend Reinvestment Plan: A company program that allows its dividends to be reinvested in additional shares.

The shares are often newly issued and may be sold at a discount from the current market price.

Dow Jones Industrial Average: The most commonly used index of stock prices. The index is computed as the sum of the prices of 30 leading industrial firms divided by a divisor that is adjusted to reflect stock splits of its components. Dow Jones indexes are also computed for utilities and transportation companies.

Equity: Assets minus liabilities.

Exercise or Intrinsic Value (Call): The price of the associated stock less the striking price of the option. With a put, the exercise value is the striking price less the price of the associated stock.

Federal Deposit Insurance Corporation: A federal agency that insures deposits at commercial banks up to $100,000.

Federal Reserve Board: The governing body of the Federal Reserve System. The seven members are appointed by the president for long and staggered terms.

Federal Reserve System: The federal agency that exercises monetary policy through its control over banking system reserves.

Fixed-Income Security: Any security that promises to pay a periodic nonvariable sum, such as a bond paying a fixed amount per period.

Fixed-Rate Mortgage: A mortgage having a constant interest rate for the life of the debt.

Futures: Contracts to buy and receive or to sell and deliver a commodity or financial instrument at a date and in accord with established rules.

Gross Income: The total income, either actual or estimated.

Growth Fund: A common stock mutual fund that seeks price appreciation by concentrating on growth stocks.

Growth Stock: The shares of a company that is expected to achieve rapid growth; such shares often carry above-average risks.

Hedging: Taking opposite positions in investments, hoping to profit or reduce risks from unrelated price movements.

Income Fund: A common stock mutual fund that concentrates on high-dividend-paying earnings.

Inflation: The rate of rise in the general price level. If, on average, $1.06 will buy what $1 would buy a year earlier, inflation is at 6 percent.

Interest: The amount a borrower pays for the use of a lender's funds; is frequently expressed as an annual percent of the principal balance outstanding and may be compounded on a daily, monthly, or annual basis.

Investment: Any asset expected to yield deferred benefits.

International Fund: A mutual fund that invests in securities of firms that are based outside the fund's home country.

Investment Company: A company that manages pooled portfolios for a group of owners.

IRA or Individual Retirement Account: A retirement plan that allows employees to set aside up to $2,000 annual into a tax-sheltered investment. Earnings on the IRA funds are either eliminated (a Roth IRA) or not taxed until they are withdrawn. The contributed sum can also be deductible from one's taxable income if the individual is not covered by a company pension and/or has a relatively low income.

Leverage: Using borrowed funds or special types of securities to increase the potential return. Leverage usually increases both the risk and the expected return.

Liability: Debt; appears on the right side of a balance sheet.

Line of Credit: Prearranged agreement from a lender to supply up to some maximum loan at prespecified terms.

Liquidity: The ease with which an investment can be converted to cash for approximately its original cost plus its expected accrued interest.

Load: The selling fee applied to a mutual fund purchase.

Margin: Borrowing to finance a portion of a security's purchase.

Marginal Tax Rate: The percentage that must be paid in taxes on the next income increment.

Maturity: The length of time until a security must be redeemed by its issuer.

Money-Market Mutual Fund: A mutual fund that invests in short-term highly liquid securities.

Money-Market Account: A type of bank or thrift institution account that offers unregulated money-market rates.

Mortgage: A loan collateralized by property, particularly real estate. The lender is entitled to take possession of the property if the debt is not repaid in a timely manner.

Mutual Fund: A pooled investment in which managers buy and sell assets, with the income and gains and losses accruing to the owners.

NASDAQ or National Association of Securities Dealers Automated Quotations: An information system that provides brokers and dealers with price quotations on securities that are traded over the counter.

Net Asset Value: The per-share market value of a mutual fund's portfolio.

Net Worth: A firm's or individual's financial position as determined by subtracting the dollar value of liabilities from that of assets.

No-Load Fund: A fund whose shares are bought and sold directly at the fund's net asset value. Unlike a load fund, no agent or sales fee is involved.

Option: A put or call that gives the holder the right but not the obligation to purchase or sell a security at a set price for a specified period.

Over the Counter: The market in unlisted securities and off-board trading in listed securities.

Par: The face value at which an issue is initially sold.

Points: A fee charged for granting a loan, especially for a mortgage or real-estate loan.

Portfolio: A holding of one or

more securities by a single owner (either institution or individual).

Premium: The amount by which a security may sell above its par value.

Prime Rate: The rate that banks advertise as their best (lowest).

Principal (of a bond): The face value of a bond.

Profit (or Loss): Net revenues minus expenses.

Prospectus: An official statement that all companies offering new securities for public sale must file with the Securities & Exchange Commission; it spells out in detail the financial position of the offering company.

Put: An option to sell a stock at a specified price over a specified period.

Rate of Return: A rate that takes into account both dividends and capital appreciation (increases in the price of the investment).

Recession: An economic downturn.

Risk: The variance of the expected return—that is, the degree of certainty (or uncertainty) associated with the expected return.

Savings Accounts: Accumulated funds, on deposit in a banking institution, that draw interest and are highly liquid.

Securities & Exchange Commission: The government agency with direct regulatory authority over the securities industry.

Second Mortgage: A mortgage debt secured by a property's equity after the first mortgage holder's claim has been subtracted from the pledged asset's value.

Securities: Paper assets representing a claim on something of value, such as stocks, bonds, mortgages, options, or commodities.

Sector Fund: A mutual fund invested in a special-interest segment of the market. Examples: utilities funds, international funds.

Stock Exchange: An organization for trading a specific list of securities over specific trading hours.

Stock Splits: Increases in the number of shares of a corporation, with a proportional reduction in the price per shares.

Striking (or Strike) Price: The amount an option holder has to pay (or will receive) to exercise an option.

Tax Shelter: An investment that produces deductions from other income for the investor, with a resulting savings in income taxes.

Term Insurance: A type of insurance without a savings feature. Rates rise with age to reflect the greater probability of death.

Thrifts: Institutions other than commercial banks that accept savings deposits and lend money to borrowers.

Time Value (Options): The excess of an option's market price over its intrinsic value.

Total Return: Dividend return plus capital-gains return.

Treasury Bills (or T-Bills): Government debt securities issued on a discount basis for the U.S. Treasury.

Whole-Life Insurance: A type of insurance policy that couples life insurance with a savings feature. Premiums are fixed, with a surplus built up in the policy's early years to meet claims that exceed premiums when the policyholders are older.

Writer (of an Option): The seller of an option.

Yield: The return of an investment expressed as a percentage of its market value.

Index

A

Alternative minimum tax: 354
America Online: 48, 279, 425, 427-428
American Express: 70-71, 73
American Stock Exchange: 268
Annual percentage rate: 74, 77
Annual reports: 232, 280, 430
Asset allocation: 5, 144-148, 152-155, 180, 182
Automobile insurance: 407

B

Balance sheet: 7, 32-33, 39, 85, 169, 231-234, 236-240, 243, 260, 262-263, 265, 288-289, 311, 317, 449
Beardstown Ladies: 4, 137-138, 296
Bond funds: 356-357
Bonds: 10, 20, 44, 87, 91, 97-102, 104, 108, 125, 129, 137, 145-146, 149-152, 154, 174-176, 182, 190, 215, 232-233, 239, 253-254, 267, 282, 353, 355-357, 361, 366-368, 384, 387, 409, 412-414, 420-421, 423, 426, 449, 451-452, 456, 461-462, 464, 473
Brokerage firms: 11, 37, 104-106, 160, 193, 197, 382, 438, 459
Browsers: 432-433
Budgeting: 28-29, 138, 321

C

Capital gains: 6, 186, 189, 193-194, 213-214, 218-219, 365, 455
Carte Blanche: 70-71
Cash-flow analysis: 256
Certificates of deposit: 10, 37, 387, 412, 418, 461, 483
Coins: 21, 371, 423
Commissions: 37, 86-87, 155, 158, 166, 191, 224, 228, 358, 457-458
Compound interest: 12, 44, 479-482, 484
CompuServe: 48, 279, 425-428
Constant-dollar plan: 174
Constant-ratio plan: 175-176
Consumer Price Index: 97, 184, 291
Corporate bonds: 104, 190, 233, 366, 462, 464
Credit cards: 18, 20-21, 32, 36, 68-72, 74, 363
Credit unions: 68-69, 77-78
Currencies: 107, 431, 450-451, 466-467
Current ratio: 124, 247, 257, 262-263, 284, 294

D

Debt-to-equity ratio: 284, 311
Deductions: 353, 360, 362-363, 384
Depreciation: 217, 219-220, 236-237, 240, 242, 245, 250, 256, 260-261, 282, 287

T

V

W

Y